CLASSIC AUTOMOBILES

TEXTS
Michael Bowler

GRAPHIC DESIGN
Maria Cucchi

EDITORIAL REALIZATION
Valeria Manferto De Fabianis
Laura Accomazzo

Library of Congress
Cataloging-in-Publication
Data available

2001 MetroBooks

ISBN 1-58663-199-3
M 10 9 8 7 6 5 4 3 2 1

Printed in Italy

For bulk purchases and special sales, please contact:
Friedman/Fairfax Publishers
Attention: Sales Department
230 Fifth Avenue, Suite 700-701 - New York, NY 10001
212/685-6610 Fax 212/685-3916
Visit our website: www.metrobooks.com

1   *Top classic sedan - 1957 Jaguar 3.4 Mk.1.*

2-3   *Ultimate future classic Ferrari - 1997 F50.*

4-5   *King of the Cobras - 1967 427 CSX.*

Contents

INTRODUCTION   page   6

CHAPTER 1
FROM 1946 TO 1950   page   16
THE MG TC, TF   page   22
ALFA ROMEO 6C-2500   page   26
MORGAN 4/4   page   30
CISITALIA GRAN SPORT   page   32
FERRARI 166   page   36
JAGUAR XK120 TO XK150   page   40
ASTON MARTIN DB2 AND DB2/4   page   44
BRISTOL 400, 402, 404   page   46

CHAPTER 2

FROM 1951 TO 1960   page 52
PORSCHE 356   page 60
LANCIA AURELIA B20   page 64
AUSTIN HEALEY 100   page 68
CHEVROLET CORVETTE 1956-1962   page 72
TRIUMPH TR2 AND TR3A   page 76
ALFA ROMEO GIULIETTA SPRINT
AND SPIDER   page 80
MERCEDES BENZ 300SL   page 84
BENTLEY CONTINENTAL S-TYPE   page 88
FORD THUNDERBIRD   page 90
MGA 1600   page 94
CADILLAC ELDORADO   page 98
ASTON MARTIN DB4 AND DB4GT   page 102
FERRARI 250GT   page 108

CHAPTER 3

FROM 1961 TO 1970   page 114
JAGUAR E-TYPE   page 124
AC COBRA   page 128
FERRARI 250GTO AND LUSSO   page 132
CHEVROLET CORVETTE 1963-1967   page 136
MGB   page 140
ALFA ROMEO SPRINT GT   page 144
LAMBORGHINI 350GT   page 146
LOTUS ELAN   page 148
ISO GRIFO GL400   page 152
MASERATI GHIBLI   page 154
RENAULT ALPINE 1600S   page 156
LAMBORGHINI MIURA   page 158
FERRARI 365GTB4 DAYTONA   page 160
FERRARI DINO 246GT   page 164
FIAT DINO 2.4 SPIDER   page 168
PONTIAC FIREBIRD   page 172
ALFA ROMEO DUETTO   page 174

CHAPTER 4

FROM 1971 TO 1980   page 176
MASERATI BORA   page 186
LAMBORGHINI COUNTACH   page 188
DE TOMASO PANTERA   page 192
FERRARI 308   page 194
PORSCHE 911 TURBO   page 196
TVR 3000   page 198
ASTON MARTIN LAGONDA   page 200
BMW M1   page 202
CADILLAC SEVILLE   page 204

CHAPTER 5

FROM 1981 TO 1990   page 206
MAZDA RX7   page 218
CHEVROLET CORVETTE 1983-1996   page 220
FERRARI TESTAROSSA 1984 AND BB512   page 224
ASTON MARTIN VANTAGE
AND VOLANTE ZAGATO   page 228
FERRARI F40   page 232
BMW Z1   page 236
NISSAN 300ZX   page 240
HONDA NSX   page 242

CHAPTER 6

FROM 1991 TO 2001 AND BEYOND   page 246
LAMBORGHINI DIABLO 5.7   page 256
BUGATTI EB110   page 260
JAGUAR XJ220   page 264
CHRYSLER VIPER   page 268
TVR GRIFFITH 500   page 272
ASTON MARTIN DB7   page 274
FERRARI 355   page 276
VENTURI 210   page 280
MC LAREN F1   page 282
BMW Z3   page 286
FERRARI F50   page 288
CHEVROLET CORVETTE
5TH GENERATION   page 292
PORSCHE BOXSTER   page 294

GLOSSARY   page 298
INDEX   page 300

An Introduction
to the World of Classic Cars

6-7 top *A rare 1950 Aston Martin, one of 13 DB1 drop head coupes.*

6-7 bottom *The best-looking model of the T-series was the TF, a 1953 1250 here.*

What is a classic car? Must it be old and rare? Must it be beautiful and expensive? Or is it just a car with class? 'Classic' in the world of art, whether architecture, painting or music, implies exceptional quality, but, in the world of cars, 'classic' means different things to different people. Any model of old Ferrari is a classic car in anyone's judgment. Some people would also call an old Vauxhall Victor a classic - there is an owners' club in the UK - but not everyone would agree. Why? It was just an ordinary car when it was new; the passing of time should not change that perception just because a few examples have been preserved. Unfortunately, the term has no standard definition, no constraint of age or price, type or style.

Broadly speaking, a classic car is a post-1945 car with some feature which set it apart from its peers, and not just the mere fact of its survival. A Ford Cortina Mk.1 is not really a classic, but the Cortina GT appeals to more than just owners of old Cortinas and it inspired the even more sporting Lotus Cortina. However if someone forms a club, even for a basic model, there are necessarily some enthusiasts who believe in the car, so it gets embraced into the general classic world whatever the purists may think.

But there are some mass-production peoples' cars that contradict the general rule. Volkswagen Beetle, Morris Minor, Citroen 2CV, Fiat 500 were technically interesting cars that generated a cult-following and have readily been accepted as classic cars, even by Ferrari owners.

CLASSIC CAR HISTORY AMERICA

If you live in America, you will have a different view. The Classic Car Club of America (CCCA) has its own definition of 'classic': "... fine or unusual cars which were built between and including the years 1925 and 1948. These very special cars are distinguished by their respective fine design, high engineering standards and superior workmanship." The CCCA have a list of acceptable cars from around the world, cars that were not mass-produced and were generally more expensive than the rest. Perhaps in response to the universal misuse of the term 'classic', these cars are now referred to as 'Full Classic', a registered CCCA trademark. The CCCA was founded in 1951 because owners of these Full Classics got fed up with being just a small class within the Antique Automobile Club of America (AACA); this had been founded in 1935 and would eventually cater for all vehicles more than 25 years old. There are over 50,000 AACA members, but only 5600 CCCA members. America is also home to the Horseless Carriage Club, a name that dates back to the turn of the last century when motor cars were built around the concept of horse-drawn carriages with a motor substituted for the horse - the dark ages. Their coverage ends at 1916, so need not concern us. Of more interest to the classic enthusiast might have been the American-based Milestone Car Society. This was formed "to promote the preservation, and restoration of domestic

and foreign automobiles made between 1945 and the end of the 1964 model year, which are distinctive because of design, engineering, performance, innovation and/or craftsmanship relative to their contemporaries." In this, a panel of judges selected cars that made a particular contribution to the history of the automobile. Covering cars from the post-war period, it was almost a chronological extension to the CCCA, except that price and rarity were not part of the decision making process. While it was a laudable attempt to separate out the more worthwhile cars, it was engulfed in the rising tide of make clubs, leaving only the name 'Milestone' behind; there is however a Milestone Car Society of California but it has no connection with the original other than the choice of name.

8-9 top *Mercedes 190SL (1955) was the little brother to the 300SL supercar.*

8-9 bottom *First of the pony cars was the Ford Mustang in 1964.*

An Introduction to the World of Classic Cars

CLASSIC CAR HISTORY REST OF WORLD

Outside America, cars built before the 1939-45 war generally have precise age-related definitions. The first such definition came from the Veteran Car Club (VCC) which was founded in 1930 and catered for cars built before 1905; these Veterans are the cars that take part in the world-renowned London-Brighton run. Then came the Vintage Sports-Car Club, founded in 1934, which looked after the cars from 1905-1930. The date of 1930 was chosen because the General Depression brought the end of many manufacturers of expensive hand-made cars. The Thirties would see mass production take over in volume terms, although some of the hand-built cars of the previous decade were able to continue.

In time, both clubs extended their ranges. The VCC began to accept cars up to 1918 and called the 1905-1918 cars Edwardians, which was a little misleading as the English King Edward VII died in 1910. The VSCC moved its end-date to 1940 but only accepted sporting cars from the

Thirties and called them Post-Vintage Thoroughbreds - cars for sporting use, but excluding such mass production sports cars as MG Midgets. The VSCC Thirties car had to be hand-built in the traditional way; more recently they have accepted certain competition cars up to 1960 which they call 'Historic'. Given such broad coverage within the two national old car clubs in England, there were some older cars that were left out. The make clubs soon followed to take care of this - Bugatti, Aston Martin, MG were all founded in the Thirties. That much is purely English history, but it was the English who were the first to appreciate the older car as a hobby rather than a cheap means of transport; English terminology and dating has led the way. As this appreciation of the older car spread to other countries, it was inevitable that an International body would be formed to try and coordinate the movement. The Federation Internationale des Voitures Anciennes (FIVA) was formed in 1966 as the world-wide extension of a previous European-only

equivalent. FIVA took note of all that had been set up before and preserved the various cut-off dates, but not necessarily the names and they accepted all cars of a given date whatever the original quality.

For FIVA, the cars built before 1905 are called 'Ancetre' (Ancestors or Forefathers), while 'Veteran' referred to the 1905-1918 group. FIVA's Vintage period conformed with the VSCC and covered 1919-1930. Initially FIVA used the term 'Classic' to describe the cars of the Thirties, but, as they expanded their interests to cater for all cars more than 20 years old, this decade became simply 'Post-Vintage'. As time went on FIVA had to find new definitions for the cars that came into their range. 'Post-war' was the name given to the 1945-60 period. After which, semantic skills ran out. The Sixties became Group F and the Seventies are Group G It was the British magazine Classic Cars, launched in 1973, which took the whole old car movement under its wing. No definition. Just a proven ability for the car to attract a following,

usually demonstrated by the formation of a club of like-minded enthusiasts for the model. Where there wasn't a club, the magazine usually inspired some owner to start one. That obviously also embraced the pre-war specialist cars of the VSCC, but it was particularly the cars excluded by that club's rules that would be called classic, the new Vintage.

While organizations such as FIVA and the Antique Automobile Club of America still require cars to be 20-25 years old to qualify for membership, classic car magazines take a broader view. Any car that is out of production has the potential to be featured and, by implication, to be considered a classic. Classic cannot be new. A new car can have classic lines - often called Retro - but it can only be called a future classic. History has shown that sporting cars earn classic status sooner than standard sedans. Almost by definition sports cars are not everyday cars. Sedan cars stay in the general transport market for much longer, getting ever cheaper until they finish in the scrap yard or someone rescues them - they gradually lose any class they had. Sporting cars

are usually more expensive, they probably cover lower mileages and are better maintained by keener owners. One might say that a car becomes a classic when it ceases to depreciate in value - the market has recognized that it is worth preserving. Well maintained sporting cars stop depreciating at a younger age than less interesting sedans. This book will also recognize a few of these future classics. Just to confuse the reader, a car might well be considered a classic in one country but not in its native country. This is particularly true of American cars where such as Ford Mustangs and Chevrolet Camaros were produced in very large numbers; but in Europe they have always stood out as something different and have achieved general classic recognition much earlier. The Citroen 2CV is just an old family run-about to the French, but it has achieved classic status in countries where it is a rarity. This is also true of the Mini, but at least that had a competition variant, the Cooper S, which merits classic recognition, even in England.

10-11 top *The 1961 Jaguar E-type had world-wide appeal*

10-11 bottom *By the time of this 1986 example, the Chevrolet Corvette had recovered the performance lost in the Seventies*

An Introduction to the World of Classic Cars

CLASSIC CAR EVENTS

Part of the joy of owning a classic car is to take it to events and compete against others. As with modern motor cars, this competition takes many forms. Classic car owners can take part in anything from a static concours through touring events, rallies, trials, hill-climbs to flat-out racing; such events will be organised by make or national clubs and commercial organizations. The Concours falls into two main categories. Most are called Concours d'Elegance which recalls the events that used to take place at the end of major rallies; this was a 'beauty contest' where judges decided on what they thought was the nicest-looking car. In the Thirties this was a good chance for coachbuilders to display their special bodies. Judging nowadays is based on how closely cars conform to the condition in which they might have left the factory - the Concours d'Etat. Pebble Beach in California is the most Internationally-known annual event and their system of marking every aspect of the car has spread around the world. A 100-point car is perfect, and many classic car dealers use such terminology in advertisements,

with perhaps less attention to detail than would be given by a truly impartial jury. Over the last 20 years there have been many regularity runs where durability of car and driver is more of a deciding factor than speed. These frequently follow the pattern of former classic competitions like the Monte Carlo Rally, the London-Sydney Marathon, the Peking-Paris or the Mille Miglia, but take somewhat longer than did the original competitors. While these are all for cars that were either built for such competitions originally or have been improved to the same period specification, there are many more events for those who wish to drive through nice scenery in original cars in the company of fellow enthusiasts without the pressure of competition. For those classic owners who want to drive against the clock, there are rallies, hill-climbs and races; these come under the overall control of the Federation Internationale de l'Automobile (FIA). The 'Historic Commission' was formed in 1974 under the presidency of Count "Johnny" Lurani, a well-known Italian competitor from the Thirties

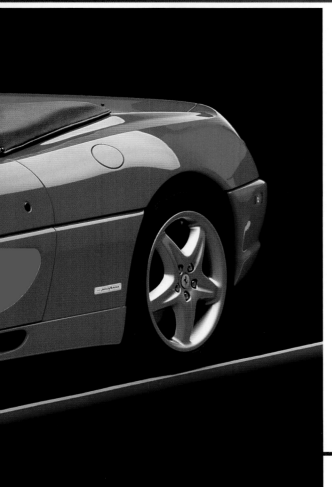

and Fifties. His committee came partly from FIVA and partly from the national clubs. All competition cars, from the beginning to the only recently obsolete, are covered in rules for which the criteria are period originality and a continuous history for that car. The rules, which are used to control modification, are based on those of the period of the car; every entrant will have a vehicle passport to show that his car has been inspected and conforms to these rules. Most European countries, Australia and America, have many race meetings, frequently attracting entries from worldwide.

While the VSCC was probably the first club to run a race meeting solely for the older car in 1937, the first truly International old-car race meeting took place in 1973 at the Nurburgring in Germany - the first of many Oldtimer Grand Prix. Certainly, there were many competition cars which generally fall outside the coverage of this book, but there were also many of the sports and grand touring road cars.

Touring cars (sedans) would join in later years. From 1973 onwards, the classic car competition world has expanded rapidly and there are European championships for rallying, hill-climbs and racing. Whatever classic car you own or decide to buy, be assured that you can do much more with it than just look at it in the garage or drive it down to the golf club. Welcome to the world of the mobile museum that is classic motoring. Long may we have the freedom to exercise our cars on the open road.

12-13 top *McLaren F1 achieved 231 mph*

12-13 bottom *Pininfarina style adds to Ferrari appeal on the 355 Spyder*

14-15 *Cadillac's 1960 Eldorado saw a reduction in chrome plate*

1946 - 1950

While the classic period is generally reckoned to start after the 1939-45 war, many of Europe's volume produced cars were only minor facelifts from 1938/9 models, their tooling costs as yet unamortised while the production machinery had sat in moth-balls for the duration of hostilities. While America did not start fighting in the war until after the attack on Pearl Harbor in December 1941, their factories had been supplying the anti-Hitler forces from 1939 with commercial vehicles and armaments. Despite this over 4 million cars were produced in 1940 and 1941. From mid 1942 all American vehicle production facilities were involved in the war effort, one of Ford's contributions being production of the Jeep – itself something of a post-war classic.

The lack of direct attack on America allowed their factories to return to vehicle production relatively quickly after the war. England was not far behind, but France, Italy and Germany all suffered major bomb damage to former car production centers.

Japan too, but their pre-war cars had made no impact outside Japan. Smaller companies could more readily consider producing new models and such new makes as Bristol and Saab emerged from airplane manufacturers.

But the return of motoring freedom was to be a slow process. Rubber and steel were hard to get.

All industries were looking for materials and governments were slow to let the automobile industries have what they needed. Nor was there the manpower to work in the factories as armies were slow to demobilize the troops. All countries had fuel rationing except the US. And then there was a shortage of dollars as America had operated the

Lease-Lend system and many allied countries were in debt – they had to export goods to America to recover. Much of Britain's early post-war production went to America and other countries before the home market could be supplied, and high national taxes were brought in to encourage exports.

Not all the cars from this, or any other, distant decade can be regarded as classics, but it was an era when many small companies started up and they necessarily produced near hand-made cars in limited numbers. So this particular five-year period saw an unusual quantity of future classics; not all of these entrepreneurial manufacturers survived through to the Sixties though.

16-17 *Riley RM sedan, 1950.*

The New Sedans

From America, there was little to attract future classic enthusiasts. The cars got bigger and V-8s more widespread albeit that some were still flat-heads (side-valves).

The Studebaker Champion, like most of the early post-war American cars, was a revised version of the successful 1942 car, but introduced a new short nose-long tail style with a much lowered roof-line in 1946. In mechanical design there was little to separate the American cars, it was style that sold them.

In 1947, Ford separated out the top end of their range by giving the new Lincoln-Mercury division some autonomy. The 1949 Mercury was a good looking car despite its heavily chromium-plated grille; with its flat-head V-8, it was popular with the hot-rodders of the day. Lincoln, which had been directed by Edsel Ford, was the top model built in European-sized numbers. The Lincoln Zephyr of the late Thirties was one of America's more striking cars, the most popular model being an elegant fast-back with a V-12 engine. The longer hand-made Continental grew out of this in 1938, continuing through to 1942. Only a few

changes were made for the 1946-1948 model years, but the cars stood out as being relatively restrained in their use of the brightwork – and a V-12 was pretty rare in those days.

Cadillac was the top of the General Motors tree. While early post-war Cadillacs were the same as those of 1941, the 1948 series were rebodied and the 'tail fin' was born. Harley Earl had set up the first in-house automotive styling studio for General Motors in 1937; impressed by the twin-boom tail plane of the Lockheed Lightning fighter, he transferred the idea to motor cars and the Cadillac was the first recipient. The 1948 cars continued with the 347 cu.in flat-head V-8s but, in 1949, Cadillac introduced the overhead valve version.

American manufacturers were relatively fortunate. There was only a four-year gap in automobile production and tastes didn't change very much over that period. But the Continentals had a much longer period of motoring stagnation. So what influenced designers when it came to starting on a new car with a clean sheet of paper? It was clear that American passenger cars were

superior in comfort, performance and style to those that had provided ordinary transport on their home markets in the Thirties. However, the American cars were just too thirsty for European fuel prices and too big for most European roads although Germany had their autobahnen and Italy too had autostrade.

So the post-war British passenger car designers adopted American styling but scaled it down. Thus running boards and separate wings (fenders) disappeared and headlights were integrated into front panels. Radiators disappeared behind false grilles. Some of the styles followed the Airline, or fastback, theme which America had adopted in the late Thirties and some of the UK designers had followed, notably Rover and Talbot. On the technical side, Britain retained their four and six-cylinder engines rather than V-8s, but took on independent front suspension and hydraulic brakes which were by no means universal in the late Thirties. Unitary construction of body and chassis was another lesson learned as essential for cheaper volume production; up-market models like Rolls-Royce and Bentley, which still used coachbuilders for bodywork, retained separate chassis.

Typical of the downsized American cars launched in 1948 was Standard's new Vanguard. In style it was quite obviously based on the 1942 Plymouth with a rounded fast-back and the adoption of fared in rear wheels. It used a new 128 cu.in 'four' that would go on to power tractors, Morgans and the Triumph TR2/3/4; the gearbox was a three-speed unit with steering column change adopted from America. Standard took over Triumph in 1944. While early post-war Standards were just continuations of the pre-war cars, the Vanguard was the sole model they produced from 1947; however Triumph was allowed to proceed a little faster and had new razor-edged sedans from 1946 using pre-war Standard engines converted to overhead valves.

They also produced the striking 1800 Roadster, a two-seater with a separate compartment behind for two more passengers in a 'dickey-seat'. The

Roadster adopted the Vanguard engine in late 1948.

Another to follow the American fast-back line was the Jowett Javelin, launched in 1946 having been built in prototype form in 1944. Although British factories were very much involved in the war effort, many were planning their post-war return to car production at the same time as producing, in Jowett's case, armaments and aero-engine water pumps. In style, the Jowett followed the looks of the Lincoln-Zephyr, and the rest of the car was well-conceived. Pre-war experience with a flat twin engine prompted the use of a water-cooled flat four engine, which was mounted ahead of the front wheels. Torsion bars were used for the suspension with wishbones at the front. With a long wheelbase, the four-door sedan was very comfortable but still agile on the road; however the small company was not able to build in the vital reliability and they ceased producing cars in 1953. Like Standard, they also produced a sporting version – the Jupiter – which used the Javelin engine in a tubular chassis under two-seater bodywork; only 850 were produced.

Jaguar were a little slow to produce an all-new sedan. Initial post-war products were uprated pre-war cars but the 1950 advent of the Mark VII saw Jaguar start their long run of success. Using the twin-cam six-cylinder 207 cu.in. engine which had been conceived during the war years, and first used in the XK120, the new generation Jaguar was a large and comfortable car styled in a European mold. In avoiding American style, Jaguar produced a car that was instantly well received in the United States.

In Sweden, Volvo introduced the fast-back PV444 with a four-cylinder engine to replace their pre-war sixes. Germany, under allied control and with a number of its factories scheduled to finish up in the Russian zone, produced the Borgward Hansa in 1949 and, of course, the Beetle and Porsche. Mercedes and BMW produced nothing new until 1951, although Mercedes made uprated 170 models from 1949.

Of the French manufacturers, Citroen retained the Traction Avant Light 15 (Onze Legere in France) through the Forties and beyond the 1955 launch of the DS19. Originally designed in 1934 it was the first effective front-wheel-drive car; it used independent wishbone front suspension with torsion

bars and a dead rear axle to give renowned fwd cornering with remarkable comfort for the period. Performance came from an overhead valve four-cylinder which would be stretched from 80 to the 116 cu.in, the size used post-war. A six-cylinder derivative was launched in 1938 and this too continued after the war. Peugeot continued with the pre-war 202, but introduced the 203 in 1947, another to follow the scaled down Plymouth theme of Standard and Volvo; it had a new 80 cu.in overhead-valve engine and all-coil suspension. It was a strong, well-built car that would sell until 1960; from 1949-53 it was the only Peugeot made. And finally, Panhard changed direction from large to small cars and produced their own brand of idiosyncratic Dynas from 1945 using designs from J.A.Gregoire. With powerful air-cooled flat twin 37.2 cu.in engines in aerodynamic shapes, they were quick and comfortable. The engine was increased to 45.7 cu.in in 1950 and 51.8 cu.in in 1952. Other specialists like DB and the German Veritas also used these for road and competition use.

In Italy, Alfa Romeo were still producing expensive cars, the 6C2500 in various forms including a competition coupe. The 1900 range was to start in 1950 to take the company into volume production with unitary construction and a new four-cylinder engine. Lancia continued with pre-war designs, the Aprilia with all-round independent suspension and its overhead camshaft narrow V-4 engine at 91 cu.in, and the smaller Ardea. Lancia too would introduce their new range in 1950 with the Aurelia, covered in the next chapter. Maserati were mostly building racing cars but a handful of road cars were built on the A6-1500 chassis.

Apart from those above, there were a number of old respected British names that continued with new looks but old engines after the war; although they are rightly regarded as classics within the UK, they made less impact on the International scene. In 1945, Riley, which had been taken over by Morris in 1938, brought in the sports sedan RM with styling reminiscent of the BMW 327 coupe; this used the pre-war 91 cu.in 'four' in a new chassis; a year later the 146 cu.in version was added. Alvis produced the TA series in 1946 and followed it up with the TB14 2-seater. AC's new sedan arrived in 1947. Lea-Francis

had new sedans and brought out a 2-seater sports in 1948. Sunbeam-Talbot, part of the Rootes group, had a range of medium sedans with sporting performance. Armstrong-Siddeley's elegant sedans and convertibles were named after the fighter aircraft produced by the group in the war. But within a decade most of these British names would be gone or merged within larger organizations.

THE BABY CLASSICS

The Austin 7 of the Twenties had been an inspirational small car in its time; it had a separate chassis, a four-cylinder water-cooled 45.7 cu.in engine and it could carry four adults. It was the first scaled down cheap car for the people, as opposed to the cyclecar which had been little better than a four-wheeled motor cycle combination. It was also produced under licence by BMW as the Dixi, Rosengart in France, Bantam in America and Datsun in Japan. In Germany Hanomag's equivalent was the 2/10 commonly called the Kommissbrot because it looked like an army loaf of bread; it only had a single cylinder engine and was limited to two people. DKW responded with a 2-cylinder two-stroke and produced the first front-wheel-drive baby-car in 1931.

The Austin 7 was still in production when Fiat conceived the first 500 – the Topolino. Giacosa had started in 1934, intending to make it a front-wheel-drive car but the constant velocity joints of the day were not good enough. He did, however, assemble the engine, transmission and independent front suspension into a single removable package – a very effective design; putting the radiator behind the 34.7 cu.in four-cylinder engine allowed a stylish sloping front. Brakes were hydraulic but the car was only a two-seater. It was, however, the logical successor to the Austin 7 and was widely exported – a small car with exceptional comfort and roadholding for its day. Production started in 1936 and was to continue after the war, with overhead valves replacing the original side valves, until 1955 when it was replaced by the rear engined 600 and then the Nuova Cinquecento (new 500) which came with an air-cooled twin-cylinder engine.

In Germany, the Beetle project was also started in 1934. While there had been a rival claimant to the first German Volkswagen in the form of the Standard

500 designed by Austrian Josef Ganz and launched in 1932, Dr.Porsche was given the contract to build the true Volkswagen after the Third Reich came to power in 1933. Both used rear engines – the Standard a transverse twin-cylinder – swing axles and a form of central backbone chassis. Dr Porsche used an air-cooled flat four and torsion bar springing instead of transverse leaf springs.

Development of the prototypes took place over 1936-39, but by the time that the cars and the new factory at Wolfsburg were ready for production, war was almost under way. During the war it had been adapted to serve as a cross-country vehicle (52,000 Kubelwagens were built between 1940-45) and as an amphibious vehicle (14,263 were produced from 1940-44). Production of the road car finally started in 1945; by March 1950 100,000 had been built. The five million came up in 1961 and in February 1972 Beetle production surpassed that of the model T Ford.

There is no doubt that Dr Porsche's German peoples' car and Giacosa's Fiat 500 inspired a lot of thought among European car producers during the war. While they were all manufacturing contributions to the various war efforts, the industry leaders were thinking ahead to the end of the conflict. They knew that ,whatever the outcome, people would be poor but they would need transport – cheap transport.

To keep the price down, production costs had to be kept to a minimum; therefore machinery should do as much work as possible to keep the labor costs low. Henry Ford had already shown the world the advantages of the production line with the Model T. In France, and inspired by the pre-war Beetle prototypes, Renault had been working on the 4CV from 1940 and prototypes were running during the war. In 1945 the company was nationalized. By 1947 a new factory was running with modern transfer machinery and the 4CV emerged at the 1947 Paris Show. Like the VW, this used a platform chassis and rear-mounted engine/gearbox but the 45.7 cu.in engine was water-cooled. It was also a four-door car. The design saved Renault and it was to be developed into the Dauphine and the R8 of later years. Somehow, though, it never inspired the same fanaticism as did the Beetle. However, there was another

French car which would become just as much loved as the Volkswagen – the Citroen 2CV.

Like the Beetle, work had started on the 2CV well before the war in 1936. While this was designed for the people, thinking was heavily slanted towards the French agricultural community. It had to carry four farmers wearing hats, be capable of taking a basket of eggs over a ploughed field and be able to carry a pig to the market. It also had to be cheap hard wearing and easy to repair. The result was the uncompromising shape with simply curved panels, a roll-back canvas roof and hinged windows. Following the theme of Citroen's Traction Avant, it too had front wheel drive and was powered by an air-cooled flat twin with 22.8 cu.in developing just 9 bhp, enough for 38 mph. Independent suspension used inter-connected leading and trailing arms with central coil springs. The springing was remarkably soft yet it was impossible to overturn the car. Prototypes were built in 1937 and production would have started in 1939 had war not intervened. Citroen destroyed all but one prototype to prevent the design being stolen. Finally it was launched in 1948. The engine was enlarged to 26 cu.in in 1954. Despite its looks, the 2CV remained in demand for many years and the final car was produced in Portugal in 1990 by which time over 5 million had been made.

18-19 Alfa Romeo 6C-2500 sedan

In England, much of the volume production was devoted to updated pre-war designs until the Morris Minor arrived in 1948. Another wartime gestation, the Minor was conceived in 1942 by Alec Issigonis who would go on to create the Mini. With conventional front engine-rear drive and a unitary chassis, the Minor was launched in 1948 using the pre-war Morris 8 side-valve engine. What set it apart from many of its rivals was that it was the first family sedan to handle like a sports car, thanks to its wide stance and rack-and-pinion steering. In 1952 it received the overhead valve engine from the new Austin A30, following the Austin-Morris merger which created BMC. The A30 was never as popular in classic terms, although its A35 derivative developed a competition following.

The last of our small classics would be the Saab 92, the first automotive product of Sweden's war-time aircraft manufacturer. In simple terms it was a much improved DKW in a unitary body/chassis unit whose engineering and styling obviously owed much to aircraft influence. Front wheel drive and two-stroke power were retained from the DKW but the engine was a 2-cylinder 45.7 cu.in unit. Design work started in 1945 and the first prototype ran a year later. Production finally started in 1949 – the first truly aerodynamic small car.

THE SPORTING CLASSICS

Where touring car designers looked to America for their inspiration and small car designers chose the most innovative solutions of the past, would-be sports car designers looked back to the pre-war competition era. Few single events were more influential than the 1940 Brescia GP, that year's Mille Miglia held before Italy joined the Axis powers. Le Mans too made its share of contribution.

The two major landmarks from the Brescia event were the success of the streamlined BMW 328s (coupes and roadsters) and the arrival of Ferrari as a constructor, although the car was actually entered as an 815 by Auto-Avio Costruzioni; the Ferrari story will be told in the special cars at the end of this chapter. The BMW coupe that won the event at over 100 mph had already won its 122 cu.in class and finished 5th overall at Le Mans in 1939.

It was one of the few coupes that had been built for racing. It was only in the late Thirties that the benefits of aerodynamic designs were beginning to be appreciated for racing machinery, particularly in such high speed events as Le Mans and the Mille Miglia. Many aerodynamic sedan Lancias and Fiats, with coachbuilt bodies, had also taken part in the Italian classic race.

At Le Mans streamlined sedan Adlers had finished sixth overall in 1937 and in 1938. Alfa Romeo had fielded a single Touring-bodied 2900B coupe in 1938 and led for most of the race. It was Touring who designed the body for the BMW and for the 1939 2500SS Alfa Romeos. While much of those aerodynamic studies took place in Germany, it was the Italians that put them into the most attractive effect.

Despite Touring's major contribution to the breed it was Pinin Farina who was credited with the creation of the Gran Turismo fast-back shape. The Cisitalia 202 Gran Sport was the product of Dante Giacosa's Fiat brain, Savonuzzi's wind-tunnel studies and Pinin Farina's styling; it was launched in 1947. It only had a tuned Fiat 1100 engine but the car could reach 100 mph. Cisitalia's Piero Dusio then became involved in a Grand Prix car project – together with Porsche – and left the country in 1948 but the car continued in production until 1952 by which time only 170 cars had been built.

A further product of the 1940 Brescia race came from the open BMWs which had finished 3rd, 5th and 6th – Alfa Romeo 2500SS had finished 2nd and 4th. The open BMW bodies had been created in Germany, again following wind-tunnel theories,

with smooth all-enveloping upper shapes and a flat underside – they were also very attractive. One of these cars was brought back to England after the war and became the prototype of the post-war Frazer Nash. Pre-war this company had built chain-drive sports cars but had imported BMWs from 1934 onwards.

Meanwhile the Bristol Aeroplane Company were, like Saab, wanting to make motor cars. Through a Frazer Nash association they acquired a useful amount of BMW knowledge which will be seen in the story of the Bristol 400 in the next chapter. Part of that knowledge was the design of the BMW 328 engine which was Anglicized and made available to Frazer Nash. While the most popular Frazer Nash was the Le Mans Replica – named after any early car finished 3rd in the French race in 1949, with a cigar-shaped body and cycle wings, the next model was the Mille Miglia, shaped very much like the Brescia race car. The Bristol engine was also used by AC and Arnolt (USA) in road cars and by such as Cooper, Lotus and Lister in racing cars.

When the original open Brescia BMW came to England it was viewed by all the manufacturers. Its style would eventually be seen on the MGA but the

most obvious lesson was put into effect by Jaguar for the XK120, launched in 1948. The lines, including the rear wheel spats, were pure BMW.

Porsche may not have been in the 1940 race but a development of the early Beetle prototypes nearly took part in a similar long-distance event before the war, but the 1939 Berlin-Rome race was cancelled. Porsche engineers had designed a coupe around VW components, but put the engine ahead of the rear axle. This coupe body was then adapted around a standard Beetle chassis for the race. After the war, Porsche started again and produced a mid-engined roadster on a tubular chassis with Beetle engine and gearbox. This single prototype, built in Austria, was sold to finance the move to Stuttgart and the production of the 356 on a Beetle chassis. Once more racing had established the breed.

It was to be the same for Aston Martin too. While the company restarted after the war with a 122 cu.in sports car based on pre-war thinking, the DB2 coupe was the first product of the merger of Aston Martin and Lagonda and this was demonstrated at Le Mans in 1949 – a fuller story comes at the end of this chapter. Lagonda too was to continue with new luxury cars based on designs by W.O. Bentley.

While they were both successful in amateur club events, neither the MG TC nor the Morgan 4/4 owed their existence to a background of International racing.

The TC was a direct continuation of the pre-war TB; the TC story is told later. Morgan had made its name with three-wheelers from 1910 but in 1936 they added the first four-wheeler using a side valve 68.5 cu.in Coventry Climax engine – some were made in France as Sandfords. At that time it was a modern-looking car but the style has never changed since then. After the war production continued using a Standard overhead valve engine of 77.3 cu.in. Both that and the TC were traditional British sports cars; they looked faster than they were, but they handled well and provided fun in lesser motor sport events. For the Morgan, though, this changed when the Plus 4 came out in 1950 using the 127.4 cu.in Standard Vanguard engine; suddenly Morgan had arrived as a true sports car.

Britain was the home of the small volume sports car. In the early post-war years, a lot of these British enthusiasts cleared the first hurdle from special builder to manufacturer rather more easily than did their counterparts overseas. In Italy, Moretti

succeeded over the next decade but reverted to making special Fiats.

Porsche had a similar start but expanded rapidly. In France, taxation soon killed off Delage, Delahaye and Talbot and it was some years before such as Alpine could start. Component suppliers in Britain were keen to expand their business even in small numbers and manufacturers were certainly willing to make engines and transmissions available to others. And there was still a coachbuilding industry.

Another new manufacturing name to profit from this attitude was Healey. Donald Healey, who had been an active motor sport competitor and was Technical Director of Triumph before the war, decided to make his own 4-seater cars. A welded box section chassis with trailing arm front suspension was equipped with the effective Riley 146 cu.in four-cylinder engine which developed 104 bhp; in 1947, a closed coupe with standard Elliott bodywork achieved 110.8 mph at Jabbeke, Belgium and claimed to be the fastest production car in the world. Healey also produced the cycle-winged two-seater Silverstone on the same chassis for just two years, 1949 and 1950, as British taxation slowed demand for more expensive cars. Healey would go on to become the second half of the better known Austin-Healey.

Allard had produced Ford V-8 powered trials specials before the war, but produced a small number of open tourers from 1947 using the flat-head Ford V-8 and the two-seater sports K-type with the same engine increased to 238 cu.in and with Ardun overhead valve conversion. The cycle-winged J2 was added in 1950 and was well received in America; mostly it used a big Cadillac engine but others could easily be fitted.

By the end of the first post-war decade, the world's industry had just about recovered from the war, although German output was still restricted apart from the Volkswagen. In 1950 the UK had made 522,000 cars of which 398,000 were exported and only 1375 were imported – a useful contribution to the balance of payments.

20-21 *Aston Martin DB2 with Bertone bodywork.*

22-23 MG TC, left and lower, was a slightly wider version of the pre-war TB. The TF added post-war elegance but not performance in the 76.2 cu.in shown below.

The MG TC, TF

Before the classic period, MG was little known outside the United Kingdom. The company had started as Morris Garages, the retail outlet near the Oxford factory. The manager, Cecil Kimber, started to produce sporting versions of the Morris Cowley from 1925. By 1930, MG was producing small sports two-seaters using Morris components – the MG Midgets with small four-cylinder engines. Six-cylinder Magnas and Magnettes followed. The Midgets were never very fast, but they had style and many owners enjoyed using them for light competition – autotests and trials.

The T-type, later called the TA, Midget arrived in 1936 with

its customary twin-channel chassis suspended on leaf springs and powered by a 78.8 cu.in 52 bhp engine from Wolseley, which Morris had owned from 1927. This engine was replaced by the stronger 76.2 cu.in Morris unit for the TB which was announced just before the 1939-45 war, so only 379 were built before production ceased.

When production restarted, MG abandoned their multi-model policy and concentrated on the new two-seater TC, which was a TB with a wider cockpit and a rear spring mounting system revised for greater reliability. Development had to be kept to a minimum to get the car into production quickly; that mattered little as there were no rivals other than pre-war cars.

The TC looked like everyone's ideal of a sports car with a strong

TECHNICAL DESCRIPTION OF THE MG TF	
YEARS OF PRODUCTION	1953-1955
ENGINE	FRONT MOUNTED IN-LINE 4-CYLINDER
BORE X STROKE, CAPACITY	2.6 x 3.5 INCHES, 76.2 CU.IN
VALVEGEAR	PUSHROD OHV
FUEL SYSTEM	TWIN SU CARBURETORS
POWER	57 BHP AT 5500 RPM
TRANSMISSION	4-SPEED, REAR DRIVE
BODY/CHASSIS	STEEL PANELS ON ASH FRAME, STEEL CHANNEL CHASSIS
SUSPENSION	SEMI-ELLIPTIC LEAF SPRINGS
TIRES/WHEELS	15 x 5.50 ON WIRE WHEELS
WHEELBASE, TRACK (F), TRACK(R)	94 x 47 x 50 INCHES
LENGTH, WIDTH, HEIGHT	147 x 60 x 53 INCHES
MAX SPEED	80 MPH
WHERE BUILT	ABINGDON-ON-THAMES, ENGLAND

radiator shape, a long bonnet, sweeping front wings, wire wheels and a slab petrol tank across the rear. The British motor industry wanted to export as much as possible and had a ready audience in the number of Allied troops still stationed in Britain. It appealed particularly to the Americans for whom it was a natural peace-time successor to the Jeep which had given many of them a taste for sporting motoring.

Of the 10,000 produced, only a third stayed in the UK and 2000 were sold in America.

By 1949, though, its pre-war design was painfully evident in the hard ride; it looked fast but its cramped cockpit and bouncy suspension was no longer fun. Even when the TB was launched in 1936 many small family sedans had independent front suspension.

So the TD came along in late 1949 using a shortened version of the chassis that had been used for the Y-type sedan from 1947. A wider front track gave added roadholding benefits, enhanced by lower fatter tires – 5.50 x 15, new rack and pinion steering and better brakes. Old-fashioned purists did not like the pressed steel wheels but they were stronger and allowed the car to sit lower. The engine, though, remained the same 76.2 cu.in unit so the TD was slower in acceleration than the TC due to the extra weight of the suspension and bumpers. However the TD looked more modern and was notably more comfortable. In its four-year life nearly 30,000 were made, including a Mk.II version with slightly more power from bigger carburetors; over 75 per cent of TDs went to America where it was as popular on the race-track as on the road. Many racing stars like Phil Hill and Richie Ginther started their track careers with an MG TD.

By 1953, such genuine post-war models as the Austin Healey 100, from the same group following the 1952 Austin-Morris merger, and

the Triumph TR2 were on the way. The TD looked old and was 20 mph slower. At that time MG were not allowed to produce an Austin-Healey rival, so the TD was just restyled with a sloping radiator grille and more flowing wing line, although still with running boards. The engine remained the same, so the TF accelerated no faster than the TC. Increasing the engine size to 89.4 cu.in in 1954 improved the performance but production stopped after a year and a half to make way for the MGA; some 9600 TFs were built, of which 3200 were the Mk.II version. The TC put the MG name on the world map and the TD strengthened the image. Although the TF was the most attractive of all, and is now the most desirable, it was too dated by 1953.

24-25 With the screen lowered to reveal the optional aero-screens, the TC looked an ideal sports car and found many American buyers.

TECHNICAL DESCRIPTION OF THE MG TC

YEARS OF PRODUCTION	1945-1949
ENGINE	FRONT MOUNTEDIN-LINE 4-CYLINDER
BORE X STROKE, CAPACITY	2.6 X 3.5 INCHES, 76.2 CU.IN
VALVEGEAR	PUSHROD OHV
FUEL SYSTEM	TWIN SU CARBURETORS
POWER	54 BHP AT 5200 RPM
TRANSMISSION	4-SPEED, REAR DRIVE
BODY/CHASSIS	STEEL PANELS ON ASH FRAME, STEEL CHANNEL CHASSIS
SUSPENSION	SEMI-ELLIPTIC LEAF SPRINGS
TIRES/WHEELS	19 X 4.50 ON WIRE WHEELS
WHEELBASE, TRACK (F), TRACK(R)	94 X 45 X 45 INCHES
LENGTH, WIDTH, HEIGHT	140 X 56 X 53
MAX SPEED	75 MPH
WHERE BUILT	ABINGDON-ON-THAMES, ENGLAND

Alfa Romeo 6C - 2500

When Carrozzeria Touring won the Grand Prix at the 1949 Villa d'Este Concours with their latest bodywork on an Alfa Romeo 6C 2500 Super Sport chassis, it was the start of a new line. It didn't matter that the model was a pre-war design; the style was what counted. It was and has remained a rare beauty.

The origins of the 6C 2500 lay in Alfa Romeo's new design of 1934, undertaken by Jano who had taken time out from race-car design to create the 6C-2300. It had a new 6-cylinder engine with a cast-iron 7-bearing cylinder block and a detachable aluminium cylinder head carrying the customary twin overhead camshafts driven by chain rather than gears or a vertical shaft. A new gearbox had synchromesh on 3rd and top gears with a freewheel. The box section frame had semi-elliptic springs all round. Alfa Romeo built the majority of the 76 bhp Gran Turismo models on a 115-inch wheelbase, while Castagna used a 126-inch chassis to make 6-seater limousines. To launch the new model, Alfa Romeo entered three Touring-

26-27 *With this Touring Superleggera bodywork, an Alfa Romeo 6C 2500SS won the Grand Prix at the 1949 Villa d'Este Concours.*

bodied Gran Turismo models in the 1934 Pescara 24-hours and took the first three places, giving rise to a new model name.

Around 760 of the 2300 were built, before the 6C-2300B came along in 1935 with an all independently sprung chassis and hydraulic brakes. The design used twin trailing arms with the Alfa Romeo combined coil spring and damper system at the front, and a swing axle at the rear with longitudinal torsion bars, a system very similar to that of Dr.Porsche's Auto-Union GP car. Turismo, Gran Turismo and Pescara continued but less than 300 were built over the three years as the company was required to build military trucks and air engines during 1935-6.

A 2nd series saw a few refinements in 1938 and the models renamed Lungo (128 inches wheelbase), with Corto and Touring's Miglia Miglia coupe on the 118 inch chassis; over 500 of these were built. Then came the 2500 in 1939 with the cylinder bores enlarged by 0.07 inch. The range continued with five and six-seater models on the 128 inch chassis and 4-seaters from Touring on the 118 inch.

Sport chassis, but a 106 inch wheelbase chassis was introduced for the 110 bhp Super Sports. These mostly went to Touring for open two-seaters, coupes and cabriolets – only 61 SS chassis were made from 1939-43. Six SS Corsa were also made by Touring; with 125 bhp, these won the 1939 Tobruk-Tripoli race but were beaten by BMW in the 1940 Mille Miglia (Brescia GP). Alfa Romeo also made almost 250 of the 6-7 seater limousines which would have been used by senior wartime officials, and a further 150 6C 2500 Coloniale open 4-seater staff-cars.

Production of the 2500 ceased in 1943. Although work had started on a prototype for the post-war period and it ultimately performed well, the facilities at the war-torn factory were not suited to the introduction of a new model, so post-war production continued with the existing 6C 2500; the only novelties were a

steering column gear-change and the welding of the steel bodywork to the chassis, creating an early form of unitary construction.

Body styling had more significant changes though and the traditional Alfa grille was made much narrower. Alfa Romeo used the 118 inch Sport chassis for a 5-6-seater which they called the Freccia d'oro (Golden Arrow) to set it apart from the pre-war models. Both 118 inch Sport and 106 inch Super Sport chassis were made available to coachbuilders; Stabilimenti Farina produced large sedan cars, Touring used the short chassis for some superb coupes while Pinin Farina produced many convertibles. Touring's shapes gradually evolved over 1947-8. Still smooth and aerodynamic in shape, they retained the separate outline of the wings but brought in tight creases curving back from the top of the wheel arch. They made the rear cabin

broader too. Then came the Villa d'Este line. Taking a 6C-2500SS chassis, they removed the rearward sweep of the front wing and just allowed the crease to give a hint of the shape; they curved the body sides under the chassis; they flattened the roof section and added rear quarter lights; and finally they integrated the grille with the wings with a raised section starting alongside the engine cover, sweeping down to include the fog lights before fading away under the headlights. It was a complicated piece of coachbuilding but it had the desired effect. While Alfa Romeo built nearly 700 Freccia d'oro models, over 400 SS chassis were sent out to coachbuilders from 1947-51; Touring built a number of coupes before the Villa d'Este line came in, so the coupe shown is indeed a rare and beautiful model.

28-29 Not all the 6C 2500SS chassis had wire wheels.

TECHNICAL DESCRIPTION OF THE ALFA-ROMEO 6C-2500SS

YEARS OF PRODUCTION	1947-51
MODELS	2-SEATER COUPE
ENGINE	IN-LINE 6-CYLINDER
BORE X STROKE, CAPACITY	2.8 X 3.9 INCHES, 149 CU.IN
VALVEGEAR	TWIN OVERHEAD CAMSHAFT
FUEL SYSTEM	THREE SOLEX CARBURETORS
POWER	110 BHP AT 4800 RPM
TRANSMISSION	4-SPEED MANUAL
BODY/CHASSIS	STEEL PANELS ON STEEL FRAME
FRONT SUSPENSION	TRAILING ARMS AND COIL SPRINGS
REAR SUSPENSION	SWING AXLE WITH TORSION BARS
TIRES/WHEELS	6.50 X 17 ON STEEL OR WIRE WHEELS
WHEELBASE X TRACK (F X R)	106.3 X 57 X 58 INCHES
LENGTH, WIDTH, HEIGHT	177 X 69.5 X 57 INCHES
MAX SPEED	100 MPH
WHERE BUILT	MILAN, ITALY

Morgan 4/4

The Morgan is an unashamedly British sports car. Conceived in the Mid-thirties, the style has hardly changed over the years until the recent launch of the Aero 8. The traditional Morgan may be too uncomfortable for some, but it always provides enjoyable motoring. From its foundation in 1910, Morgan spent the next 25 years producing three-wheeled cars. They were powered by air-cooled motor-cycle engines until 1933, when the water-cooled Ford 8 engine was added to the range. Apart from generally sound engineering, Morgan had pioneered independent front suspension, a sliding pillar system that would later be used by Lancia. The first four-wheeler arrived in 1936; four wheels and four cylinders justified the name 4/4. The engine came from Coventry-Climax; with overhead inlet and side-exhaust valves, this 68.4 cu.in engine produced 34 bhp and gave a maximum speed of 77 mph. The 4-speed Moss gearbox was separated from the engine by a short tube so that the gear lever could operate directly on the gear selectors, while the new rear axle was mounted on leaf springs set inside the chassis rails, features which stayed with the car for many years after. Additional coachwork saw steel panels laid on ash frames; the styling then was very contemporary with front wings sweeping into running boards and a long louvred bonnet going forward to a chromed radiator. A four-seater version was offered in 1937 and a new overhead valve engine of 77.3 cu.in came from the Standard Flying Ten in 1939 with 39 bhp.

30-31 *This 1947 Morgan 4/4 has the longer body to provide four seats.*

**TECHNICAL DESCRIPTION OF THE MORGAN 4/4
(STANDARD ENGINE)**

YEARS OF PRODUCTION	1939-1950
MODELS	2-SEATER, 4-SEATER
ENGINE	IN-LINE 4-CYLINDER
BORE X STROKE, CAPACITY	2.5 x 3.9 INCHES, 77.3 CU.IN
VALVEGEAR	PUSHROD OHV
FUEL SYSTEM	SOLEX CARBURETOR
POWER	40 BHP AT 4300 RPM
TRANSMISSION	4-SPEED MANUAL
BODY/CHASSIS	Z-SECTION STEEL FRAME WITH STEEL BODY PANELS ON ASH FRAME
FRONT SUSPENSION	SLIDING PILLARS AND COIL SPRINGS
REAR SUSPENSION	LIVE AXLE WITH LEAF SPRINGS
TIRES/WHEELS	5.00 x 16 ON STEEL WHEELS
WHEELBASE x TRACK (F x R)	92 x 45 x 45 INCHES
LENGHT, WIDT, HEIGHT	139 x 55 x 50 INCHES
MAX SPEED	77 MPH
WHERE BUILT	MALVERN, WORCESTERSHIRE

The post-war 4/4 used the same Standard engine in both two and four-seater models. Meanwhile Standard dropped all their pre-war engines in favor of a single 122 cu.in four-cylinder unit designed for the Vanguard. Morgan adopted this 68 bhp engine in 1950 for the Plus 4, and dropped the 4/4. By 1953, the only styling change had been the headlights blended into the front wings and the chrome grille replaced with the curved version. When the TR2 also began to use the Vanguard engine, in 90 bhp 121.4 cu.in form, Standard could not provide enough engines. Morgan brought back the 4/4 range using the side-valve 71.5 cu. in. Ford engine as the 4/4 Series 2 with the same power as the Standard. Ford continued to provide power for the 4/4 with the 60.8 cu.in Series 3 (1961), the 81.7 cu.in Series 4 (1962) and the 91.4 cu.in Series 5 (1963). The 4/4 was always more of an open tourer than a sports car, but it was just as exclusive, because Morgan never built more than 500 cars a year.

32-33 *The Cisitalia Gran Sport by Pinin Farina was one of the world's style icons. Left, a roadster version finished second in the 1947 Mille Miglia.*

Cisitalia Gran Sport

Although the Cisitalia Gran Sport was not fast, it earned its place in history as the first of the Gran Turismo line, the practical sports coupe. An example has been in the New York Museum of Modern Art since 1951 and credited to Pinin Farina who had shown the first model in October 1947 at the Milan Coachbuilders' Fair. It was a successful car, too, on the Italian race-tracks in the early post-war years thanks to light weight and good roadholding.

Cisitalia was a Turin-based industrial company established by Piero Dusio. He had been a successful racing driver before the war and, in 1934, was the Italian amateur champion; he was

also a regular Mille Miglia competitor. After the war he started to build Fiat-powered single-seaters. The little D46 used the 67.1 cu.in Fiat four-cylinder engine in a tubular space-frame chassis with Fiat independent front suspension; many Italian stars drove them.

The racer had been designed by Fiat's Dante Giacosa. Giacosa also started the design for a coupe version, based on the Savio-bodied Fiat 508C MM that was developed for the 1938 Mille Miglia. When Fiat recalled Giacosa, the work was taken on by a former Fiat engineer, Giovanni Savonuzzi. From wind tunnel studies he evolved an effective shape that would allow a tuned Fiat engine to produce 100 mph performance.

Dusio took the design to Pinin Farina. While such coupes had been built for the high speed events before the war – notably with Superleggera bodies by Touring – these all had the cabin fared into a narrow tail for better streamlining. This gave a very small rear window and no luggage space. Pinin Farina made the back of the cabin much broader, and added that subsequently familiar bulge around the rear wheels, like an animal poised to leap; the headlights were also moved outwards to the front end of the wings. In fact the cabin was too wide, resulting in a rather heavy appearance from the front, but, from the side, the proportions were perfect.

A roadster version (illustrated) was built for the 1947 Mille Miglia with rear fins similar to those that Savonuzzi had originally defined for his coupe. Driven by Tazio Nuvolari it finished second, beating the new Ferrari 125 and Maserati A6CGS, and only losing the lead to a big pre-war Alfa sedan due to heavy rain. Dusio himself entered but didn't finish, although two other Cisitalias took third and fourth places ahead of the new 1100S Fiat coupes – Giacosa's response to the Cisitalia was to produce 400 of these sporting machines. Bernabei's third-placed car recorded the fastest time from Turin to Brescia at 95 mph.

By then Dusio was involved with a Grand Prix car project. He had approached Porsche to design this in 1946, at which time Professor Porsche was interned by the French. Dusio's contract was largely responsible for providing the funds to secure Porsche's release. While the design of the four-wheel-drive supercharged 91.5 cu.in GP car was very advanced, the project consumed more money than was available and Cisitalia went into liquidation. Dusio took the project to Argentina; despite the backing of General Peron under the name of Autoar the car never raced. Although Dusio came back to Italy to re-establish Cisitalia in late 1952, he was unsuccessful; the promising start for a new manufacturer was wasted on the altar of Grand Prix aspirations.

Meanwhile Pinin Farina had built the first 100 GS using aluminium body panels. A further 70 were

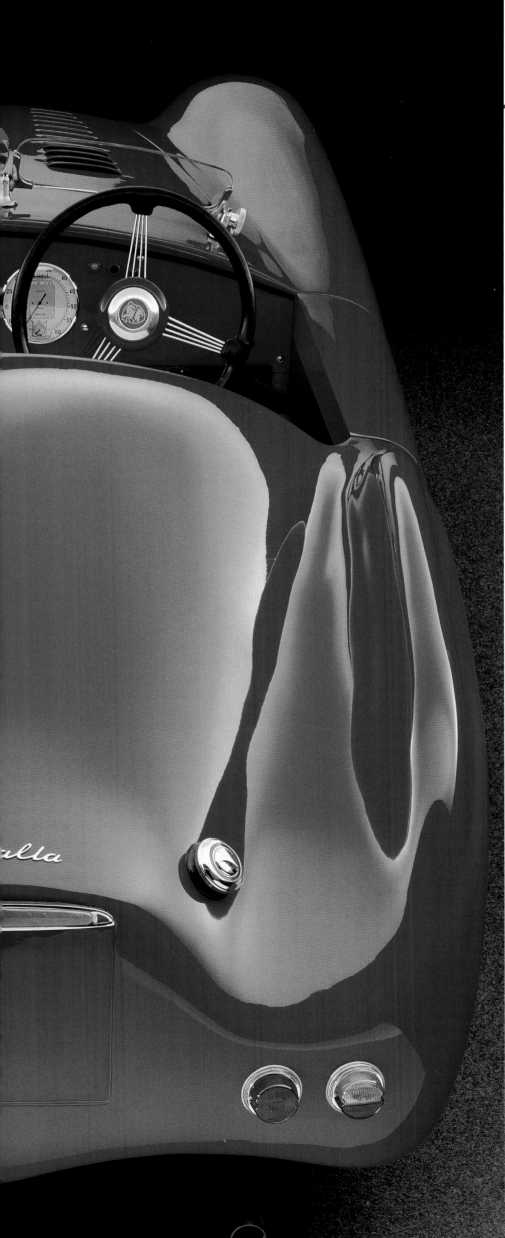

made with steel body panels by Vignale and Stabilimenti Farina who had also made some 25 examples of the Roadster (Tipo Nuvolari). Some of the Gran Sports were cabriolets. Fiat then followed up their 1100S with the 1950 Fiat 1100ES, using Pinin Farina to create a shape very close to that of the Cisitalia. Pinin Farina used the same lines for the Lancia Aurelia B20 in 1951. In automotive history, the Cisitalia GS was much more than just a Fiat-based special.

TECHNICAL DESCRIPTION OF THE CISITALIA GRAN SPORT

YEARS OF PRODUCTION	1947-52
MODELS	2-SEATER COUPE
ENGINE	IN-LINE 4-CYLINDER
BORE X STROKE, CAPACITY	2.6 X 2.9 INCHES, 66.4 CU.IN
VALVEGEAR	PUSHROD OHV
FUEL SYSTEM	TWIN SOLEX CARBURETORS
POWER	55 BHP AT 5500 RPM
TRANSMISSION	4-SPEED MANUAL
BODY/CHASSIS	ALUMINIUM OR STEEL PANELS ON SPACE FRAME
FRONT SUSPENSION	WISHBONES AND TRANSVERSE LEAF SPRINGS
REAR SUSPENSION	LIVE AXLE WITH LEAF SPRINGS
TIRES/WHEELS	5.00 X 15 ON WIRE WHEELS
WHEELBASE X TRACK (F X R)	94 X 49.5 X 49 INCHES
LENGTH, WIDTH, HEIGHT	134 X 57 X 49 INCHES
MAX SPEED	100 MPH
WHERE BUILT	TURIN, ITALY

34-35 *Cisitalia Tipo Nuvolari was named after the car in which Tazio Nuvolari finished second in the 1947 Mille Miglia*

Ferrari 166

No other make in the world generates the same universal respect as Ferrari. Whatever classic cars enthusiasts might revere, they accept that all Ferraris are classics. They represent all that is best in the Italian style from dashing good looks to competition success. While the 125 was used by many on road and track, the 166 was the first Ferrari to be offered for sale as a road car.

Through most of the Thirties, former racing driver Enzo Ferrari had run his own Scuderia Ferrari with Alfa Romeo racing cars. Following a spell as Alfa Romeo race team manager at the time of the birth of the immortal 158, Ferrari was not allowed to use the Scuderia name on cars for four years after he left in 1938. As a result the first Ferraris were the three AAC (Auto-Avio Costruzioni) 815s built out of Fiat parts, including two Fiat cylinder blocks to make a straight-8 1.91 cu.in engine, which took part in the 1940 Mille Miglia.

After the 1939-45 war, Ferrari set out to build his own cars, initially for competition. The first arrived in 1947 as the two-seater 125 either with all-enveloping bodywork or as a two-seater racing car with removable cycle-wings. Ferrari chose to use V-12 engines simply because he liked the idea, regardless of the complexity for a new manufacturer, but Modena was full of enterprising machine shops. The type number represented the capacity of a single cylinder as it

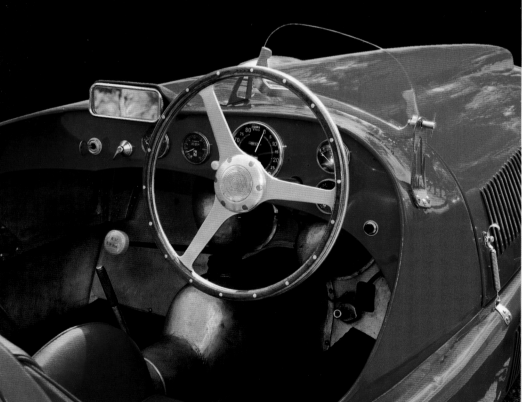

36-37 Ferrari 166MM, upper, and 166 Spyder Corsa 1948 (bottom left and bottom right).

would do for many years. Its chassis was a simple cross-braced tubular frame carrying wishbone front suspension and a live rear axle on leaf springs; a 5-speed gearbox was probably unique at the time.

For 1948 the introduction of a 122 cu.in formula 2 led to the Tipo 166 with the Colombo-designed engine increased to 121.7 cu.in. In competition form it developed 150 bhp at 7000 rpm, impressive statistics for 1948. Meanwhile Ferrari had supercharged the original 91.5 cu.in engine from the 125 for the first Grand Prix Ferrari.

The 166 Spyder Corsa was doing well in F2 races and in Sport form had won the 1948 Targa Florio and the Mille Miglia, for which the winning car had a coupe body. Some 11 of these competition chassis were built in 1948.

At the end of 1948, there were two Ferrari 166 models at the Turin Motor Show, the sports 166MM and the coupe 166 Inter, both with bodies designed by Touring and equipped with Superleggera coachwork construction. The 166MM was the first to feature the body style that was christened Barchetta, and was to be copied by AC via Tojeiro for the first post-war Ace; MM stood for Mille Miglia in honour of the 1948 victory. The 166MM earned its own place in Mille

Miglia history by winning the 1949 event in the hands of the previous year's winner Biondetti. And Chinetti put Ferrari on the Le Mans map by winning the first post-war 24-hour event in a 166M. Chinetti would become the Ferrari importer for the USA. Some of the 46 or so 166MM chassis were used for road-going coupes.

The term Inter was meant to be applied to cars for International racing but was finally used for the road cars which were built on a longer wheelbase than the MM; for these the engine was detuned to 110 bhp. Just over half of the 38 Inters had Touring coupe bodywork, but Vignale made nine coupes and Farina made four coupes and three cabriolets.

The 166 series continued to be available until 1951. However, almost identical models became 195 series in 1950, with a Touring-bodied coupe (berlinetta) winning the Mille Miglia that year from a barchetta. The 146 cu.in 195 engine was a 166 unit with a bigger cylinder bore. As before the 195 Inter used a longer wheelbase for coupes by Vignale, Ghia and Touring.

A further cylinder bore increase produced the 156 cu.in 212 series over 1951-2. Long and short chassis were called Inter and Export, with the Export intended for competition use. Some 110 chassis were built for the 212 series. Touring and Vignale built most of the 26 Export bodies in open or closed forms, while the Inters used a bigger variety of coachbuilders. Among the Inters, a number came from Pinin Farina, the first of a collaboration that has lasted through to the present day.

The 166 was Ferrari's first road car but the 212 confirmed that the Ferrari name had gained world-wide acceptance.

They may not have been the quietest or most comfortable road cars, but they had race-winning performance with Italian style.

38-39 Left, Ferrari 166 Inter by Touring. Right, 166 Inter by Stabilimenti Farina.

TECHNICAL DESCRIPTION OF THE FERRARI SPYDER CORSA	
YEARS OF PRODUCTION	1948-50
MODELS	SPYDER, SPORT, MM AND INTER
ENGINE	FRONT-MOUNTED V-12
BORE X STROKE, CAPACITY	2.36 x 2.31 INCHES, 121.5 CU.IN
VALVEGEAR	SINGLE OHC PER BANK
FUEL SYSTEM	THREE 30 DCF WEBERS
POWER	150 BHP AT 7000 RPM
TRANSMISSION	5-SPEED
BODY/CHASSIS	TWIN-TUBE STEEL CHASSIS WITH ALUMINIUM BODY PANELS
SUSPENSION	FRONT, WISHBONE AND TRANSVERSE LEAF SPRING; REAR, LIVE AXLE ON SEMI-ELLIPTIC LEAF SPRINGS
TIRES/WHEELS	5.50/6.00 x 15 TIRES; WIRE WHEELS
WHEELBASE, TRACK (F), TRACK(R)	90 x 47 x 47 INCHES
MAX SPEED	120 MPH
WHERE BUILT	MARANELLO, ITALY

YEARS OF PRODUCTION	1948-50
MODELS	SPYDER, SPORT, MM AND INTER
ENGINE	FRONT-MOUNTED V-12
BORE X STROKE, CAPACITY	2.39 X 2.31 INCHES, 121.5
VALVEGEAR	SINGLE OHC PER BANK
FUEL SYSTEM	THREE 32 DCF WEBERS
POWER	140 BHP AT 6600RPM
TRANSMISSION	5-SPEED
BODY/CHASSIS	TWIN-TUBE STEEL CHASSIS WITH ALUMINIUM BODY PANELS
SUSPENSION	FRONT, WISHBONE AND TRANSVERSE LEAF SPRING; REAR, LIVE AXLE ON SEMI-ELLIPTIC LEAF SPRINGS
TIRES/WHEELS	5.50/6.00 X 15 TIRES; WIRE WHEELS
WHEELBASE, TRACK (F), TRACK(R)	87 X 49 X 47 INCHES
MAX SPEED	120 MPH
WHERE BUILT	MARANELLO, ITALY

N.B. INTER MODELS HAD A 95-INCH WHEELBASE AND A 110 BHP ENGINE GIVING 110 MPH

Jaguar XK 120 to XK 150

For those who saw the unveiling at the Earls Court Motor Show in 1948, there was never any doubt that the Jaguar XK120 would become one of the great sporting cars in the history of motoring. In an age when most sports cars on the road still had separate wings, its all-enveloping bodywork was instantly modern, and its proportions were perfect. And it had a new 207 cu.in six-cylinder engine with twin overhead camshafts, a system previously considered as more appropriate to racing machinery. The figure 120 was chosen to represent the maximum speed the car could reach; a demonstration run in Belgium saw a standard car achieve 126 mph complete with hood and windscreen. At £988 ($3300), without the British purchase tax, it was still twice the price of an MG TC, but it was half the cost of a Frazer Nash; it was exceptional value for its performance.

Before the war, Jaguar had used engines from Standard with their own overhead-valve cylinder heads, but the twin-cam XK engine was entirely new; conceived during the latter stages of the war it was designed to give 100 mph performance to the first new sedan. In fact, the Mk.VII did not arrive until 1951. The engine would go on to serve the company for many years in 146, 231 and 256 cu.in forms, and earned them five victories in the Le Mans 24-hour race with XK120C and D-type Jaguars.

The separate chassis used deep boxed side members with cross bracing and carried wishbone front suspension with torsion bars, while the rear suspension just used leaf springs. Jaguar did not expect a big demand for the car and used traditional methods for the body with aluminium panels laid on wooden frames. When the orders flooded in, they changed the panels to pressed steel after 240 cars had been built. Most of the production from the first 18 months were exported and the car did not reach its home market until early 1950.

The striking style of the body owed much to the influence of the Italian coachbuilder Touring whose work was seen on the Alfa Romeos and BMWs in the final pre-war Mille Miglia events. A year later, a fixed head coupe became available and in 1953, a drop head coupe. The same body styles were carried through to the XK140 which arrived in 1954. For this the engine was uprated to the 190 bhp specification that had

40-41 *Graceful lines of the XK120 roadster set new standards of elegance in 1948.*

TECHNICAL DESCRIPTION OF THE JAGUAR XK120	
YEARS OF PRODUCTION	1948 - 1954
MODELS	ROADSTER AND FIXED HEAD COUPE
ENGINE	FRONT-MOUNTED IN-LINE SIX-CYLINDER
BORE X STROKE, CAPACITY	3.2 x 4.1 INCHES, 210 CU.IN
VALVEGEAR	TWIN OVERHEAD CAMSHAFT
FUEL SYSTEM	TWO SU CARBURETORS
POWER	160 BHP AT 5000 RPM
TRANSMISSION	4-SPEED
BODY/CHASSIS	BOXED STEEL CHASSIS WITH ALUMINIUM OR STEEL BODY PANELS
SUSPENSION	FRONT, WISHBONES AND TORSION BARS. REAR, LIVE AXLE WITH LEAF SPRINGS
TIRES/WHEELS	6.00 x 16 ON STEEL WHEELS
WHEELBASE, TRACK (F), TRACK(R)	102 x 54 x 53 INCHES
LENGHT, WIDT, HEIGHT	162 x 62 x 52 INCHES
MAX SPEED	120 MPH
WHERE BUILT	COVENTRY, ENGLAND

TECHNICAL DESCRIPTION OF THE JAGUAR XK150 3.4

YEARS OF PRODUCTION	1957-1961
MODELS	XK150, XK150S FHC AND DHC
ENGINE	FRONT-MOUNTED IN-LINE SIX-CYLINDER
BORE X STROKE, CAPACITY	3.2 x 4.1 INCHES, 210 CU.IN
VALVEGEAR	TWIN OVERHEAD CAMSHAFT
FUEL SYSTEM	TWO SU CARBURETORS
POWER	190 BHP AT 5500 RPM
TRANSMISSION	4-SPEED AND O/D OR AUTO
BODY/CHASSIS	BOXED STEEL CHASSIS WITH STEEL BODY
	PANELS OR STEEL BODY PANELS
FRONT SUSPENSION	FRONT, WISHBONES AND TORSION BARS
REAR SUSPENSION	LIVE AXLE WITH LEAF SPRINGS
TIRES/WHEELS	6.00 x 16 STEEL OR WIRE WHEELS
WHEELBASE, TRACK (F), TRACK(R)	102 x 51 x 51 INCHES
LENGHT, WIDT, HEIGHT	177 x 64 x 55 INCHES
MAX SPEED	124 MPH
WHERE BUILT	COVENTRY, ENGLAND

been offered as a Special Equipment option for the XK120 and it was moved forward three inches to give more space in the cockpit; for the fixed head and drophead coupes, the front seats were moved even further forward by altering the bulkhead to allow space for occasional rear seats. An overdrive was also available while an option on Special Equipment XK140s was the C-type cylinder head which would increase the power to 210 bhp. Stiffer springing and rack and pinion steering improved the handling. Heavier bumpers and fewer strips in the grille made the new model instantly recognizable. While the XK140 did not have the refreshing purity of the XK120's appearance, it was a better car for everyday use.

The steady improvement in practicality was taken several stages further when the XK150 replaced the XK140 in 1957. Restyled in the fashion of the medium sedans – 2.7 and 3.4 – the XK150 had a

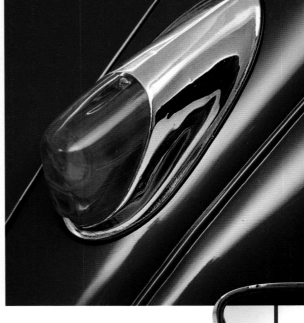

curved windscreen and was usefully wider inside. The adoption of disc brakes was a major step forward, but in other respects the specification was similar to that of the XK140. Most cars had the 210 bhp Special Equipment cylinder heads but then the S version came out with 250 bhp with triple carburetors and a higher compression ratio in 1958. A year later the engine was increased to 230.7 cu.in and the S model produced 265 bhp, the same that would power the E-type in 1961.

Of the 30,000 cars made over 12 years, the XK120 was the most popular at 12,078 followed by the XK150 at 9395 and the XK140 at 8884. The XK120 was almost the fastest car on the road in its day, but by the time of the XK150, there were many faster. But none could match the sheer value of the XK range.

Aston Martin DB2 and DB2/4

Aston Martin were one of several British companies to challenge the Italian lead in the new Grand Touring market. While traditionalists retained the belief that a sports car had to be an open two-seater with the option of a folding hood, others recognized that higher cruising speeds demanded a closed roof for long distance comfort. Aston Martin was founded in 1913 and had long made small sports cars with efficient 91.5 or 122 cu.in engines; some models were open four-seaters, and a few sedans were made in the Thirties.

Lagonda were also in the sporting market but their cars and engines were bigger; the company had won the Le Mans 24-hour race in 1935 with a 274. cu.in engine and finished third and fourth in 1939 with a 274. cu.in V-12.

In 1947 industrialist David Brown took over both companies. Both had prepared post-war designs but it was Aston Martin's prototype Atom sports sedan which provided the basis for the first production Aston Martins. The 122 cu.in Sports, later called the DB1, was launched in October 1948, together with a stark 2-seater replica of the car that had won the 1948 Spa 24-hour race; a 122 cu.in coupe was announced at the same time but not shown. However three coupes were entered for the 1949 Le Mans 24-hour race; two used the existing pushrod four-cylinder 122 cu.in engine, but a third had the 158 cu.in twin overhead camshaft six-cylinder engine that had been designed under W.O.Bentley for Lagonda. The first post-war Lagonda was announced in 1949.

While none of the three cars finished Le Mans in 1949, two went to the Spa 24-hour race two weeks later. Chinetti repeated his Le Mans victory in a Ferrari 166 and Louveau's pre-war Delage was second but the 158 cu.in Aston finished third and the 122 cu.in was fifth. British cars did well at that event as a Jowett Javelin won the touring category and HRG took the team award in the 91.5 cu.in sports class.

The success of the six-cylinder Aston Martin was enough to convince David Brown that this was his engine of the future and the DB2 was first exhibited at the New York Show in April 1950, with the engine in 105 bhp tune. The design followed the Le Mans cars closely; Lagonda's Frank Feeley had created a winning fast-back shape. Early cars had three separate grilles but this soon changed to the one-piece Omega shape. Underneath, the rectangular tube steel chassis carried Porsche-style trailing arms with coil springing at the front, and a well-located live rear axle.

A drophead coupe was available later in 1950, and in 1951 came the first use of the Vantage name for a high performance version with 125 bhp. The engine continued to be used in the competition DB3 and DB3S throughout the Fifties and was further developed to power the DBR1 to win the World Sports Car Championship in 1959. While the DB2 was highly rated as a GT car, it suffered from only having two seats with limited luggage space behind. This was rectified in 1953 with the introduction of the DB2/4; the DB2 body was lengthened and the rear roof line raised to give two small rear seats and more luggage space to which access was gained through an opening rear window.

44 Aston Martin DB2 1952 with Vantage engine.

45 *Aston Martin DB2/4 1953 with 158 cu.in engine.*

TECHNICAL DESCRIPTION OF
THE ASTON MARTIN DB2 VANTAGE AND (DB2/4)

YEARS OF PRODUCTION	1950-1954
MODELS	FIXED HEAD COUPE
ENGINE	FRONT-MOUNTED IN-LINE SIX-CYLINDER
BORE X STROKE, CAPACITY	3 x 3.5 INCHES, 157.4 CU. IN.
VALVEGEAR	TWIN OVERHEAD CAMSHAFT
FUEL SYSTEM	TWO SU CARBURETORS
POWER	125 BHP AT 5000 RPM
TRANSMISSION	4-SPEED
BODY/CHASSIS	BOXED STEEL CHASSIS WITH ALUMINIUM BODY PANELS
SUSPENSION	FRONT, TRAILING ARMS AND COILS
	REAR, LIVE AXLE, MULTI-LINK, COILS
TIRES/WHEELS	6.00 x 16 ON WIRE WHEELS
WHEELBASE, TRACK (F), TRACK(R)	99 x 54 x 54 INCHES
LENGHT, WIDT, HEIGHT	162 (169) x 65 x 54 INCHES
MAX SPEED	115 MPH
WHERE BUILT	FELTHAM, ENGLAND

Initially the engine was the Vantage 158 cu.in, but a 183 cu.in version was used from April 1954 with 140 bhp. This raised the maximum speed to around 115 mph.

The DB2-4 Mk.11 came in 1955 with minor body changes; in addition to the existing 3-door sedan and drop-head coupe styles, a 2-door fixed head coupe was available using what was effectively a hard-top on the drop-head. The body was built at the future home of Aston Martin in Newport Pagnell by Tickford, which had been bought by David Brown in 1953.

With the 1957 announcement of the DB Mk.III came the final version of the DB2; the three body styles continued to be available but the front grille adopted the revised shape of the DB3S. Disc front brakes and a redesigned engine with 162 bhp (up to 195 bhp with options) helped to make this the best of all the Atom-based models. Some 1726 were built over the ten years to 1959 when the DB Mk.III was replaced by the DB4.

Bristol 400, 402, 404

With a background in the aircraft industry extending back to 1910, Bristol chose to move into car construction after the 1939-45 war. War-time experiments with their own design proved unsuccessful, so they decided to develop an existing one. The basis of their first car was the pre-war BMW 327/80 coupe built around a 326 chassis as a result of the Thirties association between Frazer Nash and BMW. H.J.Aldington, who had acquired the Frazer Nash car company in 1928, imported BMWs which were marketed as Frazer Nash-BMWs. After the war, he acquired the rights to BMW drawings and brought BMW designer Fritz Fiedler to England to assist. Knowing that Bristol wanted to make cars, he arranged a joint venture with a view to selling the products as Frazer Nash-Bristols.

46-47 Bristol 400 of 1947, the first car from the airplane manufacturer.

In the end, Bristol made their own BMW-based cars but allowed Frazer Nash to use the Bristol engines and other components in their own sports cars which were modelled around war-time developments of the tubular-framed BMW 328. The new Bristol 400 chassis followed the design of that for the 4-door 326 – boxed steel ladder frame with sheet steel flooring. A transverse leaf spring gave independent suspension at the front, while the rear had a well-located live rear axle with torsion bars.

The body was a close copy of the one built by Autenreith for the 327; as the 326 wheelbase was 6 inches longer, the rear side window was lengthened. This also increased the rear seat space, aided further by the wider rear track of the 326 rear axle design.

For the engine, Bristol started from the 80 bhp version that was used in the sportier BMW 327 as well as in the BMW 328. A straight-6 122 cu.in, it used a side-mounted camshaft which operated valves in a hemispherical combustion chamber through cross-over pushrods and rockers; a smooth

TECHNICAL DESCRIPTION OF THE BRISTOL 400

YEARS OF PRODUCTION	1946-1949
MODELS	4-SEATER SEDAN
ENGINE	IN-LINE 6-CYLINDER
BORE X STROKE, CAPACITY	2.6 x 3.7 INCHES, 120 CU.IN
VALVEGEAR	TWIN PUSH-ROD SYSTEM WITH INCLINED OHV
FUEL SYSTEM	3 SU CARBURETORS
POWER	80 BHP AT 4200 RPM
TRANSMISSION	4-SPEED MANUAL
BODY/CHASSIS	BOXED GIRDER STEEL CHASSIS WITH ALUMINIUM PANELS
SUSPENSION, FRONT	UPPER WISHBONE, TRANSVERSE LEAF SPRING
SUSPENSION, REAR	LIVE AXLE, TRANSVERSE LINKS, A-BRACKET, TORSION BARS
TIRES/WHEELS	5.50 x 16 ON STEEL WHEELS
WHEELBASE, TRACK (F), TRACK(R)	114 x 52 x 54 INCHES
LENGTH, WIDT, HEIGHT	183 x 64 x 59 INCHES
MAX SPEED	95 MPH
WHERE BUILT	FILTON, BRISTOL, ENGLAND

engine that was very efficient. The gearbox was a Bristol design.

What Bristol did was to take the best of BMW's sporting designs and apply their aircraft expertise to build the car to the highest possible standards. Every aspect was studied and improved in design and, frequently, material specification. The result was a car that had remarkable performance when it was launched in 1947 with a maximum speed of 90 mph and new standards of ride and roadholding. Hand built, it was inevitably expensive but the company never intended to enter volume production. Only 470 were built between 1947 and 1950.

Meanwhile the 401 had been launched in 1949, a 400 with an aerodynamic body that had been proposed by Touring, Milan and refined by Bristol who used the Touring Superleggera principle of small body frame tubes around which the aluminium panels were wrapped. The improved shape with the same 85 bhp brought the maximum speed up to 95 mph. Some 600 were built from 1949 to 1952. Additionally there were just 21 of the convertible 402. Outwardly the 403 was almost identical to the 401 but the engine was increased to 100 bhp and improvements were made to the gearbox, suspension and brakes. From 1953-55, around 275 were made.

Also launched in 1953 was the 404, a fastback 2-seater coupe on a shortened 403 chassis. Where the early cars had respected their BMW origins with a version of the German company's grille, the 404 looked to Bristol's own origins by using a front intake shaped like that for a jet engine. And the rear of the car featured small fins; being based on those of the Bristol 450 Le Mans racer, these were more aerodynamic in origin than the stylistic devices of the American sedans. For the 404, the 122 cu.in engine was given 105 bhp, enough for 110 mph; it was a fast car for its day and earned the title of

TECHNICAL DESCRIPTION OF THE BRISTOL 402	
YEARS OF PRODUCTION	1949-1953
MODELS	4-SEATER CONVERTIBLE
ENGINE	IN-LINE 6-CYLINDER
BORE X STROKE, CAPACITY	2.6 X 3.7 INCHES, 120 CU.IN
VALVEGEAR	TWIN PUSH-ROD SYSTEM WITH INCLINED OHV
FUEL SYSTEM	3 DOWNDRAFT SOLEX
POWER	85 BHP AT 4500 RPM
TRANSMISSION	4-SPEED MANUAL
BODY/CHASSIS	BOXED GIRDER STEEL CHASSIS WITH ALUMINIUM PANELS
SUSPENSION, FRONT	UPPER WISHBONE, TRANSVERSE LEAF SPRING
SUSPENSION, REAR	LIVE AXLE, TRANSVERSE LINKS, A-BRACKET, TORSION BARS
TIRES/WHEELS	5.50 X 16 ON STEEL WHEELS
WHEELBASE, TRACK (F), TRACK(R)	114 X 52 X 54 INCHES
LENGHT, WIDT, HEIGHT	192 X 67 X 60 INCHES
MAX SPEED	100 MPH
WHERE BUILT	FILTON, BRISTOL, ENGLAND

Businessman's Express. Unfortunately only 50 of them could afford it.

For the 405, Bristol stretched the 404 shape back to the standard wheelbase size and, for the only time, produced a 4-door model to replace the 403. After 340 of the 405, including 43 two-door convertibles by Abbotts of Farnham, the 406 emerged as a more conventional-looking sedan with two doors; by now comfort was beginning to add weight, so the engine was increased to 134 cu.in, but the performance was no longer class-leading. A 311 cu.in Chrysler V-8 was installed in the 406 to create the 407 from 1962, and all succeeding Bristols have used Chrysler engines.

50-51 *The 404 Businessman's Express, a shortened 405.*

TECHNICAL DESCRIPTION OF THE BRISTOL 404

YEARS OF PRODUCTION	1953-1955
MODELS	2+2 COUPE
ENGINE	IN-LINE 6-CYLINDER
BORE X STROKE, CAPACITY	2.6 X 3.7 INCHES, 120 CU.IN
VALVEGEAR	TWIN PUSH-ROD SYSTEM WITH INCLINED OHV
FUEL SYSTEM	3 DOWNDRAFT SOLEX
POWER	105 BHP AT 5000 RPM
TRANSMISSION	4-SPEED MANUAL
BODY/CHASSIS	BOXED GIRDER STEEL CHASSIS WITH ALUMINIUM PANELS
SUSPENSION, FRONT	UPPER WISHBONE WITH TRANSVERSE LEAF SPRING
SUSPENSION, REAR	LIVE AXLE, TRANSVERSE LINKS, A-BRACKET, TORSION BARS
TIRES/WHEELS	5.50 X 16 ON STEEL WHEELS
WHEELBASE, TRACK (F), TRACK(R)	96 X 52 X 54 INCHES
LENGHT, WIDT, HEIGHT	159 X 68 X 56 INCHES
MAX SPEED	110 MPH
WHERE BUILT	FILTON, BRISTOL, ENGLAND

1951 - 1960

CLASSIC SEDANS

Although most of the car producing nations were well under way by the end of the previous decade, there was still a far greater demand than supply. Waiting lists were common, even in the USA. As a result there was not the pressure on manufacturers to make frequent changes to models, although Americans still expected it to be obvious that they had the latest car, so minor changes had to be made at minimal investment to differentiate the model years. By the middle of the Fifties, basic transport was generally available and manufacturers had time to enhance their ranges with more specialist models, the ones that would become future classics. In America it was the period of the high performance V-8 when ever larger engines were inserted to satisfy the demand for rubber-burning acceleration at the local drag-strip or even just at the traffic lights. Technological progress saw the introduction of disc brakes and more general use of radial ply tires in Europe. Curiously, America lagged behind in such primary safety features, but

concerned themselves more with driving comfort aids like automatic transmission, power steering, air-conditioning and large spacious interiors.

In styling, America remained the most influential center; ever-larger tail fins were a memorable feature of the Fifties. Around the world, the old coachbuilding firms were suffering as the separate chassis was replaced by the high volume unitary construction. France had all but lost its coachbuilding industry with the demise of the Grandes Makes like Delage and Talbot. English coachbuilders were more artisan than original but there were enough makes around still using a separate chassis. It was the Italians who saw the way ahead. They could see that their future lay in providing a styling service and in building smaller runs of specialist cars that would not be economical for major manufacturers. By working with the manufacturers they were able to have the cars taken off the production line before they were finished; they then completed the bodywork themselves. Bertone's production of

the Alfa Romeo Giulietta Sprint was a notable example – Spider and SS versions also came from Bertone. At the top end of the scale Aston Martin went to Touring to generate the shape for the new DB4 and built the cars under Touring's Superleggera licence.

Italian coachbuilders were very much involved in the styling, and frequently body building, of most of the Italian cars apart from those within Fiat. The first Lancia was the Aurelia which arrived in 1950 to be followed, a year later, by the coupe version with fast-back styling by Pinin Farina – an enlarged Cisitalia with four seats. Pinin Farina went on to design the open Spider version too.

It was a Pinin Farina design that was to lead to the R-type Bentley Continental of 1952 using the same basic fast-back shape. The Torinese coachbuilder had made a special body for Jean Daninos who would head the Facel Vega firm; this was

52-53 Lancia Flaminia 2500 Zagato 1959-1961.

shown at Paris in 1948. Before the war Bentley had experimented with similar shapes. The new Continental followed these overall lines but gave them added grace with twin sweeping wing lines tailing into restrained fins. With an uprated version of the old six-cylinder 274 cu.in R-type engine, it was good for 115 mph. The style continued into the S-type. By 1959, HJ Mulliner had built 193 Continentals on the R-type chassis and over 400 on the next model, the S-type. This was introduced in 1955 when Rolls-Royce brought out the matching Silver Cloud in 1955, the first Rolls to be available with standard bodywork, something that the company had already done with the first post-war Bentley, the Mk.VI. Underneath was a new but still separate chassis which allowed continued freedom for coachbuilders. With the 1959 S2 and Silver Cloud II came a new engine, the 378 cu.in V8. The S3 and Cloud III came with twin headlamp style in 1962 and both were replaced by the first unitary-construction T-type and Silver Shadow in 1965.

Other old-established English firms like Alvis and Rover continued to develop their big sedans and Alvis used the Swiss coachbuilder Graber to provide the basis of their new TD21 in 1958; Graber had been building special bodies on the TC21 from the Mid-fifties. Rover's single shape policy had started in 1949 with the Rover 75 with a six-cylinder 128 cu.in engine; in 1953 came the 90 and the 60, the latter with a four-cylinder engine.

The range was to continue through 80, 95, 100, 105 and 110 versions until 1964 by which time over 130,000 of these middle-class P4 sedans had been built. The larger 183 cu.in P5 appeared in 1959.

Although post-war MG production was initially taken up with the TC, MG launched the Y-type Magnette sedan in 1947. This had been designed pre-war with independent front suspension on its box-section chassis. Using a single carburetor version of the TC engine, it was a lively performer; it was uprated in 1951 to YB specification.

This was followed by the ZA Magnette which used the 1952 Wolseley 4/44 body – which had been powered by the 76.2 cu.in MG sports engine – fitted with an MG grille and the BMC B-series 91.5 cu.in engine, which gave it very good performance. Badge-engineering had arrived in the British Motor Corporation and would be seen at its worst with the next generation Austin, Morris, Riley and MG sedans all using the same bodies and engines – not classics.

1951 - 1960

In classic terms, however the most notable British sedan arrival was that of the Jaguar 2.4 in 1955. The Mk.VII had been in production from 1950 and would be replaced by the similar Mk.VIII in 1957. The 2.4 was the 'little Jaguar', a compact 4-door sports sedan using a short-stroke version of the famous XK 207 cu.in from the bigger car; it was also Jaguar's first unitary-bodied sedan.

The 207 cu.in engine was added to the range in 1957 making a fast car very fast for its day. The Mk.II arrived in 1959 with a wider rear track and deeper side windows; there was also the option of a 231 cu.in engine which gave genuine 125 mph performance. A 152 cu.in Daimler V-8 version was added to the range in 1963. The 'softer' S-type came in 1964 but the Mk.II cars continued on till 1968. Almost 130,000 of the Mk.I and II were built.

Big Fiat sedans of the period were sturdy but hardly classics. However Alfa Romeo's 1900 was

notable for the being the first volume production sedan for the nationalized company. Announced in 1950 it had a unitary construction, independent wishbone front suspension and a well-located live axle. The new 116 cu.in four-cylinder engine retained the Alfa hallmark of twin overhead camshafts but these were chain driven. It wasn't the quietest or most comfortable car but it was certainly sporting with 100 mph performance from the basic 90 bhp engine. Later TI and TI Super versions had 100 and 115 bhp respectively and these engines were used in the Sprint and Super Sprint versions which were produced as rolling platforms for the coachbuilders. Over 17,000 4-door sedans and 1800 Sprint chassis were produced in the 1950-1958 period. It was an important classic for Alfa Romeo. The Giulietta which came out in 1955 was preceded by the sporting versions in 1954 and is covered in more detail later in the chapter.

In Sweden, Saab continued to produce the two-stroke 92, changing to the 93 in 1955 with the introduction of a 45.7 cu.in 3-cylinder engine and dead axle rear suspension; the 95 estate followed in 1959 with the engine up to 51.8 cu.in, which the 96 used in 1960. Volvo added the 4-door Amazon or B120 in 1956 using the PV444 engine increased to 97 cu.in. The 1958 PV544 continued the PV444's hump-backed shape in a thoroughly revised model which earned the 109 cu.in engine in 1961. The Amazon Sport (B 122S) came in 1958 with 4-speeds and 88 bhp, with the two-door 121 following in 1961. Although these cars were made in fairly high volumes (PV444 196,000; PV544 440,000; B120-122 564,000), the production runs were spread over long periods and the cars were very well built.

In France, Citroen produced the epochal DS19 in 1955 with many advanced features which were to justify keeping it in production for 20 years with few changes. The chassis was a steel structure to which the body panels were bolted; the style was exceptionally aerodynamic. Although the engine was initially the old long-stroke 122 cu.in, this was replaced in 1966 by short stroke 'fours' of 122 and 140 cu.in. It was unique in using hydraulic power to operate its

variable height all-independent suspension, the clutch for its semi-automatic transmission, the brakes and steering servo. Over the 20 years, 1.4 million were built including a number at their English assembly plant. The hydraulic circuitry may not make it the easiest of classic cars to maintain, but it was a true milestone design.

American classics of the period are generally regarded as those from the top end of the manufacturers' ranges. In the Fifties these were the high performance models or those produced in more limited numbers. As one of the smaller manufacturers, Studebaker set out to impress by style for which Raymond Loewy was responsible. The early post-war range was uplifted in 1950 with the circular radiator intake theme and clean lines uncluttered by chromework, quite unlike any other. The 1953 coupe designs – Starliner and Starlight – were even more remarkable.

The Cadillac Eldorado and the Lincoln Continental were the major contenders in the luxury car market. The Cadillac used excessive chrome and styling gimmicks but the Lincoln was more restrained, more European. At the other end of the market, Chevrolet launched the Corvair

compact in 1959 as a response to the success of the imported Volkswagen. Like the Beetle it used a rear-mounted air-cooled 'boxer' engine, but, being American, it was somewhat larger and had six cylinders; it was also very European in style. Unfortunately the design also adopted the Beetle's swing-axle rear suspension, which could make the car very unstable in cornering; American safety crusader Ralph Nader effectively killed the car and even a revised rear suspension system couldn't overcome the market resistance – there were some nice-looking models in the range.

In performance terms, though, the 1955 Chrysler 300 was the real classic. It was Chrysler's answer to the Ford Thunderbird, itself a response to Chevrolet's Corvette. Chrysler, though, gave sports car performance in sedan style and the hemi-headed 329 cu.in V8 produced 300 bhp, making the 300 the most powerful production car in the world at the time. For 1956 the engine was increased to 354 cu.in and 355 bhp for the 300B, and for the 1957 300C there was a 390 cu.in 390 bhp option. Chevrolet's reply to this was the Bel Air, restyled for 1957, using the new 280 cu.in small-block V-8 with fuel injection and 283 bhp for the top range model. This too was destined to become an American classic.

MINI CLASSICS

The Suez fuel crises of the Mid-fifties was responsible for the near success of another breed, the bubble-car or microcar, a latter-day evolution of the Twenties cyclecars. Like their forerunners they were powered by motor cycle engines but these were three-wheelers taking advantage of tax concessions for motor cycles and sidecars – some produced four-wheel versions as well. In Britain, there were Bond, Reliant and Berkeley of whom Reliant went on to make a proper car – the Scimitar – and Berkeleys were sports cars. In Germany, Messerschmitt took over production of the Fend invalid car while BMW acquired the

rights of the Italian Iso bubble car, and used BMW single cylinder motor cycle units. This Isetta became the twin-cylinder 600 4-wheeler, which then grew into the successful 700 in sedan and coupe forms from 1959. By the end of the decade, though, the bubble car had died as mini cars were almost as small but did everything so much more comfortably.

One was the new Fiat 500. The Fiat 500 Topolino had effectively been replaced by the rear-engined 600 in 1955 but the Nuova 500 came in 1957 as the Italian 'peoples' car'. With its air-cooled 29.2 cu.in 13 bhp twin-cylinder engine also rear-mounted, it was a neat and attractive little 2-door minicar which could just take four adults.

A 30.4 cu.in version arrived in 1958 and the model continued on through various forms until the 500R came out in 1972 using an 18 bhp version of the new 36.2 cu.in twin from the 126. Although Fiat did not produce tuned versions, Carlo Abarth sold ready-modified 500 and 600 models as Fiat-Abarths, such as the 695SS or the OT1000.By the end of its production in 1977, over 4 million new 500s had been built.

Like the Topolino it lasted twenty years. In France the 2CV continued, but Renault added the Dauphine to the range in 1956 and brought in the Dauphine Gordini in 1960. It used the same basic layout as the 4CV which continued on into 1962.

The trend-setting Mini arrived in 1959. With a 34 bhp 51.7 cu. in. version of the Morris Minor A-series engine mounted transversely on top of the gearbox, it was carefully packaged to seat four people in reasonable comfort and provide some luggage space. Front-wheel-drive and firm rubber cone suspension gave it remarkable roadholding too. The Mini-Cooper arrived in 1961 with 60.8 cu.in and 55 bhp, followed in 1963 by the various Cooper S models (59.1 cu.in - 65 bhp, 65.3 cu.in - 68 bhp, 77.8 cu.in - 75 bhp); they were extremely successful in all forms of motor sport too. Along the way came more luxurious Riley and Wolseley versions too.

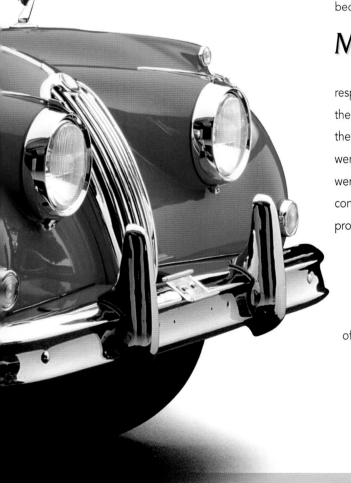

54-55 Jaguar XK140 roadster 1954-1957.

In its various forms the Mini was to continue until 2000, over 30 years and still an example to many. Maybe the basic Mini is hardly a collectable classic but genuine Cooper versions are much sought after.

GRAND TOURERS

Following the birth of the Grand Touring breed, exemplified by the Cisitalia, Aston Martin and Porsche 356 of the late Forties, the Fifties saw a rapid growth in this niche market. The Grand Tourer was for those who wanted to travel long distances at high speed with enough luggage for a week-end in a sporting car, but without the drawbacks of open air motoring or the noise of soft-tops. Some manufacturers just made fixed head coupe versions of their open sports cars, like the MGA or Jaguar XK120. Others offered detachable hard-tops, or Targa-tops like the Triumph TR4.

But many built proper GTs. As most of these cars were in limited volumes they retained separate chassis which allowed the remaining coachbuilders to build special bodies. The Ferrari name was established in racing and the early Ferrari GTs were built for such long distance races as the Mille Miglia or Carrera Panamericana, usually with Touring or Vignale bodywork. Pinin Farina's first work on a Ferrari was a 212 Inter roadster in 1952. Ferrari's first series of cars were all based on the smaller Colombo-designed V-12, but as Grand Prix racing had shown that large normally aspirated engines were better than small supercharged ones, the bigger Lampredi-designed V-12 was used for the road cars as well. The first genuine road-going Ferrari with no racing aspirations was the 342 America of 1952 with a 200 bhp 250 cu.in V-12; only six were built and Pinin Farina built the three coupes. The earlier 340 America had used the same engine in 220 bhp form but was also used for sports-car racing as MM or Mexico versions; Ghia, Touring and Vignale had provided the bodywork. The 375 America with 300 bhp came in 1953 and Pinin Farina produced most of the twelve cars that were built using a variety of different styles.

All GTs are classics. All Ferraris are classics. It is not possible to include every Ferrari in a general work. Although these three models were produced in very small numbers, they represent the start of the big fast road-going Ferraris. Once Ferrari had established an agreement with Pinin Farina, production numbers began to grow. The 250GT Europa of 1954 was the first of these – around 40 were built. This was followed by 77 of the 250GT Berlinetta Tour de France from 1956-59 before the arrival of the 250GT short wheelbase (SWB) Berlinetta – the classic racing GT. Ferrari called his racing GTs Berlinettas while his road cars were referred to as coupes. Coupes, cabriolets and Spyders on the longer 250GT chassis were all in production before the end of the decade.

Ferrari did not have a monopoly in Italy, though. Fiat then made a tentative foray into the GT market with the Otto-Vu (V8). Fiat engineers had designed a 122 cu.in 70 degree V-8 as a possible engine for touring cars. When this idea was shelved they created a small GT coupe around a tubular and sheet steel chassis with all-independent suspension and showed it at Geneva in 1952. Fiat built around 115 cars from 1952-54. At that point Zagato, who had already re-bodied five or six cars, acquired a further 25 units, some as complete cars, some as rolling chassis. Over the years to 1959 Zagato converted these to lightweight coupes, mostly for national competition; Elio Zagato won the Italian 2000GT championship in 1955 and 1959. Siata used their own chassis and installed Otto-Vu running gear; they built 56 Siata 208s. Fiat's little coupe did not have a big following outside Italy but it was an effective little car capable of 120 mph.

Of greater significance though was the Maserati 3500GT which arrived in 1957. The Maserati brothers had been producing competition cars since 1926 and sold many of them to private customers, but this was not enough to keep the company going so the firm was sold to the Orsi family in 1938. After the war the brothers set up OSCA. Initially they concentrated on small competition sports cars using their own engines. Formula Junior single-seaters were added in 1959. Twin-cam OSCA engines were built by Fiat for the 1500S and 1600S sports cars from 1959-66 and OSCA used them in their own GT cars using local coachbuilders.

Meanwhile Maserati continued to produce such successful competition cars as the 250F GP car and the 300S and 450S sports-cars. They hand-built a few road cars too, but it wasn't until they withdrew from racing in 1957 that they took road cars seriously and produced the 3500GT. The engine followed the design principles of the six-cylinder racing units but used chain-drive for the camshafts rather than gears; the road-going 213

cu.in engine was also used in the 350S sports-racing cars. With a tubular chassis frame, bodies were built by Touring (2+2) and Vignale (open Spider on a shortened chassis). The 213 cu.in engine was further refined and fuel injection was added in 1962 for the 3500GTI – the first car to use the GTI name. In 1959 road-going versions of the 450S V-8 power unit were used in a limited run of 32 5000GT coupes. Maserati had arrived on the road car scene.

In Germany, Porsche continued to produce their Beetle-based coupes as well as competition RS sports cars. BMW didn't start post-war production until 1952 and then produced large comfortable sedans and tourers in their new 500 series – developments of the last of the pre-war 300 series. However the launch of the 502 with a new V-8 engine in 1954 marked progress. Coupe and cabriolet versions of this arrived with the 503 in 1956 when BMW also launched the two-seater 507; although only 253 of this were produced, it was one of the finest designs of the Mid-fifties with handsome Goertz bodywork and the V-8 engine

increased to 195 cu.in with 150 bhp. It was available with a factory hard-top, hence its inclusion in this GT section. Mercedes were also slow to start post-war production with a new version of the 170 sedan. The memorable 300SL arrived in 1954 as the road-going version of the 1952 Le Mans winner – more later – but the similarly-styled sporting 190SL was more affordable; with a 4-cylinder ohc 105 bhp 116 cu.in engine, it would reach 118 mph.

French taxation had all but killed the established grandes makes of Delage and Delahaye – a few were produced before they died in 1954 – but Darracq (now Talbot) continued to produce fast road-going GTs in small numbers until 1960, using successively their own 152 cu.in 4-cylinder engine, a Ford V-8 side valve and the 152 cu.in version of BMW's V-8. However a new grande make arrived in 1954; Facel emerged from the Forges et Ateliers de Construction d'Eure et Loire which produced body panels for Panhard, Simca and Ford. Using a 275 cu.in 180 bhp Chrysler V-8, the Facel Vega was a luxury GT in the old tradition. With ever larger Chrysler engines, the Vega was developed through to the FVS (1957) into the HK500 with up to 360 bhp from 384 cu.in in 1962.

A four-door Excellence had been available from 1957 but the line came to an end in 1964 after 1270 V-8s had been built. Reason for the failure was an attempt to enter the small sports-car market with the Facellia, initially with their own 4-cylinder twin-cam 97 cu.in; when this proved unreliable some were produced with the 110 cu.in Volvo engine and a few were fitted with the Austin-Healey 3000 engine. But by then the company had lost too much money and production ceased after 1250 Facellias had been built.

Somewhat in the same mold was the Spanish Pegaso as the product of a nationalized company that was and still is producing commercial vehicles.

It was designed by Wilfredo Ricart who had worked with Alfa Romeo for ten years. The Z102 used a separate chassis with wishbone and de Dion suspension; the in-house V-8 was used in a variety of sizes over the 1951-8 production period with a minor redesign in 1955 to change from gear to chain cam-drive for the Z103. Bodies were built by Touring and Saoutchik as well as in Spain. It was an expensive way of advertising Pegaso lorries.

The English had their Aston Martin DB2 in its various 2/4 and drop-head variations as the only

56-57 1957 Porsche Speedster with Carrera engine.

1951 - 1960

serious challenger to Ferrari's GT reputation in the Mid-fifties. Their products came even closer in 1958 when Aston Martin unveiled the DB4 as a direct rival to the Ferrari 250GT. Meanwhile, like Facel, the Jensen company emerged from making bodies for others to establish their own make. Pre-war they had built a few attractive sedans and tourers using the Ford V-8, Nash straight-8 and even Lagonda V-12 engines and continued post-war using Austin's 244 cu.in straight-6. Jensen built 2573 examples of the Austin A40 sports and would go on to make the big Austin-Healeys but in 1954 they showed their own 4-seater GT, the 541, retaining the big Austin engine and a number of other Austin components. It was a striking design and was technically interesting in that it used a fiberglass body on top of a substantial twin-tube chassis. The de Luxe version in 1956 saw Jensen as the first manufacturer to use four-wheel disc brakes. In 1957 the 541R brought in rack and pinion steering and a more powerful engine; the final revision was the 1960 541S, four inches wider and with the option of a GM Hydramatic automatic transmission. While the engine was hardly a thoroughbred, the 541 series was a welcome addition to the classic scene.

Fiberglass provided the basis for two more English GT cars, the TVR and Lotus Elite, both aimed at the younger enthusiast. TVR had produced some 20 2-seater coupes with proprietary fiberglass bodywork on a tubular chassis using A40 components but, in 1958, they produced the first Grantura using Coventry Climax, Ford or MGA engines. A new space-frame chassis carried Beetle front suspension at both ends and, with a neat and very short two-seater coupe, began a production run of around 100 cars; the Mk.II (1960-1) continued with the same chassis but rack-and-pinion steering and the IIA (1961-2) had disc brakes with the later MGA engine, the production total of these second series cars being around 400. Lotus had grown from special builders to small producers of competition sports cars, but 1957 saw them established as road-car manufacturers. The low, stark Lotus 7 was the ultimate enthusiast's road car for competition use and has continued through without a break into the somewhat faster Caterham 7 of today. With the Elite they broke new ground, using a monocoque

body/chassis unit of fiberglass; the suspension used Colin Chapman's racing designs and the engine was the lightweight 74.4 cu.in Coventry Climax FWE. With attractive aerodynamic styling, the Elite made a big impression at its 1957 launch; 112 mph from just 75 bhp was a significant pointer to the way ahead. By 1963 over 1000 had been produced. Both TVR and Lotus were, of course, considerably outnumbered by Alfa Romeo's successful Giulietta Sprint GT which had emerged in 1954.

SPORTS CARS

In the Fifties, England was the center stage of affordable sports car production. Following the worldwide acceptance of the MG TC and the Jaguar XK120, other manufacturers, large and small, joined in to provide America in particular with a type of motoring which their own companies were unable to produce.

MG went on to produce the 2-seater TD in 1950, using independent front suspension from the Y-type sedan, still with the same 76.2 cu.in engine. When the slightly more modern looking TF arrived in 1953, it was already outdated by a rival product from within the same newly merged Austin-Morris (BMC) company – the Austin-Healey 100 which came out the same year. Increasing the MG TF's capacity to 89.4 cu.in did not offset the decline of the make's appeal; it still had the pre-war running-board style, where the Austin-Healey had all-enveloping bodywork. It was to be 1955 before the MGA appeared to broaden MG appeal once more.

Meanwhile, the Triumph TR2 had also arrived in 1953, another with the integrated wing-line. While this used the same basic engine as the Standard Vanguard and the Morgan Plus 4, the Triumph's engine

capacity was reduced to 121.4 cu.in to make it more suitable for competition. Competition inspired the creation of the AC Ace in 1954 and led to the birth of the Cobra in 1961. More detailed studies of the MGA, big Healeys, Triumph TR2 and AC Cobra appear later.

Jaguar continued to produce the XK120 until the very similar XK140 appeared in 1954. The XK150 came in 1957 bringing more space and comfort under a considerably revised shape.

The XK120 had performed well in national competitions in England and America, but Jaguar wanted to promote their name on the International racing scene, targeting the Le Mans 24-hour race as the most famous. The XK120C (competition) was ready for Le Mans 1951; it used a tubular frame chassis with XK120 front suspension but the live rear axle was better located and the body was more streamlined.

The C-type, as it was soon called, duly won its first Le Mans and repeated this in 1953. Seeking

even more speed for Le Mans, Jaguar developed the D-type with even less drag; the engine was still basically the same famous XK unit but had dry-sump lubrication; the chassis used a monocoque center section with aircraft-style rivets. Le Mans victories were repeated in 1955, 1956 and 1957. The D-type was to lead directly to the famous E-type in the next decade.

But there was still more to come from Britain. By 1956, BMC were producing the successful MGA and Austin-Healey, but these were quick cars. There was a gap at the bottom of the market for a cheap and economical two-seater, which was where the original MG Midget had come in. The Austin-Healey Sprite arrived in 1958 with the BMC A-series engine in an all-new monocoque chassis and the famous frog-eye headlights on the bonnet-top – nearly 50,000 were built before the Mk.II came in 1961 together with the MG Midget equivalent. Although the Sprite name came to an end with the

Mk.IV in 1971, the MG Midget continued through further development until 1979. Some 225,000 Midgets and 130,000 Sprites were built.

While Daimler would join Jaguar in 1960, they were independent at this stage. The company had generally produced fairly luxurious cars but made a handful of the Barker Special Sports Coupes from 1949-52. They returned to the sports car market in 1959 with the SP250 (originally Dart) using a fiberglass body and a new small 152 cu.in V-8 with a conventional steel chassis.

From 1961 chassis and body were strengthened but the SP250 ceased production in 1963 after 2645 had been built. It was an interesting sporting machine and Jaguar used that engine in Daimler versions of the Mk.II sedan. Last of the British sporting cars to appear in this decade was the Sunbeam Alpine. The name first appeared on an open two-seater version of the Sunbeam-Talbot 90; introduced in 1953, it had some rallying success but production stopped in 1955 for the building of a new range of sedans of which the 68 bhp 91.5 cu.in Sunbeam Rapier was the most notable and had considerable competition success. The Alpine used the Hillman Husky platform and uprated Rapier running gear with 2+2 sports-car bodywork. By 1968 it had gone through five development series and 70,000 cars were produced. Along the way, an American 256 cu.in Ford V-8 had been inserted into the Mark IV to create the Tiger in 1964. Nearly 6500 were built before the 286 cu.in Ford was used for the Tiger II which added a further 571 cars to the production run. The V-8 power made a real sports car out of the rather tame Alpine.

In Italy, Fiat made some attempt to stem the all-British tide. The early post-war Fiat 1100S was a rounded GT based on the pre-war 1100 chassis; after only 400 models, this was replaced by the 1100ES with Pinin Farina bodywork very similar to that of the Cisitalia – only 50 models were made during 1950/1. Fiat followed this up with the 1100TV Trasformabile in 1955, an open two-seater based on the unitary construction 1100TV (Turismo Veloce) sedan, but only 1030 were built in two years. The bigger-engined 1200 convertible took them through to the end of 1959 after a low run of 2363 cars. Fiat took their next little sports car more seriously using the then new 1100 as a base clothed in Pinin Farina bodywork.

Early 1959 saw the new 1200 cabriolet which was joined by the 1500 using the OSCA 91.5 cu.in twin-cam engine in the same basic car for 38% more power. In 1963, the 1200 was replaced by the 1500 from the new 1500 sedan and given front disc brakes, and the 1500 OSCA (called 1500S in hindsight) became the 1600S with discs all round and a 5-speed gearbox from March 1965. Over 7 years, Pinin Farina built some 37,500 of which 3000 were coupes, and of this total around 4000 were OSCA-powered. Local rivals Alfa Romeo had changed from the 1300 Giulietta Spider to the 1600 in 1962.

While all of Europe was flooding their market with sports cars, the Americans had not been totally idle. However the two comparable cars that were produced – the Chevrolet Corvette and the Ford Thunderbird – were hardly in the same mold as the nimble European sports cars.

The Corvette was notable for the first volume use of fiberglass for bodywork when it came out in 1953. The Thunderbird might have been aimed at the Corvette but the company changed direction to create a new niche market, the two-seater personal car; it was more of a two-door Lincoln when it arrived in 1955. Both these cars are covered in greater detail later. As the Fifties closed, world production had increased immeasurably and car design had marched on towards new levels of comfort and performance. Not every one has been proved to be a classic though.

58-59 Mercedes 300SL with the famous 'gullwing' doors.

Porsche 356

All makes have to start somewhere but Porsche's rise from the humble origins of a modified Volkswagen Beetle to the supercars of today has been a major transformation. In fact, the Beetle was just one design project for Professor Ferdinand Porsche who had earlier worked on the powerful Mercedes sports cars of the late Twenties and went on to design the Auto Union Grand Prix cars of the Thirties. The Volkswagen project started in 1934 and by 1936 the first prototypes were running. When a Berlin-Rome race was announced for September 1939, Porsche was given permission to produce three streamlined VWs; being Porsche, the company had already sketched a sporting coupe using the VW engine ahead of the rear axle. The Berlin-Rome cars used this body but on a Beetle chassis with the engine tuned to 40 bhp. War caused the race to be cancelled, but the idea lived on.

The Porsche engineering consultancy had been moved to Gmund in Austria in 1944. After the war, shortage of parts and other projects delayed a return to the sporting VW. But finally it was the Professor's son, Ferry, who ordered the work to start. The first and only prototype was completed in May 1948, an open roadster with the VW engine ahead of the rear axle, but production of the rear-mounted Porsche started immediately; all the mechanical parts were well proven as Beetle production had been under way for three years. The first coupe was finished in September 1948.

60-61 *Speedster fitted with 1600 Super engine.*

While the concept of putting the engine and transmission package at one end of the car was well suited to carrying people and luggage in a compact sedan car, and is now the universal system, it is not ideal for a sports car where a near-equal weight distribution gives fundamentally safer handling. Putting the package behind the rear wheels is even less safe than is the modern system of front wheel drive. With the Volkswagen, and hence the Porsche, the rear suspension with swing axles was inferior to the trailing arm front suspension. While all round independent suspension was good for the ride quality, the unbalanced suspension and weight distribution combined to make it easy to spin a Porsche if you take a corner too fast. Ever since the first car, Porsche have had to develop the cars around this problem. To a large extent they have succeeded but a rear-engined Porsche always demands respect from its driver.

For the new car Porsche made their own steel platform chassis, almost a foot shorter than the Beetle's. On this was mounted the Beetle front suspension, the Porsche-patented trailing arms, and the complete engine, gearbox and rear suspension package from the Beetle.

TECHNICAL DESCRIPTION OF THE OF PORSCHE SPEEDSTER

YEARS OF PRODUCTION	1956-1962
MODELS	ROADSTER
ENGINE	REAR-MOUNTED FLAT-FOUR
BORE X STROKE, CAPACITY	3.2 x 2.9 INCHES, 96.5 CU.IN
VALVEGEAR	PUSHROD OHV
FUEL SYSTEM	TWO SOLEX 32PBI CARBURETORS
POWER	75 BHP AT 5000 RPM
TRANSMISSION	4-SPEED
BODY/CHASSIS	STEEL PLATFORM CHASSIS WITH STEEL BODY PANELS
FRONT SUSPENSION	TRAILING ARMS AND TORSION BARS
REAR SUSPENSION	SWING AXLES AND TORSION BARS
TIRES/WHEELS	5.60 x 15 ON STEEL WHEELS
WHEELBASE, TRACK (F), TRACK(R)	83 x 51 x 49 INCHES
LENGHT, WIDT, HEIGHT	156 x 65 x 48 INCHES
MAX SPEED	110 MPH
WHERE BUILT	STUTTGART, GERMANY

In Beetle form, the 69 cu.in flat-four air-cooled engine gave 25 bhp at 3300 rpm. With an eye to racing in the 67.1 cu.in class, Porsche reduced the capacity to 66.2 cu.in but increased the compression ratio and installed twin carburetors to reach 40 bhp at 4200 rpm. This was clothed in a hand-beaten aluminium body designed by Erwin Kommenda. Conditions and supplies in that part of Austria were not good for the production of cars and only 50 were made in two years before the company negotiated a return to Porsche's old premises in Stuttgart. From 1950, all the cars had steel bodies and production started at 60 cars a month. Porsche had arrived and the cars were quickly recognized for their ability to cruise quietly and comfortably at speeds very close to their maximum of 80 mph.

For a sporting machine, more power was obviously needed. Early in 1951 the engine was bored out to 78.4 cu.in which added another 10 per cent to the power, and in October that year came a 90.7 cu.in version using roller bearings to give 60 bhp at 5000 rpm. For this a long-stroke crankshaft was made which would last the life of the 356 series. A plain-bearing 1500 came in 1953 with 55 bhp, while the roller-bearing 1500S continued with 70 bhp; the equivalent 1300S had 60 bhp.

The first cabriolet was offered in 1951 but the American market wanted a sleeker model. The 1952 America was followed in 1954 by the famous Speedster, a cabriolet with a cut-down windscreen.

When the 356A arrived in 1956, the V-screen had been replaced with a curved one, quarter-lights had been added, wider 15-inch wheels were fitted, the handling was improved and the bigger engine were increased to 97.6 cu.in Minor styling and engineering changes denoted the 356B in 1960 and 356C in 1963. The final 1600SC with 95 bhp was the ultimate 356, very far removed from its Beetle ancestry.

TECHNICAL DESCRIPTION OF THE PORSCHE CARRERA 2000GS

YEARS OF PRODUCTION	1960-1964
MODELS	COUPE
ENGINE	REAR-MOUNTED FLAT-FOUR
BORE X STROKE, CAPACITY	3.2 x 2.9 INCHES, 119.9 CU.IN
VALVEGEAR	FOUR OHC
FUEL SYSTEM	TWO TWIN-CHOKE SOLEX 40P11
POWER	140 BHP AT 6200 RPM
TRANSMISSION	4-SPEED
BODY/CHASSIS	STEEL PLATFORM CHASSIS WITH STEEL BODY PANELS
FRONT SUSPENSION	TRAILING ARMS AND TORSION BARS
REAR SUSPENSION	SWING AXLES AND TORSION BARS
TIRES/WHEELS	6.5 x 18 INCHES ON STEEL WHEELS
WHEELBASE, TRACK (F), TRACK(R)	83 x 51 x 49 INCHES
LENGHT, WIDT, HEIGHT	156 x 65 x 51 INCHES
MAX SPEED	135 MPH
WHERE BUILT	STUTTGART, GERMANY

62-63 *Top, Speedster with Carrera engine. Lower, 356 Carreras used 91.5, 97.6 and 122 cu.in engines with 4-cam heads.*

Lancia Aurelia B20

The Lancia B20 is one of the few cars that have gone down in history as a motoring landmark. It had that rare combination of advanced design and a shape that would also start a new fashion. And its performance was as strong as its visual appeal.

Since their foundation in 1906 Lancia have had a long history of producing cars that set trends. The 1922 Lambda pioneered unitary body/chassis construction and featured a narrow V-4 engine with a single cylinder head. The Aprilia was the first popular sedan to have all-independent suspension and a streamlined body when it arrived in 1937. Despite the death of the founder, Vicenzo Lancia, that year, innovation continued after the war.

The new Aurelia B10 sedan, announced in 1950, was mostly the work of Vittorio Jano, who had joined Lancia in 1938 after many years in charge of Alfa Romeo engineering. The Aurelia's specification included a V-6 engine, independent rear suspension using semi-trailing arms with coil springs and a 4-speed gearbox in unit with the differential; this transaxle helps to keep the weight evenly distributed between the front and rear of the car. The front suspension retained the familiar sliding pillar and coil spring system that had been introduced on the Lambda. The engine was actually the work of one of Jano's engineers, De Virgilio, who extended the V-4 philosophy to produce the world's first production V-6, a 107 cu.in unit producing 56 bhp. As this had its cylinder banks set at 60 degrees, the heads were separate and the valves were operated by a central camshaft and pushrods.

For 1951, Lancia decided to add the coupe B20 to the range using a chassis some 8 inches shorter. This was assigned to Pinin Farina – he would become Pininfarina in 1961. Drawing upon the lines of his 1947 Cisitalia GT, he created the fastback B20 which was a masterpiece of clean and effective design. For this, and as an option for the B21 sedan, the engine size was increased to 121.4 cu.in with 75 bhp for the B20 (70 bhp for B21). For the 1952 2nd series, Farina added four inches to the rear to improve its lines and the engine output was increased to 80 bhp; the 3rd series in 1953 included the B20 2500GT with its capacity increased to 149.5 cu.in and 118 bhp. For the final 4th series in 1954, the rear suspension was changed to use a de Dion tube on leaf springs, a design proven on the sports-racing D24 to improve stability.

Even in tuned 122 cu.in form, the B20 had already established itself in competition with a 2nd overall in the 1951 Mille Miglia; in 1952 an Aurelia was 3rd and three Aurelias finished 1,2,3 in the Targa Florio. Meanwhile the factory had started to make special competition coupes called D20 to match the B20. Using a 183 cu.in V-6 with twin overhead camshafts they won the Targa Florio again for Lancia in 1953. The victory was repeated in 1954 with the open D24.

The final version of the Aurelia took the sports-racing car design number and became the B24 Spyder, another elegant Farina creation; as this was strictly a 2-seater, the wheelbase was shortened by a further 8 inches. In fact it was also available in cabriolet form with a windscreen more suited to a soft top.

The sedan Aurelia became the Series II in 1954 with a 140 cu.in engine and also adopted the de Dion rear axle. However production ceased in 1955 after some 30,000 Aurelias had been produced and the Flaminia took over. The coupe continued until 1958 by which time 3600 examples had been assembled by Pinin Farina. It was a superb example of Lancia engineering and also helped to establish Farina as a designer for volume production road cars.

The B20 may have had its origins in the sedan Aurelia, but its design was so well executed that it became a GT car in its own right. In England the price for the 2500GT was the same as that for an Aston Martin and its performance was very similar. It certainly had as much appeal to the motoring cognoscenti of the day.

TECHNICAL DESCRIPTION OF THE
LANCIA AURELIA B20 2500GT 1954

YEARS OF PRODUCTION	1951-1958
MODELS	FASTBACK GT
ENGINE	FRONT-MOUNTED V-6
BORE X STROKE, CAPACITY	3 X 3.3 INCHES, 149.5 CU.IN
VALVEGEAR	PUSHROD OVERHEAD VALVES
FUEL SYSTEM	WEBER TWIN-CHOKE CARBURETOR
POWER	118BHP AT 5000 RPM
TRANSMISSION	4-SPEED TRANSAXLE
BODY/CHASSIS	MONOCOQUE STEEL BODY/CHASSIS WITH SOME ALUMINIUM PANELS
SUSPENSION	FRONT, SLIDING PILLAR AND COILS REAR, DE DION AXLE, LEAF SPRINGS
TIRES/WHEELS	6.5 X 16 INCHES ON STEEL WHEELS
WHEELBASE, TRACK (F), TRACK(R)	104 X 50.5 X 52 INCHES
LENGHT, WIDT, HEIGHT	160 X 61 X 53.5 INCHES
MAX SPEED	112 MPH
WHERE BUILT	TURIN, ITALY

N.B. FOR THE SPYDER (1954-1958), THE WHEELBASE WAS SHORTENED TO 96.4 INCHES

Austin Healey 100

After the failure of the A90 Atlantic to appeal to appeal to the export market, Austin's Leonard Lord invited Jensen, Frazer Nash and Healey to produce design proposals using Austin A90 components. The Healey 100 used most of the A90 running gear, including steering, brakes and suspension, and made an instant impact at the 1952 British Motor Show.

Before the end of the show, Lord and Donald Healey agreed terms and the Austin-Healey 100 became a belated star of that 1952 show. Healey would help to develop the cars, produce special variants and receive royalties, Jensen would make the body/chassis units and final assembly would take place at the Austin factory in Longbridge, Birmingham.

The long stroke A90 engine (3.4 x 4.3 inches, 162.3 cu.in) was really more suited to commercial vehicles than to sports cars, but 90 bhp at 4000 rpm was enough to make the Austin-Healey a genuine 100 mph car. The A90 with the same engine could only reach 92 mph.

As the gearbox also came from the heavier A90 it had a very low first gear ratio.

The Healey solution was to remove the first gear selector and use an overdrive for the upper two ratios, an added benefit being that the three gearbox ratios all had synchromesh. When Austin introduced the A90 Six, the Healey adopted its 4-speed gearbox and retained the overdrive for third and top.

Where the Healey scored particularly was in its appearance. Healey's Gerry Coker had designed a body with just the right mixture of long bonnet and muscular rear haunches. Another appealing feature was the clever adjustment for the angle of the windscreen. The soft top was straightforward and removable side-screens were to remain a feature until the Convertible of 1962.

The first big Healey (BN1) went into production in 1953. As Austin Healeys had finished 12th and 14th at Le Mans in 1953, special Le Mans kits were offered with bigger carburetors and a new camshaft for 100 bhp or, with high compression pistons, 110 bhp. After 10,688 cars the BN2 came in mid-1955 with the new gearbox; cars fitted when new with the Le Mans kit became 100M, which

68-69 The factory-built 100M was based on the BN2 with 4-speed gearbox.

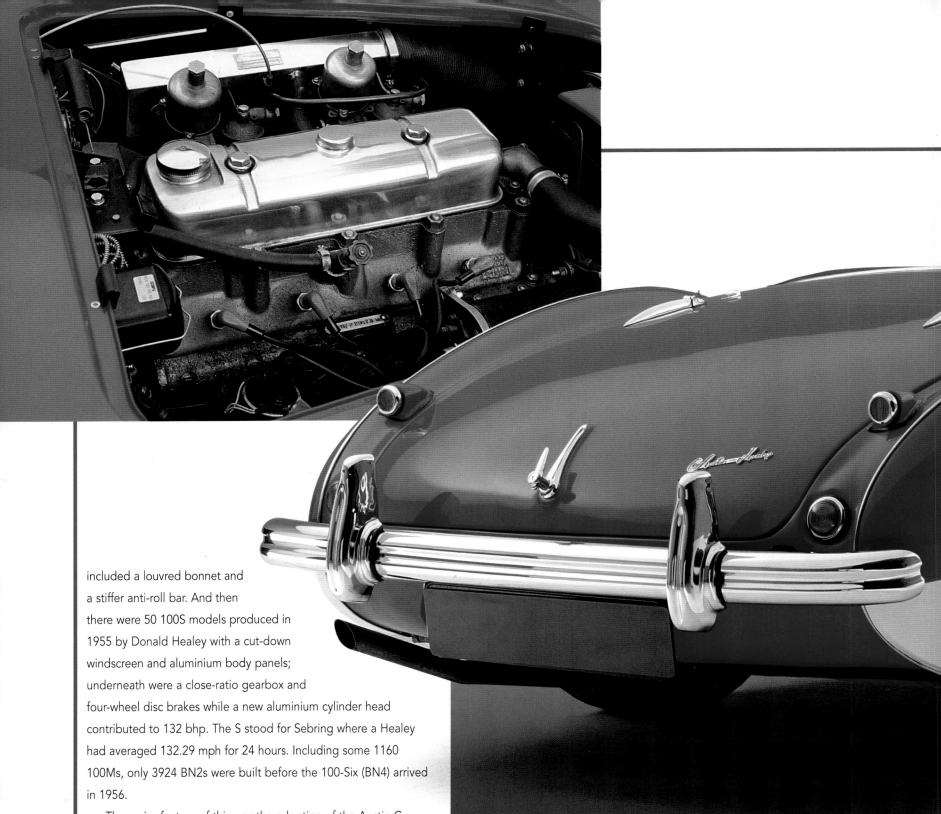

included a louvred bonnet and a stiffer anti-roll bar. And then there were 50 100S models produced in 1955 by Donald Healey with a cut-down windscreen and aluminium body panels; underneath were a close-ratio gearbox and four-wheel disc brakes while a new aluminium cylinder head contributed to 132 bhp. The S stood for Sebring where a Healey had averaged 132.29 mph for 24 hours. Including some 1160 100Ms, only 3924 BN2s were built before the 100-Six (BN4) arrived in 1956.

The major feature of this was the adoption of the Austin C-series 158 cu.in six-cylinder engine from the A90; initially this had the standard Austin cylinder head with siamesed inlet ports and 102 bhp but a new cylinder head with six inlet ports, bigger valves and a higher compression ratio was used from October 1957 with 117 bhp. The original chassis was lengthened by two inches to allow two occasional child seats and the windscreen became fixed. Of the 15,400 100-Sixes, 4150 were BN6 two-seaters, introduced in 1958, with the child seats removed and the battery repositioned.

First of the Healey 3000s came in 1959 with the C-series engine at 177.6 cu.in and 124 bhp; front disc brakes were fitted. By now, BN7 were two-seaters and BT7 were the 2+2 variety. These classifications continued into the 3000 Mk.II (1961-62) with triple SU carburetors and 131 bhp, but a Mk.IIA (BJ7) took over from 1962-64 which reverted to twin larger carburetors and 129 bhp. However the main feature of the BJ7 was that it was a Convertible with curved windscreen, quarter lights and wind-up windows; the soft top used three, not two, hoops and sat in its own well behind the child seats. The rear seat back could fold down to create a luggage platform – the big Healey had finally become civilized.

The last version was the Mk.III (BJ8) which were all Convertibles and had 150 bhp from even larger carburetors and a new camshaft. Just 1390 Phase I cars were built in early 1964 before the Phase II came out with the rear suspension revised to provide more ground clearance; radius arms replaced the old Panhard rod and the leaf springs were reset.

The Phase II was the most popular of all the big Healeys with 16,322 produced out of a total 42,926 of the 3000. At the end of 1967 new safety and emissions legislation brought an end to one of England's finest post-war sports cars.

70-71 *The BN2 had rear reflectors above the lights.*
Engine air-box has a badge to show that the Le Mans kit is fitted.

TECHNICAL DESCRIPTION OF THE AUSTIN-HEALEY 100M

YEARS OF PRODUCTION	1955-56
MODELS	SPORTS 2-SEATER
ENGINE	FRONT-MOUNTED IN-LINE 4
BORE X STROKE, CAPACITY	3.4 x 4.3 INCHES, 162.3
VALVEGEAR	PUSHROD OVERHEAD VALVES
FUEL SYSTEM	TWIN SU CARBURETORS
POWER	110 BHP AT 4500 RPM
TRANSMISSION	4-SPEED AND OVERDRIVE
BODY/CHASSIS	STEEL CHASSIS, INTEGRAL BULKHEADS
	AND DETACHABLE BODYPANELS
SUSPENSION	FRONT, WISHBONES AND COILS
	REAR, LIVE AXLE WITH LEAF SPRINGS
TIRES/WHEELS	5.90 x 15 ON STEEL WHEELS
WHEELBASE, TRACK (F), TRACK(R)	90 x 49 x 51 INCHES
LENGHT, WIDT, HEIGHT	151 x 60.5 x 49.2 INCHES
MAX SPEED	110 MPH
WHERE BUILT	LONGBRIDGE AND WARWICK, ENGLAND

Chevrolet Corvette 1956 - 1962

In the aftermath of the war, the British motor industry spearheaded the export drive to America, providing sports cars to a country whose major manufacturers had yet to appreciate the values of this niche market; the American industry was accustomed to working in larger numbers, although, as in England, there were some enthusiasts building specials around such as the Kaiser-Frazer Henry J chassis. General Motors started to rectify the situation in 1951, planning the Corvette around a low-volume facility away from Detroit but making full use of the mass production hardware.

Styled under the legendary Harley Earl by Bob McLean, the body was to be built in the new medium of fiberglass which had the benefit of much lower tooling costs than the normal metal pressing system. A new box-section chassis was designed in the Chevrolet R&D department under suspension specialist Maurice Olley and used stock steering, braking and suspension units. The best available engine was the existing Chevrolet 235 cu.in 'six' which produced 115 bhp at 3600 rpm in standard form; as they wanted to match Jaguar's 160 bhp for the Jaguar XK120, this had to be uprated in the usual speed-shop fashion – higher compression, new camshaft with solid lifters, triple carburetors – to reach 150 bhp. This engine was normally attached to the two-speed Powerglide

automatic transmission, so this was chosen despite its unsporting character.

The Corvette was originally shown at the GM Motorama in early 1953. It was mid-1953 before development was completed and GM began a pilot production run of 300 cars at Flint in Michigan; production moved to a new facility in St.Louis, Missouri for 1954. While the Corvette could exceed 100 mph, and accelerate as well as an Austin-Healey 100, it was not a sports car when it came to the corners. However, performance took a step in the right direction with the 1955 model; the new 265 cu.in small block V-8 became a 195 bhp option and a 3-speed manual transmission was offered towards the end of 1955. By the end of this first generation of the Corvette, only 4640 had been built – it was just enough to keep the model alive and moving towards the new generation.

Regarded as the father of the true

72-73 Chevrolet Corvette 1959 retained the 1958 change to 4 headlights.

Corvette, Zora Arkus-Duntov had arrived at Chevrolet in 1953 and had little influence on the first model, but he improved the handling with minor suspension changes to make it more track-friendly for the new generation in 1956. The V-8 engine output was increased to 210 bhp with the option of 225 bhp with a second 4-barrel carburetor, and the 3-speed manual transmission became standard.

With the restyling the second generation Corvette had a much more positive air. The tail lost its little fins and became more rounded with its profile matching concave side sculptures behind the front wheels and the headlights moved to the front of the wings.

Wind-up side windows and an optional hard-top broadened its appeal. Revealed at the January 1956 Motorama, the new car suddenly achieved instant sporting credibility when it was revealed that Duntov had recorded 150 mph at Daytona Beach with a virtually standard car. Annual production for 1956 at 3467 cars was the start of a steady growth that would reach 14,531 by the end of the model in 1962.

The story of 1957-62 was one of ever-increasing performance with a few minor body changes. For 1957, the V-8 was increased in capacity from 265 to 283 cu.in and offered in four states of tune from 245 to 283 bhp. The latter was achieved with the temperamental Rochester fuel injection which was only fitted to 240 cars that year. A four-speed manual gearbox came in too. The 283 continued to be used until it was increased again to 327 cu.in in the final year with 250-340 bhp available, or 360 bhp with an improved version of the fuel injection.

Body changes during the period covered twin headlights which increased the width and the front overhang, plus new bumpers and restyled interior (1958), mesh grille and duck-tail (1961) and

removal of the chrome trims around the side sculpture (1962).

Meanwhile, Duntov continued work on the car's road behavior. The live axle suffered wind-up with the ever-increasing power, so radius arms were added to it in 1959. The ride had become less comfortable, so springs were softened in 1960 and anti-roll bars were fitted to restore the roll stiffness.

Regular Performance Options (RPO) were always available for those who wanted to adjust their cars.

By the end of its ninth year, the Corvette had become a strong muscular sports car, faster than most European products and Chevrolet could sell all they were able to make.

TECHNICAL DESCRIPTION OF THE CHEVROLET CORVETTE 1959	
YEARS OF PRODUCTION	1956-1962
MODELS	SPORTS 2-SEATER
ENGINE	FRONT-MOUNTED V-8
BORE X STROKE, CAPACITY	3.8 X 2.9 INCHES, 283 CU.IN
VALVEGEAR	PUSHROD OVERHEAD VALVES
FUEL SYSTEM	ROCHESTER 4-CHOKE CARBURETOR
POWER	245 BHP AT 5000 RPM
TRANSMISSION	3-SPEED (4-SPEED OPTION)
BODY/CHASSIS	STEEL CHASSIS, FIBERGLASS BODYWORK
SUSPENSION	FRONT, WISHBONES AND COILS REAR, LIVE AXLE WITH LEAF SPRINGS
TIRES/WHEELS	6.70 X 15 ON STEEL WHEELS
WHEELBASE, TRACK (F), TRACK(R)	102 X 57 X 59 INCHES
LENGHT, WIDT, HEIGHT	177 X 72.8 X 50 INCHES
MAX SPEED	125 MPH
WHERE BUILT	MISSOURI, USA

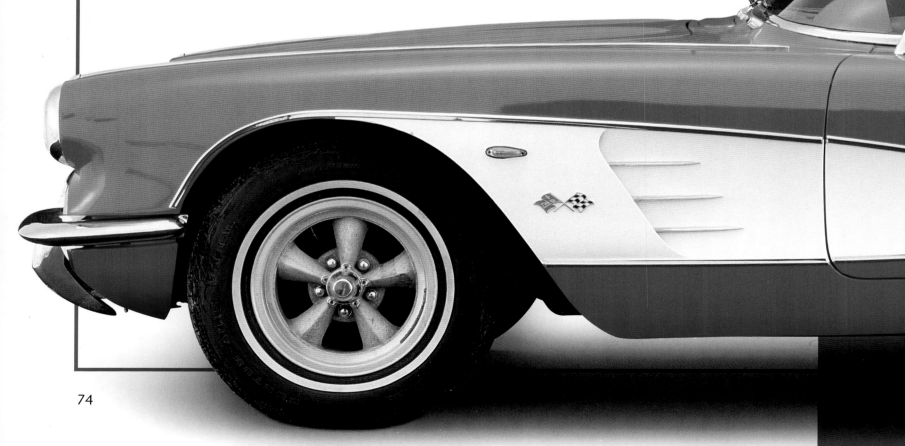

74-75 *Two-tone paint was an option.*
Alloy wheels are later addition.

Triumph TR2 and TR3A

Standard bought Triumph in 1944. Before the war, neither make had produced sporting machinery in any volume, although Standard had supplied Jaguar with engines and chassis. After the war, Standard brought out the Vanguard sedan with a 128 cu.in engine which was quickly adopted by Morgan for the Plus Four in 1950; Morgan had used a Standard engine in the 1939 4/4 but side-valve Ford engines after the war.

Standard-Triumph's first sporting attempt after the war was with the 1800 Roadster which came out in 1946 based on the pre-war Standard 14 engine and chassis. After 2500 were made, the engine was replaced by the Vanguard 128 cu.in in 1948 as the 2000 Roadster. After 2000 of these, production stopped in 1949 as a new sports car, based on the Vanguard chassis, was to be launched in 1950. When it was shown in October, nobody liked it, so plans were cancelled.

Two years later, what was later called the TR1 was shown with a modified pre-war chassis and a 75 bhp version of the Vanguard engine, under a body best described as short-tail TR2.

76 *A prototype Triumph TR2 with covered rear wheels reached 114 mph at Jabbeke in 1953.*

By March 1953, after considerable engine and chassis development the definitive 90 bhp TR2 was shown at Geneva, its engine reduced to under 128 cu.in for competition classes.

Sporting credibility was acquired in May with a 115 mph run at Jabbeke and production started slowly in July. Development had been rather too short and in autumn 1954 the chassis was strengthened by raising the bottom of the door and widening the sills.

Successes in rallies and races did much to promote the strength and performance of the TR2; in 1954 they won the RAC rally and took the Manufacturers Team Prize in the Alpine Rally. At Le Mans one finished 15th in 1954, and three finished 14th, 15th and 19th in 1955.

While the TR2 was destined for American sales these did not really build up until the TR3 was launched in October 1955; this was basically a TR2 with an egg-box grille, sliding panel side-screens and 95 bhp from bigger carburetors. A year later a new cylinder head had taken this to 100 bhp while disc brakes were fitted at the end of 1956.

A new full-width grille, doors and trunk lid with external handles, denoted the TR3A which arrived in early 1958. By mid-1958 the 130.4 cu.in engine became an option, although few were actually fitted at the factory. By the end of the decade, the TR3A was losing its appeal; rivals offered more comfort and more performance. Only 405 were delivered in 1961, the year Leyland took over, but by then the TR4 was on the way, being announced in September 1961.

While the 130.4 cu.in engine and chassis were basically unchanged, the front and rear tracks were widened to allow the body width to be increased by 2.5 inches, the gearbox had synchromesh on all ratios and the steering used rack-and-pinion gearing. Italian Michelotti designed the new body with a uniquely versatile roof and considerably more space for occupants and luggage. The top was a two-piece hard-top with a fixed rear window frame and a removable metal top panel which could be replaced by a soft top – the Surrey top. Passengers also had wind-up windows, a better heater and fresh air vents. The TR4 was a very big improvement over the earlier cars and gained a considerable increase in sales.

During his work for Triumph, Michelotti also designed a new body for the TR3A chassis and a number were produced by Vignale as the Triumph Italia. There was also a TR3B available on the American market; uncertain of the reception which the TR4 would get, American dealers asked for the TR3A shape to be continued in 1962 using the all-synchromesh gearbox – over 3300 were built before the more practical TR4 was appreciated.

It was 1965 before the Triumph chassis gained independent rear suspension with the TR4A, still using the 130.4 cu.in engine to carry the semi-trailing arm rear suspension that had been used on the Triumph 2000. Once again some American customers wanted to retain the old design, so a number went to America with the new chassis adapted to take the old live axle.

TR5 followed in 1967 with the 152.5 cu.in six-cylinder engine from the Triumph sedan and this was rebodied to Karmann's design for the TR6 in 1969.

TECHNICAL DESCRIPTION OF THE TRIUMPH TR2 and (TR3A)	
YEARS OF PRODUCTION	1953-55 (1958-61)
MODELS	SPORTS 2-SEATER
ENGINE	FRONT-MOUNTED IN-LINE 4
BORE X STROKE, CAPACITY	3.2 x 3.6 INCHES, 121.4 CU.IN
VALVEGEAR	PUSHROD OVERHEAD VALVES
FUEL SYSTEM	TWIN SU CARBURETORS
POWER	90 (100) BHP AT 4800 (5000) RPM
TRANSMISSION	4-SPEED AND OVERDRIVE
BODY/CHASSIS	STEEL CHASSIS, INTEGRAL BULKHEADS AND DETACHABLE BODYPANELS
SUSPENSION	FRONT, WISHBONES AND COILS REAR, LIVE AXLE WITH LEAF SPRINGS
TIRES/WHEELS	5.50 x 15 ON STEEL WHEELS
WHEELBASE, TRACK (F), TRACK(R)	88 x 45 x 45.5 INCHES
LENGHT, WIDT, HEIGHT	151 x 55 x 50 INCHES
MAX SPEED	104 (110) MPH
WHERE BUILT	COVENTRY, ENGLAND

78-79 *TR3A brought in full-width grille.*
Wire wheels were an option.

TRIUMPH

Alfa Romeo Giulietta Sprint and Spider

Stretching back to 1910, the Alfa Romeo heritage was one of fast cars and competition success until the all-conquering Tipo 159 became ineligible for Grand Prix racing at the end of 1951.

While the company continued to race sports cars during the Fifties, the future was to be sedan cars with coupe and spider derivatives produced in large numbers. The heritage ensured that even the sedan cars had good sporting characteristics.

First of these had been the medium-size 1900 series which ran from 1950-58; Touring produced a 2-door coupe and Pinin Farina made the cabriolet – only 1800 of these short-chassis variants were built out of a total of 19,000. Work started on the smaller Giulietta in 1952.

Like the 1900, this had a monocoque chassis, a twin-cam engine (79.3 cu.in), a well-located live axle and sporting performance.

As Alfa Romeo were owned by the Italian state, IRI (Institute for Industrial Reconstruction) decided to raise money for Alfa Romeo in 1953 with a bond issue; they offered new Giuliettas as prizes. Alfa Romeo had completed work on the platform but was still developing the rest of the car, so they arranged for Bertone to have platforms to build a two-door version; planned for low numbers, the Sprint did not require the same level of tooling and the early ones were produced in

the traditional handbuilt way. So the Sprint came out in 1954, almost a year before the sedan Giulietta. It was an instant success. No-one had expected the demand to be so great, so Bertone had to build a new production factory in Grugliasco outside Turin.

While the Giulietta used a single carburetor and a 7.5:1 compression ratio to give a conservative 53 bhp, the Sprint had 80 bhp due to a higher compression ratio at 8.5:1 and a twin-choke downdraft carburetor. When the Veloce version was added in 1956, the compression ratio was further increased and twin double-choke Weber carburetors were fitted to give 90 bhp. Over the six years,

80-81 *Bertone's Giulietta Sprint, left, was the first of the line in 1954. The Spider followed a year later.*

Bertone built more than 25,000 of which 3058 were Sprint Veloces.

Pinin Farina was given the task of producing the open sports car – the Spider. For this, an all-new body was designed for which the Giulietta chassis was shortened by 5 inches; the new car was introduced just three months after the sedan. Some 14,300 Giulietta Spiders were built with a further 2900 Veloce versions with more power.

Bertone added to the range in 1959 with the dramatic Sprint Speciale, modelled on his BAT concept cars (Berlina Aerodinamica Tecnica); although the prototype had been shown as a concept car in 1957, the decision to produce it took another two years. The first 153 Giulietta SS were built in Bertone's Turin factory using aluminium bodywork, but the rest of the 1460 total were built in Grugliasco with steel bodywork. Sprint, Spider and SS were much used in Italian racing, but the SS was no lighter than the Sprint. This was rectified by Zagato who brought out the most successful Giulietta of all at the end of 1959; the SZ was much lighter than the others and 200 were built to conform to the rules for competition GT cars. Both SS and SZ used the shorter Spider platform with 100 bhp engines and 5-speed gearboxes.

In 1962, Alfa Romeo replaced the Giulietta with the Giulia, using a 95.8 cu.in version of the superb little engine with bigger pistons and a longer stroke crankshaft. At that time, no other manufacturer offered a twin overhead camshaft engine in a small family sedan. The new square-looking body was mounted on a Giulietta chassis lengthened by 5 inches and fitted with 4-wheel disc brakes and a 5-speed gearbox. Bertone and Pinin Farina continued to build their Giulietta bodies – Sprint (7083-off), Spider (6961-off) and SS (620-off) – but used the new engine with disc brakes on the front and called them Giulias. In fact, the Sprint reappeared with a 1300 engine in 1964 together with a Giulia Spider Veloce with 112 bhp.

While the Giulietta and Giulia sedans may become classics, the models made by the coachbuilders Bertone, Pinin Farina and Zagato are already appreciated as classics.

82-83 *Spider, by Pinin Farina, displays the typical twin-cam engine.*

One of the most desirable cars of the Fifties, the Mercedes 300SL was directly derived from the racing coupe that won Le Mans in 1952. Having been one of the dominant duo of pre-war Grand Prix racing, Mercedes began to plan a return in 1951. They started to design a car for 1952 but the formula changed and they had to wait until the rules changed again for 1954. Meanwhile there was sports car racing. Jaguar had won the 1951 Le Mans 24-hour race with the C-type; this used a tubular chassis frame with running gear from the production XK120.

Like Jaguar, Mercedes could only use running gear from the production line as there was no time to design new components. So the new car was based around the six-cylinder 300 series which had been launched in 1951. As the engine potential was necessarily limited, the car had to be as light and streamlined as possible. To keep the overall weight down, Mercedes' previous race design work was put to good use and they made a new space-frame chassis to take

Mercedes Benz 300SL 1954 - 1957

the front and rear suspension of the production 300S, as well as the engine and 4-speed manual gearbox. Drum brakes were improved by using the Alfin system of ribbed aluminium drums with steel liners.

Others had shown the aerodynamic benefits of using closed coupes for long-distance sports car racing, particularly in the Mille Miglia and at Le Mans, so the new 300SL – Super Light – had closed bodywork. The drag factor of 0.25 was lower than any other coupe and much lower than that of open cars. The frontal area was kept low by inclining the six-cylinder 183 cu.in engine at 50 degrees to the vertical. As small tube space frames lose a lot of their strength if they have big spaces for door ways, the engineers evolved the gull-wing doors hinged in the center of the roof. Initially the lower edge of the doors was the bottom of the window frame; it was only when it came to Le Mans and the prospect of quick driver changes, that the doors were deepened.

In its standard form, the 300 engine produced 115 bhp at 4500 rpm using a compression ratio of 6.4:1. With a new camshaft, 8:1 compression and 3 downdraft Solex carburetors, the output was improved to 171 bhp at 5200 rpm. The new car was shown to the press in March 1952, only nine months after the Mercedes board approved the project. In May, three 300SLs ran in the Mile Miglia and finished second and fourth; the leading Ferrari 250S, also a coupe, had 230 bhp. Factory 300SLs finished 1-2-3 at Bern, also in May; new ones with modified doors went to Le Mans and finished 1-2.

For a 10-lap race over the twisty Nurburgring where low drag was less important than light weight and more power, the coupes became roadsters and finished 1,2,3. The final 1952 event for the 300SLs was the Carrera Panamericana, two coupes and a roadster; as at Le Mans they defeated the Ferraris and finished 1,2. It had been an impressive debut year. Although development continued after the season, the

84-85 *Always known as the Gullwing, the Mercedes 300SL was developed from the racing cars.*

proposed 1953 campaign was cancelled in favor of preparation for the Grand Prix cars.

Instead, the factory responded to the request of the American importer Max Hoffman to produce road-going replicas of the 300SLs; he also instigated the production of the similar-looking 190SL based on the floorpan of the 180/220 series with a 4-cylinder engine developing 105 bhp.

The new 300SL used very much the same design as had the earlier racing versions, although, inevitably the weight was increased from the competition 1914 lb to 2557 lb – the Jaguar E-type coupe would be 2513 lb in 1961. The major change was for the engine with a power increase from around 175 bhp to 220 bhp with the sports camshaft and direct fuel injection. The 300SL was first shown at New York show in February 1954 and production started that autumn. By 1957, 1371 road-going cars had been produced with a further 29 lightweights for competition use.

In 1957, the 300SL coupe was replaced by the Roadster, still using a space-frame chassis. Its major change was the adoption of the low-pivot swing axle which would have been used on the 1953 competition cars, and was used for the GP car. With a compensating spring to reduce rear roll stiffness, this considerably improved the handling. When disc brakes were adopted in 1961, the 300SL Roadster was a match for the E-type but more than twice the price. By 1962, 1858 had been built.

TECHNICAL DESCRIPTION OF THE MERCEDES-BENZ 300SL

YEARS OF PRODUCTION	1954-1957
MODELS	2-DOOR COUPE
ENGINE	FRONT-MOUNTED IN-LINE SIX
BORE X STROKE, CAPACITY	3.3 x 3.4 INCHES, 182.8 CU.IN
VALVEGEAR	SINGLE OVERHEAD CAMSHAFT
FUEL SYSTEM	BOSCH FUEL INJECTION
POWER	220 BHP AT 5800 RPM
TRANSMISSION	4-SPEED
BODY/CHASSIS	TUBULAR SPACE FRAME
SUSPENSION	FRONT, WISHBONES AND COIL SPRINGS
	REAR, SWING AXLE WITH COIL SPRINGS
TIRES/WHEELS	6.50 X 15 ON 5.5K STEEL WHEELS
WHEELBASE, TRACK (F), TRACK(R)	94.5 X 54 X 56 INCHES
LENGHT, WIDT, HEIGHT	178 X 70 X 51 INCHES
MAX SPEED	155 MPH
WHERE BUILT	STUTTGART, GERMANY

86-87 Low frontal area and low drag gave a 155 mph top speed from 220 bhp.

Bentley Continental S-type

Bentley is one England's more illustrious makes; the Bentley was the archetypal Vintage sports car, big, powerful and well engineered to last. After five victories at Le Mans, they were taken over by Rolls-Royce in 1931, but their sporting reputation has never been forgotten. From 1931, Rolls-Royce and Bentley cars have shared components even though the models looked very different through the Thirties. After the war, most Rolls models had a matching Bentley with just a radiator change, but there have been a number of models that have been uniquely Bentley.

The R-type Continental was the first of these. The 10-foot chassis, shared by the Bentley R-type and the Rolls-Royce Silver Dawn, was available to individual coachbuilders, but it was H.J.Mulliner who was given the

YEARS OF PRODUCTION	1956-59
MODELS	FIXED HEAD COUPE, CONVERTIBLE
ENGINE	IN-LINE 6-CYLINDER
BORE X STROKE, CAPACITY	3.7 X 4.4 INCHES, 298.2 CU.IN
VALVEGEAR	INLET OVER EXHAUST
FUEL SYSTEM	TWIN SU CARBURETORS
POWER	NOT PUBLISHED
TRANSMISSION	4-SPEED OR AUTO
BODY/CHASSIS	STEEL FRAME, STEEL BODY PANELS
FRONT SUSPENSION	WISHBONES AND COIL SPRINGS
REAR SUSPENSION	LIVE AXLE AND LEAF SPRINGS
TIRES/WHEELS	8.00 X 15 ON STEEL WHEELS
WHEELBASE, TRACK (F), TRACK(R)	123 X 58 X 60 INCHES
LENGTH, WIDTH, HEIGHT	212 X 72 X 62 INCHES
MAX SPEED	120 MPH
WHERE BUILT	CREWE, ENGLAND

88-89 *The S-type Continental, a 1957 example here, continued the line established by the R-type in 1952.*

more powerful version for the new Continental. Its aerodynamic body had origins in pre-war work by van Vooren. After the war, Bentley's Paris distributor commissioned Pinin Farina to produce a 2-door fast-back sedan along the same lines. What appeared at the 1948 Paris Motor Show was an enlarged Cisitalia GT of rather cleaner proportions with the belt-line running from headlight to tail-light in a single integrated sweep, a line that was recognizable in the 1951 Lancia Aurelia. The factory moved the headlights inwards towards a narrower vertical radiator and created separate sweeps around each wheel arch, running into small fins at the tail. As the chassis was still the same length as the sedans, it could still take four people in comfort. The 278.6 cu.in engine was mildly tuned, the gearbox was given

close ratios and a higher back axle ratio was fitted; the prototype had been taken round Montlhery's banked track at 118 mph. When the Continental was launched in 1952, it was called the fastest four-seater in the world. After Bentley had made 208 Continental chassis, of which only 15 had not received H.J.Mulliner bodies, the company introduced the Bentley S-type and Rolls-Royce Silver Cloud in 1956 with the 299 cu.in engine that had been used in later R-types. Although the new chassis was 3 inches longer, Mulliner continued to produce the fast-back shape, and others, until the V-8 powered S2 arrived in 1959. From 1957, the S-type Continental chassis had been made available to other coachbuilders including Rolls' own Park Ward. So not every Continental is a Mulliner fast-back.

Ford Thunderbird

General Motors were the first to react to the rising tide of imported British sports cars when they launched the Corvette in 1953. In fact, Ford had reacted in 1951 but were slower to convert the project from paper to metal; it was the Corvette launch that prompted them to reopen the file. And having watched the Corvette's slow sales due to poor straight line performance, Ford chose to use V-8 power from the start in 1955 but also provided a higher level of comfort. This may have made the Thunderbird slower round the corners, but it was faster on the drag-strip and sold in much greater numbers. Although the Corvette gained a V-8 option in the same year that the Thunderbird was launched, Ford had obviously found a better interpretation of what the American buyer wanted from his home-grown personal two-seater. The Thunderbird was styled within Ford by Frank Hershey. Based on a new chassis frame with the same wheelbase as the Corvette, the T-bird had a slender elegance that was as attractive as anything from Europe. No trace of Jaguar, Ferrari or Triumph marred its lines. Underneath, the suspension was just standard Ford with wishbone independent front suspension and a simple live axle at the rear. Sporting performance came from the drive-train. Where the Corvette started with a six-cylinder engine coupled to a 2-speed automatic transmission, Ford chose a V-8 and fitted a manual 3-speed gearbox with overdrive, offering a 3-speed automatic as an option; they had finally replaced the old flat-head V-8 in 1954. In fact the top option was the 292 cu.in from the Mercury range with 193 bhp, but 239 cu.in and 256 cu.in versions were also available in some markets. For 1956, the smaller unit was increased to 272 cu.in with 200 bhp and the Mercury engine increased to 312 cu.in and 245 bhp. The horsepower race was on and Ford took the lead from GM when the big engine was also offered with a Paxton supercharger to give around 300 bhp. Despite the T-bird's long tail, there was still not enough luggage space, so for 1956 the spare wheel was taken out and

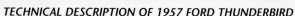

mounted under a cover with its own bumper extension, like the Lincolns. The optional hard-top came with a choice of the famous port-holes in its sail panel for 1956 and appealed to 80 per cent of the 15,000 buyers. The 1957 cars were distinguished by the arrival of more pronounced flared fins at the rear.

Although 1957 sales reached 21,380 cars, against the Corvette's 6340, this was not enough to justify the extra production lines, so Ford responded by making the T-bird into a 4-seater for 1958 – Big Bird. This added 11 inches to the wheelbase and 20 inches to the overall length; the extra 815 lb was overcome by using Ford's new big-block V-8 with 332 cu.in or, as the top option, at 352 cu.in and 300 bhp. The new style reflected the fins and chrome era with a massive plated grille at the front, four headlights and the spare wheel still carried outside the bodywork.

Although the Big Bird had lost the slim elegance of the previous

YEARS OF PRODUCTION	1955-57
MODELS	2-SEATER ROADSTER
ENGINE	FRONT-MOUNTED V-8
BORE X STROKE, CAPACITY	3.6 X 3.3 INCHES, 271.9 CU.IN
VALVEGEAR	PUSHROD OVERHEAD VALVES
FUEL SYSTEM	SINGLE FORD CARBURETOR
POWER	200 BHP AT 4400 RPM
TRANSMISSION	3-SPEED AND O/D
BODY/CHASSIS	STEEL BOX-SECTION FRAME
SUSPENSION	FRONT, WISHBONES AND COILS
	REAR, LIVE AXLE WITH LEAF SPRING
TIRES/WHEELS	7.10 X 15 ON STEEL WHEELS
WHEELBASE, TRACK (F), TRACK(R)	102 X 56 X 56 INCHES
LENGTH, WIDTH, HEIGHT	163.5 X 69 X 51.5 INCHES
MAX SPEED	115 MPH
WHERE BUILT	DETROIT, USA

90-91 *Marilyn Monroe's T-bird carries the 1956 Model Year hallmarks of the external spare wheel and the port-hole hardtop.*

92-93 Restrained fins denoted the 1957 model. The 1959 Big Bird, left, has the optional tonneau cover covering the rear seats.

car, the sales almost doubled in the first year to nearly 38,000 units, so Ford's market research had paid off.

The 1959 cars had a few changes with a horizontal bar grille replacing the honeycomb but, of greater significance was the arrival of the power-operated hood, placing the T-bird more firmly in the luxury market. However the hard-top was preferred by the majority of buyers. Performance was still a strong selling point, though, as the top engine option was increased yet again to 430 cu.in using an engine from the Lincoln range. For the 1961 face-lift, the T-bird reverted to elegance with a mildly pointed front end and less chromium plate, and there was only one engine option – the 390 cu.in. Although four seats appealed to the majority of buyers, there were still some who wanted a two-seater Ford, so an option was created by covering the rear seats with a fiberglass tonneau cover complete with fared head-rests, just like a Fifties sports-racing car.

The spare wheel disappeared inside the trunk again. Successive face-lifts in 1964 and 1967 brought more luxurious fittings but the Mustang had arrived in 1964 so the T-bird gradually became just another sports sedan. Chevrolet had won the battle to produce the sports car that America lacked.

TECHNICAL DESCRIPTION OF 1959 FORD THUNDERBIRD	
YEARS OF PRODUCTION	1958-59
MODELS	4-SEATER ROADSTER
ENGINE	FRONT-MOUNTED V-8
BORE X STROKE, CAPACITY	3.9 X 3.4 INCHES, 352 CU.IN
VALVEGEAR	PUSHROD OVERHEAD VALVES
FUEL SYSTEM	SINGLE FORD CARBURETOR
POWER	300 BHP AT 4600 RPM
TRANSMISSION	3-SPEEDS
BODY/CHASSIS	STEEL BOX-SECTION FRAME
SUSPENSION	FRONT, WISHBONES AND COILS
	REAR, LIVE AXLE WITH LEAF SPRING
TIRES/WHEELS	8.00 X 14 ON STEEL WHEELS
WHEELBASE, TRACK (F), TRACK(R)	113 X 60 X 57 INCHES
LENGTH, WIDTH, HEIGHT	205 X 77 X 53 INCHES
MAX SPEED	125 MPH
WHERE BUILT	DETROIT, USA

MGA 1600

The MGA was the sports car that the Abingdon factory wanted to build instead of the TF for 1953. When Austin and Morris merged in 1952 to form BMC, Austin was given the sports-car responsibility and allowed to continue with the external development which would become the Austin Healey in October 1952. MG had to continue with a further improvement to the TD to make the TF which, even with the 89.4 cu.in XPEG engine in 1954 was too old-fashioned and slow to make any impact against the Austin-Healey and Triumph.

It could all have been so different. MG's Syd Enever had produced a special-bodied MG TD for privateer George Phillips to race at Le Mans in 1951. Although it retired with engine problems that year, it was the shape of the MGA to come. With a widened chassis to lower the seating, it was presented as EX175 to BMC management in late 1952, after the launch of the Austin-Healey. It was turned down. TD sales had begun to decline and the TF did little to boost MG sports car production.

However, alongside the TF on the 1953 Motor Show stand was an MG sedan, the ZA Magnette; although this looked like a Wolseley 4/44 with an MG radiator, it was fitted with a 60 bhp 90.8 cu.in version of the B-series engine which had been used by the Austin A40 in 73.2 cu.in form from 1949; the Wolseley equivalent was fitted with the 76.2 cu.in XPAG MG engine. EX175 with the bigger B-series engine could easily have been ready for 1953. As it was, the poor reception for the TF eventually forced the BMC management to re-establish an MG design office and the prototype MGA (EX182) was finally shown to the public in June 1955 – a team of three were about to run at Le Mans that year.

The car was finally launched in September 1955 and during the London Show, a near-standard MGA put over 100 miles into an hour round Montlhery. For the MGA the ZA engine was given bigger carburetors to increase the output to 68 bhp, a modification later used for the ZB Magnette. It was a straightforward but effective open sports car with the typical English curves, the long sweep over the front wheels blending into a separate sweep over the rear ones – actually, like the XK120, these were based on the pre-war Touring designs for BMW. With a 91.5 cu.in engine it wasn't intended to be as fast as the Austin-

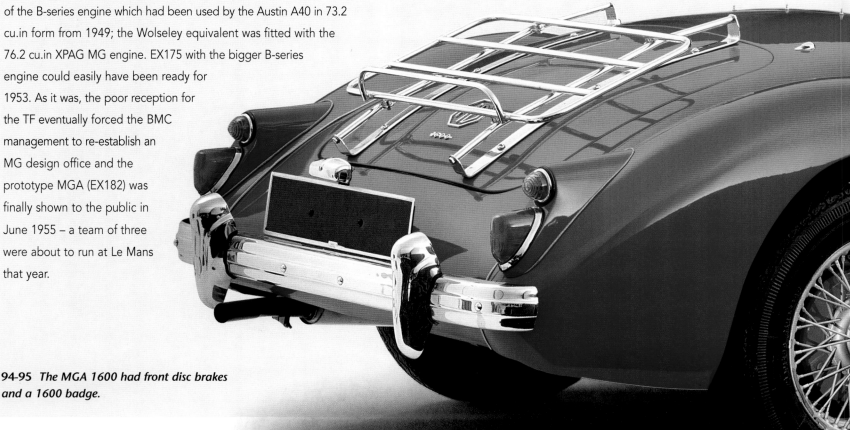

94-95 The MGA 1600 had front disc brakes and a 1600 badge.

Healey, Triumph or Jaguar but 95 mph was enough for most people.

In the USA the new MG soon achieved wider acclaim than did the TC and established a new level of production at Abingdon. In the first full year (1956) more than 13,000 were built, more than four years of the TC. When the fixed head coupe was shown in late 1956, its better aerodynamics took the maximum speed to 100 mph.

The factory competition department continued to be active in racing and rallying with the MGA and the Magnette. And they were still involved in record breaking with special streamlined bodies powered by modified production engines.

One of these experimental power units was used for a new model, the MGA Twin-Cam which was launched in 1958 in open and coupe forms; basically a B-series enlarged to 96.8 cu.in and fitted with a new twin-cam cylinder head, this gave 108 bhp which took the maximum speed through 110 mph. Center lock wheels hiding all-round disc brakes ensured that the Twin-Cam was easily distinguished from the

TECHNICAL DESCRIPTION OF THE MGA 1600

YEARS OF PRODUCTION	1959-61
MODELS	SPORTS 2-SEATER
ENGINE	FRONT-MOUNTED IN-LINE 4
BORE X STROKE, CAPACITY	2.9 x 3.5 INCHES, 96.8 CU.IN
VALVEGEAR	PUSHROD OVERHEAD VALVES
FUEL SYSTEM	TWIN SU CARBURETORS
POWER	80 BHP AT 5500 RPM
TRANSMISSION	4-SPEED
BODY/CHASSIS	STEEL CHASSIS, SEPARATE BODY
SUSPENSION	FRONT, WISHBONES AND COILS
	REAR, LIVE AXLE WITH LEAF SPRINGS
TIRES/WHEELS	5.60 x 15 ON WIRE WHEELS
WHEELBASE, TRACK (F), TRACK(R)	94 x 47.5 x 49 INCHES
LENGTH, WIDTH, HEIGHT	156 x 58 x 50 INCHES
MAX SPEED	100 MPH
WHERE BUILT	ABINGDON-ON-THAMES, ENGLAND

TECHNICAL DESCRIPTION OF THE MGA 1600 MK.11

YEARS OF PRODUCTION	1961-62
MODELS	SPORTS 2-SEATER
ENGINE	FRONT-MOUNTED IN-LINE 4
BORE X STROKE, CAPACITY	2.9 X 3.5 INCHES, 98.9 CU.IN
VALVEGEAR	PUSHROD OVERHEAD VALVES
FUEL SYSTEM	TWIN SU CARBURETORS
POWER	86 BHP AT 5500 RPM
TRANSMISSION	4-SPEED
BODY/CHASSIS	STEEL CHASSIS, SEPARATE BODY
SUSPENSION	FRONT, WISHBONES AND COILS
	REAR, LIVE AXLE WITH LEAF SPRINGS
TIRES/WHEELS	5.60 X 15 ON WIRE WHEELS
WHEELBASE, TRACK (F), TRACK(R)	94 X 47.5 X 49 INCHES
LENGTH, WIDTH, HEIGHT	156 X 58 X 50 INCHES
MAX SPEED	104 MPH
WHERE BUILT	ABINGDON-ON-THAMES, ENGLAND

normal MGA. Although the car performed well in racing, the engine was not as reliable in service as the push-rod unit and the model was discontinued in 1960 after only 2111 had been built – the problems were mostly due to the engine's need for 100-octane fuel which wasn't always available and early engines used too much oil.

For 1959 the bore of the ordinary push-rod B-series engine was increased to that of the Twin-Cam to make the MGA 1600 with 80

bhp and front disc brakes were fitted.

The final version came in 1961 with the bore increased still further to give 98.9 cu.in and 86 bhp while a modified grille gave the Mark II a distinctive appearance. By mid-1962, 101,081 MGAs had rolled off the Abingdon production line, a record then for a single model of sports car. Over half these were the 1500, while the 1600 Mk.II was the rarest, excluding the Twin-Cam, with only 8719 built. Declining sales reflected customer demand for a new car with a little more performance and comfort – the MGB came in late 1962.

Cadillac Eldorado

Cadillac is one of the oldest American car companies having been founded in 1902 by Henry Leland; the name had come from a Frenchman who had established Detroit in 1701 and it is his coat of arms that is still used by Cadillac. The company became a part of William Durant's General Motors (GM) when that was set up in 1909, along with Buick, Cadillac, Oldsmobile and Oakland – Chevrolet became a part of GM in 1918. Cadillac was chosen as the engineering center of GM and was making the finest American cars before the 1914-18 war. It was Leland who established the Cadillac motto which still adorns the factory entrance gates – Craftsmanship a creed, accuracy a law.

Cadillac has continued to make fine cars in the traditional way; there is much more manual work on the Cadillac lines than anywhere else in GM. Although much of the basic chassis and the running gear come from GM stock, many body panels and the interior design are unique to Cadillac and production numbers are much smaller than those of Chevrolet. Cadillac, though, continued to have its own engines and, even today, the all-aluminium Northstar V-8 is unique to Cadillac and a variant of that engine was used to power the Cadillac sports

98-99 *The Eldorado was always exclusive but the Brougham was very rare and only 700 were built in two years.*

racing cars at Le Mans 2000, 50 years after Cadillac had finished 10th there with a standard coupe. That Fifties engine, first shown in 1949, was a new 331 cu.in V-8 which was also made available for the English Allard sports car.

The same year, Cadillac launched the tail fin which would grow in size throughout the Fifties. GM's head of styling, Harley Earl, had been impressed by the design of the Lockheed Lightning P38 fighter airplane with its twin-boom tail. The new style for 1949 featured small fins on the tail and bomb-shaped bumper guards at the front and rear.

The Eldorado convertible was added in 1953 to celebrate the 50th anniversary of the launch of the first car, so the model used a special gold chevron. It was the height of luxury with leather upholstery, two-way power seats, power steering, automatic transmission, seeker radio, power windows, concealed soft-top, wrap-round windscreen and wire wheels; many of these features heralded the future. It was expensive and exclusive; only 532 were produced in 1953, 2150 in 1954 and 3950 (with bigger tail fins) in 1955.

Emphasising their tradition of craftsmanship, Cadillac began to use such coachbuilding names for their models as Sedanca de Ville, Coupe de Ville and Brougham, even if they didn't always match the

early motoring definitions. De Ville used to imply open front seats with a closed rear section, coupe being a shorter version of the Sedanca. The Brougham, after Lord Brougham's nineteenth century one-horse close carriage, was similar to a Coupe de Ville but usually shorter and with razor-edged styling for the closed compartment. Cadillac chose to use Coupe de Ville on the 2-door coupe from which the Eldorado was derived, and used Brougham for the four-door Fleetwood and Eldorado. Both had the pillarless construction, opening the side window area completely between quarter lights.

The Eldorado Brougham grew out of one of Harley Earl's 1953 show cars. Its external novelties included a brushed stainless steel roof, tinted glass and four headlights, while the chassis was the shortest of all Cadillacs.

Power steering, automatic transmission and power assisted brakes were regular Cadillac features, but the Brougham was the first car to use air suspension with an electrically driven compressor

pressurizing air in rubber domes – a short-term feature as the system leaked. Power was provided by the Cadillac V-8 increased to 365 cu.in with 325 bhp, a necessary output given a weight of over 2.75 tons.

For interior comfort, the Brougham had air conditioning, separate front and rear heating, powered front seat for driver adjustment and easier access, power door locks, power trunk lid, vanity case and a perfume atomiser in the rear armrest. The Eldorado Brougham was Cadillac's flagship to match the Lincoln Continental, but sold just 704 cars in the two years of its production.

As such small numbers could not justify the assembly space, newly styled 1959 cars were built by Pinin Farina in Italy but only 200 of these were made in two years. The true successor to the 1958 Eldorado Brougham was the less lavishly equipped Fleetwood Brougham displaying the biggest vertical fins of all, but the near-horizontal fins on the 1959 Chevrolet Biscayne are actually more attractive.

TECHNICAL DESCRIPTION OF THE CADILLAC ELDORADO	
YEARS OF PRODUCTION	1957-1958
MODELS	4-DOOR SEDAN
ENGINE	FRONT-MOUNTED V-8
BORE X STROKE, CAPACITY	3.9 x 3.5 INCHES, 364.4
VALVEGEAR	PUSHROD OVERHEAD VALVES
FUEL SYSTEM	SINGLE CARBURETOR
POWER	325 BHP AT 4800 RPM
TRANSMISSION	4-SPEED AUTOMATIC
BODY/CHASSIS	STEEL BOX-SECTION FRAME
SUSPENSION	FRONT, WISHBONES AND AIR SPRINGS
	REAR, LIVE AXLE WITH AIR SPRINGS
TIRES/WHEELS	6.70 x 15 ON STEEL WHEELS
WHEELBASE, TRACK (F), TRACK(R)	129.5 x 61 x 61 INCHES
LENGHT, WIDT, HEIGHT	210 x 80 x 55 INCHES
MAX SPEED	110 MPH
WHERE BUILT	DETROIT, USA

Aston Martin DB4 and DB4GT

The arrival of the Aston Martin DB4 at the 1958 London Motor Show put Britain back near the top of the high performance Grand Tourer league, alongside the Ferrari 250GT and the Mercedes 300SL. Styled by Touring of Milan, the DB4 looked like a proper GT and it was a genuine 140 mph four-seater, too.

Following a pre-war range of small sporting cars, the DB2/4 had successfully established Aston Martin as a high performance

car manufacturer but, by the Mid-fifties, the 120 mph maximum speed was no longer fast. Aston Martin had begun work on the DB2/4 replacement in 1954. Initially this was a perimeter frame with wishbone front suspension and a de Dion axle, but when the project was taken to Touring, they asked for a conventional platform as a better base on which to mount their tubular steel body frame – the superleggera system. By the time the first prototype was completed

108-109 *Short wheelbase 250GT California Spyder had the same specification as the 250GT SWB. Engine, inset, develops 270 bhp.*

110-111 *Short Wheelbase Berlinetta was a classic road car.*

TECHNICAL DESCRIPTION OF THE FERRARI 250GT SWB

YEARS OF PRODUCTION	1959-1962
MODELS	2-SEATER COUPE
ENGINE	FRONT-MOUNTED V-12
BORE X STROKE, CAPACITY	2.8 X 2.3 INCHES, 108.1 CU.IN
VALVEGEAR	SINGLE OVERHEAD CAMSHAFT PER BANK
FUEL SYSTEM	3 WEBER TWIN-CHOKE CARBURETORS
POWER	270 BHP AT 7000 RPM
TRANSMISSION	4-SPEED
BODY/CHASSIS	STEEL TUBE WITH ALUMINIUM OR STEEL BODYWORK
SUSPENSION	FRONT, WISHBONES AND COILS REAR, LIVE AXLE WITH LEAF SPRINGS AND RADIUS ARMS
TIRES/WHEELS	6.00/7.00 X 16 ON WIRE WHEELS
WHEELBASE, TRACK (F), TRACK(R)	94.5 X 53.3 X 53.1 INCHES
LENGHT, WIDT, HEIGHT	163.5 X 66 X 50 INCHES
MAX SPEED	155 MPH
WHERE BUILT	MODENA, ITALY

For early GT racing, the models just had to come from a recognized manufacturer. But by 1957, FIA rules stated that it was necessary to build 100 similar GT cars in 12 months in order to qualify for International GT racing; the chassis and running gear had to be identical on all of them but the body style could be closed or convertible. After the first 100, individual bodies could be used provided they weighed the same and internal measurements matched the regulations. Ferrari qualified by combining all models on the same chassis.

The 250 series was a steady evolution from the original Colombo-designed 166 V-12. This became the 225 by increasing the bore from 2.67 to 2.7 inches, 165.6 cu.in for some 20 cars in 1952, mostly for competition use. One of these coupes used a 250 engine – 2.8 inch bore – to win the 1952 Mille Miglia; it was the basis of the 250MM that followed in 1953, but only 35 or so of these were built.

First of the real road cars bearing the 250 number was the 1953 Europa, the majority of the small run being with Pinin Farina coupe bodywork; although this was still a 12 x 15.2 cu.in, it was based on the longer (Lampredi) design which was used for the larger capacity engines.

The short-block (Colombo) 250 was used for the next 250GT Europa for 1955; they were the first of the 2-seater Ferraris to use coil springs in the front suspension as all had previously used a transverse leaf spring. Most of the 36 were Pinin Farina coupes.

The arrival of the 1956 250GT (Boano), styled by Pinin Farina but built by Boano, saw the first Ferrari to be produced in any quantity; around 130 were built up to 1958. Although the engine produced 220 bhp at 7000 rpm, it was very much a road car. As the GT competition cars became more specialized, road cars were no longer

dual-purpose machines. A 250GT cabriolet came in 1957 as an open version of the Boano-bodied cars. A similar, but faster, open version of the Berlinettas was called a 250GT California Spyder from 1958. The 250GT (Boano) was replaced by the 250GT Coupe in 1958 (350 over 3 years) . This gave way in 1960 to the 250 GT 2+2 also known as the 250GTE. This was Ferrari's first family car built to attack the Aston Martin and Maserati market – despite the extra seats it still used the 102-inch wheelbase. Over 950 of these were built in three series over 1960-63; they may not have the sporting appeal of the Tour de France and SWB cars but they are an affordable classic Ferrari built in exactly the same way.

For competition Ferrari had turned the 250GT Boano into the 250GT Berlinetta, often referred to as the Tour de France model; this had the same 102-inch wheelbase twin-tube chassis with a revised version of the short-block engine. Some 90 of these were built with minor body variations from 1956-59 and mostly with headlights behind plexiglass. However a final seven were built with the headlights exposed at the front of the wings and two of these were run at Le Mans in 1959; one finished 4th behind the earlier version, the GT category winner. With the shape thus proven, Ferrari then launched the 250GT Short Wheelbase (SWB), on the same chassis shortened to a 94-inch wheelbase and fitted with Dunlop disc brakes. The live rear axle was still carried on leaf springs but radius arms improved its location. Competition versions had aluminium bodywork, but over half the 160 produced were steel-bodied road cars. The 250GT SWB certainly lived up to expectation on the track providing many victories in 1960 and 1961.

112-113 *Short Wheelbase Berlinetta had many victories in GT races.*

1961 - 1970

THE ARRIVAL OF THE JAPANESE

With the Sixties came European rationalization as lesser manufacturers found it difficult to compete with the majors, although very small makers like Morgan, Alpine and TVR still retained autonomy, thanks to the those majors who were keen to supply components. The decade also saw the rapid expansion of Japanese car production with exports to America as their first major target.

At the start of this decade Japan was still an emergent car producing nation. The Fifties saw co-operation with western companies to import production technology quickly. Nissan produced the Austin A40, followed by the A50; Mitsubishi made Kaiser-Frazer Jeeps; Isuzu made Hillman Minxes

and Hino made Renault 4CVs – no classics there.

By 1960 production had reached 308,000 of which over half were sub-22 cu.in economy cars; imports were minimal, mostly through taxation, partly because the roads were still in a rough state. Even by 1970 very few out-of-town roads were metalled, but by then production had grown to 3.2 million and a few classics had emerged; Italian styling companies helped many on the way.

Nissan's first sports car was the 1959 Datsun Fairlady S211. Fairlady sports models and their equivalent Silvia coupes continued through the Sixties; the 1962 97 cu.in Fairlady grew to 122 cu.in. Already Nissan was making an impression on the

International rally scene, finishing the decade with victory for 1600SSS sedans in the 1970 East African Safari – a tribute to the lessons learnt on their own country's poor roads. The 240Z, arriving in 1969, would continue in the same vein; with its six-cylinder engine and independent suspension all round it was the natural successor to the big Austin-Healey 3000, particularly on the American market.

Honda had made considerable impact in the motor cycle world during the Fifties and only produced their first car in 1962; this S500 two-seater used such motor cycle technology as an 8000 rpm roller-bearing four-cylinder engine and chain drive to the rear wheels. Just two years later,

114-115 *Marcos produced the 1800 in 1964 with a wooden chassis and a Volvo 109 cu.in engine.*

Honda became the first Japanese manufacturer to enter Formula One racing. By 1966, the S500 two-seater had grown to become the exportable S800.

Mazda too were late into car production; their first car – a 22 cu.in 2-seater coupe – came in 1960, but they were soon into larger cars and the Bertone-styled 1500 sedan was being exported from 1967. They had also taken out a Wankel licence from NSU and produced the Cosmo or 110S sports coupe from 1967, followed by the R100 coupe both using the nominally 122 cu.in twin-rotor unit. Toyota used Yamaha to build just 351 examples of the striking Toyota 2000GT as a slightly scaled down Jaguar E-type between 1966-8. The Celica came in 1969 as the first of Toyota's own sporting machines.

In Britain Ford USA created Ford of Europe and took over the reins of Ford UK, General Motors had long controlled Vauxhall (and Opel), and Chrysler invested in the Rootes group (Humber, Hillman, Sunbeam, Singer) from 1964 before the final take-over came in 1973. So half the British motor industry was controlled from America. That left the British Motor Corporation (Austin, Morris, MG, Riley, Wolseley) and Leyland Motor Corporation (Standard, Triumph) still as major players. BMC took over Jaguar in 1966, Leyland took over Rover in 1967 and the two corporations merged in 1968. Many of these names would die, while others increasingly shared components.

While there many notable British launches in the decade, the arrival of the Jaguar E-type in 1961 was the highlight, an instant performance icon at a very reasonable price. In the small car world, the Mini was still supreme, but Rootes tried hard to challenge with the Hillman Imp using a lightweight 53 cu.in Coventry-Climax engine in the back, but it was not a commercial success, although it performed well in racing and rallying; from 1963-76 over 440,000 were built of which the fast-back versions – Singer Chamois coupe and Sunbeam Stiletto – still have some appeal.

Italy saw some change too. Fiat continued to supply most of the Italian market and Alfa Romeo remained under state control. Lancia survived most of the decade but finally became a part of Fiat in 1969. Maserati came to a technical agreement with Citroen from 1968, and in 1969 Fiat took a 50% shareholding in Ferrari. Of more lasting influence was the arrival of two new manufacturers; both de Tomaso and Lamborghini started making road cars in 1965.

In Germany, Mercedes had been the majority shareholder in the Audi group from 1956 but Volkswagen took this over in 1964. NSU joined Audi in 1969. While the Isetta, 600 and 700 had kept BMW going during the latter half of the Fifties, the Sixties saw BMW establish themselves as makers of real cars from 1962.

French production combined the utilitarian with the sophisticated as exemplified by Citroen's range from 2CV to the SM, the latter fruit of the Maserati alliance arriving in 1970; the DS19 became a DS21 in 1965 including a new short-stroke 134 cu.in engine to replace the 122 cu.in which had been designed in 1934. Peugeot brought in the 4-series, which included the nicely styled 122 cu.in 504 Coupe and the Safari-winning 404 sedan. Renault launched their 2CV rival with the fwd R4 in 1961, and the rear-engined R8 gradually replaced the Dauphine, whose sporting Floride derivative then became the Caravelle. Gordini continued his tuning association with the R8 Gordini which became a rallying success. Alpine took over the Renault competition mantle towards the end of the decade using the R8-engined A110 coupe, which was to have considerable rallying success. It was even more successful when it used the 1600 engine from the new Renault 16 which emerged in 1965 as the first real hatchback.

There was no corporate change in America, but it was the decade that saw the publication in 1965

1961 - 1970

of Ralph Nader's safety crusading book 'Unsafe at any Speed'. Although this had little major effect until the Seventies, sales of the Chevrolet Corvair and the VW Beetle were badly affected – both rear-engined cars with swing axle suspension. Meanwhile the Sixties saw the best of the American muscle cars with ever larger engines dropped into the 'compacts' – slightly down-sized versions of the regular sedans.

Then came the 'pony' car revolution headed by the Ford Mustang in 1964, pony being a small horse like a mustang. Chevrolet continued to produce the Corvette two-seater, which became a genuine high-performance car with the big 427

cu.in V-8 engines, and also introduced the largest-engined front-wheel-drive car in the Oldsmobile Toronado.

Ford took its motor sport aspirations onto the International scene with the GT40, which won Le Mans from 1966-69 in its various guises. The Sixties was really the last decade in which the average enthusiast could reasonably service and subsequently restore his own car. By the Seventies, emission legislation required so much hardware to be added that even simple engines became complicated to work on. And fuel injection systems were much harder to look after than carburetors.

Classic Sedans

If you wanted ultimate straight-line performance from a sedan, it had to come from America. Even if European cars could mostly outhandle them and outbrake them on the touring car race tracks, Ford's Falcons, Galaxies and Mustangs could win by brute power and the Chevrolet Camaro was just as effective.

America had two major performance outlets, NASCAR racing around the oval tracks and the drag-strip, official or unofficial. Both were all about flat out maximum power. Arguably Chrysler started the hot-rod ball rolling with the 300 in the late Fifties and Chevrolet responded with the Bel Air. Big engines meant big cars. However the arrival of

the 'compacts' brought new opportunities to get a better power/weight ratio.

When General Motors dropped their biggest V-8 with 390 cu.in and 325 bhp into the 1964 Pontiac Tempest and called it the GTO, the muscle car era had arrived. Oldsmobile replied with the 4-4-2, an F85 compact with the 330 cu.in. engine; a year later it had a 400 cu.in and in 1970 came the 455.

Chrysler further developed the 'hemi-head' V-8 to 427 cu.in for the Dodge Charger and Plymouth Belvedere. Most striking of all was the 1970 Plymouth Superbird with a low-drag nose and a high wing on the tail; nearly 2000 of these NASCAR specials were built. Dodge's equivalent was the Charger with a Superbee style and the same engine choice. Ford put the 429 427 cu.in into Galaxies and Fairlanes. The trend continued through to 1972. Any one of these over-engined compacts is a classic today.

America introduced another new breed in 1964 with the Ford Mustang, the American 2+2. It was a trend perhaps started with the Studebaker Golden Hawk with its supercharged 286 cu.in engine in 1957. Ford's 1955 Thunderbird had provided fast personal transport for two with all mod cons and had the option of a supercharged V-8 in 1957. When the T-bird became a four-seater, it lost its elegance and youth appeal.

Ford still wanted a car that looked sporting, but could provide a range of performance; it also had to be affordable for the young and as appealing as the sports car imports.

Developed from the Falcon, the Mustang came in 1964 in open and hard-top four-seater forms with engines that ranged from a 101 bhp 170 cu.in six to the 260 cu.in V-8 with 164 bhp; by the end of the year the 271 bhp 289 cu.in engine was available. Ford had a head start with two years of pony car sales before the arrival of General Motors' Chevrolet Camaro and Pontiac Firebird, Chrysler's Plymouth Barracuda and the Mustang's cousin, the Mercury Cougar.

While NASCAR racing was still the popular outlet for the muscle cars, a new form of road-racing started in 1966 – Trans-Am, a name soon to be annexed by Pontiac. This rapidly bred the same horsepower race and the big V-8s were soon available in the pony cars.

Last of the performance Mustangs was the 1971 Boss 351 with 347 cu.in; there had earlier been a very limited run of Boss 429s with the 427 cu.in Ford engine. There were Shelby Mustangs too in GT-350 and GT-500 form.

Also worthy of note was the 1963 Buick Riviera – Buick's belated answer to the 4-seater Thunderbird. Initially with the 402 cu.in V-8, it was powered by a 427 cu.in version by 1965 and was capable of nearly 130 mph – it still only had drum brakes though. GM's new styling boss, Bill Mitchell, had removed all the Fifties fins and produced a very elegant 2-door, 4-seater coupe. The lines were carried through to another pair of notable GM classics – the front-wheel-drive Oldsmobile Toronado (1966) and the Cadillac Eldorado (1967) – both two-door luxury coupes with 427 cu.in engines. One of GM's more lasting contribution to the Sixties was the aluminium 213 cu.in V-8 which was only briefly used by Buick, but has been a great success for Rover, who bought the rights to it in 1963.

In the luxury world, the 1961 Lincoln Continental was one of the best ever for its combination of elegance and equipment. Cadillac's 1965 Fleetwood was equally restrained – one of Mitchell's outstanding designs. That was the year when Rolls-Royce brought out the Silver Shadow with the matching T-series Bentley, both powered by revised versions of the Silver Cloud's 378 cu.in V-8. Although these used unitary construction, there was still scope for coachbuilt versions; Mulliner Park Ward produced the 2-door coupe in 1966 and convertible in 1967 – both called Corniche from 1971. Last of the variants before the 1977 Shadow II was the Camargue with Pininfarina bodywork.

Mercedes' response to the Rolls' claim of "Best Car in the World" was the 1964 600 limousine, complete with all possible comforts and a 384 cu.in V-8, but of more lasting classic appeal was the 300SEL 6.3; the 300 bhp engine from the 600 was dropped into the long wheelbase 300 sedan in 1967 to produce a German muscle car – over 7000 were built.

One of the features of the Sixties was the growth of sedan car racing and rallying as a means of make promotion – works teams rather than enthusiastic amateurs.

Controlling this on an International level was the work of the FIA (Federation Internationale de l'Automobile); they had originally drawn up rules in 1954 which demanded minimum levels of production and listed allowed changes. In 1960 they introduced a system whereby the specifications and production numbers would be confirmed by FIA visits to the factories before homologation forms were issued. So manufacturers had to produce limited numbers for general sale of cars that they wanted to use for competition – the homologation specials.

Following their total performance philosophy, Ford was particularly active through the Sixties and the competition successes of the homologation specials was reflected on all models in the range. In 1962 the Cortina was just another family sedan, but the arrival of the Cortina-Lotus in January 1963 saw the first of the homologation specials, just two months ahead of the Mini Cooper S and the Cortina GT. The Cortina-Lotus engine was one that had been announced for the Lotus Elan in October 1962. The GT engine was also used in the Capri (1961) and the Corsair (1964). In 1967 Ford changed the Cortina body-style and introduced the 97 cu.in cross-flow engine. Cortina 1600GT and Cortina-Lotus continued but an addition to the range was the 1600E, a 1600GT with Cortina-Lotus running gear and Executive luxury fittings.

In 1968 Ford replaced the Anglia with the Escort which had more competition derivatives – 1300GT, Mexico (1600GT engine), Twin-Cam (Lotus engine) and the RS1600 with the Cosworth BDA engine.

116-117 *Ferrari 250GT Lusso of 1964.*

This was the first of the classic RS (Rallye Sport) models, all of which rate as classics.

Then came the second generation Capri in 1969 as a European Mustang with a large number of options including engines from 79 cu.in to V-6 183 cu.in; competition versions came from Germany with the RS2600 and Britain with the RS3100, both of which recorded many track successes. The last of the Capris rolled off the lines in 1987.

Other contributions to the British classic sedan ranks came from Rover with the 2000 in 1963 and Jaguar who introduced the XJ6 range in 1968, both of which would continue well into the next decade. An unusual rival in this class came from the house of NSU; the German company had launched an open version of the 36 cu.in Sport Prinz with a nominal 61 cu.in single-rotor Wankel engine as the Wankel Spider in 1963 as a pilot exercise. It was interesting but made little impact.

The 1967 launch of a spacious 4-door, front-wheel-drive, aerodynamic sedan was a considerable contrast, given NSU's history of motor cycles and small rear-engined cars. The 122 cu.in twin-rotor Wankel engine made a very good car doubly interesting. It was a German Citroen DS19 with a wheel at each corner to give a comfortable ride, excellent ZF power steering and semi-automatic transmission.

Sadly, NSU never truly sorted out the lubrication problems of the rotor-tip seals, even after the 1970 introduction of a Mark II, and only 37,000 had been built by 1977.

A number were subsequently converted in the after-market with 103 cu.in Taunus V-4 engines and transmissions. In fact NSU had been absorbed by the VW group in 1969 and NSU's planned K70 intermediate car was launched as a VW K70 in 1969 with a 97 cu.in version of the smaller NSU – another power pack that can replace the rotary unit.

But the major news in Germany was the resurgence of BMW, starting with the four-door 1500 in 1962; its single overhead camshaft 'four' with hemi-head valve disposition was a design that

served the company well and with independent suspension all-round it was a very modern car. An 1800 followed in 1963 together with a limited run of 1800TISA 130 bhp models for racing; a 2000 came in 1966 with the 2000TI and injection 2000tii in 1969. The two door 1600-2 (later 1602) range began in 1966, leading to the 2002 and 2002ti (1968), 2002tii (1971) and 2002 turbo (1973). Meanwhile the old V-8 cars had continued through to the Sixties and the Bertone-styled 3200CS coupe came out in 1962 for a 3-year run of 600 units; and the 700 lasted until 1965.

The first coupe from the new range came in 1965 with the 2000C and more powerful 2000CS; the style of its rear half owed much to the 3200CS, but the front panel with pronounced wrap-round headlights was not a success. In 1968 BMW launched the new 6-cylinder cars, bringing in the 2800CS coupe with a revised front panel that was far more successful than its predecessor. It was an incredible range of cars to launch and produce in a single decade, and many of them have become classics.

From Sweden, Saab had brought in the 38 bhp

52 cu.in engine for the 96 in 1960, then added the GT850 to the range in 1962 with triple carburetors and 55 bhp; this was called the Saab Sport in the UK and the Monte Carlo in the USA. The 96 proved to be a remarkable rally car in the hands of Erik Carlsson, winning the Monte Carlo Rally twice and the RAC Rally three times. A 96 even finished 12th overall at Le Mans in 1959. Emission pressures saw the 2-stroke finally replaced by the 91.5 cu.in Ford V-4 for 1967, but rally victories continued. The old shape continued to be produced in Finland until 1980, but the new 99 had arrived in 1969, still front-wheel-drive but using the inclined 4-cylinder engine from Triumph; this too would have its share of rally successes including some with turbocharged 250 bhp engines. Competition did much to develop and promote the classic sedans of the Sixties.

118-119 *Aston Martin DB4 GT Zagato from 1961.*

GRAND TOURERS

While Ford's adoption of the term GT to add to their faster Cortina somewhat devalued the initials, the FIA didn't help either. They instituted a GT championship in 1962 for which there were

minimum dimensions specified and a requirement that at least 100 were built per year; thus, many open sports cars also became GTs.

But the market still knew that real Gran Turismos were built to carry two – or two plus two occasional children – far and fast in entertaining comfort.

Some of the Sixties GTs were designed around such racing requirements.

The Ferrari 250GTO (1962) was the lightweight streamlined version of the 250GT SWB, and the Lusso (luxury) was its roadgoing equivalent. Jaguar built special lightweight versions of its E-type roadster. Aston Martin raced re-bodied versions of the DB4GT. The Ford GT40 (1965) was a mid-engined

coupe built to race against Ferrari's 275LM, and the GT40 Mk.III was the road-going version.

Most of the GTs, though, were built as fast tourers and some were genuine four-seaters. Aston Martin changed the DB4 for the DB5 244 cu.in in 1963 and lengthened the chassis for the DB6 in 1965. While the 4-seater DB6 was still in production, Aston Martin brought in the DBS(1967) to provide more back seat space; the DBS V-8 followed in 1969, the start of a range that would run through to 1989.

In search of cheap high performance, four British manufacturers made cars with American engines under Italian coachwork; the AC 428 had a Ford 427 cu.in under Frua bodywork and Gordon Keeble had a Chevrolet engine under a Bertone skin – a combination that was also used for the Iso Rivolta and its two-seater Grifo version.

The Jensen CV-8 with Chrysler power had replaced the 541 in 1962 and the new Interceptor used the same engine with Vignale bodywork from 1966; the FF version was the first to offer four-wheel-drive in a road car. And from 1961 Bristol used a special Chrysler 311 cu.in V-8 for the 407; the identically-bodied 406 had seen the final 134 cu.in development of the famous 'six'.

Jensen had also been responsible for the assembly of the Saint's Volvo P1800 for its first three years (1961-63) before production was transferred to Sweden as the 1800S. In 1968, it had the 122 cu.in B20 engine and the 1800E (for Einspritz-injection) came in 1969. The sporting estate 1800ES arrived in 1971. Overall nearly 47,500 1800s were produced, of which 8000 were estates, and the majority of production went to the USA.

The sports estate theme had been pursued by Reliant in England. A 3-wheeler manufacturer, they had entered the sports car market in 1962 with the fiberglass-bodied Sabre using a 103 cu.in Ford engine, then the 158 cu.in Ford 'six'. This somewhat ugly car was transformed by Ogle into the Scimitar GT in 1966. The Ford V-6 was available in 1967 and in 1968 the Scimitar GTE was launched as a four-seater estate car. Perhaps the first sports estates were the 12 'shooting brakes' specially built on the Aston Martin DB5 by coachbuilder Harold Radford from 1964.

It was certainly Aston Martin that put the first opening hatch-back, as opposed to a 2-door estate car, into production with the DB2/4 in 1953. Jaguar adopted the same system for the 1961 213 cu.in XKE coupe and continued it on the 2+2 that came in 1966 by which time the 256 cu.in engine was fitted. The V-12 came in 1971.

A scaled down E-type coupe was built by Triumph as the GT6 from 1966 using the 122 cu.in 'six' from the Vitesse and Triumph 2000 in what was basically the Herald chassis, complete with swing axle rear suspension; from 1968 the Mk.II had revised rear suspension and became a nice little car.

Triumph's other sporting GT was the elegant Stag which arrived in 1970; based on the 2000 chassis, but with a single-cam 183 cu.in V-8, it followed the Mercedes 230SL theme of having a removable winter hard-top with a soft-top concealed under a metal cover. Having invented the Gran Turismo breed, Italy continued to make a significant contribution to the GT ranks, encouraged by their coachbuilders who were always ready to produce niche models on sedan platforms. Ghia's 2300 coupe on the six-cylinder Fiat 1800/2100/2300 platform was a wonderfully elegant creation which had power and sound to match, particularly with the 136 bhp Abarth conversion. It lasted from 1961-68, by which time the Fiat 124 Sport had taken over (1967) with a Pininfarina-styled Spider to back it up. Both used twin-cam 87 cu.in versions of the standard 124's pushrod 67 cu.in 'four'; this was increased to 98 cu.in in 1969 and 107 cu.in in 121 cu.in, while the Spider carried on from 1978 with a 122 cu.in engine. Nearly 180,000 Spiders and 280,000 Sport coupes were produced. At the same time, budget sports Fiats were being produced on the rear-engined 850 platform initially with the 51 cu.in unit (1965-68) and then with 55 cu.in (1968-73); Fiat designed the coupe (343,000 produced) and Bertone the Spider (125,000 produced). This was a golden decade for sporting Fiats as the company also produced the Fiat Dino in both Coupe (Bertone) and Spider (Pininfarina) forms – see separate chapter.

Round the corner in Turin, Lancia had replaced the Aurelia with the 152 cu.in Flaminia back in 1956 – this became a 171 cu.in from 1964. From 1958 Pininfarina produced some elegant bodies for the

short wheelbase coupe and also for the 109 cu.in flat-four front-wheel drive Flavia, which arrived in 1961 (122 cu.in from 1969).

The narrow V-4 front-wheel-drive 73 cu.in Fulvia came in 1964; the little coupe versions, using 79 and 97 cu.in engines, were very effective rally cars and were still in production in 1975, some time after Fiat's 1969 take-over. All three of these Sixties models were also available with Zagato bodywork.

At the other end of the Turin-Milan autostrada, Alfa Romeo were doing much the same as Fiat, albeit in smaller volumes. The bigger cars continued with the 122 cu.in 'four' exchanged for a 158 cu.in 'six' in 1962, with bodies still from Touring, Bertone and Zagato, the 2600SZ being one of Zagato's finest designs, ranking alongside their Aston Martin DB4 GT. The Giulietta Sprint, Spiders and SS became Giulias with the 97 cu.in engine in 1963 but a new Sprint GT came in with Bertone bodywork – one of his best shapes which would last through 106 cu.in and 122 cu.in versions until the Mid-seventies. Pininfarina's Duetto Spider would continue through to 1993. Zagato built the competition Giulia TZ (Tubolare Zagato) of which 112 were the TZ1 followed by 12 of the lower and lighter TZ2 (1963-67); they followed this up with 1500 of the Sprint GT

Zagato (1969-75) using 79 and 97cu.in engines.

Down the road from all this volume production activity was Modena, the home of Ferrari and Maserati, to be joined in 1963 by de Tomaso and in 1964 by Lamborghini.

Together they were to produce an incredible range of vehicles – all destined to be classics. Vehicle homologation and crash-testing had yet to arrive, so there were no constraints on adding a constant stream of variations on basic themes. All four were able to produce rolling chassis of varying lengths, with different engines, leaving the coachbuilders to finish the cars.

De Tomaso produced the mid-engined Mangusta (Ford 286 cu.in V-8) in 1967 which became the Pantera in 1969, and the following year saw the first of their front-engined road cars – the Ford V-8 powered 4-door Deauville. Lamborghini started with the front-engined 350GT with Touring bodywork in 1964, followed it with the 400GT in 1965, to which was added a 2+2 version; the mid-engined Miura (Bertone) came in 1967 and the Islero (Marazzi) replaced the 400GT 2+2 in

120-121 Jaguar E-type 3.8 roadster from 1962.

1968. Tubular frames were replaced by sheet steel platforms when the four-seater Espada (Bertone) was launched at the same 1968 show.

Maserati's collection moved on from the 3500 GTI, the first car to use those initials following the adoption of fuel injection in 1962. A short chassis Spider version of this had been bodied by Vignale in 1959; Vignale then added a roof to produce the Sebring in 1963. The same year, the 4-door Quattroporte, using a tamed version of the racing V-8, emerged from the house of Frua, who also produced the two-seater Mistral (open and closed) on a further shortened 3500GTI frame. Vignale made a luxury four-seater Mexico using the V-8 in 256 and 286 cu.in forms from 1965; then Ghia produced the memorable Ghibli (286 and 298 cu.in V-8) in 1966, which was followed by Vignale's similar-looking fast-back four-seater Indy in 1968. It was Maserati's most prolific period, brought to gradual rationalisation by the Citroen merger of 1969. The first product of this was the 1970 Citroen SM which used a new Maserati four-cam V-6 164 cu.in engine in a sporting development of the DS.

Like the rest of the Modena group, Ferrari had begun to take their road cars seriously in this decade and produced a remarkable variety, all with Pininfarina bodywork. From the short-wheelbase 250GT, Ferrari moved on to the lighter and faster competition 250GTO, and then developed the luxury (Lusso) equivalent. Using the last development of this engine was the 275GTB and 275GTS (Berlinetta and Spider), Ferrari's first road car with no competition aspiration; the four-cam 275GTB/4 from 1966 was the most desirable of this range. A new 244 cu.in V-12 single-cam engine was used to power the 330 range from that year with 330GTC and 330GTS (Coupe and Spider). An enlarged engine for 1967 brought in the long-wheelbase 365GT 2+2 to which 365GTC and 365GTS were added in 1968. A year later came the flag-ship 365GTB/4 Daytona coupe with twin-cam heads, followed by the 2+2 version – the 365GTC/4 in 1971.

Meanwhile Ferrari had introduced the mid-engined Dino 206GT in 1968 using the 122 cu.in engine that Fiat had put into production for them, and followed that with the 146 cu.in version that Fiat had developed as more suitable for road use; the beautiful Dino 246GT arrived in 1969 as the affordable Ferrari to take on Porsche.

The German company had introduced the Porsche 911 to replace the old Beetle-based 356 in 1963. Using a flat-six air-cooled engine mounted in the familiar place at the rear, the 911 was an instant success which has forever remained a sporting icon; more power and controllability have been added over the years. Porsche also designed the mid-engined 914 as a Volkswagen sports car of which 120,000 were produced from 1970-75; their own version, using the 911 engine, was the 914/6 made in much smaller numbers.

Around the corner in Stuttgart, Mercedes-Benz had finished production of the specialized 190SL and 300SL in 1963 and introduced the 140 cu.in 230SL as a sporting version of the new 220 sedan range. The 2-seater was sold as a roadster, but came with a substantial fully-trimmed hard-top, which gave it GT comfort. The 250SL came in 1966 and the 280SL in 1968 with successive enlargements of the six-cylinder engine. Coupe (250C and 280C) and convertible versions of the sedans were further classics from the make.

A further German GT came from the unlikely source of Opel, which, like General Motors' British subsidiary Vauxhall, had steadfastly ignored the sporting scene. Opel's Rallye-Kadett was the first step in 1966. The 2-seater fastback Opel GT followed in 1967, based on the revised Kadett platform. It was offered with 67 or 116 cu.in engines; over 100,000 were built, of which 60 per cent went to the USA, by the time production finished in 1973. Preceding the Ford Capri, coupe versions of the Rekord (1966) and Commodore (1967) were attractive scaled-down versions of the Oldsmobile Toronado.

1961 - 1970

On their home territory, General Motors continued to produce the Chevrolet Corvette in gradually increasing numbers – 11,000 in 1961 rising to 38,800 in 1969. The second series gave way to the Sting Ray in 1963, the first with independent rear suspension, and another body change in 1968 gave Targa-top and convertible versions. Gradually losing its battle with the big three, Studebaker took on the Corvette market with the 2+2 Avanti (1962), an amazing piece of sculpture in fiberglass by Raymond Loewy. The company had foreseen the compact market with the 1959 Lark and used a shortened version of this chassis with their own 286 cu.in V-8, offering a Paxton supercharger option; front disc brakes were the first seen on an American car. Financial problems saw the company close its American plant after some 4500 Avantis had been built; however the design was taken over by two dealers who continued to produce the car with Chevrolet power for many years.

SPORTS AND SPECIALIST GT

While many manufacturers were offering GT cars and then making a convertible version, there were still some making roadsters first and then perhaps adding the fixed head model later. Fastest of the true roadsters was undoubtedly the AC Cobra, which emerged from the marriage of the Fifties AC Ace and the 256 cu.in Ford V-8 in 1961. By the time that AC adopted the strengthened chassis that Ford had designed to take 427 cu.in power, the AC 289 had become a very desirable sporting machine.

As recounted in a previous chapter, the Sunbeam Tiger (1964-67) used the same 256 cu.in engine and the Tiger II followed with the 286 cu.in V-8.

Morgan, too, adopted American V-8 power in 1968 with the Plus 8, but this was the ex-Buick 213 cu.in that Rover had acquired. Over thirty years later, they are still using the same engine in 238 cu.in and 280 cu.in forms in almost the same chassis.

Before the V-8, Morgan were still using the Triumph 'four' which had been around since the

days of the Standard Vanguard.

Triumph continued to use this engine for their own TR3 and TR3A (1955-61); a handful of TR3As with Michelotti fixed head bodies were built by Vignale and sold as Triumph Italias. When the TR4 arrived in 1961 with new Michelotti bodywork, including a targa-top version, the engine had been enlarged to 130 cu.in. By then the chassis was getting old and uncomfortable, so the TR4A came in 1965 with independent rear suspension which gave some improvement. The TR5 followed in 1967 using the Triumph 2500 six-cylinder engine with fuel injection within the same bodywork. The body was redesigned by Karmann for the 1969 TR6, which proved to be the most popular of all the real TRs as nearly 92,000 were produced over the next 8 years.

From 1962, Triumph were also represented in the small sports car market with the Spitfire, a neat and popular two-seater based on the Herald sedan. With a twin-carburetor 70 cu.in 63 bhp engine, it was fast enough and agile. Successive developments saw the Mk.II in 1964 and the Mk.III with a 79 cu.in 75 bhp engine in 1967. The Mk.IV came in 1971 with the engine changed to the later 1500TC unit in 1975 to overcome the power loss due to emission controls. Its major rival throughout was the MG Midget which initially used the BMC A-series engines (58, 67 and 77 cu.in) through to 1974 until it, too, adopted the same Triumph 1500 engine. By 1979 both had been axed.

MG had replaced the MGA with the MGB in 1962 using an 110 cu.in version of the BMC B-series engine in a new unitary construction sports car; the MGBGT followed in 1965. The MGC came along in 1967 with a new 183 cu.in engine in a vain attempt to replace the big Healey; over half a million MGBs were produced but only 9000 MGCs in 1967-69. The B would continue in production to 1980.

While the MG was a traditional unsophisticated sports car, Lotus set new standards of performance, ride and roadholding with the Lotus Elan which replaced the Elite in 1962. The Elan, with a fiberglass body on a steel backbone chassis, was small and light, which

allowed the 95 cu.in Ford twin-cam to give impressive performance. A fixed head coupe joined the range in 1965 and the Elan +2 came in 1967. In between Lotus found time to produce the Europa (1966), a mid-engined GT 2-seater using the Renault 16 drive-train reversed – the first affordable mid-engined production car.

Among Britain's other small specialist producers, TVR produced a new Mk.III chassis in 1962 with wishbone suspension, and adopted the 109 cu.in MGB engine and transmission when that became available in 1963. From 1964 the body was modified to give a cut-off Manx tail for the 1800S. This was displaced in 1967 by the Vixen series with Ford Cortina GT power; the Vixen S2 of 1968 saw a longer wheelbase which was also used for the Tuscan, the 286 cu.in Ford-engined model which had started life in America as the Griffith. By the end of the decade the Tuscan was also available with the 183 cu.in Ford V-6. Marcos had also joined the ranks of the small GT cars. Early cars used wooden chassis and body of questionable beauty, but the 1964 Marcos 1800, styled by Denis Adams, was a very attractive machine. The chassis still used marine quality plywood but the body was fiberglass and a Volvo 110 cu.in engine was used. A 91.5 cu.in Ford Cortina GT engine was also offered and a tuned 100 cu.in version replaced the Volvo unit in

1966. For 1969 a Ford V-6 version became available and a steel space-frame chassis replaced the wooden one. Marcos also tried to enter the luxury four-seater GT market with the Mantis, using a Triumph 2500 engine, but this was not a success.

Marcos were also responsible for the Mini-Marcos, probably the best of a number of fiberglass monocoque units designed to take the transverse Mini engine and subframes.

While this installed the engine at its customary end, the Unipower GT had its own space-frame chassis and installed the Mini engine and transmission behind the driver; it was an effective little car – forerunner of the Fiat X1/9 – but only some 70 or so were made from 1966-69.

Two other well-engineered and good-looking British GT cars deserved to last longer than they did. The 2-seater Rochdale Olympic was created by the designer of the Lotus Elite in 1960 and used the same fiberglass monocoque principles with

Riley 1.5 components under very aerodynamic lines; a Phase II version came in 1963 using the Cortina GT engine. The Tornado Talisman was a small 4-seater GT which used the 81 cu.in Ford engine from 1961 – an attractive little car which went very well in British sedan car racing.

Small GT cars were not just a British preserve. In Sweden, Saab had introduced the Sonett II using the two-stroke 850GT fwd engine in a small coupe in 1966; a year and 260 cars later, the V-4 engine replaced the two-stroke as it had done for the 96. From 1967-69 1610 of these were produced.

A minor redesign of the fiberglass body accompanied the Sonett III and 8365 were built before the end in 1974.

In France, the Panhard-powered fiberglass-bodied DBs had become Renault-powered Rene Bonnets in 1962; Le Mans and Missile used 67 cu.in R8 and 51 cu.in Dauphine power trains converted to front wheel drive, while the Djet mounted the R8 engine

amidships. Matra took the company over at the end of 1964 and continued with the Djet, gradually improving its performance. A new mid-engined coupe, the Matra MS530, came in 1967 using the 103 cu.in Ford V-4. Alpine continued their Renault association with the A110 coupe and Simca produced a nice coupe on the rear-engined Simca 1000. Italian tuner Abarth was to take this development further with Abarth-Simca 1300GT and 2000 coupes.

And in South Africa, the GSM Delta was another pretty little GT car using fiberglass bodywork on a tubular frame. This was powered by a tuned Ford Anglia 105E engine and proved very effective on the race circuits. The arrival of glassfibre certainly gave small manufacturers the chance to produce properly styled cars at a reasonable price during the Sixties.

122-123 *Triumph TR4 of 1962 was shaped by Michelotti.*

Jaguar E-type

When it was launched at Geneva in 1961, the Jaguar E-type set new standards for the ideal sports car, just as the XK120 had done 13 years earlier. The engine was a development of the original, but everything else was new. With independent rear suspension from the saloon Mk.X – announced 5 months later – it had good roadholding with ride comfort unmatched in a sports car. Its aerodynamic body shape, developed from the race-winning D-type, ensured that it had effortless high speed performance. And it was considerably cheaper than the Aston Martin DB4 and Ferrari 250GT which were the only cars of similar performance.

Jaguar had actually started work on the new car in 1957 using a development of the center monocoque D-type chassis with aluminium panels and a tuned 146 cu.in XK engine. A major feature of E1A,

TECHNICAL DESCRIPTION OF THE JAGUAR E 3.8

YEARS OF PRODUCTION	1961-1965
MODELS	ROADSTER AND COUPE 2-SEATER
ENGINE	FRONT-MOUNTED IN-LINE 6
BORE X STROKE, CAPACITY	3.4 x 4.1 INCHES, 230 CU.IN
VALVEGEAR	TWIN OVERHEAD CAMSHAFTS
FUEL SYSTEM	THREE SU CARBURETORS
POWER	265 BHP AT 5500 RPM
TRANSMISSION	4-SPEED
BODY/CHASSIS	STEEL MONOCOQUE
SUSPENSION	FRONT, WISHBONES AND TORSION BARS
	REAR, WISHBONE, DRIVE-SHAFT AND COIL SPRINGS
TIRES/WHEELS	6.40 x 15 ON 5K x 15 WIRE WHEELS
WHEELBASE, TRACK (F), TRACK(R)	96 x 50 x 50 INCHES
LENGTH, WIDTH, HEIGHT	175 x 65 x 48 INCHES
MAX SPEED	143 MPH
WHERE BUILT	COVENTRY, ENGLAND

124-125 *The Jaguar E-type, launched in 1961, gave remarkable performance for its price.*

though, was the independent rear suspension which initially used twin wishbones before the upper one became a fixed length drive-shaft. The second level of prototype was E2A which might have been used for Jaguar's return to sports-car racing in 1958/9. Although Jaguar decided not to race, they allowed American Briggs Cunningham to use the car for Le Mans 1960. For this it was fitted with a dry sump D-type unit reduced to 183 cu.in but with fuel injection and an aluminium cylinder block.

The production E-type followed the basic design of E2A closely. The chassis used the D-type's central monocoque but extended it rearwards to be able to carry a separate rubber-mounted cradle for the differential, inboard disc brakes, coil springs and suspension links including the drive-shaft. Fore and aft wheel location was provided by a pressed steel trailing arm with large rubber bushes. At the front, the D-type system of a separate space-frame bolted to the monocoque was continued, as were the torsion bar springs. The body design showed a front section just like that of E2A, but the doors were bigger and the tail section was lower. Both the roadster and the fixed head coupe were developed in the wind tunnel.

The engine was identical to that used in the 3.8 XK150S with 265 bhp (gross) together with the 4-speed gearbox, a Moss unit still with unsynchronised first gear. Since the car weighed only 2520 lb, the performance was good for its day with 0-60 mph in 7.0 sec. This sounds slow now, but the E-type only had four gears and a speed range of 150 mph, so first gear was high. The first E-types to be tested achieved almost 150 mph, but they used higher gearing from racing tires and had a little more power than standard; standard E-types with normal gearing were limited to 144 mph.

Private entrants raced the early E-types with factory assistance and these were a match for the Ferrari 250GT in short races, but could not keep up with the GTO in 1962. Jaguar eventually produced a car for International GT competition in 1963. The original homologation form allowed aluminium or steel for chassis and bodywork, so the competition one used aluminium. However the later extension included bigger Dunlop wheels, Girling brakes, ZF 5-speed gearbox, dry sump lubrication, D-type cylinder head, aluminium cylinder block, Weber carburetors or fuel injection. Although the engine could

produce 340 bhp with all the extras, the competition Jaguar E was never as fast as the Ferrari 250GTO or the AC Cobra that took over. Jaguar built up just 14 of these 'lightweight' E-types for private entrants.

When the E-type 4.2 arrived in 1965, it had improved brakes and the gearbox gained synchromesh on first gear. Although the maximum power was still quoted as 265 bhp, and the top speed of the two models remained the same, the new one had more torque which improved drivability. Up to that point the E-type had always been a two-seater. In 1966, a 2+2 joined the range with its wheelbase increased by 9 inches and the height by 2 inches. Radial tires were fitted and automatic transmission was also offered for the first time.

Series II cars followed in 1968 with exposed headlights, a larger radiator intake to provide extra air for the optional air conditioning, revised bumpers and optional power assistance. Series III cars came in 1971 with the new 323 cu.in V-12, a change which was necessary to overcome the power lost due to emission controls. The final E-type rolled off the lines in 1973 after 56,000 six-cylinder cars and 15,300 with the V-12.

TECHNICAL DESCRIPTION OF THE JAGUAR LIGHTWEIGHT COUPE

YEARS OF PRODUCTION	1961-1965
MODELS	ROADSTER AND COUPE 2-SEATER
ENGINE	FRONT-MOUNTED IN-LINE 6
BORE X STROKE, CAPACITY	3.4 x 4.1 INCHES, 230 CU.IN
VALVEGEAR	TWIN OVERHEAD CAMSHAFTS
FUEL SYSTEM	FUEL INJECTION
POWER	344 BHP AT 6000 RPM
TRANSMISSION	5-SPEED
BODY/CHASSIS	ALUMINIUM MONOCOQUE
SUSPENSION	FRONT, WISHBONES AND TORSION BARS
	REAR, WISHBONE, DRIVE-SHAFT AND COIL
	SPRINGS
TIRES/WHEELS	7.00L & 7.25L x 15 ON 7 & 7.5 IN ALLOYS
WHEELBASE, TRACK (F), TRACK(R)	96 x 53 x 55.5 INCHES
LENGTH, WIDTH, HEIGHT	175 x 65 x 48 INCHES
MAX SPEED	168 MPH
WHERE BUILT	COVENTRY, ENGLAND

N.B FIGURES FOR LIGHTWEIGHT COUPE ARE THOSE FOR THE 1964 LE MANS CAR

AC Cobra

When the Cobra-Ford took the FIA World GT championship in 1965, its chassis design was more than twelve years old. Variously known as a Shelby Cobra or AC Cobra powered by Ford, it was effectively an AC Ace with a big Ford V-8 engine. The Ace story started with a special chassis that John Tojeiro had designed to take the engine and gearbox from his MG TA. With twin steel tubes and box-section

cross members at each end, it carried independent suspension along the lines of the racing Coopers which had used the transverse leaf spring and lower wishbones from the Fiat 500 (Topolino).

Cliff Davis bought a Cooper-MG complete with a Ferrari 166 Barchetta body style and used an identical body for his Tojeiro-Bristol chassis. A similar car with a body style only slightly changed from that of Touring's masterpiece was finally shown to AC in mid-1953. With a few changes to equip it for the road and AC's own 122 cu.in six-cylinder engine, it was on the AC stand at the Earls Court Motor Show in October. As announced it developed 85 bhp.

One of many enthusiasts who raced their Aces was Ken Rudd, who first used a Bristol engine and gearbox in 1956. AC offered the

102 bhp 100B from October that year and also fitted disc front brakes. The 120 bhp 100D came in 1957, and the 100D2 raised this to 128 bhp. The new Ace-Bristols became very successful race cars too, particularly in American sports car racing. When Bristol engines ceased to be available, Rudd inserted a pushrod 158 cu.in Ford Zephyr unit which AC were happy to adopt as an option from October 1961; Rudd's tuning company offered this in various states of tune with 100 to 170 bhp.

Meanwhile former racing driver Carroll Shelby wanted to use an American V-8 engine instead of the Bristol units and approached AC in September 1961. With Ford assistance two examples of the new 221 cu.in V-8, which was very little heavier than a Bristol engine, were sent to AC, who completed the installation relatively easily, using a

Borg Warner gearbox and Salisbury differential; a modified chassis had thicker main tubes, stronger differential mounting, new hubs and kingpins and various bracing plates, but retained the leaf springs. The first prototype ran in England in January 1962. By the time it arrived in America, Shelby had decided to call it the Cobra. By the end of February it had been tested with the new 260 cu.in engine and was announced to the US press in April. They were instantly successful on the race track, developing 260 bhp in standard form or up to 330 bhp in full race trim.

**128-129 *The 1963 AC Cobra 289 retained the original leaf
springs of the AC Ace.***

The first 75 cars used the 260 cu.in. engine before the 289 cu.in came in mid-1963 with a little more power but usefully greater torque. All the Cobras this far had been sold in America but two cars had been sent to AC; one of these raced at Le Mans, as an AC Cobra Ford, in 1963 and finished 7th, fourth in the GT category behind three Ferrari 250GTOs. It had been homologated at the beginning of 1963.

For 1964, Shelby produced the more aerodynamic Daytona coupe for a serious onslaught on the GT championship. Only six were to be built. Using the rules to advantage, the mountings for the alternative body style considerably stiffened the chassis. Ferrari managed to win that year but the Cobra-Fords won in 1965.

A further development in late 1964 had been a new coil sprung chassis designed by Ford to take the 427 cu.in Ford V-8 with 425 bhp, but Shelby did not build enough over that winter to achieve homologation and continued racing with the old chassis and engine. The 427 was finally homologated for 1966. As Shelby was already involved in the Ford GT40 programme, the Cobra 427 was never really developed into a racing car, although 480 bhp semi-competition cars

were sold, but it was an extremely fast road car. Later cars had the 'softer' 390 bhp 428 engine. However AC acquired surplus chassis in 1966 and installed the 286 cu.in engine, selling this as the AC 289 as Ford had acquired the rights to the Cobra name. It was actually the best of the V-8 engined ACs, but only 27 were built. In all 655 leaf-sprung Cobras were built and, eventually, around 320 of the 427/428.

130-131 *Simple chrome bars protected the vulnerable aluminium bodywork.*

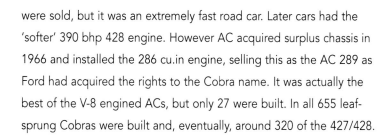

TECHNICAL DESCRIPTION OF THE AC COBRA 289	
YEARS OF PRODUCTION	1963-1965
MODELS	SPORTS 2-SEATER
ENGINE	FRONT-MOUNTED V-8
BORE X STROKE, CAPACITY	3.9 x 2.8 INCHES , 288 CU.IN
VALVEGEAR	PUSHROD OVERHEAD VALVES
FUEL SYSTEM	HOLLEY CARBURETOR
POWER	271 BHP AT 5750 RPM
TRANSMISSION	4-SPEED
BODY/CHASSIS	TUBULAR CHASSIS, ALUMINIUM BODY
SUSPENSION	FRONT, TRANSVERSE LEAF AND WISHBONE
	REAR, TRANSVERSE LEAF AND WISHBONE
TIRES/WHEELS	6.40 x 15 ON WIRE WHEELS
WHEELBASE, TRACK (F), TRACK(R)	90 x 51.5 x 52.5 INCHES
LENGTH, WIDTH, HEIGHT	151 x 61 x 49 INCHES
MAX SPEED	150 MPH
WHERE BUILT	ABINGDON-ON-THAMES, ENGLAND

Ferrari 250GTO and Lusso

When the 250GTO was first shown in 1962, it was the most beautiful Ferrari yet produced. The Lusso, which was effectively its roadgoing equivalent, was even better even if it lacked the racing charisma. Time has since seen many good looking products of the Pininfarina-Ferrari liaison, but the last two of the long 250GT line have never lost their appeal.

Throughout the Fifties and Sixties, the Le Mans 24-hour race was Mecca for manufacturers. A good performance in the ultimate endurance race brought invaluable prestige to both make and model. Ferrari took it even more seriously than others. When Le Mans brought in a separate GT category in 1959, Ferrari was there; a 250GT won in 1959 and the 250GT SWB won in 1960 and 1961.
In fact, wherever there was a GT race, the SWB usually won it.

For 1962, the FIA turned the World Sports Car Championship of Makes into a Manufacturers GT championship; even though Le Mans and other events continued to run sports cars and, from 1963, GT prototypes, they were not part of an FIA championship. Ferrari was already prepared for this as they had been working on a purpose-built

132

132-133 *The 1963/4 Lusso was a graceful marriage between the front of the 250GT Berlinetta and the rear of the 250GTO to make a luxury 2+2.*

GT car from late 1960. However, the rules required 100 identical models to have been built in 12 months; the FIA would issue a certificate of homologation. Once the model was homologated, special bodies could be used provided the car still weighed within 5 per cent of the weight of the standard model; options could be listed on a separate sheet.

Ferrari took this to the limits. The 1962 car had a new body, 6.5 inches longer and 3 inches lower, which had been developed in a wind tunnel. Two different carburetor set-ups were allowed within the original 100 cars, so six Weber carburetors were used instead of three. Options included a 5-speed gearbox, a transverse Watt linkage for the rear axle and a dry sump for the engine, which enabled a lower bonnet line. The basic chassis remained the same. The standard 250GT had been homologated in June 1960, just before Le Mans that year. Ferrari had to get the new options homologated, so the application form showed the standard 250GT SWB with the option list. When confirmation came back from the FIA, "250GT Omologato"

was written on the papers and the 1962-4 competition cars have been known as 250GTO ever since. Just 36 were built with the 183 cu.in engine. Jaguar went through exactly the same process for the E-type and its evolution, which was always known as the "Lightweight E-type". Aston Martin never quite made 100 of the DB4GT before producing the Zagato and Project 214 variants.

So the 250GTO was aerodynamically better than its predecessor with less lift and less drag. Its roadholding was also better due to the lower center of gravity and the new rear axle linkage which freed the leaf spring from its task of lateral location. That the car was also 250 lb lighter came within the allowed tolerance. With the engine output increased to 300 bhp it was considerably faster and Ferrari won the GT championship in 1962 and 1963. They won in 1964 too with a different body style which allowed wider wheels; it was modelled on the 250LM, a mid-engined GT car which Ferrari had hoped to homologate, but the FIA would not accept that it was just another

250GT evolution; as Ferrari never made 100 LMs it ran as a prototype with a 201 cu.in engine – usually called a 275LM – before being accepted into the 50-off Sports category in 1966 along with the Ford GT40. By the end of 1964, though, Ferrari's 183 cu.in engine was being outpaced by bigger American V-8s, so development ceased on the 250GTO.

Meanwhile Ferrari continued to build 2+2 road cars based on the earlier 250GT. The two-seater GT market was covered by the steel-bodied 250GT SWB until the end of 1962. A proper road car was then evolved as the 250 GT Berlinetta Lusso, still on the 2.4-metre wheelbase, but with the engine moved forward to gain interior space. By this time all Ferrari road cars were designed by Pininfarina and the Lusso was an appealing mixture of the front of a 250GT SWB married to the rear of a GTO. It was only in production for 18 months but 350 were built. It was the final swan song of the 250GT as the next generation 275 arrived in 1964.

TECHNICAL DESCRIPTION OF THE FERRARI 250GTO

YEARS OF PRODUCTION	1962-1964
MODELS	2-SEATER COUPE
ENGINE	FRONT-MOUNTED V-12
BORE X STROKE, CAPACITY	2.8 x 2.3 INCHES, 180 CU.IN
VALVEGEAR	SINGLE OVERHEAD CAMSHAFT PER BANK
FUEL SYSTEM	6 WEBER TWIN-CHOKE CARBURETORS
POWER	300 BHP AT 7500 RPM
TRANSMISSION	5-SPEED
BODY/CHASSIS	STEEL TUBE WITH ALUMINIUM BODY
SUSPENSION	FRONT, WISHBONES AND COILS
	REAR, WATT LINKAGE
TIRES/WHEELS	6.00 & 7.00 x 15 ON WIRE WHEELS
WHEELBASE, TRACK (F), TRACK(R)	94.5 x 53.3 x 53.1 INCHES
LENGTH, WIDTH, HEIGHT	173.5 x 66 x 49 INCHES
MAX SPEED	165 MPH
WHERE BUILT	MODENA, ITALY

134-135 *The GTO was built solely for competition and had no concessions to comfort*

Chevrolet Corvette 1963 - 1967

The Sting Ray era produced what was probably the most classic of all the Corvettes with its combination of exciting elegant lines, effective suspension and raw high performance. The range included a coupe for the first time while the roadster had an optional hard top; and there was the usual selection of RPO extras to enable anyone to tailor his own specification.

While the first two generations of America's sports car saw a progression from the two-seater personal tourer to a very fast sporting machine, these early Corvettes lacked the technical sophistication of their European equivalents when it came to the chassis. Although Ferrari was still using a live rear axle with leaf springs, ride comfort was less important in a Ferrari than roadholding. Aston Martin had much better live axle location. When the Jaguar E-type emerged in 1961 with a simple and effective independent rear suspension, the sporting world had to accept that a comfortable ride need not compromise roadholding.

Chevrolet had evolved a similar principle on experimental cars, so the third generation Corvette, like the Jaguar, used the drive-shaft as an upper link; a lower link controlled the camber angle, and wheel torques were absorbed in a forward extension of the hub carrier. Front suspension and steering continued

with adapted Chevrolet parts; the one area where the new Corvette was behind the times was in the retention of drum brakes, however disc brakes became standard in 1965. These new suspension parts required a new chassis which was a stiffer ladder frame.

Engine choices continued where the old model had stopped with the 327 cu.in. V-8 developing 250-360 bhp. In response to the demands of Corvette racers trying to keep up with the 427 cu.in Cobra, Duntov managed to insert the big-block V-8 into the engine compartment as a 1965 option; a bonnet-top bulge was needed to clear the taller engine, and side exhaust systems became an

option. The first big-block unit was the 396 cu.in with a massive 425 bhp; a year later this was increased to 427 cu.in with 390-435 bhp variations. By 1967, the racers could order the L88 engine as an RPO to make the ultimate Corvette; with aluminium heads, racing camshaft and strengthened bottom end the 427 cu.in unit developed around 560 bhp.

The body continued to be made in GRP and had been styled by Bill Mitchell around an earlier Sting Ray race car. The 1963 coupes had a divided rear window but the division was removed the following year. From almost every angle the production Sting Ray was a superb-looking car, open or closed but the front was too high; with concealed headlights there was no feature to break up the sharp prow. But, beautiful or not, the new Corvette sold 50% more in 1963 than had its predecessor the year before and would keep up a steady growth until it was replaced by an even more successful model in 1968.

Despite a steady rise in sales, Chevrolet brought out a new look Corvette for 1968. Modelled on Mitchell's 1965 Mako Shark II, the

new body had a much lower nose still with retractable headlights and Coke-bottle effect in its sills and waistline.

With a vertical rear window set between sail panels, it anticipated Jaguar's similar treatment for the XJS. The roof had a pair of removable panels but a convertible was also available until 1975. From 1978, the rear window returned to conventional fast-back shape. Chrome bumpers had disappeared in favor of soft front and rear panels for 1973.

Underneath the chassis was stiffened for the new car and wider wheel rims were used. Initially engine options continued as before with 327 and 427 cu.in, including the L88 and from 1969 a new racing ZL-1 with an aluminium cylinder block; however the 327 was increased to 350 cu.in for 1969, a stronger but softer engine with hydraulic valve lifters. A similar treatment was applied to the big-block engine option with an increase to 454 cu.in for 1970.

The 4th generation Corvette – Stingray from 1969-1978 – kept its performance image until the 1973 models when emission equipment took its toll on horsepower figures.

This didn't slow demand, though, as production continued to grow and 1979 saw almost 54,000 cars produced. The model ran through to 1983 but it was the pre-1973 cars that provided the classics.

YEARS OF PRODUCTION	1963-1967
MODELS	COUPE AND CONVERTIBLE
ENGINE	FRONT-MOUNTED V-8
BORE X STROKE, CAPACITY	3.9 X 3.2 INCHES, 326 CU.IN
VALVEGEAR	PUSHROD OVERHEAD VALVES
FUEL SYSTEM	CARTER 4-BARREL CARBURETOR
POWER	250 BHP AT 5500 RPM
TRANSMISSION	3-SPEED
BODY/CHASSIS	STEEL CHASSIS, FIBERGLASS BODYWORK
SUSPENSION	FRONT, WISHBONES AND COIL SPRINGS
	REAR, WISHBONES, FIXED LENGTH DRIVE-SHAFTS AND TRANSVERSE LEAF SPRING
TIRES/WHEELS	6.70 X 15 ON STEEL WHEELS
WHEELBASE, TRACK (F), TRACK(R)	98 X 56.3 X 57 INCHES
LENGTH, WIDTH, HEIGHT	175 X 69.6 X 50 INCHES
MAX SPEED	130 MPH
WHERE BUILT	MISSOURI, USA

138-139 *With concealed headlights,
the Sting Ray's sharp prow is set too high.*

MGB

The 7-year production run of over 100,000 MGAs came to an end in 1962. When the MGB took over it was not expected to last another 18 years and over half a million models. While this extended run was largely due to the mergers that took BMC into British Leyland, a contributory factor was the expected American ban on open cars; British Leyland assumed the MGB would come to a natural end when it could no longer be imported into America, and had designed the TR7 coupe as the replacement for the MGB and the TR6. When the open cars were reprieved, the MGB just continued to sell.

However higher production numbers were always expected for the MGB, so the design used unitary construction. Mechanically the car was a developed MGA with the same 4-speed gearbox, independent front suspension and a live rear axle, but the B-series engine was enlarged to 109 cu.in and the wheels were smaller; with 94 bhp, this was enough to make the MGB a genuine 105 mph car. The major improvements were to comfort with wind-up windows, a better ride, more interior and luggage space. As before, though, a lot of the expected fittings were optional extras – heater, headlamp flasher, anti-roll bar, cigar lighter, wing mirror, folding (rather than removable) roof among them – so don't be surprised if such things are missing if you buy an early one. Original road testers thought the car was a great improvement over the MGA even if the character had become more touring than sporting.

A year later overdrive was offered as an extra. While a factory hard-top was soon available, the B followed the A with a coupe version in 1965; an attractive design created with some help from Pininfarina, the MGB GT had a useful hatchback and rear seat space for 7-year-olds. By this time the B-series engine had been given five main bearings, using the engine that had been revised for the Austin 1800 saloon; the power output was unchanged.

As the Austin Healey 3000 was about to go out of production because it would no longer pass American safety standards, MG added the MGC in 1967, using an engine from the big Austin 183 cu.in saloon.

The extra length of this unit forced a change to torsion bar front suspension, but the only outward change from the MGB were bulges

in the bonnet top to allow for a bigger radiator and the front carburetor. Although, on paper, the engine specification looked almost the same as that for the big Healey – 145 bhp at 5500 rpm and 170 lb.ft at 3500 rpm against 150 bhp at 5250 rpm and 173 lb.ft at 3000 rpm – it was a very poor design; overlarge ports gave it very little low speed torque and it was also very heavy, adding 330 lb to the front end of an MGB. The result was considerable understeer, heavy steering and an unresponsive engine. It lasted just two years with 4542 roadsters and 4457 GTs, the latter being the nicer car.

For 1970, in an attempt to modernize the MGB, the chrome grille gave way to a matte black open version, Rostyle wheels were fitted, the seats were changed and a heater had at last become standard.

140-141 *The interior of this 1963 roadster has been personalised with a sports steering wheel and a wooden gear lever knob.*

The biggest change came in 1973 when the MGB GT was available with the 213 cu.in Rover V-8 in 137 bhp Range Rover form; using the stronger MGC gearbox but retaining the MGB front suspension, this was a much better car than the MGC with a 125 mph maximum; it should have been a great success.

However British Leyland stopped it going to America where it might have competed against the Triumph Stag and Jaguars, Europe was beset by petrol price rises and Rover needed their V-8 engines for the SD1, so the car ceased production in 1976 after only 2591 had been built.

Meanwhile the MGB was still being sold in America, for which the output had been stifled to 85 bhp. Legislation also necessitated a change to energy absorbing front and rear bumpers for 1975; while this was cleverly done, classic enthusiasts prefer the chrome bumper MGB.

It was because the MGB had already become a classic that the MG RV8 emerged in October 1992, an updated MGB roadster powered by the 237 cu.in 190 bhp Rover V-8. British Motor Heritage had acquired the tooling for MGB roadster bodyshells for use in restoration; by 1992 over 3000 old MGBs had benefitted. The project was taken further by Rover Special Projects who skilfully modernized the style with flared wings, bigger wheels, soft end panels and a luxury interior; although it was still the old MGB underneath, the RV8 was an appealing car that relaunched MG into the sporting market. By 1995, the planned 2000 had been sold.

TECHNICAL DESCRIPTION OF THE MGB

YEARS OF PRODUCTION	1962-1980
MODELS	SPORTS 2-SEATER
ENGINE	FRONT-MOUNTED IN-LINE 4
BORE X STROKE, CAPACITY	3.1 X 3.5 , 109 CU.IN
VALVEGEAR	PUSHROD OVERHEAD VALVES
FUEL SYSTEM	TWIN SU CARBURETORS
POWER	95 BHP AT 5500 RPM
TRANSMISSION	4-SPEED
BODY/CHASSIS	STEEL MONOCOQUE
SUSPENSION	FRONT, WISHBONES AND COILS
	REAR, LIVE AXLE WITH LEAF SPRINGS
TIRES/WHEELS	5.60 X 14 ON WIRE WHEELS
WHEELBASE, TRACK (F), TRACK(R)	91 X 49 X 49 INCHES
LENGTH, WIDTH, HEIGHT	154 X 60 X 49.5 INCHES
MAX SPEED	106 MPH
WHERE BUILT	ABINGDON-ON-THAMES, ENGLAND

The Giulietta Sprint had been a landmark design as much for its looks as for its place in history, the first in the new line of volume production Alfa Romeos. The same shape had become a Giulia Sprint in 1962 with disc front brakes and the 95 cu.in engine.

A year later came one of Bertone's finest shapes, the Giulia Sprint GT, based on a Giulia chassis shortened by 5 inches to almost the same wheelbase as the Sprint's Giulietta-based chassis. However the overall length was 4.7 inches longer, which allowed the Sprint GT to be a full four-seater with reasonable luggage space. The lines were very similar to those that Bertone had used for the 2000 Sprint in 1960 – very clean, modern and lasting. It was the first car to be built at Alfa Romeo's new Arese factory. In its initial form the engine developed 106 bhp using two twin-choke Weber carburetors. This was enough to give it a maximum speed around 110 mph.

As Alfa Romeo wanted to continue taking part in GT racing, Zagato were asked to produce a Giulia-based competition car. The resulting beautiful Giulia TZ (Tubolare Zagato) used the Giulia engine and gearbox, but the chassis was a space frame which carried independent rear suspension. From 1963, some 120 were built, of which the last 10 were in fiberglass, before a handful of even lower

TZ2s were produced for competition in 1965. Zagato continued their Alfa Romeo involvement by using the Giulia Spider (Duetto) chassis as a base for retro versions of the famed Alfa Romeo 1750 Zagato of 1929-1933; 92 of these neo-classics were built from 1965.

Meanwhile Bertone continued to produce the Giulia Sprint until 1964 when it was also offered with the 79 cu.in engine. The first Sprint GT variant came in March 1965 at the Geneva Show, the Giulia GTC (Cabriolet), which managed to retain all the appeal of the Sprint GT with a well-planned folding roof. Later that year came the Giulia GTA, a GT lightened (Allegerita) for competition with aluminium body panels and a 115 bhp engine. The GTA won the European Touring Car Challenge in 1966 and 1967, and produced further modifications for the GTAm which used an oil pressure driven supercharger.

A Giulia GTV with a little more power came in April 1966 and, as there were tax advantages for smaller engines, a 1300 GT Junior was added to the range in September that year. When Alfa Romeo brought in the 1750 saloon, a name evoking the Thirties sports cars, with a 108 cu.in engine, this was used to create the 1750GTV in 1968. The only noticeable body change was the adoption of four headlights. With 122 bhp, its maximum speed went up to 112 mph.

Alfa Romeo Sprint GT

The final version came in 1971 with the 122 cu.in engine (2000GTV) giving 132 bhp and 115 mph. The car still looked as modern as it had in 1963 but its suspension was beginning to show its age. This was eventually rectified with the next generation Alfetta GT (1974) with a new Bertone body style – a new 2000GTV would follow for 1976 using the Alfetta's de Dion rear axle.

Meanwhile Zagato had finished building the TZ series and the limited run of the 1750 GS, so turned their attention to a roadgoing coupe to follow in the steps of the Giulietta SZ. They built road-going equivalents to the TZ with a similar style by Ercole Spada from 1969 – his last for the Milanese coachbuilder. Using the shorter Duetto sports car platform, 1108 Junior Z 1300s were built before the 97 cu.in engine was inserted in 1972 – production ceased in 1975 after 402 had been built. Many were subsequently modified using the bigger engines from the GTVs. Over the 1965-1972 period Zagato also produced some 2900 Fulvia Sports for Lancia.

While the Giulietta launched Alfa Romeo into volume production, the Giulia in all its forms gave the company its well-deserved International reputation. The original Duetto was still being produced by Pininfarina until 1993 as the 2000 Spider Veloce.

TECHNICAL DESCRIPTION OF THE ALFA ROMEO GIULIA SPRINT GT	
YEARS OF PRODUCTION	1963-1968
MODELS	COUPE 4-SEATER
ENGINE	FRONT-MOUNTED IN-LINE 4
BORE X STROKE, CAPACITY	3 X 3.2 INCHES, 95 CU.IN
VALVEGEAR	TWIN OVERHEAD CAMSHAFTS
FUEL SYSTEM	TWO WEBER TWIN-CHOKE CARBURETORS
POWER	106 BHP AT 6000 RPM
TRANSMISSION	5-SPEED
BODY/CHASSIS	STEEL MONOCOQUE
SUSPENSION	FRONT, WISHBONES AND COILS REAR, LIVE AXLE WITH RADIUS ARMS AND A-BRACKET, COIL SPRINGS
TIRES/WHEELS	155 X 15 ON STEEL WHEELS
WHEELBASE, TRACK (F), TRACK(R)	93 X 51.5 X 50 INCHES
LENGTH, WIDTH, HEIGHT	161 X 62 X 52 INCHES
MAX SPEED	110 MPH
WHERE BUILT	MILAN, ITALY

144-145 *Alfa Romeo Sprint GT was one of Bertone's great designs. With thr famous twin-cam engine, a 5-speed gearbox and a well-located live rear axle, it went as well as it looked.*

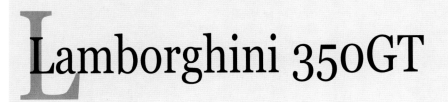

Lamborghini 350GT

The story of Ferruccio Lamborghini's arrival in the automobile world is well known. Dissatisfied with Ferrari's service to road car owners, and denied the chance to discuss this with Enzo, he resolved to usurp Ferrari as king of the road. With successful businesses in tractors and industrial climate control, he had the necessary backing. Next he needed people. In March 1962, he brought in from Maserati Giampaolo Dallara, to be chief engineer, together with Paulo Stanzani – they would evolve the chassis and running gear.

For the new engine Lamborghini contracted Giotto Bizzarini (former project director for the Ferrari GTO); Bizzarini had his own business and was already working on the forthcoming Iso Rivolta. The engine had to be a V-12 with dry sump lubrication and four cams – Ferrari engines only had two – and had be more powerful than the regular Ferrari 250 series. It is said that Bizzarini had previously designed a 91.5 cu.in V-12 and scaled this into the 213 cu.in; it was certainly a very quick process as the first engine was running in May 1963 producing over 100 bhp per 61 cu.in.

Bizzarini had hoped the programme would also include racing, so the engine was strong enough for even more power, but Lamborghini was never interested in taking on Ferrari at that level. With Bizzarini's task completed, the refinement of the engine became Dallara's responsibility. With ZF gearbox and Salisbury final

drive the rolling tubular chassis was sent to Carrozzeria Sargiotto in Turin to build a two-seater coupe to the design of Franco Scaglione, former head of Bertone styling. This 350GTV was shown at the Turin Show in November 1963. Partly because this was all done in a very short space of time, the result was not pretty; the lines lacked harmony and the show car was poorly made.

With little enthusiasm amongst press and public, Lamborghini cancelled production plans and took the project to Superleggera Touring, who could also build the bodies. The Touring design was very similar but they improved the relationship between side and rear windows, balanced the front and rear with more rounded lines, fitted oval headlights instead of previously concealed ones and had the front wheels moved forward by 3.9 inches. Since the new debut was at Geneva in March 1964, there wasn't time to make major alterations; accordingly, it wasn't one of Touring's more memorable works but it was better than the original 350GTV. Dallara meanwhile had removed the dry sump which raised the engine, requiring side-draft carburetors rather than the original vertical ones. The car was well received by all.

During the next year, a 244 cu.in version became available as the 400GT with 320 bhp; there were 108 350GTs and 23 400GTs, of which 20 had steel body panels. Lamborghini extended the range in 1966 with the 2+2, using the same wheelbase, but converting the

padded luggage bench to two extra seats. This was skilfully achieved by lifting the body (now steel) by 2.6 inches, adjusting the front wheel arch and deepening the sills to lower the floorpan. Reversing the mounting of the rear wishbones gave extra internal width. The 350/400GT had various front intake treatments but the 2+2 adopted the horizontal bars, quarter-bumpers with no over-riders, and the four round headlights that had been required for the American market. Engine power remained the same but Lamborghini now used their own gearboxes and final drives. Over 1966-68, 224 of these were built.

Meanwhile Touring had financial problems due to steel-worker problems in 1962, followed by cancellation of two Rootes Group projects. Receivership in 1964 was followed by closure in early 1967, so the later 400GT 2+2 were built by ex-Touring employees who had moved to previous sub-contractor Mario Marazzi.

To replace the 400GT 2+2, Lamborghini stayed with Marazzi who used a two-door version of a full four-door proposal drawn up by Touring in 1966. The Islero emerged in 1968, an understated design with the concealed headlights of the 350GTV; it was a 2+2 on the previous 400GT 2+2 chassis but slightly shorter. Viewed alongside the full four-seater Espada, a striking Bertone design based on the Marzal show car, it was not exciting in 1968, but, thirty years on, the Islero looks the nicer car. The Islero S came in for 1969 with an improved

interior and a more powerful engine with 350 bhp. There were 225 Isleros of which just 100 had the S engine. The Islero did not last long and was replaced in 1970 by the Bertone-designed Jarama which continued until 1976, the last of the front-engined Lamborghinis.

TECHNICAL DESCRIPTION OF THE LAMBORGHINI 350GT

YEARS OF PRODUCTION	1964-1966
MODELS	2-SEATER COUPE
ENGINE	FRONT-MOUNTED V-12
BORE X STROKE, CAPACITY	3 x 2.4 INCHES, 211 CU.IN
VALVEGEAR	TWIN OVERHEAD CAMSHAFT PER BANK
FUEL SYSTEM	6 WEBER TWIN-CHOKE CARBURETORS
POWER	270 BHP AT 6500 RPM
TRANSMISSION	5-SPEED
BODY/CHASSIS	STEEL TUBE WITH ALUMINIUM BODY
SUSPENSION	FRONT, WISHBONES AND COILS
	REAR, WISHBONES AND COILS
TIRES/WHEELS	210 x 15 ON WIRE WHEELS
WHEELBASE, TRACK (F), TRACK(R)	100.4 x 54.3 x 54.3 INCHES
LENGTH, WIDTH, HEIGHT	182 x 68 x 48 INCHES
MAX SPEED	145 MPH
WHERE BUILT	BOLOGNA, ITALY

Lotus Elan

When Colin Chapman's new Lotus Elan appeared at the London Motor Show in October 1962 it seemed just a cleverly designed roadster replacement for the Elite coupe. Like the Elite it was also available in kit form which avoided the British purchase tax at the time. It wasn't until it was tested by the motoring press that it became clear that the Elan was a breath of fresh air in sports car design.

It had independent suspension all round, not just to demonstrate race technology, but to provide a hitherto unmatched combination of sports car ride and roadholding; it was softly comfortable for the bumps but well damped to prevent sudden body movement; and it clung to the road with its suspension designed to keep the tires at optimum angles. It was small and light, so its 105 bhp engine gave good acceleration; although the final drive gearing was too low for effortless motorway cruising, the car was designed to be fun to drive – straight roads are not fun.

As a company, Lotus began producing cars for sale in 1952 but, for the first five years, they were competition cars – trials or racing – which could be used on the road. The first genuine road car was first shown in October 1957; the Lotus Elite (type 14) could also be raced. It used three large fiberglass moldings bonded together to create a monocoque with steel inserts and tubes for mounting the mechanical components. It was powered by a special version of the Coventry Climax FW series which the competition cars had been using; the 74 cu.in FWE developed 75 – 105 bhp in road to race states of tune. Beautifully shaped, it was a remarkable car and proved its effectiveness in the Le Mans 24-hour race by winning its class from

1959-1964, including 8th overall at 99.5 mph in 1962. Exciting though it was, the Elite was not the strongest nor the most reliable of cars; from 1958-1963, they built 1050, but the next car had to be stronger.

While fiberglass was an effective material for the body, it was not appropriate for a load-bearing road-car chassis. So the Elan retained a fiberglass body but used a separate backbone chassis of deep section to maintain torsional strength. Suspension used a pair of wishbones at the front,

---

TECHNICAL DESCRIPTION OF THE LOTUS ELAN

YEARS OF PRODUCTION	1962-1966
MODELS	2-SEATER SPORTS
ENGINE	FRONT-MOUNTED IN-LINE 4
BORE X STROKE, CAPACITY	3.2 x 2.8 INCHES , 95 CU.IN
VALVEGEAR	TWIN OVERHEAD CAMSHAFTS
FUEL SYSTEM	TWIN WEBER 40DCOE CARBURETORS
POWER	105 BHP AT 5500 RPM
TRANSMISSION	4-SPEED
BODY/CHASSIS	STEEL BACKBONE, FIBERGLASS BODY
SUSPENSION	FRONT, WISHBONES AND COIL SPRING
	REAR, COIL SPRING STRUT AND WISHBONE
TIRES/WHEELS	4.50 x 13 ON 4.5 IN RIMS
WHEELBASE, TRACK (F), TRACK(R)	84 x 47 x 48 INCHES
LENGTH, WIDTH, HEIGHT	145 x 56 x 45.5 INCHES
MAX SPEED	110 MPH
WHERE BUILT	CHESHUNT AND HETHEL, ENGLAND

148-149 *Original Lotus Elan had few luxuries but was a very efficient sports car. Headlights were lifted by vacuum control.*

while the rear used a MacPherson strut and lower wishbone; rubber couplings in the drive-shaft absorbed plunge and transmission shocks.

By this time Lotus had some recognition within Ford as the Lotus 18, 20, 22 had all been successful in Formula Junior with Ford 105E engines. Chapman wanted a twin-cam engine for the Elan and Harry Munday designed a suitable head for the the 81 cu.in 109E 3-bearing block. Ford heard of the project and offered the 5-bearing 91 cu.in 116E block which was to be announced in September 1962. Lotus used this twin-cam 1500 in the sports-racing Lotus 23 and surprised the bigger cars in the rain at Nurburgring 1000Km in May 1962. The Elan was announced and the first twenty so cars were sold with the 91 cu;in engine giving 100 bhp. All these were converted to the definitive 95 cu.in for which the block was bored out to the maximum replacement piston size.

An Elan S2 came in November 1964 with such refinements as electric windows, wooden fascia and bigger brakes. The S3 arrived a

year later in fixed head coupe form (Lotus 36), so the open S2 continued until June 1966. The type 45 Elan (drophead S3 and S4) came in March 1968 continuing through to 1973 by which time some 10,000 had been built. Special Equipment 115 bhp engines were offered from January 1966 and 126 bhp Sprint versions became available at the end of 1970.

Stretching the Elan wheelbase by 12 inches, widening the track by 7 inches and adding nearly two foot to the overall length produced the Lotus 50 Elan +2 four-seater in 1967 using the Special Equipment engine. A +2S with more comfort and no kit-purchase option came in 1968, being replaced by the +2S 130 in 1971 using the Sprint engine. The final +2S 130/5 denoted the 5-speed option offered from October 1972 until the end of the line in 1974 after 5168 of the +2 had been produced.

150-151 *With the longer and wider Elan +2, the family man could enjoy Lotus performance and roadholding.*

TECHNICAL DESCRIPTION OF THE LOTUS ELAN +2

YEARS OF PRODUCTION	1967-1974
MODELS	4-SEATER COUPE
ENGINE	FRONT-MOUNTED IN-LINE 4
BORE X STROKE, CAPACITY	3.2 X 2.8 INCHES, 95 CU.IN
VALVEGEAR	TWIN OVERHEAD CAMSHAFTS
FUEL SYSTEM	TWIN WEBER 40DCOE CARBURETORS
POWER	118 BHP AT 6000 RPM
TRANSMISSION	4-SPEED
BODY/CHASSIS	STEEL BACKBONE, FIBERGLASS BODY
SUSPENSION	FRONT, WISHBONES AND COIL SPRING
	REAR, COIL SPRING STRUT AND WISHBONE
TIRES/WHEELS	165 X 13 ON 5.5 IN RIMS
WHEELBASE, TRACK (F), TRACK(R)	96 X 54 X 55 INCHES
LENGTH, WIDTH, HEIGHT	69 X 66 X 47 INCHES
MAX SPEED	115 MPH
WHERE BUILT	CHESHUNT AND HETHEL, ENGLAND

Iso Grifo GL400

When it first appeared at the Turin Show in 1963, the Iso Grifo A3L (Lusso) was a strikingly beautiful car, which had been styled by Giugiaro during his time with Bertone. With Chevrolet's 327 cu.in V-8 producing 365 bhp, it was a high performance machine with a top speed of 161 mph, considerably faster than Aston and Jaguar could manage with their highly tuned six-cylinder engines.

The Iso Grifo was the 2-seater coupe based on a shortened chassis from the Iso Rivolta which had been launched at Geneva in March 1962. Iso had made their name from Isetta scooters and bubble cars in the Fifties when the company was owned by Count Renzo Rivolta. His son, Piero, wanted to return to car manufacture for the Sixties and approached Giotto Bizzarrini to design a chassis for a fast but comfortable 4-seater sports saloon; Bizzarrini had been project director for the Ferrari 250GTO but had set up his own Societa Autostar in 1962.

Facel Vega had started the trend of using American power in European bodies in 1954. Gordon Keeble, Bristol, AC and Jensen would follow in the early Sixties. In fact the first was the Gordon GT, which might be called the father of the Iso Rivolta. John Gordon had been the Managing Director of Peerless, making four-seater coupes with space-frame chassis, fiberglass bodywork and Triumph engines from 1957-1960. This had been designed by Bernie Rodger, who went on to refine the car further as the Warwick GT (1960-1962) while Gordon went in a different direction – same concept but faster and more luxurious. He had a new chassis designed by Jim Keeble, once more a space frame, but stronger to take a Chevrolet V-8. In 1959 they took this to Bertone, for whom Giugiaro produced his first work; the Gordon GT was shown with steel bodywork at Geneva in March 1960.

Financial problems then delayed its production for four years, after which time it used a fiberglass body and became a Gordon Keeble – some 140 would be built under two different company owners. Bizzarrini and Rivolta were obviously aware of the Gordon GT by the time they started on the Iso Rivolta. It was very close to what they

TECHNICAL DESCRIPTION OF THE ISO GRIFO GL400	
YEARS OF PRODUCTION	1969-1974
MODELS	2-SEATER COUPE
ENGINE	FRONT-MOUNTED V-8
BORE X STROKE, CAPACITY	4.2 X 3.6 INCHES, 425 CU.IN
VALVEGEAR	PUSHROD OVERHEAD VALVES
FUEL SYSTEM	ONE 4-BARREL HOLLEY CARBURETOR
POWER	406 BHP (GROSS) AT 5400 RPM
TRANSMISSION	4-SPEED
BODY/CHASSIS	STEEL PLATFORM, STEEL BODYWORK
SUSPENSION	FRONT, WISHBONES AND COIL SPRINGS
	REAR, DE DION AXLE WITH RADIUS ARMS
	AND PANHARD ROD
TIRES/WHEELS	205 X 15 ON ALLOY WHEELS
WHEELBASE, TRACK (F), TRACK(R)	98.5 X 55.5 X 55.5 INCHES
LENGTH, WIDTH, HEIGHT	174.7 X 69.5 X 47 INCHES
MAX SPEED	161 MPH
WHERE BUILT	MILAN, ITALY

wanted. Bizzarini designed a fresh chassis using pressed sheet steel rather than a space frame, fitted wishbone front suspension and a de Dion axle with Panhard rod lateral location rather than the Gordon's Watt linkage. All round disc brakes were inboard at the rear.

The engine was Chevrolet's latest 327 cu.in V-8 in either 300 or 340 bhp form with a Warner 4-speed gearbox, both of which the Gordon Keeble would later adopt. And Giugiaro, for Bertone, provided a body similar to that of the Gordon GT but more modern. In fact, the wheelbase was 4 inches longer for the same overall length, and the roof provided 2 inches more headroom. The result was shown in late 1962 and production started in 1963 – it was a remarkably good car and 800 were built before it gave way to the 2-door Lele and 4-door Fidia in 1969.

For the Turin Show in November 1963, Bizzarrini shortened the Rivolta chassis by 7.8 inches for Giugiaro to create the beautiful Iso Grifo A3L (Lusso). A sleeker more aerodynamic A3C (Corsa) was also shown for which Bizzarini had moved the engine rearwards; Piero

Drogo designed and built the 29 cars bearing the Iso name. Grifo A3C models competed at Le Mans in 1964 (14th) and 1965 (9th).

Bizzarrini returned to his own business in 1964, changing the name to Societa Prototipi Bizzarini and, with Iso agreement, started to make the A3C as a Bizzarrini 5300GT or Strada as road cars with a little restyling from Giugiaro. By 1969, 155 had been built. Meanwhile production of the Grifo A3L did not start until 1965. The standard A3L would be known as the GL365, as it used the 365 bhp engine with solid valve lifters for more revs and power – the 300 bhp Rivolta engine was an option.

The GL400 was added in 1969 with the Corvette's 406 bhp 427 cu.in engine; installing this big block engine required an unsightly hump on the bonnet. The Grifo continued until 1974 when Piero Rivolta sold out to American interests which shortly collapsed. The Grifo was the car that ensures the name will be remembered; Bertone built 411 of them of which 90 were GL400s.

153

The Ghibli was one of Maserati's greatest road cars, the best and almost the last of the real Italian breed. The fastback coupe body, designed by Giugiaro during his three-year period at Ghia, is as elegant today as it was when the world first saw the car at the 1966 Turin Show. Beautifully finished inside too with plenty of leather, deep pile carpet and air conditioning as an option. Further appeal and some noise came with a race-bred 286 cu.in four-cam dry-sump V-8 giving 320 bhp, enough to exceed 160 mph; for later models, the V-8 was increased to 298 cu.in with a little more power and usefully more torque. The usual transmission choice was the manual ZF 5-speed, but an automatic was available.

Supporting all this was still an old-fashioned tubular chassis – like Ferrari – but this one still had a live rear axle mounted on leaf springs. Although the American muscle cars of the period were similarly equipped, most of Europe's supercars had rear wishbones or at least a De Dion axle. Contemporary reports, though, suggest that ride and roadholding were as good as the rivals. Production of the Ghibli started slowly during 1967. A year later it was joined by the lovely slender convertible version. Over a seven year production life, 1150 coupes and just 125 convertibles were built.

For the first 30 years of its life from 1926, the company had existed largely on the sale of single seater and sports racing cars to private competitors, with only a handful of the early post-war A6 cars equipped with coupe bodywork for road use. In 1937, the Maserati brothers had sold out to the Orsi group who moved the factory to Modena in 1941; however the contract retained the brothers' services until 1947, at which point they returned to Bologna and set up OSCA, leaving Omer Orsi to take over the reins.

Before the Maseratis departed they designed a 6-cylinder 122 cu.in engine which was fitted in sports-racing and road coupe models; it then became the basis of the A6GCM which was a strong contender in the 122 cu.in Grand Prix period of 1952-3. When the 152 cu.in GP formula came in 1954, Colombo further developed the six-cylinder unit with a new chassis, and the legendary 250F was born to establish Maserati's racing tradition in the top level during 1954-1957; a further development of this engine was used in the 300S, to be joined by

Maserati Ghibli

the 450S with a new 274 cu.in V-8 engine. The straight six and the V-8 engines were to provide the basis of power units for road cars from then until the arrival of the Biturbo in 1982.

The first of these road cars was the Touring-bodied 3500GT 2+2, announced in 1957 with the six-cylinder engine giving 220 bhp, later 235 bhp in GTi fuel injection form. Vignale made spider versions on a shorter wheelbase, then produced the fixed head 3500GTiS (Sebring) on the Spider chassis; around 2700 of the various 3500 models were produced. The Frua-styled 2-seater Mistrales, open and closed, were the last to use the straight-six engine in 225 cu.in 245 bhp and 244 cu.in 255 bhp forms; with a further shortened chassis, these were the nicest of the six-cylinder cars.

The first road use of the former racing V-8 was for a few 5000GT models, mostly with Allemano fixed-head bodies, which arrived in 1959 using a 350 bhp 298 cu.in version in the longer 3500GT chassis. It was used in the Quattroporte from 1963, and the Vignale Mexico 2+2 from 1966, both using the V-8 in either 260 bhp 256 cu.in or 290 bhp 286 cu.in forms. Ghibli and Spider derivative followed in 1966

154-155 *Long and low, the Ghibli was the best-looking of all the Sixties Maseratis; here, a 1971 Ghibli SS.*

and 1968, when the Vignale-bodied Indy 2+2 was added to the range as a slightly stretched Ghibli.

Although Maserati could sell a large number of different models by producing two chassis lengths and various engines and leaving the rest to the coachbuilders, some order was restored when Citroen acquired the company in 1969. Their main interest was in using Maserati to build their new V-6 engine for the SM. Using some Citroen components, they brought in the Bora for 1971, and the Merak for 1972, both with ItalDesign bodies (Giugiaro).The Khamsin 2+2 (Bertone) went into production in 1974 with the 298 cu.in V-8 and was the first front-engined Maserati road car to feature independent rear suspension; effectively replacing both the Indy and the Ghibli, the Khamsin was to continue in production until the new generation arrived.

TECHNICAL DESCRIPTION OF THE MASERATI GHIBLI	
YEARS OF PRODUCTION	1970-1974
MODELS	2-SEATER COUPE AND CONVERTIBLE
ENGINE	FRONT-MOUNTED V-8
BORE X STROKE, CAPACITY	3.7 X 3.5 INCHES, 300 CU.IN
VALVEGEAR	TWIN OVERHEAD CAMSHAFTS PER BANK
FUEL SYSTEM	4 WEBER TWIN-CHOKE CARBURETORS
POWER	355 BHP AT 5500 RPM
TRANSMISSION	5-SPEED
BODY/CHASSIS	REINFORCED STEEL TUBE CHASSIS WITH STEEL BODY PANELS
SUSPENSION	FRONT, WISHBONES AND COILS REAR, LIVE AXLE AND LEAF SPRINGS
TIRES/WHEELS	205 X 15 ON 6.5 IN. ALLOY WHEELS
WHEELBASE, TRACK (F), TRACK(R)	100.3 X 56.6 X 55.9 INCHES
LENGTH, WIDTH, HEIGHT	180.7 X 70.8 X 45.6 INCHES
MAX SPEED	160 MPH
WHERE BUILT	MODENA, ITALY

Alpine Renault 1600S

Until the Alpine-Renault 1600S started to win International rallies outright at the turn of the decade, few outside France were familiar with this compact two-seater coupe with its Renault engine pushed out behind the rear axle. It was very low with seemingly little space inside for two large people wearing helmets, but it kept on winning. Alpine driver Andruet became European Rally Champion in 1970 and the team won the International championship in 1971.

The Sixties had seen the start of the homologation specials for racing and rallying, the limited edition models produced in just enough numbers to qualify for FIA homologation – Mini Cooper S and Lotus Cortina. Renault 8 Gordini and Lancia Fulvia HF were European replies to the British. Then came the Escort Twin-Cam and RS1600, but the rules also allowed GT cars with fewer seats and smaller numbers. So rallies accepted the front drive Lancia Fulvia coupe and the rear-drive Porsche 911 and the Alpine A110.

The A110 arrived in 1962. John Redele had set up the Societe des Automobiles Alpine in 1955 at the Renault dealership of his father. After several years competing with a Renault 750, including winning his class in the Mille Miglia, Redele produced the A106 in 1956. This used the 750 running gear with a fiberglass 2+2 coupe body; when the Dauphine came out the engine was increased to 51 cu.in. The 1957 A108 was the cabriolet version available. By 1960, Redele had evolved the steel tube backbone chassis that was to characterise all subsequent Alpines. New body styles for the 2+2 GT4 coupe and convertible came in 1961, with the convertible on a shorter wheelbase. The same chassis length was used for the new A110 2-seater coupe for 1962.

As state-owned Renault was still only producing 61 cu.in cars for the people, the Alpine's performance appeal was somewhat limited. The turning point came with the introduction of the Renault 16 in 1965. Although this was a front wheel drive car, the layout was the same as for the Renault 8; the engine was behind the gearbox. The 89 cu.in engine was ideal for the Renault Alpine; with a little tuning the A110 was moving up the rally leader boards. When the 95 cu.in TS engine became available in 1968, Redele returned to rallying with the 1600S and the financial help of Renault. A 3rd place in the 1969 Monte Carlo Rally and 1,2,3 in the 1969 Alpine Rally was the start of an amazing rally career for the little blue cars. By now Renault were 30% shareholders and Alpine was Renault's competition department.

Alpine had started very much like Porsche. Both used humble saloon cars as the base for their first GT cars, but by the time the A110 arrived, Porsche were about to produce the 911. Although there were technically very different, and you could buy two Alpines for a Porsche, both proved ideal for the loose surface roads which were increasingly used for rallies. The rear engine package gave good traction and tight controllable handling, but neither was as successful on the race tracks where greater grip upset the rear suspension. On the road this was not important and the A110 was fun, despite the hard ride and noisy engine.

Although the A110 was to continue through until 1977, Alpine brought in the A310 at Geneva 1971 as a 2+2 using the same Renault 16 running gear under a new distinctive shape. The body was still a fiberglass shell mounted on a tubular back-bone frame, but the rear suspension now featured double wishbones. It was bigger, more comfortable and trimmed to proper GT levels. Alpine had finally become a serious producer of internationally acknowledged performance cars.

By the Mid-seventies Renault owned 87% of Alpine whose production then included A110s, A310s and R5 Alpines – the 1975 total was 4500 vehicles; the A110 ceased in 1977 by which time some 7200 had been built over 14 years. The A310, with the PRV 164 cu.in V-6 from 1980, became the GTA in 1985 with 160 bhp or 200 bhp using a turbocharger. Alpine were still regarded as the French Porsche but they didn't sell enough and the last Alpine was built in 1994.

156-157 Neat and aerodynamically efficient, the 1600S (1969 here) won many International rallies.

TECHNICAL DESCRIPTION OF THE RENAULT ALPINE 1600S

YEARS OF PRODUCTION	1968-1973
MODELS	2-SEATER COUPE
ENGINE	REAR-MOUNTED 4-CYLINDER
BORE X STROKE, CAPACITY	3 X 3.3 INCHES, 95 CU.IN
VALVEGEAR	PUSHROD OVERHEAD VALVES
FUEL SYSTEM	TWIN WEBER CARBURETORS
POWER	138 BHP AT 6000 RPM
TRANSMISSION	4-SPEED
BODY/CHASSIS	BACKBONE STEEL CHASSIS AND FIBERGLASS BODY
SUSPENSION	FRONT, WISHBONES AND COIL SPRINGS REAR, SWING AXLE AND COIL SPRINGS
TIRES/WHEELS	165 X 13 ON ALLOY WHEELS
WHEELBASE, TRACK (F), TRACK(R)	83 X 51.6 X 53.2 INCHES
LENGTH, WIDTH, HEIGHT	151.6 X 61 X 44 INCHES
MAX SPEED	130 MPH
WHERE BUILT	DIEPPE, FRANCE

Ferruccio Lamborghini had achieved the first stage of his Ferrari rivalry in launching the fast and comfortable 350GT in 1964. While Lamborghini had no intention of going racing, engineers Stanzani, Dallara and Wallace evolved the Miura as a road car that might be raced – it never was. They had a superb engine in the V-12 and they could design and build any necessary transmission. Comfort required equal space for both passengers without the intrusion of wheel arches into the foot-well, a problem with the genuine racing Ford GT40 and Ferrari 250LM. To avoid a long wheelbase they turned the engine, through 90 degrees, and then built the transmission into the rear side of the block-cum-crankcase – a very large and complex single casting which could only have been achieved in Italy at that time. The problem of connecting the gear lever to the back of the engine was solved by passing the linkage under the crankshaft. As low engine height was not as important for a mid-engined car, the unusual and efficient downdraft inlet porting of the 400GT could be used to maximum advantage with matching triple-choke Weber carburetors mounted vertically; with a higher compression ratio, output rose to 350 bhp. This mechanical masterpiece was mounted in a pressed steel monocoque chassis liberally pierced for lightness and strength

– a plate with flared edges to holes is stiffer than a flat plate. Engine and front suspension were mounted on square tube sub-frame extensions, the suspension using double wishbone and coil springs all round.

Lamborghini duly gave his approval and the rolling chassis was unveiled at the Turin Show in November 1965. Even without a name or a body it was a sensation. During 1965, Touring was still making bodies for the 350GT; they produced some studies which were unquestionably heralds of the final Miura shape. With Touring still in the hands of the receiver and unable to guarantee future production, these thoughts were taken to Bertone. It was Marcello Gandini, to whom the Miura design is always attributed, who refined the Touring designs.

The definitive shape, a classic mid-engined fastback, was shown at Geneva in March 1966. Features inspired by development included bonnet-top vents to let hot air out of the radiators, ducts in the sills to feed air to the rear tires, scoops in the rear edge of the doors feeding air through the B-posts to the engine intakes and the slatted rear 'window' to let hot air out of the engine compartment; there was a vertical rear window between the sail panels to keep the engine noise out. The 'flatfish' headlights, with black strakes above and below them were the least clever part of a striking design. Lamborghini had only expected to

Lamborghini Miura

make perhaps 25 a year, prestige advertisements for the GT cars, but demand was far greater. The first cars were delivered in early 1967 and their performance was sensational with a maximum speed around 170 mph. And they handled very well too with less than 60 per cent of the weight on the rear wheels but, after 125 cars, the chassis was stiffened using sheet steel 10 per cent thicker. After 475 of the P400, the P400S came in 1969 with anti-squat rear suspension and 370 bhp at 7700 rpm with new camshafts and bigger carburetors; there were around 140 of these. The output was further increased to 385 bhp in 1971 for the P400SV, for which the sump was made deeper to lessen the effects of oil surge in fast cornering, and the oil for the gearbox and engine was separated by a partition to allow different oil for a limited slip differential; other SV changes included widened rear bodywork for wider tires, ventilated disc brakes and headlamps which were no longer surrounded by eyelashes. Meanwhile, Ferruccio Lamborghini's businesses were suffering in the general climate and he sold 51 per cent to Swiss interests in 1972, disposing of the remaining 49 per cent a year later to another Swiss. Following the 1971 showing of the Countach, the new owners killed the Miura, but then took another three years to get the Countach into production. After 150 of the SV and a total run of 762, the Miura died too soon.

158-159 *The Miura was the first road-going mid-engined supercar.*

TECHNICAL DESCRIPTION OF THE LAMBORGHINI MIURA P400	
YEARS OF PRODUCTION	1966-1969
MODELS	2-SEATER COUPE
ENGINE	MID-MOUNTED V-12
BORE X STROKE, CAPACITY	3.2 x 2.4 INCHES, 239 CU.IN
VALVEGEAR	TWIN OVERHEAD CAMSHAFT PER BANK
FUEL SYSTEM	4 WEBER TRIPLE-CHOKE CARBURETORS
POWER	350 BHP AT 7000 RPM
TRANSMISSION	5-SPEED
BODY/CHASSIS	SHEET STEEL WITH ALUMINIUM BODY
SUSPENSION	FRONT, WISHBONES AND COILS
	REAR, WISHBONES AND COILS
TIRES/WHEELS	210 x 15 ON ALLOY WHEELS
WHEELBASE, TRACK (F), TRACK(R)	98.6 x 55.6 x 55.6 INCHES
LENGTH, WIDTH, HEIGHT	172 x 69.3 x 41.3 INCHES
MAX SPEED	170 MPH
WHERE BUILT	BOLOGNA, ITALY

Ferrari 365GTB4 Daytona

In presenting the 365GTB4 Daytona at the Paris Show in October 1968, Ferrari and Pininfarina were making a clear statement to the world in general, and Lamborghini in particular, that, even if the engine was still at the front, Maranello could still make sensational road cars.

Logically, the 365GTB4 should have been just a 365GTC with the 4-camshaft engine.

Fortunately, it wasn't. The mid-engined Miura had stolen Ferrari's prime position for two years, and Ferrari needed a reply.

So the Daytona had a style like no other Ferrari before, an exciting mixture of a long aggressive chisel nose with a flat top and powerful haunches extending all the way from the rear wheels to the top of the front windscreen. It exuded power and it was faster than the Miura.

It looked good, big too, yet its wheelbase was the same as all the Berlinettas from the 250 GT SWB through the 275 series. The 275GTB (Berlinetta)and GTS (Spider), announced at the 1964 Paris Show, were the first Ferraris to be designed purely as road cars. Although the chassis structure followed the familiar tubular principles, its design had finally moved with the times and Lamborghini, and had independent rear suspension; this allowed Ferrari to group the gearbox, now with five speeds, and final drive unit into a single transaxle to keep the weight distribution more even. The body style retained 250GTO lines with pronounced curves above the rear wheels and an inset cabin.

Two years later, the 1966 Paris Show hosted the launch of the 275GTB4 denoting four overhead camshafts; it was Ferrari's first four-cam road car, three years after Lamborghini's.

With 300 bhp at 8000 rpm it would run to 160 mph. Of the 275 series which ran into 1967, some 450 were GTB, 200 GTS and 350 GTB4. The 275GTB4 launch had extended the life of the 275 by a year, so it overlapped with the new 330 range which had been presented in March 1966. With a new longer block, the 300 bhp 244 cu.in two-cam V-12 was used to power the 330GTC (Coupe) and GTS. The chassis was still very like that of the 275, but the drive-shaft was now enclosed in a torque tube.

Pininfarina's new body style had a lower straight waistline, deeper windows, a tail with a separate trunk and an oval grille more like a Superamerica. Around 600 330GTC and 100 330GTS were built from 1966-68 when the 365 engine came in.

The 330 engine had been used in the sports-racing 330P in 1964; the factory continued to develop this engine for their own team in 1965 but produced a 268 cu.in 365P for the non-works teams.

For 1967 the 330P4 had four cams, three-valve twin-plug heads

and fuel injection to generate 450 bhp at 8200 rpm; private entrants made do with 380 bhp at 7300 rpm using carburetors and single-cam 365s. Ferrari used sports car racing to develop designs that could be adapted for road use later. On the way, they won the world sports car championship three times in those four years, including victory at Daytona.

The first production car to use a 268 cu.in single-cam V-12 was the 365GT 2+2, an extremely elegant Pininfarina stretch of the 330GTC. The 330GTC and GTS had to wait another year until late 1968 to be uprated to 365-series. However, the big event of that year was the October arrival of the ultimate two-seater coupe, named Daytona after Ferrari successes there; racing experience dictated the engine specification.

The 365GTB4 engine (268 cu.in) had twin-cams per bank but only two valves, six carburetors and dry sump lubrication; at 352 bhp it was 30 more than the single-cam cars.

The chassis was basically that of the 330/365GTC. And the style set it off to perfection.

On early cars the headlights were set behind a band of clear plastic running across the nose, but American laws required proper glass, so the plastic was replaced by painted metal and the headlamps were concealed. aOther variants included a convertible – 100 only – and the 365GTC4, a 2+2 Daytona with less horsepower and a revised front end which was available in 1971/2 following the phasing out of the previous 2+2.

But the Daytona stayed in production until 1974; over 1300 were built in that six-year period.

162-163 The Daytona Spyder was just as attractive but lost the brutal appeal of the coupe.

TECHNICAL DESCRIPTION OF THE FERRARI 365GTB4 DAYTONA	
YEARS OF PRODUCTION	1968-1974
MODELS	2-SEATER COUPE AND CONVERTIBLE
ENGINE	FRONT-MOUNTED V-12
BORE X STROKE, CAPACITY	3.1 X 2.7 INCHES, 267 CU.IN
VALVEGEAR	TWIN OVERHEAD CAMSHAFTS PER BANK
FUEL SYSTEM	6 WEBER TWIN-CHOKE CARBURETORS
POWER	352 BHP AT 7500 RPM
TRANSMISSION	5-SPEED
BODY/CHASSIS	TUBULAR CHASSIS WITH STEEL AND ALUMINIUM BODY PANELS
SUSPENSION	FRONT, WISHBONES AND COILS REAR, WISHBONES AND COILS
TIRES/WHEELS	205 X 15 ON ALLOY WHEELS
WHEELBASE, TRACK (F), TRACK(R)	94.5 X 56.5 X 56 INCHES
LENGTH, WIDTH, HEIGHT	174 X 69.2 X 49 INCHES
MAX SPEED	175 MPH
WHERE BUILT	MODENA, ITALY

163

Ferrari Dino 246GT

The Dino 246 was the first to prove that the racing-inspired concept of placing the engine behind the driver could produce a perfect road car. It went fast, cornered well and looked beautiful in its Pininfarina clothes. Mid-engined road cars before it had tail-heavy handling, poor rearward visibility and no storage space. The Dino's handling and stability were superb; the driver's view through glazed sail panels and the neat curved vertical rear window was more than adequate; and there was a good luggage space behind the transverse engine. Its 146 cu.in V-6 would power the car to around 150 mph and reach 60 mph in 7 seconds.

The V-6 engine had an impeccable pedigree. It started life as a Formula Two (F2) engine for the 1957 91 cu.in formula, co-designed by Vittorio Jano and Ferrari's son Alfredino, who sadly died in 1956 before the engine had raced. The 65-degree four-cam V-6 became the Dino in his memory. While it did not do particularly well as an F2 engine, it went on to power Mike Hawthorn to his 1958 Grand Prix world championship in 146 cu.in form.

When GP rules changed to 91.5 cu.in for 1961, the original Dino engine was used before the team switched to a wider angle V-6. When F2 reverted to 91.5 cu.in, the engine had to have a production cylinder block of which 500 had been made. Ferrari persuaded Fiat to produce a limited run of front-engined sports cars in time for Ferrari to use the engine during 1967; the Pininfarina Fiat Dino sports

car arrived in November 1966 with the V-6 in 122 cu.in form and the Bertone coupe came in March 1967.

Ferrari had been using the V-6 in sports car racing in 1965/66. Pininfarina used a 206P to show a special concept GT in October 1965, following it with another a year later. Ferrari had been seeking an entry-level car to take on the Porsche 911 market and adopted Pininfarina's GT shape and changed the engine from longitudinal to transverse mounting; this was launched at Turin in November 1967 as the Dino 206GT – not using the Ferrari name. The aluminium bodies were built by Scaglietti and production started in mid 1968 – around 150 were built over the next year.

Meanwhile Fiat had dutifully turned out many more of the Fiat Dino 2.0 than were required for the F2 rules, but had also been developing the version they would have preferred to build if there had not been such a rush to build the first 500. The result was a very much revised chassis and the V-6 aluminium block was exchanged for a

164-165 *Although created by Ferrari, the Dino 246GT was never called a Ferrari by the factory. This did not stop some owners putting a Ferrari badge on the car.*

quieter and stronger cast iron 146 cu.in. The new Fiat Dino 2.4 was announced at the 1969 Turin Show, where the new (Ferrari) Dino 246GT, with a steel body, was also making its first public appearance. It was to continue in production until 1975, having been joined by the Targa-top 246GTS in 1972, and just over 3000 were built.

By the time the 246GT was around, the original purpose of productionising the V-6 had been forgotten. Ferrari eventually used it in mid-1967 F2 races with no success. They had a better year in 1968 with few results until they won the last two European races of the year, and went on to take three out of four of the Argentine Temporada races. In 146 cu.in form, the engine did well for Chris Amon in the 1968 Tasman series and he won the championship in 1969. There was just one more achievement for the same basic power unit; the Dino engine/transmission package was used for the Lancia Stratos which won the World Rally Championship from 1974-1976, 20 years after the original first ran.

But Ferrari moved on from the V-6 to a V-8, two thirds of the 365 V-12, but with its overhead camshafts driven by toothed belt. In 1973, this was installed in the Bertone-designed 308 GT4 which had an extra 8 inches in the wheelbase to carry four people. The 246GT was replaced by the 308GTB in 1975, initially with fiberglass bodies

but with steel from 1977 when the 308GTS Spider came along and the cars became Ferraris. The GT4 lasted until 1980, and the 308GTB and 308GTS until 1985 having gathered fuel injection in 1980 and 4-valve heads from 1982.

TECHNICAL DESCRIPTION OF THE DINO 246GT

YEARS OF PRODUCTION	1969-1974
MODELS	246GT AND 246GTS 2-SEATER
ENGINE	MID-MOUNTED V-6
BORE X STROKE, CAPACITY	3.6 X 2.3 INCHES, 147 CU.IN
VALVEGEAR	TWIN OVERHEAD CAMSHAFTS PER BANK
FUEL SYSTEM	THREE WEBER CARBURETORS
POWER	195 BHP AT 7600 RPM
TRANSMISSION	5-SPEED
BODY/CHASSIS	TUBULAR CHASSIS, STEEL BODY
SUSPENSION	FRONT, WISHBONES ANDCOIL SPRINGS
	REAR, WISHBONES AND COIL SPRINGS
TIRES/WHEELS	205/70VR14 ON 6.5 IN ALLOY WHEELS
WHEELBASE, TRACK (F), TRACK(R)	92 X 56 X 55 INCHES
LENGTH, WIDTH, HEIGHT	165 X 67 X 44 INCHES
MAX SPEED	148 MPH
WHERE BUILT	MARANELLO, ITALY

166-167 *The Dino 246GT performed as well as it looked.*

Fiat Dino 2.4 Spider

Through the Fifties Fiat had only dabbled in sports cars. Producing just a handful of the early 1100/1200 and 8V, they missed out on the big post-war American demand. Fiat were not prepared to tool up for lower volumes, so any sports car had to use a saloon platform and have its body built by one of the coachbuilders. It was Pininfarina who produced the 1200/1500/Oscar series of cabriolets from 1959 - 66 and built 37,500 of them over the seven year period. It was Ghia who pushed through the 2300S from 1961.

Serious sporting thoughts began with the little rear-engined 850 saloon launched in May 1964. Fiat styled and built the attractive coupe, Bertone styled and built the Spider; both were launched

together in March 1965. Fiat had read the market right and they were a success in America. By 1973, 342,873 coupes and 124,660 Spiders had been made, including the 55 cu.in Sport version from 1968.

The Fiat 124, launched in April 1966, had been scheduled for similar derivatives from its inception. Its engine had been designed by Lampredi (back at Fiat from Ferrari) as a pushrod 73 cu.in unit that could be stretched and fitted with a twin-cam head. The 124 Sport had a 87 cu.in twin-cam unit. The fixed head coupe was built within Fiat and the Spider, on a shortened platform, at Pininfarina.

While this was being planned, Ferrari had persuaded Fiat to produce at least 500 sports cars with the Dino V-6 engine as soon as

168-169 *The Fiat Dino 2.4 (1969 here) was a much better car than the 1966 2.0 model although fewer were made.*

possible; this would allow Ferrari to use the engine block in their Formula Two racing cars in 1967. So Fiat took over development and production of the 65-degree four-cam V-6 for which Lampredi settled on a 122 cu.in capacity, still with the aluminium block. Fiat engineers created a suitable platform from available parts but used a new rear suspension – a live axle on single leaf springs with rear radius arms and telescopic dampers ahead of and behind the axle.

Heavily committed to producing the complete 124 coupe in house, Fiat subcontracted the body building of both Dinos; Bertone made the delightful four-seater coupe and Pininfarina made the shorter and beautifully curvaceous Spider.

Both Spiders were launched at Turin in November 1966, and both coupes at Geneva in March 1967. Although the Fiat Dinos were twice the price of the 124 Sports, they were very well received.

They had style, performance and pedigree with a real race-derived engine. Pininfarina had built 1163 Spiders and Bertone 3670 coupes by 1969, when Fiat launched the Dino they would have built without the rush to build 500. The Dino 2400 was launched in November 1966, alongside Ferrari's Dino 246GT. In mid-1969 Fiat had acquired 50 per cent of Ferrari, and final assembly of the new car was transferred from Turin to an extension of the Maranello factory.

The new 146 cu.in engine retained just the basic design details of the V-6 with 65 degree vee-angle and four chain-driven cams; its 3.6 x 2.3 inches dimensions compare with 3.3 x 2.2 inches for the 122 cu.in and 3.3 x 2.7 inches of the original F1 engine in both its 1958 and 1966 forms. The block was made of cast iron which was heavier but quieter and easier to make without the removable liners; the major virtue was the improved drivability with the peak torque at 4600 rpm rather than 6000 rpm. The extra 20 bhp was also a bonus.

170-171 *Although the engine was used by Ferrari, the Dino 2.4 was always a Fiat.*

The previous gearbox had been a 2300 4-speed converted to five speeds with an additional casing. The new one was a ZF 5-speed box shared with the new Fiat 130. This car also supplied the new independent rear suspension – a MacPherson strut with, effectively, a lower wishbone. Outwardly there were no changes but the new 2400 was a much better car than its predecessor.

Despite that, sales of both models were lower over a similar production period than for the 122 cu.in. Just 420 Spiders and 2398 coupes were built before the line finished in 1973. Doubtless Ferrari put more effort into selling their own more expensive Dinos. Meanwhile both Fiat 124 Sport models continued to sell well. The engine grew to 98 cu.in in 1969 and 107 cu.in in 1972. The coupe finished in 1975 after nearly 280,000 units, while the Spider (almost 130,00 to 1978) rolled on into a 122 cu.in version to maintain the American sales until 1983.

TECHNICAL DESCRIPTION OF THE FIAT DINO 2.4 SPIDER

YEARS OF PRODUCTION	1969-1973
MODELS	SPIDER AND LWB 4-SEATER COUPE
ENGINE	FRONT-MOUNTED V-6
BORE X STROKE, CAPACITY	3.6 X 2.3 INCHES, 147 CU.IN
VALVEGEAR	TWIN OVERHEAD CAMSHAFTS PER BANK
FUEL SYSTEM	THREE WEBER CARBURETORS
POWER	180 BHP AT 6600 RPM
TRANSMISSION	5-SPEED
BODY/CHASSIS	STEEL MONOCOQUE
SUSPENSION	FRONT, WISHBONES AND COIL SPRINGS
	REAR, MACPHERSON STRUT, TRANSVERSE
	LINK AND TRAILING ARM
TIRES/WHEELS	185 X 14 ON 6.5 IN ALLOY WHEELS
WHEELBASE, TRACK (F), TRACK(R)	90 X 54.5 X 53 INCHES
LENGTH, WIDTH, HEIGHT	162 X 67.4 X 50 INCHES
MAX SPEED	128 MPH
WHERE BUILT	MARANELLO, ITALY

Pontiac Firebird

When Ford introduced the Mustang in April 1964, General Motors hoped their revised Chevrolet Corvair would be more appealing than a rebodied Ford Falcon. By August, when 100,000 Mustangs had been sold, they started work on their Mustang rival, determined to make it faster, more comfortable and more stylish. The Camaro was an all-new car; it used a unitary body chassis but with a rubber-mounted front sub-frame. By the time the Camaro hit the showrooms in September 1966, it had more options available than the Mustang. Ford brought out the Mercury Cougar, with a longer platform, as their high-style Mustang.

Pontiac initially ignored the new compact sports youth market. NASCAR successes still appealed to the young and they used competition names on their big 2-door sports coupes. Tempest Le Mans, Catalina Grand Prix while speed record venue Bonneville was used for the biggest cars – these early Sixties coupes are particularly attractive future classics. Then came the magnificent GTO muscle car for 1963 with a 389 cu.in V-8 in the Le Mans coupe. However, Pontiac finally gave in and joined the Camaro development programme in early 1966; the Firebird used the Camaro's center section and added its own front end and rear panels, but retained the slightly different Pontiac engine range.

The Firebird, named after earlier turbine-powered concept cars, went on sale in February 1967 as a coupe and a convertible. The engine choice ranged from the 165 bhp 230 cu.in. overhead cam six-cylinder through a 250 bhp 326 cu.in V-8 to the 400 cu.in with 325 bhp. By then the Mustang was available with a 390 cu.in. 335 bhp

unit and you could get a Shelby Mustang GT-500 with the 428 cu.in with 350 bhp.

Ever since the early days of NASCAR, the American market had responded to racing success – win on Sunday, sell on Monday. With the rise in the pony car market, the SCCA launched the Trans-American Championship in 1966 for cars with 304 cu.in engines and the manufacturers joined in. The Shelby Mustang won comfortably in the first year but had to work harder in 1967 to beat the Mercury Cougar and the new Camaro Z-28. The Camaro beat the Mustang in 1968 with the American Motors Javelin not far behind. The Camaro won again in 1969 from the Mustang Boss 302, but the Firebird had joined in to take third. In 1970 Mustang took the honours from the two Chryslers, Dodge Challenger and Plymouth Cuda, with Camaro and Firebird trailing. By 1971 the major manufacturers had left the scene and Javelin won the final year before the championship switched to private entries.

Entering the Trans-Am championship for 1969 justified a new Firebird model, the Trans-Am which has been the top model ever since. Although the racers used 302 cu.in engines, the Trans-Am model had the 335 bhp 400 cu.in engine, together with sports suspension and a choice of two colors, white with blue stripes or blue with white stripes – American racing colors. The 1969 Firebirds had bumpers replaced by the new plastic front end which was also seen on the Judge

172-173 Pontiac's Firebird (1968 400 illustrated) had smoother style than the sister Chevrolet Camaro.

derivative of the GTO; Pontiac had pioneered the Endura deformable front panel made from polyurethane.

Firebird and Camaro were both rebodied in 1970 with European-style long bonnet, short fastback tail and dropped the convertible. Firebird sales never reached Mustang levels but had been comfortable; 82,000 in 1967 went to 107,000 in 1968, 87,000 in 1969 but only 48,000 in 1970. This reflected the decline in the overall pony car market which had made up 13 per cent of US sales in 1967, 9.2 per cent in 1969 and 3.4 per cent in 1972. The Mustang had peaked at 550,000 in 1967 but was down to 127,000 in 1972.

To maintain the high engine outputs on lower octane fuels,

engine sizes were increased in 1971 and the 455 cu.in became the Trans-Am's standard unit, still with 335 bhp. Production went up to 53,000, but was back to 30,000 in 1972.

Ford also claimed the same power for their 1971 Boss Mustang 351 – the last performance Mustang.

High performance was no longer acceptable. By 1975, the Mustang had become a small car, the Cougar was too big and Chrysler and Javelin had left the market to the Firebird and Camaro, which continued to survive on style before the power resurgence of the Nineties.

TECHNICAL DESCRIPTION OF THE PONTIAC FIREBIRD 400	
YEARS OF PRODUCTION	1967-1968
MODELS	2-DOOR COUPE
ENGINE	FRONT-MOUNTED V-8
BORE X STROKE, CAPACITY	4.1 X 3.7 INCHES, 400 CU.IN
VALVEGEAR	PUSHROD OVERHEAD VALVES
FUEL SYSTEM	SINGLE CARBURETOR
POWER	325 BHP (GROSS) AT 5000 RPM
TRANSMISSION	3-SPEED AUTOMATIC
BODY/CHASSIS	STEEL BODY AND CHASSIS
SUSPENSION	FRONT, WISHBONES AND COIL SPRINGS
	REAR, LIVE AXLE AND LEAF SPRINGS
TIRES/WHEELS	7.75 X 14 ON STEEL WHEELS
WHEELBASE, TRACK (F), TRACK(R)	108 X 60 X 60 INCHES
LENGTH, WIDTH, HEIGHT	189 X 74 X 49.6 INCHES
MAX SPEED	130 MPH
WHERE BUILT	DETROIT, USA

Alfa Romeo Duetto

Few cars remained in production as long as the Alfa Romeo Giulia Spider; the seductively-shaped two-seater was launched at Geneva in 1966 with a 97 cu.in engine and finally retired in 1993 using the 122 cu.in version of an engine that had long ceased to be used in any other Alfa Romeo. With various adjustments over the years, the design looked almost as fresh and modern at the end as it had done 27 years earlier. Over 120,000 of the various models were built by Pininfarina.

Following Alfa Romeo's replacement of the Giulietta with the new boxy Giulia saloon in 1962, Bertone took 6.2 inches out of its platform to create the Giulia Sprint GT; Pininfarina's Giulietta-based Giulia Spider continued rather longer until the new car took over in 1966, with the Sprint GT chassis shortened a further 3.9 inches. The name Duetto was the product of a Europe-wide competition.

The styling theme, which Pininfarina carried forward from an earlier show car, was the principle of oval cross sections decreasing towards each end, with a shallow central scoop running along most of the side of the car. In fact the name didn't last long in Alfa terminology as the 1750 (106 cu.in) engine was introduced a year later and the Duetto became simply a 1750 Spider Veloce. But most people continued to call the car Duetto until the shapely tail was cut short during 1970 – Pininfarina had made some 15,000 cars by then.

Power outputs generally matched those of the equivalent Sprint GT or GTV. In 97 cu.in form, the Alfa engine gave 109 bhp, enough for a maximum speed of 111 mph. It was a good all-round performer. When the Giulia changed into the 106 cu.in, the 108 cu.in GTV engine with 122 bhp powered the Spider to 118 mph. The short-tail 1750 became the 131 bhp Spider 2000 in 1971, but it was still possible to get 97 cu.in and even, for a time, 79 cu.in versions.

The next significant change came in 1983 with a new full width rubber front bumper shaped around the lower half of a new Alfa shield. A large rubber molding was attached to the rear panel, with an aerodynamic lip matching the front chin-spoiler; American market bumpers were 2 inches longer. For 1986, a skirt was added along the sills, finally destroying the original oval section, and a more

174-175 *Pininfarina's delightful Duetto shape lasted for 27 years with no major change.*

pronounced spoiler was added under the front bumper. By this time, the 1600 still had 104 bhp and the 2000, with fuel injection, gave 128 bhp or 117 bhp to American regulations.

The final change came in 1990 with car colored soft bumpers and a smoother rounder tail. With the familiar scoop along the sides, it looked more like the original Duetto than any of its interim versions. It was finally phased out when it became uneconomical to develop the old engine for modern emission regulations.

TECHNICAL DESCRIPTION OF THE ALFA ROMEO DUETTO (1750 SPIDER)

YEARS OF PRODUCTION	1966-1967 (1967-1971)
MODELS	SPORTS 2-SEATER
ENGINE	FRONT-MOUNTED IN-LINE 4
BORE X STROKE, CAPACITY	3 x 3.2 INCHES, (3.1 x 3.4) 95 CU.IN (108)
VALVEGEAR	TWIN OVERHEAD CAMSHAFTS
FUEL SYSTEM	TWO WEBER TWIN-CHOKE CARBURETORS
POWER	109 BHP (122) AT 6000 RPM (5500)
TRANSMISSION	5-SPEED
BODY/CHASSIS	STEEL MONOCOQUE
SUSPENSION	FRONT, WISHBONES AND COILS
	REAR, LIVE AXLE, RADIUS ARMS, A-BRACKET,
	COIL SPRINGS
TIRES/WHEELS	155 x 15 ON 4.5 IN STEEL WHEELS
WHEELBASE, TRACK (F), TRACK(R)	88 x 51.5 x 50 INCHES
LENGTH, WIDTH, HEIGHT	169 x 64 x 51 INCHES
MAX SPEED	111 MPH (118)
WHERE BUILT	TURIN, ITALY

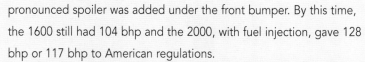

1971 - 1980

SAFETY LEGISLATION AND EMISSIONS CHANGE PERFORMANCE ATTITUDES

The Seventies were expected to continue the expansion of the Sixties, but a world fuel crisis and legislation had other ideas. The Arab-Israeli war of October 1973 restricted fuel supplies and increased costs throughout the world; almost overnight big-engined cars lost credibility and prices of old classic ones fell drastically. America brought in the 55 mph limit to save fuel in 1974. There was a near-repeat when the Shah of Persia was deposed in 1979, but by then manufacturers were working hard to improve efficiency of cars and engines.

Legislation came from America in two forms. Los Angeles air pollution was blamed on the motor car, resulting in lead free fuel and catalytic converters in California from 1975. The American performance market

was instantly stifled and all manufacturers started making European-style compacts. There were a few big-engined cars like the 500 cu.in Cadillac Fleetwood or the 457 cu.in Lincoln Continental but they could only generate 200 bhp and had nothing to commend their appearance either. Apart from a few muscle car developments from the previous decade, hardly a classic emerged from the USA after 1972 – all looks and no go.

Then Nader's safety crusade of the Sixties resulted in a steady flow of crash-test regulations and the convertible was almost banned; US manufacturers were certainly expecting it and stopped designing roadsters. Even European makers stopped making soft top cars for the US, as America had long been their biggest market. However, the ban never came in and convertibles resumed their popularity in the early Eighties.

THE HOT HATCHES

In small cars the Mini influence was spreading, not just for its front wheel drive but also for its transverse engine position. It also bred the supermini, the next size up with cars like the Renault 5 (1972), Ford Fiesta (1976) and the Autobianchi A112 (1969) which acted as the prototype for the Fiat 127 (1971) – all 3-door hatchbacks. The front-wheel-drive theme was developed further in the next size up of which BMC's

own 1100/1300 series had been the forerunners from the early Sixties – a little more space and a five-door option. The Simca 1100 (1967) and the Fiat 128 (1969) were in the same mold. But what really made the hatchback breed was the Volkswagen Golf which arrived in 1974. Ford were slow to follow; the rear-drive Mk.2 Escort ran from 1975-80 and it was 1980 before the front-drive Mk.3 arrived.

None of these small cars were classics in their standard forms, but the faster models have already generated a classic following. Front wheel drive cars had such good roadholding that they could easily handle more power, so a mini muscle-car revolution took place. First away was the VW Golf GTI, a year after the standard Golf launch, with a 96 cu.in fuel-injected 110 bhp 'four'.

Ford's XR3 Escort came in 1980 with 96 bhp. Renault brought the 5 into line with the R5 Alpine or Gordini with 85 cu.in and 93 bhp, and added a 5 Turbo in 1979 with the turbocharged 85 cu.in engine mounted in the middle and now producing 160 bhp. This was another homologation special developed for rallying.

Some retained rear wheel drive for their superminis, though. Vauxhall had added the Chevette as their supermini in 1975, but produced a limited run of Chevette HS2300s in 1979 with special 16-valve heads for rallying. Talbot took a different route for the Sunbeam and acquired 134 cu.in Lotus 16-valve engines for the Sunbeam-Lotus which was another rallying success; the Talbot had

been designed under Chrysler ownership but Peugeot took over in 1978.

Fiat took a slightly different view. They left International rallying to sports machinery, like the 124 Spider and Lancia Stratos, or the 131 Abarth Rally (1976), so stayed out of the mini-muscle horsepower race and provided extra style instead. While the 128 was available with 67 and 79 cu.in engines, they added a 3-door fastback, the 128 coupe sport, on a shortened platform from 1971-1975 and changed it in 1975 for the 3P (tre porte) to make a hatch-back. Calling in Bertone for a Spider version again, they finished up with the mid-engined X1/9.

Meanwhile Alfa-Romeo opened a new plant in southern Italy to create the remarkable Alfasud, Alfa's first front wheel drive car, which used a flat-four engine of 72 cu.in from 1971. Although the Alfasud would be enlarged to 91.5 cu.in, the model that appealed was the Alfasud Sprint, a fastback 2+2 designed by ItalDesign of which over 100,000 would be built.

Actually, VW had taken a leaf out of the Italian book in producing the Golf-based 3-door fastback Scirocco at the same time (1974) as the standard car; both the Golf and Scirocco were also shaped by ItalDesign.

The arrival of all these hot hatches and coupe derivatives virtually killed the youth sports-car market. They had all the convenience of a family four-seater with plenty of performance; they were far more practical and insurable than an open sports car.

176-177 Star personalization – the overstated grille on Presley's 1973 Cadillac Fleetwood is not quite the way Cadillac built it.

FAMILY SEDAN COUPES

Racing and rallying continued to produce sporting and desirable versions of the family sedans. Triumph's 1965 1300 front-wheel-drive car gradually evolved into the rear-drive Dolomite with the 113 cu.in overhead cam slant-four engine that had been used for the 1971 Saab 99; the Dolomite Sprint emerged in 1973 with a 16-valve 122 cu.in 127 bhp version and was highly successful in British sedan car racing.

Vauxhall's Firenza coupe 122 cu.in superseded the Viva GT in 1970 to join the Capri market. The 1972 Firenza Sport SL came with a 140 cu.in version of the belt driven ohc 'four'. Under the guiding hand of tuning expert Bill Blydenstein, this had become a successful sedan racer; lessons learnt were carried through to a new attractive Firenza coupe for 1974. This 'droop-snoot' car had a full width flat front panel with headlights set behind plastic and a deep air-dam; a tuned 131 bhp 140 cu.in was attached to a ZF 5-speed box and sports suspension was fitted. Sadly, it became a limited edition special as Vauxhall only produced 204. The balance of the aerodynamic fronts were used up on 197 Sportshatch models based on the Magnum (big Viva) 2300 estates in 1975 – an equally rare classic.

Until General Motors' first world car arrived in 1974 as the Chevette, Kadett (1976) or Gemini, Opel still had a fair amount of autonomy and were free to develop their own Capri rival; the Manta coupe arrived in late 1970 as a fastback version of the Ascona using 72, 115 cu.in 4-cylinder engines. A Rallye version was available, the SR and the GTE following later. Evolutions of the Ascona and Manta continued for many years.

In 1981 the homologation special Manta 400 arrived with 144 bhp from 146 cu.in; the same specification was available in the Ascona 400 which also had its share of rallying success. Like the Capris and Cortinas, the top end of the Ascona and Manta ranges have their classic following.

Fiat joined the same market through Lancia which they had taken over in 1969. The Lancia Beta came in late 1972 as a fastback sedan using versions of the twin-cam Fiat 125 engine mounted transversely on top of a 5-speed gearbox co-developed with Citroen. The coupe version followed in 1973 on a shortened platform with notchback styling similar to the Fulvia coupe, while 1975 saw the Spider and the High Performance Estate (HPE). The Lancia Gamma, a longer Beta with the 122 cu.in and a further enlarged 146 cu.in engines, came in 1976 using similar styles to those of the Beta, a fast-back sedan and an elegant notch-back coupe. The Beta was a good car in its day, but they all suffered badly from rust due largely to Fiat's use of second-rate steel at the time, so there may not be many still in existence.

Alfa Romeo had phased out the Giulia with the restyled 1750 in 1968 and made it into the 2000 for 1971; the Alfetta came in 1972 with the 1750 engine, but with a rear-mounted gearbox and de Dion rear suspension.

The important derivative was the Bertone-styled Alfetta GT which arrived in 1974 with the 109 cu.in 4-cylinder. By 1977, this had become the 2000GTV finally replacing the Giulia-based GT. When the Alfa 6 came out in 1979 with a new 152 cu.in V-6 engine, this provided an appropriate power plant for the 2000GTV to create the GTV6 2.5 – the last classic sporting Alfa Romeo before Fiat took over the company in 1986.

Toyota continued to produce the Celica as a Carina coupe with 97 cu.in engines, and added a lift-back. Toyota twin-cam engines had dominated formula 3 in this period and a 122 cu.in version of this engine became

BIG SEDANS AND COUPES

an option in the new 1977 range.

A few large sedans deserve classic status in their own right, but the coupes that were derived from the rest have also become classics. Typical of classic sedans were the Bristol 411, Aston Martin Lagonda, Ferrari 400, Rover SD1 and Jaguar XJC, while such coupes as the Jaguar XJS, BMW 3.0CS, Fiat 130 all came from less appealing sedan models.

Bristol had moved on from the first Chrysler-engined 407, through the 408 (1963) with mild body differences and improved headroom, the 409 (1965), and the 410 (1967) before the 411 arrived in 1969 with radial tires and its Chrysler engine up to 383 cu.in. The 411 moved through five series from 1969-77 with the Series III (1972) notable for its headlights set within the grille.

The first major change of shape since the 406 came with the 412 convertible in 1975; the body design by Zagato was an enlarged version of the Pininfarina-styled Beta Spider which Zagato were building for Lancia at the time. It had the same style of targa-roof and the same half hard-top at the rear, which could be replaced for summer use with a soft-top, but the B-pillar carried a small window for rear passengers. It was very much a car for all seasons like the Triumph Stag. A turbocharged

178-179 *Beta Monte Carlo (Scorpion in USA) was Lancia's equivalent to the mid-engined Fiat X1/9 and was later used as the basis for the 037 rally car of the early Eighties.*

version came in 1980 as the 412 Beaufighter. Meanwhile Bristol made a major change to their sedans as well when the fast-back 603 replaced the last of the 411s in 1977; this gave way to the bodily similar Brittania and turbocharged Brigand in 1982. Bristol has always been a small company evolving their cars by steady development; they accomplished a lot in the Seventies.

Aston Martin had been renowned for their high-speed grand tourers from the DB2 onwards; the Lagonda sedans based on that were highly regarded, but four-door versions of the DB4 and DBS Aston Martin under the Lagonda name were less successful. The DB4-based Rapide was also styled by Touring, but only 55 were made from 1961-64 as they were too expensive to make and upset production of the DB4.

When a 4-door version of the DBS V-8 finally went into production in 1974 as the V8 Lagonda, the company was going through a change of ownership and only seven of this desirable sedan were built.

Aston Martin's new owners immediately set about creating a new Lagonda, similar underneath to the Aston Martin V-8, but with completely new razor-edged body styling by William Towns; inside were advanced digital instrumentation and touch-sensitive switchgear. Launched in 1976, it was eventually put into production in 1978. Fuel injection replaced the downdraft Weber carburetors in 1986 and the instrumentation was changed to TV screens in 1984. When the body's razor edges were rounded off and a new front was added in 1987, the instruments were changed again to a liquid crystal display; this

was the final and best interpretation of the Lagonda. While the Lagonda does not have as much classic appeal as the equivalent Aston Martin, it has very much the same character for considerably less money.

There might have been another big 4-door sedan in the Monica, an Anglo-French project that was to use big Chrysler V-8s in a space-frame chassis under bodywork resembling the Ferrari 365GT4. The two parties were Jean Tastevin of the French railway company CFPM and Chris Lawrence, an engineer well known in the Morgan racing world. Sadly, production never really got under way after various motor show launches, but a number of prototypes were built and tested by the press. If you find one, it is worth keeping, as it was an excellent concept.

Another to use Chrysler engines in low volume

production runs was Peter Monteverdi in Switzerland. The first road-car, the High Speed , was launched in 1967 using a 439 cu.in V-8 (or the 427 cu.in Hemi) in a steel frame with Frua building the bodies to Monteverdi's design. The car was so well received that Monteverdi had to find another coachbuilder who could produce more cars. Frua claimed the shape was his, so Monteverdi had to redesign it in 1969 for Fissore to build. The 375S 2+2, 375L 4-seater, 375C convertible (also Palm Beach cabriolet) and a 4-door Limousine (375/4) followed from 1970-75. They were well-built high-class cars, very much in the style of Jensen for whom Monteverdi was the Swiss importer. He also built a handful of the mid-engined Hai 450SS using the Chrysler Hemi engine.

Ferrari had originally joined the 4-seater sedan car market with the 330GT 2+2 in 1963 and followed this with the bigger-engined 365GT 2+2 in 1967; these were semi fastback cars with limited rear headroom. Pininfarina produced considerably more headroom for the more formal 365GT4 2+2 in 1972, but only 470 were built before the 292 cu.in 400 appeared in 1975 – the first Ferrari to be sold with automatic transmission, manual optional. It stayed in production for 10 years before being replaced by the 412 in 1985.

Rover may not naturally follow Ferrari in classic thinking, but the 1976 Rover SD1 was quite deliberately styled to look like a 4-door Ferrari

Daytona, and successfully too. Four and six-cylinder versions were sold, but the only one with classic pretensions was the 3500 which used the Rover aluminium V-8 engine with 157 bhp. Fuel injection was added to give 193 bhp to the 1982 3500 Vitesse, which was the basis for a successful racing sedan.

Jaguar's coupe based on the Series 2 XJ6 eventually came out in 1975 after a 1973 launch. In XJ6C and XJ12C (XK 256 cu.in 'six' and 323 cu.in V-12) forms, the coupe used the sedan wheelbase, but with only two doors, and the side windows dropped down fully to give a pillarless appearance. By 1977 production had stopped after 6505 XJ6C and only 1873 XJ12C; it wasn't the easiest of cars to produce to Jaguar's high standards of quietness, but it was always destined to be a classic Jaguar.

The XJS V-12 had also been launched in 1975 just as the XJC started production and the V-12 E-type stopped. On a shortened XJ6 platform, it was better suited to the 2+2 GT market than was the coupe, but it was never regarded as a replacement for the E-type. The XJS would continue through until the arrival of the XK8 in 1996. Along the way came the coupe-cabriolet in 1983, together with the option of the 219 cu.in twin-cam AJ6 engine; the true cabriolet followed in 1988, while the engine sizes were increased to 244 cu.in (AJ6) and 366 cu.in (V-12) in 1991. The XJS had all the attributes of a classic car but lacked the elegance of the big sedans or the

style of the E-type; the wide headlights ruined the appearance of the front – the American version with twin round lamps was better – and the rear sail-panel with a near vertical rear window may look good on a Dino, but it is clumsy on the XJS. The notchback cabriolet and convertible looked much better and the estate conversion by Lynx was the most elegant of all bodies seen on the XJS.

Fiat took a similar route into the big coupe market in 1971 with the graceful Pininfarina 2-door version of the Fiat 130, which had been an odd mixture of an ugly body concealing a nice engine (176 cu.in V-6 increased later to 195 cu.in) and good all-round independent suspension; on the same wheelbase as the sedan, the coupe was a spacious four-seater with the elegant lines of a Ferrari. However only 4500 were built between 1971 and 1977.

De Tomaso continued the technical collaboration with Ford and used the 347 cu.in V-8 in the front-engined 1970 Deauville 4-door, and added the Longchamp 2-door on a shortened wheelbase in 1972, both designed by Tom Tjaarda at Ghia. By this time de Tomaso had owned Ghia from 1967 and had also taken over Vignale in 1969 for its production

180-181 *This 1980 Porsche 911SC Targa has borrowed the whale-tale wing from a Turbo.*

space. Ghia had also produced the styling for the 1968 Iso Fidia 4-door sedan, but Iso went to Bertone for the 1969 Lele 2+2; both cars started with Chevrolet engines but used Ford 347 cu.in by 1973.

In Germany, Mercedes and BMW also produced coupe versions of their big sedans. BMW had started their new coupe range with the 2800CS in 1968. In 1971 they changed the numbering system and brought in the 182 cu.in 3.0CS, CSi and CSL – Coupe Sport with injection or lightness from aluminium panels. A 2500CS was added in 1974 as an economy model. BMW changed the numbering system again in 1972 with the introduction of the 5-series sedans; the 3-series were added in 1975 and 1976 saw the latest coupe, the 6-series, in 630CS/CSi and 633CSi forms; with its wheelbase 3.5 inches longer than the 5-series it was a comfortable 4-seater.

Mercedes had continued the 230SL theme through to the 280SL which ceased in 1971. Meanwhile the new generation Mercedes had been launched in 1968 and had included the 300SEL 6.3. When a new 213 cu.in V-8 was announced in 1971 it became an option for the 280SE/SEL but, more importantly it powered the new 350SL followed within the same year by the

14 inches longer SLC to give fixed head seating for four – perhaps the nicest of the SL range. At last the sporting Mercedes had an engine worthy of its looks and roadholding to match with a redesigned rear suspension. The 450SL and SLC were added in 1973 with an economy 280SL and SLC twin-cam six-cylinder in 1974; a rather less economical 450SLC 5.0 joined the range in 1977 with 240 bhp. The 450SLC had a resounding success in the 18,500 miles Round South America Rally in 1978 taking the first two places and a 450SL 5.0 took second place in the 1979 Safari rally. For 1980, the range was rationalized with a 204 bhp 231 cu.in V-8 and a 231 bhp 305 cu.in V-8 to produce 380SL and 500SL. The SLC was dropped in favor of the 380 and 500SEC in 1981, an elegant two-door S-class with pillarless side windows.

The American muscle car era was to continue through to 1973. Ford took the Mustang on through Mach 1 and Boss 302 and 429, with the final fling being the 1971 335 bhp Boss 351. Mustang II came in 1974 as a four-seat coupe with just 88 and 100 bhp options; even the 1976 305 cu.in engine only produced 134 bhp. The Pontiac Judge of 1970 was the ultimate

GTO with its plastic molded front end, rev counter on the back of the bonnet, a wing on the tail and a 400 cu.in V-8 with 366 bhp. By 1971 the power was on the way down as GM put all its cars onto low-octane fuel in preparation for the arrival of unleaded petrol.

THE REAL GTs

By now anyone could afford a GT as the majority were just sedans with style. But there were still a handful of true Grand Touring 2+2 built for that sole purpose. Porsche continued to develop the 911 and brought out the first of the Turbos in 1975 complete with wide rear wheels and a big wing at the back; by 1977 the 260 bhp 183 cu.in had been exchanged for a 300 bhp 201 cu.in and the car could exceed 155 mph.

In 1971 Porsche had actually thought of replacing the 911 with a new front-engined four-seater, the 928, using a big 274 cu.in V-8 with an automatic transmission option to satisfy the American market. Fortunately the 911 was never replaced and the 928 found its own niche when it finally arrived in 1977; it had been delayed while Porsche decided to put the 924 into production following the withdrawal of VW-Audi from that project.

Porsche's 928 market was then occupied by the Ferrari 400 and the various large sedan coupes mentioned above, plus Aston Martin. While the DB6 Mk.II carried on into 1970, the DBSV-8 was in full production with its 315 bhp 323 cu.in V-8 using fuel

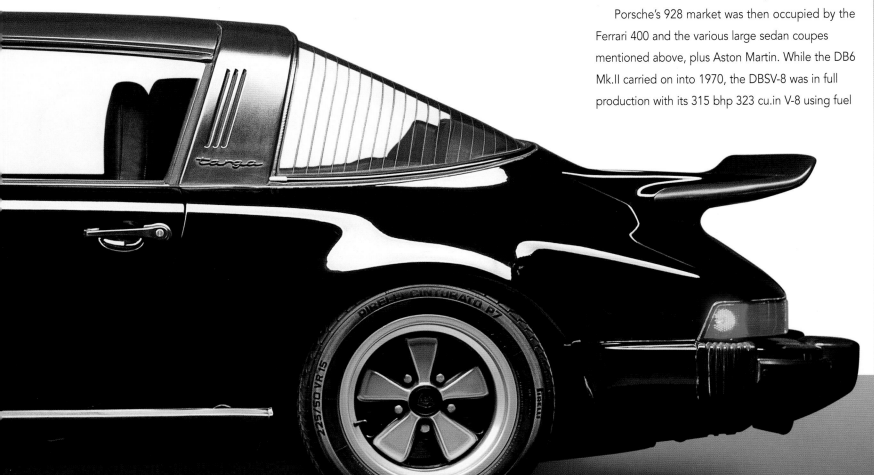

injection. The Vantage version with 375 bhp and downdraft Weber carburetors came in 1977, and the convertible Volante followed a year later.

A worthy newcomer to this scene was the Bitter CD, which had started life as an Opel styling exercise for the 1969 Frankfurt Show; it was based on a short wheelbase version of the Opel Diplomat which used a 232 cu.in Chevrolet V-8 and had de Dion rear suspension. The concept was taken over by former Opel racer, Erich Bitter, who launched the CD (Coupe Diplomat) as a 2+2 in 1973; Baur of Stuttgart built the elegant fast-back bodies. Bitter continued his Opel association and introduced the Bitter SC2 (Senator Coupe) in 1979 using the 183 cu.in engine from the Senator with the 4WD option. A convertible SC2 followed in 1981 and a 231 cu.in option in 1983. Alfa Romeo too put a toe in the exclusive coupe market with the Montreal which had started as Bertone's show car for the Canadian Expo 67. Alfa Romeo took it over and inserted a detuned version of the engine which had powered the company's sports racing Tipo 33, a 158 cu.in all aluminium 4-cam V-8 coupled to a ZF gearbox. It was finally launched in 1971 but fell victim to the 1973 fuel crisis. Lamborghini's striking 4-seater Espada continued through from 1968 to 1978, but they replaced the Islero with the 2+2 Jarama (Bertone) using a shortened Espada platform which now used sheet steel rather than the traditional tubular frames. These front-engined Lamborghinis are underrated in the classic world; they are mechanically strong but the electrical components can let them down.

The Maserati Mexico, Ghibli and Indy continued through to the Seventies until Citroen's rationalization phased them all out in favor of the Bertone-bodied Khamsin using the 298 cu.in V-8. It was the first front-engined Maserati with independent rear suspension and featured Citroen-style power steering and braking. A practical and good looking 2+2, it was destined for an 8-year production span until de Tomaso's Biturbo took over.

Although Citroen had traditionally produced cars for the people and advanced comfortable sedans, they had ignored the high performance GT market; acquiring access to Maserati technology gave them instant high performance engines and GT market acceptability. Maserati's four-cam V-6 was reduced to 164 cu.in to avoid a steep taxation rise at 170 cu.in and was coupled to Citroen's own gearbox. The rest was pure Citroen with the hydraulic system providing suspension control and power for brakes and steering. It was a remarkable high performance grand tourer with effortlessly quiet cruising ability. Nearly 20,000 were built before Peugeot took over Citroen in 1975 and stopped its production.

THE SPECIALIST SPORTS CARS

Almost any of the limited volume sporting cars has become a classic, although some are more expensive than others. Included here are the two-seater GTs, wherever their engines are situated, and the open two-seaters.

In production numbers, Britain and Italy were probably equal contributors, but Britain made the greater variety. MG continued to produce the MGB and the Midget, but had to add plastic bumpers to both to comply with American regulations in 1974, at which point the Midget became a Mk.III and adopted the 90 cu.in engine from the Triumph Spitfire, the sister company within the Leyland organization. The disappearance of the MGC in 1969 had left a performance gap in the range until the 1972 arrival of the MGB GTV-8; Rover's 213 cu.in V-8 was squeezed into the engine compartment and the aged MGB had instant 125 mph performance. Despite Rover being part of the same group, politics intervened and the V-8 was withdrawn when the Rover SD1 was launched in 1976, so only 2591 GTV-8s were produced. The car did of course make a welcome return in 1992 as the RV8, using new bodyshells from British Motor Heritage; this time it was a roadster.

Triumph themselves ran the TR6 through until 1976 in both PI (Petrol Injection) form and with carburetors plus rubber bumpers for the US. The various Leyland sports models were all reaching the end of their lives, so the decision was taken to produce a single corporate sports car with the USA remaining the prime market. In the early Seventies it was feared that convertibles would succumb to American roll-over laws, so the TR7 was designed as a monocoque coupe and would use the 122 cu.in 4-cylinder already used in the Dolomite and the Saab. The new car arrived in January 1975 in the USA, but the home market had to wait until May 1976. Eventually the fears of a convertible ban went away and a TR7 convertible came out in

1979. The last of 112,375 TR7s emerged in late 1981.

Part of the corporate strategy had been to build a TR8, using the Rover V-8 in a TR7 with a bonnet bulge and wider tires. Leyland's problems delayed its arrival until 1979 in America only where it had fuel injection for California and carburetors in the other states. The convertible version virtually replaced the coupe at the end of that year. Then came the second OPEC petrol price rise and big engines suddenly lost their appeal; coupled with an adverse exchange rate, this killed the profitability of the US market and the TR8 ceased in early 1981 after only 2700 had been built, none of them for the home market.

The TR7 styling was not its strong point. It was such a wedge shape that the driver couldn't see anything in front of the screen; separate federal bumpers and the strange crease between the wheels didn't improve its looks – the convertible was far better balanced. It was certainly a modern car in its general behavior but it was a major departure from the high performance TR5 and TR6 that had preceded it. The TR8 was intended to rectify that but market and management combined to prevent that happening.

The TR7 wasn't the only British sports car to suffer from relying too much on the US market. The 1970 Jensen-Healey was supposed to be the replacement for the big Healey 3000 which could no longer pass crash regulations. Jensen were still making the Chrysler-engined Interceptor in its various forms including a convertible and the FF 4WD model. They had also been building the big Healey for British Leyland. Teaming up with Donald Healey to produce a new car was a mutually convenient solution, particularly as Jensen was now largely owned by the Healey's biggest American importer, Kjell Qvale.

Donald Healey already had the basis of a new car on the stocks using Vauxhall running gear under a neat and comfortable two-seater body. By the time of the 1972 announcement, the engine had changed to Lotus' 4-valve 122 cu.in, which had started as a development of the 45 degree slant-four Vauxhall engine, and the gearbox came from Chrysler. It was a nice car but the build quality was not good enough and the engine was unreliable. Most of its problems were cured after the first 800 or so cars with the Mk.2 from August 1973. A 5-speed Getrag box replaced the Chrysler 4-speed in 1974 and a hatch-back Jensen GT was added to the range in July 1975. Not helped by the early engine problems, US sales of the Jensen Healey had not been as good as planned, and there were too many engineering projects being financed as well; in May 1976 Jensen ceased production. Over the four years, 10,926 Jensen Healeys were sold (7709 USA, 1914 UK and 830 other exports), of which 473 were GTs (202 UK). A sad end to a promising design, but a classic nevertheless.

The main beneficiary of the Jensen project was Lotus, for whom Jensen had effectively developed their engine. They had also learnt from their own work with the 1969 racing Lotus 62, outwardly a Europa, using the 122 cu.in engine which was then still called the LV (Lotus-Vauxhall) 240. The Europa had been given an S2 designation in 1968, but the Renault engine was replaced by the Lotus twin-cam in 1971. The first production Lotus to use the ex-Jensen 122 cu.in engine was the 1974 Elite, followed in quick succession by the Eclat (1975) and the first of the long-running Esprit (1976). Before these were all given the 134 cu.in version in 1980-1981, Lotus had supplied this engine for the Sunbeam Lotus rally car. If you have an early Jensen-Healey with engine problems, find a Lotus dealer.

The British sports car industry was beset by problems through the Seventies. The Welsh Gilbern had started in 1960 as a fiberglass bodied coupe powered by the BMC A-series engine, followed by the B-series MGA and MGB engines. A new body accompanied the 1966 Genie which came with Ford V-6 power. The similar Invader came in 1969, with a Mark II and an estate car following in 1971. By then the company ownership had changed several times and the doors were closed in 1973.

Ginetta fared rather better. Like Gilbern and TVR they used a space-frame chassis with fiberglass

182-183 *Lotus Esprit came in S2 form in 1978 with this new air-dam and rear valance and a change of alloy wheels.*

bodywork. They had made their name with the little road sports racing G4 powered by Ford Anglia 60 and from 1964 Cortina 91.5 cu.in. Over 500 were built between 1961-69; a later version appeared from 1981-84, and it reappeared with independent rear suspension as the G27 in 1985. It is again being made today by subsequent owners of the company. Their next popular road car was the G15 which ran from 1968 to 1974; using the rear-engined 53 cu.in Hillman Imp power train, over 800 were made. TVR continued to develop their models at a remarkable rate of progress despite still only selling around 1000 per year. A heavily revised and stronger chassis came in 1972 with a new longer body to create the M-series for (Ford) 1600M, (Triumph) 2500M and (Ford V-6) 3000M range. A turbocharged version of the 3000M came in 1975, the hatchback Taimar in 1976 and a convertible in 1978. Then 1980 saw the launch of the new TVR Tasmin, part of the story of the next decade.

AC had continued to produce variations on the Cobra theme throughout the Sixties but had little luck with the Frua-bodied AC 428, which had been launched in 1965 as a convertible and 1966 as a coupe. The bodies were built in Italy and Frua had problems producing the required quantity. Then came the 1973 fuel crisis and the market disappeared as did the 428 after only 80 had been built – 29 coupes and 51 convertibles. AC's bread-and-butter was in making three-wheeled cars for disabled motorists, so the early failure of the 428 was not a major setback. However, seeking an alternative car to make, they made a move into the modern world of mid-engined sports cars with the ME3000. Starting with the privately designed mid-engined prototype Diablo with an Austin Maxi 106 cu.in engine, AC mounted a Ford V-6 transversely behind the driver and Hewland built a special gearbox. The result was a nice looking car but it took a long time to get into production and the first car was finally delivered in 1979; only 82 were made before the design was sold to a Scottish company who built another 30. A rare classic that should have lasted longer.

Meanwhile in Italy, mid-engined sports

machinery was very much in fashion. Fiat made a bigger Fiat X1/9 in the form of the Lancia Beta Monte Carlo, which was launched in 1975, the ex-125 engine increased to 121 cu.in, and placed behind the driver. Also mid-engined, the Lancia Stratos was built for rallying and won the World Championship in 1974-76; with the Ferrari Dino 246 power-train mounted in a space-frame chassis under Bertone bodywork, some 500 were produced from 1972 to 1974. The Stratos ceded the task of Fiat's rallying flagship to the 131 Fiat-Abarth, but it was a development of the Monte Carlo that was to take over from that in the Eighties.

From Modena, Ferrari further developed the Dino 246GT theme with the 308GT4 in 1974 as a Bertone-bodied 2+2 using a 183 cu.in V-8. The 246GT replacement came with the 308GTB in 1975, followed by GTS (1977) and fuel injection versions in 1980. The final variation came in 1982 with the 4-valve head (QV) versions before the 328 came in 1985. Not to be outdone by Lamborghini and Maserati, Ferrari followed the mid-engined route with the Daytona replacement, the 365GT4/BB. This used a flat-12 with belt-driven camshafts and 387 were built from 1973-76 before the BB512 arrived with a bigger engine.

Lamborghini had produced around 750 Miuras before the Countach arrived in 1973; this now used

the 244 cu.in V-12 mounted longitudinally under another breathtaking Bertone body. In various forms it would last for 16 years until the Diablo arrived in 1990. They also produce the little Lamborghini, the mid-engined Urraco, using a transverse V-8 to allow room for +2 seating; the P250 (152 cu.in) and the P300 (183 cu.in) accounted for 700 cars from 1972-1979.

Maserati's first mid-engined road car was the 1971 Bora, using the regular 298 cu.in V-8 in a pressed steel chassis with bodywork by ItalDesign. It was followed a year later by the outwardly similar Merak; with a 183 cu.in version of the Citroen SM V-6 in the back, there was just enough space for two small rear seats. Like the Khamsin, this featured Citroen power brakes. Although Citroen withdrew from Maserati and De Tomaso took over in 1975, these models would continue until the end of the decade.

The Maserati engine and Citroen gearbox was also seen in the back of the Ligier JS2, a fiberglass-bodied two-seater GT. Former French rugby player Guy Ligier had driven in Formula One but expanded

his construction company to produce road cars.

The 1969 JS1 (named after Jo Schlesser) was a competition coupe with a 109 cu.in Cosworth FVC, but the JS2 which emerged in 1971 initially used a 158 cu.in Ford V-6 coupled to a Citroen SM after gearbox, the following year it had the 158 cu.in SM engine. This then grew to the Merak's 183 cu.in capacity for 1974 by which time Ligier was assembling the SMs for Citroen. Around 300 JS2 were made.

France's main constructor of fiberglass coupes was still Alpine who continued to make the A110 until 1977 using Renault 79 and 97 cu.in engines. They added the A310 to the range in 1971 to create a 2+2 using basically the same chassis and 97 cu.in running gear. The engine was still mounted behind the axle like the Porsche 911. When Renault introduced the R30, the A310 was able to adopt the 164 cu.in V-6 package from 1980 to give the car a performance more suited to its style.

Having taken over Rene Bonnet and produced the Ford-powered M530, Matra formed an association with Chrysler at the end of 1969. In 1973, this resulted in the Matra-Simca Bagheera, a neat little mid-engined fiberglass coupe, powered by an 84 bhp Simca 79 cu.in engine; a notable feature was three seats across the car in a total width of 68 inches. Power rose to 90 bhp when the 88 cu.in Simca engine became available. Peugeot-Citroen took over Chrysler Europe in 1979, so the Bagheera became the 2-seater Talbot Murena using the 97 cu.in Talbot engine, which could produce up to 120 bhp.

In Germany, the only low volume manufacturer was Porsche who introduced the 924 in 1976. Originally an Audi-VW project, the 2+2 924 was powered by a 122 cu.in single cam four-cylinder; the aftermath of the 1973 fuel crisis and a change of VW management in 1975 caused them to cancel the car. Porsche continued with it, developing it through Turbo and Carrera GT into the 1981 944. While the rest of the German coupes were derived from sedans, the exception was to be the mid-engined BMW M1, derived from BMW's 1972 Munich Olympics show car; it finally arrived in 1978, eventually being built by ItalDesign – a separate story.

In Japan Mazda continued their work on the twin-rotor Wankel-powered cars and the 110S coupe (Cosmo) stayed in production until 1972. Wankel engines, increased to a nominal 140 cu.in,

powered the top end of the various model ranges – RX-2 on the Capella 616 (1970), RX-3 on the Grand Familia 808 (1971), RX-4 on the Luce 929 (1972) and RX-5 on the Cosmo 121(1975). But the next classic was the RX-7, or Savanna coupe, which arrived in 1978 with very attractive fast-back lines; the 140 cu.in Wankel produced 130 bhp for Japan but 110-115 bhp for the more emission conscious markets. In 1983, the turbocharged fuel injected version gave 165 bhp and a serious performance increase.

The first RX-7 came to an end in 1985 with nearly half a million cars produced.

The RX-7 was clearly aimed at the Datsun 240Z which was still going well in the early Seventies, but increasing luxury and stifled power made its successors, the 260Z (1974) and 280Z (1975), rather less sporting – there were also 2+2 versions. The 280ZX (1978) was the first major revision with a new body and independent rear suspension but it was still slower than the original 240Z; this was only rectified when a turbocharger option was added in 1981.

And America's sports car? The Corvette's basic body style remained the same throughout the Seventies, but the chrome bumpers disappeared in favor of a soft front end in 1973 and 1975 was the last year for the roadster.

Power figures are a little confusing as the previous claims had been for gross bhp, but these were net figures from 1973; the combination of emission controls and honesty made the contrast even greater. In 1970, the small block 350 gave 300-370 bhp and the 427 had 390 bhp (the 1969 options had included a high compression 430 bhp). Solid valve lifter engines disappeared for 1973 and the 454 was down to 275 bhp. By 1975 there was just the 350 cu.in engine with 165 bhp or 205 bhp with the optional transistorised ignition – half the power of the real Corvettes. That was the story of the Seventies, safety and emission legislation made a big impact in America, but the rest of the world was not far behind in accepting that high performance had become anti-social.

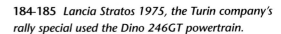

184-185 *Lancia Stratos 1975, the Turin company's rally special used the Dino 246GT powertrain.*

185

Maserati Bora

186-187 *First shown at Turin 1971, the Bora was the star of the show.*

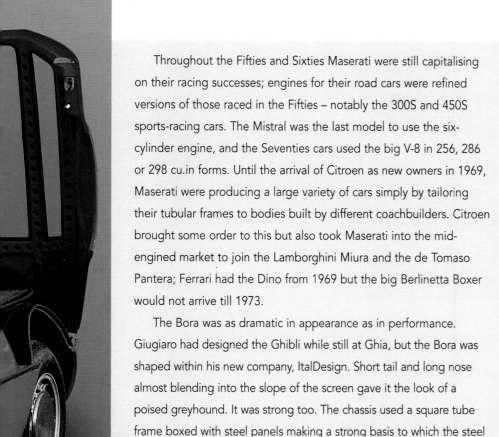

Throughout the Fifties and Sixties Maserati were still capitalising on their racing successes; engines for their road cars were refined versions of those raced in the Fifties – notably the 300S and 450S sports-racing cars. The Mistral was the last model to use the six-cylinder engine, and the Seventies cars used the big V-8 in 256, 286 or 298 cu.in forms. Until the arrival of Citroen as new owners in 1969, Maserati were producing a large variety of cars simply by tailoring their tubular frames to bodies built by different coachbuilders. Citroen brought some order to this but also took Maserati into the mid-engined market to join the Lamborghini Miura and the de Tomaso Pantera; Ferrari had the Dino from 1969 but the big Berlinetta Boxer would not arrive till 1973.

The Bora was as dramatic in appearance as in performance. Giugiaro had designed the Ghibli while still at Ghia, but the Bora was shaped within his new company, ItalDesign. Short tail and long nose almost blending into the slope of the screen gave it the look of a poised greyhound. It was strong too. The chassis used a square tube frame boxed with steel panels making a strong basis to which the steel body shell was welded – a handmade monocoque. Separate sub-frames carried front suspension and power train plus rear wishbone suspension.

The engine was the all-aluminium 286 cu.in V-8 with four downdraft Weber carburetors developing 310 bhp. This was mated to a 5-speed transaxle from ZF, who also supplied the rack and pinion steering. A Citroen touch came with a hydraulic pressure accumulators to power the pop-up headlights, pedal box adjustment, seat vertical movement and the brakes – the least appropriate feature of such a muscle car. There was more luggage space than in most mid-engined cars, because the spare wheel was carried in a cradle above the gearbox, allowing the front compartment to take a number of cases.

It was reasonably quiet too, as the vertical rear window is double-glazed, but very firm suspension transmitted a lot of road noise on coarse surfaces. Some details let it down though; optional air conditioning was poor, headlights did not match the performance, the engine compartment got covered in road dirt and the fuel consumption was heavy.

But the car was designed for performance and it had plenty. It would reach 60 mph in 6.5 seconds, 100 mph in under 15 seconds and go on to a maximum speed around 160 mph. It was well received in the market place and nearly 500 would leave the Modena factory over the next seven years, the later ones with 298 cu.in engines.

Despite the change of Maserati ownership from Citroen to de Tomaso in 1975, the Bora and its SM-powered Merak equivalent continued through till 1978 and 1979 respectively. They have been underrated classics.

TECHNICAL DESCRIPTION OF THE MASERATI BORA

YEARS OF PRODUCTION	1971-1978
MODELS	COUPE 2-SEATER
ENGINE	MID-MOUNTED V-8
BORE X STROKE, CAPACITY	3.6 x 3.3 INCHES, 287 CU.IN
VALVEGEAR	FOUR OVERHEAD CAMSHAFTS
FUEL SYSTEM	4 WEBER TWIN-CHOKE CARBURETORS
POWER	310 BHP AT 6000 RPM
TRANSMISSION	5-SPEED
BODY/CHASSIS	STEEL TUBE FRAME, STEEL BODY
SUSPENSION	FRONT, WISHBONES AND COIL SPRINGS
	REAR, WISHBONES AND COIL SPRINGS
TIRES/WHEELS	215/70 x 15 ON 7.5 IN. ALLOY WHEELS
WHEELBASE, TRACK (F), TRACK(R)	102.4 x 58 x 53 INCHES
LENGTH, WIDTH, HEIGHT	171 x 69.6 x 44.5 INCHES
MAX SPEED	160 MPH
WHERE BUILT	MODENA, ITALY

Lamborghini Countach

Ferruccio Lamborghini was born under the sign of Taurus, the bull in the badge. Miura was a breed of fighting bulls; Countach is what the Piedmontese say when a beautiful woman slinks into view – it was what Bertone said when he first saw Marcello Gandini's design in the flesh. Striking though the Countach is to look at, it had much more than just style when the car was first shown at the 1971 Geneva Show. The Miura was still in production, but as the Countach was expected to be on sale a year later, the Miura was phased out over that period. Unfortunately it took another three years to develop, by which time Automobili Ferruccio Lamborghini had been sold to Swiss partners to enable Lamborghini to return to tractors. It was to go into liquidation and be sold twice again before Countach production finished in 1990; Chrysler took over in 1987.

Countach design started with a clean sheet of paper, just retaining the basic Miura principles of a mid-engined supercar. The Miura's ingenious layout had the V-12 mounted transversely with

TECHNICAL DESCRIPTION OF THE LAMBORGHINI COUNTACH LP400	
YEARS OF PRODUCTION	1974-1978
MODELS	COUPE 2-SEATER
ENGINE	MID-MOUNTED V-12
BORE X STROKE, CAPACITY	3.2 x 2.4 INCHES, 239 CU.IN
VALVEGEAR	FOUR OVERHEAD CAMSHAFTS
FUEL SYSTEM	SIX WEBER TWIN-CHOKE CARBURETORS
POWER	375 BHP AT 8000 RPM
TRANSMISSION	5-SPEED
BODY/CHASSIS	STEEL TUBE FRAME, ALUMINIUM BODY
SUSPENSION	FRONT, WISHBONES AND COIL SPRINGS
	REAR, WISHBONES AND COIL SPRINGS
TIRES/WHEELS	FRONT, 205/70 x 14 ON 7.5 IN. ALLOYS
	REAR, 215/70 x 14 ON 9.5 IN. ALLOYS
WHEELBASE, TRACK (F), TRACK(R)	96.5 x 59.1 x 59.8 INCHES
LENGTH, WIDTH, HEIGHT	163 x 74.4 x 42.1 INCHES
MAX SPEED	180 MPH
WHERE BUILT	BOLOGNA, ITALY

188-189 *First of the line, this first prototype was shown at Geneva 1971 before development added ducts and scoops; it is the pure shape that Gandini designed.*

190-191 *Last of the line, the 1989 Countach S Anniversary celebrated 25 years of the company's vehicle production. Body changes made it the sleekest of all.*

the gearbox behind; the Countach mounted the same engine fore and aft with the gearbox in front, putting the lever very close to the driver. From drop gears a drive-shaft passed through the sump to a crown wheel and pinion within the sump casting; while this raised the overall center of gravity, there were other benefits. The engine for the prototype LP500 had been stretched to 305 cu.in but the production LP400 retained the Miura's 244 cu.in V-12 with 375 bhp.

The Countach was conceived as a limited run supercar to promote Lamborghini technology, so the prototype was built in a labour-intensive fashion with a space-frame and a steel body welded to it adding strength. The reception at Geneva showed that there would be great demand, so the space-frame was strengthened to carry an unstressed aluminium body.

Following GT40 thinking, the Miura had used a sheet steel tub but this was not as stiff as it could have been and it was liable to corrosion. The Countach frame, ideal for low volume, used a large number of steel tubes over the full length of the chassis.

While the beetle-wing doors were retained for production, the original purity of Gandini's lines was lost during development. Aerodynamic tests deepened the nose and scoops and NACA ducts for the rear mounted radiators replaced the grilles behind the doors. Original tire testing had been with low profile Pirelli tires, but these were slow to get into production and the LP400 used 70% profile Michelins. When the low and wide P7 became available, the clean

side of the car was broken by wheel-arch eyebrows and the front ones were blended into an air dam; with revised suspension, the P400S came out in 1978, still with the same power.

The Countach finally received its 305 cu.in engine in 1982; although this was actually a 289 cu.in, the car was labelled LP500S. The increase had been necessary to restore the power lost through emission equipment. The first true power increase came in 1985 with 455 bhp for the LP5000S QV; new four-valve cylinder heads put the carburetors into the center of the vee and the engine was increased to 315 cu.in.

The American version with catalysts and fuel injection gave 425 bhp. Maximum speed had increased from around 180 mph to nearer 190 mph. Over the 4 years of the LP400 only 150 Countach were produced, with 466 of the LP400S from 1978-82. The LP500S saw 323, but the LP5000S QV was the most long-lived and the most popular with 610 produced. In 1989 the company brought out the Anniversary model to celebrate 25 years of car production.

A 25 year badge was mounted on the rear panel. Underneath, it was still the 5000S QV but various changes had been made to the bodywork by Lamborghini. Although the original designer Gandini had no input, the restyling was very successful. It continued in production for one more year.

Over its 16 years, the Countach remained the iconic supercar.

TECHNICAL DESCRIPTION OF THE LAMBORGHINI COUNTACH LP500S QV	
YEARS OF PRODUCTION	1985-1990
MODELS	COUPE 2-SEATER
ENGINE	MID-MOUNTED V-12
BORE X STROKE, CAPACITY	3.3 X 2.9 INCHES, 315 CU.IN
VALVEGEAR	FOUR OVERHEAD CAMSHAFTS
FUEL SYSTEM	SIX WEBER TWIN-CHOKE CARBURETORS
POWER	455 BHP AT 7000 RPM
TRANSMISSION	5-SPEED
BODY/CHASSIS	STEEL TUBE FRAME, ALUMINIUM BODY
SUSPENSION	FRONT, WISHBONES AND COIL SPRINGS
	REAR, WISHBONES AND COIL SPRINGS
TIRES/WHEELS	FRONT, 225/50 X 15 ON 8 IN. ALLOYS
	REAR, 345/35 X 15 ON 12 IN. ALLOYS
WHEELBASE, TRACK (F), TRACK(R)	96.5 X 60.5 X 63.2 INCHES
LENGTH, WIDTH, HEIGHT	163 X 78.1 X 42.1 INCHES
MAX SPEED	191 MPH
WHERE BUILT	BOLOGNA, ITALY

NB LP5000S FOR THE AMERICAN MARKET USED WEBER FUEL INJECTION GIVING 426 BHP

De Tomaso Pantera

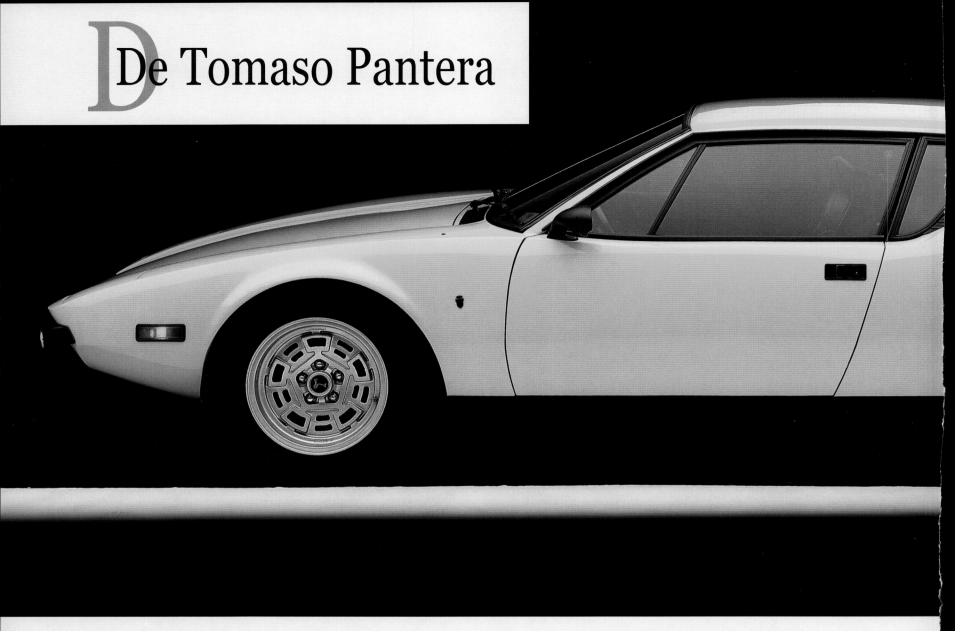

When the production Ford GT40 won Le Mans in 1968 and 1969 and Ford then launched the mid-engined Ford-powered de Tomaso Pantera in early 1970, it seemed like there was a link; it was only a very indirect one. Ford had tried to buy Ferrari in the early Sixties as they wanted an Italian sports car maker to take them into racing and production of GT cars. When the bid failed, Ford bought into Eric Broadley's Lola GT project and the Ford GT40 was born in 1964.

However Ford still wanted an Italian involvement and eventually signed an agreement with Alejandro de Tomaso in September 1969 for technical cooperation between Ford of America, Ghia and de Tomaso who would build concept cars and niche vehicles for Ford. The first of these would be the Pantera, to be built at the rate of 5000 a year with de Tomaso retaining the right to non-American sales. If de Tomaso had been able to build as many cars as planned, and if they had been built as well as Ford expected, the Le Mans successes would have been used to promote sales through Ford's Lincoln Mercury dealers. As it was, the Pantera was not fully developed when it was put on the market and the 1973 oil crisis severely restricted demand.

De Tomaso had joined the ranks of Italian sports car builders back in 1963. The first offering was the mid-engined Vallelunga of which 180 were built; this used a backbone chassis to which was bolted a 97 cu.in Ford Cortina engine which took all the rear suspension loads through arms on the transaxle bell-housing. The theme was extended at the

1965 Turin Show with the display of a sports-racing car using a bigger backbone which carried a 271 bhp Ford Mustang engine; although this was never raced, it formed the basis of the de Tomaso Mangusta for which Giugiaro drew up the body while he was working at Ghia. Production started in 1967 with Ghia building the bodies in Turin and de Tomaso fitting the power train in Modena. Although Ghia had the contract to build the Giugiaro-designed Maserati Ghibli, they were in financial trouble and de Tomaso acquired the company.

Meanwhile, Ford's search for an Italian supercar led them to Ghia, via the Ghibli, and came to look at the Mangusta in 1969, at which time Tom Tjaarda had just completed a scale model of a new Ford-powered sports car. Tom had left Ghia in 1961 but returned as Head of Styling in 1969. Ford didn't like the Mangusta engineering but thought more highly of the Tjaarda car.

Dallara was poached from Lamborghini to redesign the chassis which followed contemporary racing practice with a sheet steel monocoque center section with strong sills; Ford's latest 351 cu.in V-8 was attached to the rear and mated to a ZF transaxle. This acted as a sub-frame under the steel body. The result was a reasonably priced supercar which performed very well. As Ghia didn't have enough space to build the bodies in the required quantity, de Tomaso acquired the nearby Vignale factory in late 1969. Within a year, Ford owned 84% of de Tomaso's Ghia/Vignale/Pantera operation.

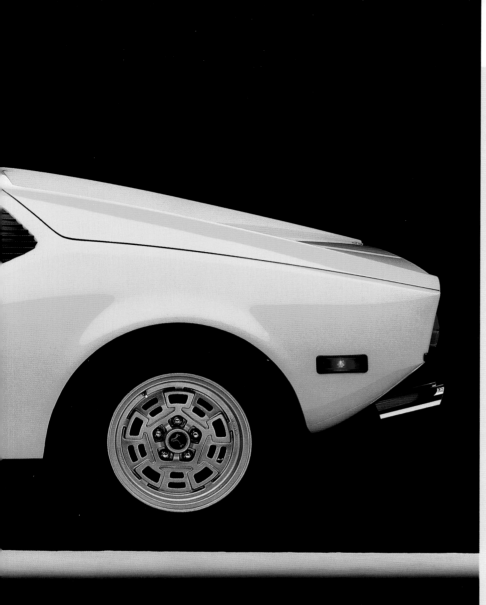

TECHNICAL DESCRIPTION OF THE DE TOMASO PANTERA

YEARS OF PRODUCTION	1970-1974
MODELS	2-SEATER COUPE
ENGINE	MID-MOUNTED V-8
BORE X STROKE, CAPACITY	3.9 x 3.4 INCHES, 351 CU.IN
VALVEGEAR	PUSHROD OVERHEAD VALVES
FUEL SYSTEM	AUTOLITE 4-BARREL CARBURETOR
POWER	330 BHP AT 5400 RPM
TRANSMISSION	ZF 5-SPEED
BODY/CHASSIS	UNITARY STEEL CHASSIS AND BODY
SUSPENSION	FRONT, WISHBONES AND COIL SPRINGS
	REAR, WISHBONES AND COIL SPRINGS
TIRES/WHEELS	185/70 & 215/70 x 15
	ON ALLOY WHEELS
WHEELBASE, TRACK (F), TRACK(R)	106 x 57.5 x 57 INCHES
LENGTH, WIDTH, HEIGHT	167.5 x 71 x 43.5 INCHES
MAX SPEED	155 MPH
WHERE BUILT	MODENA, ITALY

192-193 *The Pantera was sold through Lioncoln-Mercury dealerships in the USA until 1974 when Ford gave the project back to de Tomaso, who continued to produce variations on the same theme until 1990.*

In the first year of production, nearly 300 Panteras were sold in Europe. However Ford had to carry out further development before American approval came 1971. Sales were slower than anticipated, with 1550 in 1972 and 2030 in 1973; and then came the energy crisis. With the prospect of stricter emission laws in 1975, Ford stopped importing the Pantera and closed the Vignale plant in late 1974. De Tomaso had released his minority shareholding to Ford in early 1973 but retained the European sales rights for the Pantera.

European sales had dropped from 508 in 1973 to 78 due to the energy crisis. When Ford closed the Vignale plant de Tomaso collected the work in progress and continued to make the Pantera in Modena for the next 20 years with occasional refinements as new engines or new tires came in.

In 1990, the bodywork was restyled by Gandini and the engine had changed to the Ford 302 cu.in V-8 using fuel injection to give 305 bhp. It was as fast as the original. Although the Pantera never achieved the appeal of a Ferrari or Lamborghini, it remains a very affordable supercar.

Ferrari 308

The Fiat and Ferrari Dinos had stemmed from the desire of Ferrari to run a V-6 engine in 1967 Formula 2 racing. Fiat built some 4830 122 cu.in Dinos from 1966 to 1969 with orders for the Bertone-bodied Fiat Dino Coupe 2+2 being three times greater than those for the Pininfarina-bodied Fiat Dino Spider. Ferrari's own Dino 206GT finally emerged for 1969; at the end of that year Fiat brought out the heavily revised Dino 2.4, and the Ferrari Dino became the 246GT. The same year had seen Ferrari move under Fiat control, one consequence of which was that production of the Fiat Dino 2.4 was moved to an extension of the Ferrari factory.

By then, the V-6 was coming to the end of its days with emission controls becoming tighter, so the Fiat Dinos were scheduled to finish at the beginning of 1973, leaving vacant production space at Maranello. It was logical to combine these events with the desire to pitch a Dino 2+2 against the Porsche 911 as well as the Lamborghini Urraco P250 from the other side of Modena – both with rear seat accommodation; accordingly Ferrari went to Bertone for the new 308GT4. It is probable that Fiat had some influence over this, as the cessation of the Fiat Dino coupe would leave a hole in Bertone's production line; Bertone had also been let down by the failure of the Lamborghini Urraco to reach its planned production levels.

Ferrari needed a more impressive engine than the aged V-6 for the small range, and the heavier body of a 2+2 certainly required more power. Scaling a V-8 from the 268 cu.in V-12 was exactly what Lamborghini should have done for the Urraco; with a change in vee-angle, Ferrari's 90-degree 183 cu.in V-8 had the same bore and stroke dimensions as the 365GT engines and shared many components. The only design change was to adopt the toothed belt drive for the four camshafts as the flat-12 engine was already using. With four downdraft Weber carburetors it produced 250 bhp. Like the Dino 246, the engine was mounted transversely with the gearbox behind it. Italian taxation was responsible for the 208GT4 with 170 bhp.

The chassis followed the Dino principles with a space frame which was stretched by 8.2 inches and widened. Bertone's design was neat and functional and was actually very similar to the Urraco in its proportions, its glazing and the details of the two separate rear deck openings for engine and luggage space.

It has been an underrated car which is really very practical and has most of the feel of a proper sporting Ferrari. Over 3000 308GT4 were made, and some 800 208GT4, before they were replaced by the Pininfarina Mondial in 1980.They were finally allowed to be called Ferrari in 1978.

The next logical step was to install the 308 engine into a new version of the Dino 246GT. In effect this used the wide-track 308GT4 chassis

shortened to the same length as the 246GT. The new 308GTB arrived in 1975 using the GT4 engine fitted with dry sump lubrication for European cars. Pininfarina effected a delightful marriage of the shapes of the previous Dino and the new Berlinetta Boxer. The latter used fiberglass bodywork below its belt line, but the 308GTB used this material for the complete bodyshell until mid-1977 when it was replaced with steel. The Targa-top Spider 308GTS followed in 1977, with all markets using the wet sump engine. Again a 122 cu.in version was available for the Italian market. Demands for increasing emission control brought a change to fuel injection across the Ferrari range, denoted by 308GTBi and 308GTSi in 1980; this lost some power to 214 bhp (205 bhp for the USA), but this was largely recovered by the 1982 adoption of 4-valve heads to give 240 bhp with quattrovalvole written on the rear panels. At this point the Italian version had a turbocharger added to give 220 bhp.

The arrival of fuel injection had also seen the changeover from the GT4 to a new Pininfarina-designed Mondial 8. To give more space for rear passengers the wheelbase was lengthened by 3.9 inches and the roofline raised 3.1 inches. The shape retained some of the GT4 features but the more curved waistline and the pronounced air dam improved the appearance. This also adopted four valve heads in 1982, and in 1984 came the Mondial cabriolet, still with rear seat space. The following year the 308 engine was increased to 195 cu.in for the 328 range.

TECHNICAL DESCRIPTION OF THE FERRARI 308GTB

YEARS OF PRODUCTION	1975-1980
MODELS	COUPE 2-SEATER
ENGINE	MID-MOUNTED V-8
BORE X STROKE, CAPACITY	3.1 X 2.7 INCHES, 180 CU.IN
VALVEGEAR	FOUR OVERHEAD CAMSHAFTS
FUEL SYSTEM	FOUR WEBER CARBURETORS
POWER	255 BHP AT 7600 RPM
TRANSMISSION	5-SPEED
BODY/CHASSIS	STEEL TUBE FRAME, STEEL BODY
SUSPENSION	FRONT, WISHBONES AND COIL SPRINGS
	REAR, WISHBONES AND COIL SPRINGS
TIRES/WHEELS	205/70 X 14 ON 6.5 IN. ALLOY WHEELS
WHEELBASE, TRACK (F), TRACK(R)	92.1 X 57.5 X 57.5 INCHES
LENGTH, WIDTH, HEIGHT	167 X 68 X 44 INCHES
MAX SPEED	154 MPH
WHERE BUILT	MARANELLO, ITALY

NB FOR THE 308, FUEL INJECTION WAS INTRODUCED IN 1980 AND 4-VALVE HEADS IN 1982

194-195 *The 308 used a wider version of the Dino 246GT chassis with an even more elegant shape. Early 308GTB bodies were in fiberglass.*

Porsche 911 Turbo

When the Porsche 911 Turbo was unveiled at the 1974 Paris Show, it started a new trend of spectacularly powerful road cars. At that time the 911's flat-6 air-cooled engine had been increased to 164 cu.in with the standard car producing 150 bhp, the 911S 175 bhp and the highly tuned Carrera RS had 210 bhp. The Turbo had a 183 cu.in engine and 260 bhp but was just as tractable as the standard car. It proved that turbocharging was a very effective way of increasing performance without having a big engine. Although BMW were the first manufacturer to sell a turbocharged production car with the 1973 2002, they only made 1672 of them as a basis for competition versions . Porsche gave credibility to the cult-following that was to keep growing long after BMW had dropped the idea.

Porsche have always promoted their name through racing, particularly by using their production cars in endurance races and rallies. While the 911 was designed as a road car and then raced and rallied in its various forms, the Porsche Turbo 930 was introduced because the factory wanted to use it and its derivatives for racing. Production was necessary if the model was to take part in the new GT championship which was scheduled to start in 1976.

Porsche customers had already monopolised the existing championship with the 164 cu.in Carrera RSR. By 1973 they had worked out the turbo way ahead.

When the 1969-72 305 cu.in World Sports Car Championship came to an end, Porsche took the successful 917 across the Atlantic to the Can-Am races where rules were less restrictive; they used open versions of the 917 with the 274 or 305 cu.in flat-12 engines of the earlier cars. Competing against the McLarens with big 488 cu.in Chevrolet engines, Porsche engineers closed the power gap by turbocharging the existing engines rather than make bigger ones; for the 917-30, the engine was increases to 329 cu.in and turbocharged to produce 1100 bhp; they won the Can-Am championship in 1973.

Having used the 183 cu.in block in a prototype RSR to win the Targa Florio and come 4th at Le Mans in 1973, the next year's project was to use a turbocharged version running against the 183 cu.in sports prototypes, two-seater Grand Prix cars. Because it was very reliable, the Carrera Turbo finished in the top six in six races, including second at Le Mans. The car thus had a strong racing pedigree by the time it was launched in October that year.

The new GT racing rules were for Group 3 (1000-off road cars), Group 4 (400-off) and Group 5 (Groups 3 and 4 cars with further modifications). By the end of 1975, the necessary 400 of the 930 Turbo road car had been built and Porsche were ready to start the season with the 930 brought up to 934 and 935 racing specifications. Both won their championships and the 934 was equally unbeatable in American racing series.

The racing versions proved that the concept was reliable, despite the engines being developed to over 500 bhp; with only 260 bhp in road trim, the 911 Turbo was going to be as long-lasting as any other Porsche. It still looked like a 911 from the side, but it needed much wider wheel arches to accommodate wider tires, and a big rear wing improved the stability at high speed.

But despite all that power it was very tractable, with so much torque that Porsche only gave it four speeds. Inside, it was more comfortably equipped than any 911.

Porsche rationalized their range for 1978 to produce just two basic models, the 911SC with the 183 cu.in engine, and the Turbo with an increase to 201 cu.in and 300 bhp in European trim, or 280 bhp for America. The car stayed in more or less this form throughout the Eighties, although a Targa-top version was added in 1988. The model came to an end in 1989, but this was only to allow the introduction of the new Carrera 2 and Carrera 4 models.

By 1990, the Turbo was back still with a 201 cu.in engine but with further modifications, the power was raised to 320 bhp. With, finally, a five-speed gearbox it would accelerate even faster, reaching 60 mph in just 4.7 seconds. The original 1975 Turbo took 6.1 seconds. All the 911 designs have been classics, but the Turbo has been just a little more so.

TECHNICAL DESCRIPTION OF THE PORSCHE 911 TURBO 3.0

YEARS OF PRODUCTION	1975-1977
MODELS	COUPE 2 + 2
ENGINE	REAR-MOUNTED FLAT 6
BORE X STROKE, CAPACITY	3.7 X 2.7 INCHES, 182 CU.IN
VALVEGEAR	TWO OVERHEAD CAMSHAFTS
FUEL SYSTEM	BOSCH FUEL INJECTION AND
	TURBOCHARGER
POWER	260 BHP AT 5500 RPM
TRANSMISSION	4-SPEED
BODY/CHASSIS	STEEL MONOCOQUE
SUSPENSION	FRONT, MACPHERSON STRUTS, COILS
	REAR, TRAILING ARMS, TORSION BARS
TIRES/WHEELS	FRONT, 205/50 X 15 ON 7 IN. ALLOY
	WHEELS REAR, 225/50 X 15 ON 8 IN.
	ALLOY WHEELS
WHEELBASE, TRACK (F), TRACK(R)	89.4 X 56.3 X 59.1 INCHES
LENGTH, WIDTH, HEIGHT	168.9 X 69.7 X 51.2 INCHES
MAX SPEED	155 MPH
WHERE BUILT	STUTTGART, GERMANY

196-197 *Although originally announced as the PorscheTurbo, the design type number for this 911 was actually 930.*

TVR 3000

Through the early post-war years, Britain was home to a large number of special builders, people who created sporting cars around the running gear or even complete chassis of older cars. Many perished, Lotus and TVR survived. After an early series of cars using their own chassis and Austin A40 parts under proprietary fiberglass body shells, TVR built their own tubular backbone chassis and fiberglass body from 1958; they used Volkswagen front suspension with a choice of engines of which the Coventry Climax was most popular. Having produced around 500 of these Grantura Mk. I, II and IIA, the Blackpool-based company moved on to the Mk.III in 1962 with a new chassis carrying all-round wishbone suspension and the MGA engine.

The 1800S, with the MGB engine, came in 1964. Meanwhile, the company sold the Griffith in America from 1963-1965 using a 286 cu.in Ford V-8; this became the Tuscan V-8 from 1967-1970. Ford engines powered the other models too, the 183 cu.in Tuscan V-6 and the Vixen with the Cortina GT unit. Emission regulations dictated a change from the Ford V-6 to the Triumph 2500 twin carburetor engine for the American market in 1971.

The early Sixties saw TVR go through several changes of ownership but from 1966 this had stabilised under the Lilley family. They had introduced the Tuscans and Vixens including lengthening the very short wheelbase in 1968; but it was not until 1970 that they had sufficient confidence to invest in the next generation of cars and bigger premises in which to build them. By the time the new M-series came in late 1971, some 1800 of the previous chassis had been built over nine years.

The new chassis followed the TVR tubular frame principles but was stronger and easier to make. The new body had a longer nose which allowed the spare wheel to be mounted on top of the sloping radiator instead of taking up internal luggage space. The sharply cut-off Manx tail, introduced in 1964, gave way to a more slender version. All the glass was carried over from the previous model. By the time the changeover had taken effect, TVR produced the 1600M, 2500M and 3000M from late 1972. The 2500M became the export model as the Triumph TR6 had been certified for America; 950 were sold from 1972-77, by which time TVR had certified the 3000M.

In the seven years of the M-series models, 2480 were built from 1972-79, more than had been built in the previous 14 years. TVR were beginning to appeal to the wider market. Although the 1600M was no faster than the Sixties cars, the 3000M was capable of nearly 125 mph and could reach 60 mph in 7.5 seconds. There was little advantage in having the slower car so the 1600M was dropped in 1977; however some wanted even more performance.

Developing 128 bhp at 4750 rpm, the Ford Essex V-6 was not a very sporting engine in the Sixties, but it had been considerably improved (138 bhp at 5000 rpm) by the time the 3000M came along. The revised engine was also better able to withstand more power and Broadspeed developed a suitable turbocharger installation; installed in a TVR, this developed 230 bhp at 5500 rpm – enough to lift the performance to 140 mph and reduce the 0-60 mph time to 5.8 seconds. The Turbo option was announced at the 1975 London Motor show.

Getting luggage into a TVR was always difficult as there was no direct access to the space behind the seats. For those who wanted to travel, this was finally corrected in 1976 with the hatchback Taimar, which soon outsold the outwardly identical 3000M. The only model missing from the line-up was a convertible. This finally came in 1978 with the body considerably modified. The door tops were changed to take removable sliding glass side-screens, the tail was altered to provide a lockable trunk, and the windscreen was changed to take the quick-action soft-top. It was an instant success and 270 were built in the two years before the M-series changed over to the new Tasmin. The Turbo option was offered on all models but it was expensive and only 63 were sold. While the 3000M was the biggest seller with 654 produced, Taimar and Convertible would have surpassed it given more time.

TECHNICAL DESCRIPTION OF THE TVR 3000

YEARS OF PRODUCTION	1972-1979
MODELS	COUPE 2-SEATER
ENGINE	FRONT-MOUNTED V-6
BORE X STROKE, CAPACITY	3.6 X 2.8 INCHES, 182 CU.IN
VALVEGEAR	PUSHROD OVERHEAD VALVES
FUEL SYSTEM	ONE TWIN-CHOKE WEBER CARBURETOR
POWER	138 BHP AT 5000 RPM
TRANSMISSION	FORD 4-SPEED
BODY/CHASSIS	STEEL TUBE FRAME, FIBERGLASS BODY
SUSPENSION	FRONT, WISHBONES AND COIL SPRINGS
	REAR, WISHBONES AND COIL SPRINGS
TIRES/WHEELS	185 X 14 ON 6 IN. ALLOY WHEELS
WHEELBASE, TRACK (F), TRACK(R)	90 X 54 X 54 INCHES
LENGTH, WIDTH, HEIGHT	134 X 64 X 47 INCHES
MAX SPEED	121 MPH
WHERE BUILT	BLACKPOOL, ENGLAND

198-199 *This TVR Convertible (sometimes 3000S) was only in production from 1978-1979.*

Aston Martin Lagonda

Long before it joined forces with Aston Martin, Lagonda had established its own history. Founded in 1905, some 15 years before Aston Martin started to make cars, Lagonda made fast 4-seater tourers and, from the early Thirties, comfortable sedans. Aston Martin generally produced sports cars. When David Brown merged the two in 1947, it was Lagonda's Bentley-designed engine that set Aston Martin on its GT path. In the Fifties Lagondas retained their own comfortable sedan identity, sharing their engine, until 1957.

Making a 4-door Aston Martin sounds a simple procedure in a low volume manufacturing environment, but it was another four years before the first stretched Aston Martin came out as the Lagonda Rapide. It differed from the DB4 in having the 244 cu.in engine that would be used in the DB5, it had a de Dion rear axle and the body, also designed by Touring, was a totally different style. However, it had such a disruptive effect on the DB4 production line that only 55 were built over its three year life. David Brown built a single 4-door DBS V-8 in 1969 but it was left to new owners to return to the project in 1974; although this was a relatively simple stretch, the changing fortunes of the company were against it.

New owners came in 1975 after just seven of this Aston Martin Lagonda had been built.

The new management started on the Lagonda straight away with the brief that a 2-door version would be the next Aston Martin.

Actually Aston designer William Towns drew the 2-door car first, but the owners wanted to start with the 4-door version. Just eight months later, the prototype was on display at the 1976 Earls Court show. It was a remarkable piece of design; long and slender with razor-edge styling, it caught the imagination of luxury car buyers worldwide. It had the Aston Martin virtues of the 323 cu.in V-8 and excellent roadholding, coupled with 4-door 4-seat luxury; it also had electronic switchgear and digital instrumentation, the two areas that would prove major problems throughout the car's life, despite fundamental changes.

However the masterpiece of styling proved less than ideal when it came to fitting everything inside. Aston's talented engineers achieved the task but development took rather longer than expected and it was mid-1978 before the first car was handed over, only for the computer to fail at the public ceremony. Following an electronic redesign, new cars finally reached customers in early 1979, just in time for the fuel crisis. However, with energetic salesmanship, the Lagondas found ready buyers in the Middle East which did much to keep the company going over a difficult period.

October 1984 saw the switchgear improved and the instrumentation replaced by three TV tubes, computer driven but rather ahead of their time in an automotive environment. They were replaced with vacuum fluorescent screens in 1987, finally successful. Fuel injection had replaced the four Weber carburetors in early 1986 to increase the power for European markets to 300 bhp.

The only major external change came in 1987. In response to safety legislation which declared that its razor edge styling was too sharp for errant pedestrians, William Towns rounded the edges of his original design, removing also the belt-line crease, and continuing the sill panels below the doors.

With six exposed lights across the front, rather than the pop-up type, the car became somewhat easier to make; it lost its slender grace but it was still a fine-looking car.

At the end of 1987, new owners Ford moved in as the Virage was about to replace the long-running Aston Martin V8; built on a shortened Lagonda chassis this was the final stage of the 1976 plans. Making way for the new Aston, the last Towns Lagonda emerged in 1990, after just 645 had been built over an 11-year period. They were grand cars but never achieved the same acclaim as the Aston Martins. A few bespoke Lagondas have subsequently emerged from the Aston Martin service department as 4-door and estate versions of the Virage and its successor.

200-201 *An early production car, this 1979 Lagonda shows the sharp lines of William Towns' creation.*

TECHNICAL DESCRIPTION OF THE ASTON MARTIN LAGONDA	
YEARS OF PRODUCTION	1978-1985
MODELS	SEDAN 4-SEATER
ENGINE	FRONT-MOUNTED V-8
BORE X STROKE, CAPACITY	3.9 X 3.3 INCHES, 325 CU.IN
VALVEGEAR	FOUR OVERHEAD CAMSHAFTS
FUEL SYSTEM	FOUR TWIN-CHOKE WEBER CARBURETORS
POWER	260 BHP AT 5500 RPM
TRANSMISSION	CHRYSLER 3-SPEED AUTOMATIC
BODY/CHASSIS	STEEL MONOCOQUE, ALUMINIUM PANELS
SUSPENSION	FRONT, WISHBONES AND COIL SPRINGS
	REAR, DE DION AXLE AND COIL SPRINGS
TIRES/WHEELS	235/70 X 15 ON 6 IN. ALLOY WHEELS
WHEELBASE, TRACK (F), TRACK(R)	115 X 59 X 59 INCHES
LENGTH, WIDTH, HEIGHT	208 X 71.5 X 51.2 INCHES
MAX SPEED	140 MPH
WHERE BUILT	NEWPORT PAGNELL, ENGLAND

BMW M1

The M1 is unique in BMW history as the only car which the company built specifically for racing. BMW had long had a sporting reputation but this had been built on touring cars, tuned for competition, or the success of their engines in racing machinery built by others – including such as the McLaren F1. The M1 was planned to take on Porsche in the long distance sports car races. It used the production six-cylinder engine increased to 213 cu.in; equipped with 4-valve heads and fuel injection this gave 277 bhp at 6500 rpm for the road. This was mated to a ZF transaxle and fitted in a space-frame chassis for which the fiberglass bodywork had been designed by Giugiaro.

Although Giugiaro had drawn up the M1's final shape, it was based on the Turbo concept car that BMW presented for the Munich Olympics in 1972; designed by BMW's Paul Bracq, this 'experimental safety vehicle' had side impact bars in its gull-wing doors and soft end panels mounted on rams among many safety features, but it was the mid-engined layout that was of particular interest. The familiar four-cylinder 122 cu.in was mounted transversely and fitted with a turbo-charger to give around 200 bhp; it was this engine, in 170 bhp form, that was fitted to the 2002 turbo the following year. The shape also provided styling cues for the M1; the black belt-line and the low slender nose were features that Giugiaro would adopt. The two prototypes were used to assess mid-engined handling advantages, useful knowledge for the new BMW Motorsport division which was founded in 1973; it was from this department that all the M-series cars would come – the M635CSi used the M1's engine.

International sports car racing in the late Seventies was based on production GT cars. For Appendix J Group 3 you had to make 1000 a year, Group 4 demanded 400 over two years, Group 5 was for cars of Groups 1-4 so heavily modified that they only had to retain the basic shape of the car and the standard engine block. Some races, notably Le Mans, had a class for Group 6 which was for full racing two-seaters with restrictions on the different types of engine – race, turbocharged race, stock-block. Initially BMW had built some turbocharged 3.0CSLs for Group 5 and nearly beat the Porsche 935 in the 1976 Manufacturers Championship.

However, the 3.0CSL was really too old for this form of racing, but BMW continued to use it in Group 2 events, winning the European Touring Championship for Makes and Drivers from 1975-1979. They were waiting for the M1. In Group 4 tune this could develop 470 bhp, so it had a theoretical chance against the Porsche 934, and the mid-engined layout gave it potentially better roadholding. And turbocharged versions with up to 850 bhp could challenge for Group 5 victory.

TECHNICAL DESCRIPTION OF THE BMW M1	
YEARS OF PRODUCTION	1978-1981
MODELS	COUPE 2-SEATER
ENGINE	MID-MOUNTED IN-LINE SIX
BORE X STROKE, CAPACITY	3.6 x 3.3 INCHES, 210 CU.IN
VALVEGEAR	TWO OVERHEAD CAMSHAFTS
FUEL SYSTEM	BOSCH FUEL INJECTION
POWER	277 BHP AT 6500 RPM
TRANSMISSION	ZF 5-SPEED
BODY/CHASSIS	STEEL TUBE FRAME, FIBERGLASS BODY
SUSPENSION	FRONT, WISHBONES AND COIL SPRINGS
	REAR, WISHBONES AND COIL SPRINGS
TIRES/WHEELS	FRONT, 205/55 x 16 ON 7 IN. ALLOYS
	REAR, 225/50 x 16 ON 8 IN. ALLOYS
WHEELBASE, TRACK (F), TRACK(R)	100.8 x 61 x 62 INCHES
LENGTH, WIDTH, HEIGHT	172 x 72 x 45 INCHES
MAX SPEED	160MPH
WHERE BUILT	MUNICH, GERMANY

202-203 **The delay in the start of production stopped the M1 challenging the Porsches in GT races.**

Having decided to build the M1 in late 1976, BMW contracted Lamborghini to develop and produce it, as low volume work was better suited to the Italian company who were looking for outside work. After much useful work in 1977, Lamborghini had financial problems and couldn't build the cars.

Production finally started after a year's delay with Giugiaro's ItalDesign company sub-contracting manufacture of the tubular chassis and fiberglass bodywork, joining the two and trimming the interior. Baur of Stuttgart then installed the mechanical components and completed the trim.

So it wasn't until 1980 that the required 400 were built, by which

time the racing rules were set to change for 1982; these no longer suited the M1 which was too heavy for the new formula.

Meanwhile BMW had launched the M1 at the 1978 Paris Show and arranged the Procar series for 1979; Group 4 M1s had their own races at Grands Prix. It certainly gave the M1 instant publicity and justified 50 or so racing versions being built. They had some success in other races, but the loss of those two years meant that the M1 never had the chance to tackle the Porsches seriously in Group 4 racing or the faster Group 5. Despite that, the M1 was a superb 160 mph road car in the supercar mold. It looked the part and it was well built with luxurious trim.

Cadillac Seville

American manufacturers were so beset by emission and safety legislation during the Seventies that few cars of that period generated any lasting classic appeal. The established big cars lost performance and style. And the new smaller ones were slow and functional. It was only towards the end of the decade that any design confidence returned to create possible future classics.

Apart from the rare sports cars, most of the American classics come from the mid-size coupes, Firebirds and Mustangs, or the high performance 2-door sedans like the Sixties muscle cars.

Some achieve classic status because their style sets them apart from others of similar performance, like the early Sixties Buick Riviera. Some have great technical merit, like the Oldsmobile Toronado. Only a few big four-door sedans earn a place in classic lore.

It is a combination of style, technical merit and the high standards of Cadillac production that sets the 1980 Cadillac Seville apart from other big sedan cars. Cadillacs were as near hand-built as possible within a GM production line and the numbers were correspondingly lower, the cars rarer. "Craftsmanship a creed, accuracy a law" was the motto established by the company founder, and this has remained true since 1902.

Cadillac was generally used to lead the way in GM engineering. Perhaps it was to protect the Cadillac name from possible failure that it was left to Oldsmobile to pioneer the use of front-wheel-drive with powerful engines with the 1965 Toronado. A Cadillac Eldorado followed two years later using the same technology and slightly different style. The two cars continued until 1978 before they were replaced by smaller and lighter equivalents bearing the same names. These both retained the same system of front wheel drive with chain drive from the torque converter to the side-mounted gearbox ; following the Toronado success, GM used front wheel drive on many models but mostly with a transverse V-6.

Independent rear suspension was also a new feature for 1978 together with the option of the 347 cu.in V-8 petrol engine converted for diesel fuel. Perhaps because they had been prime targets of the Nader consumerism campaign, GM invoked all manner of technology to reduce emissions and fuel consumption. This had also inspired the 1976 Seville, the shortest Cadillac for many years; it was old technology, though, with a rear drive live axle, drum rear brakes and the 347 cu.in petrol V-8 producing 180 bhp – in 1978 it would produce 105 bhp as a diesel.

Although the wheelbase and overall length remained the same on the Seville's 1980 replacement, it used the latest technology with independent self-levelling rear suspension, the V-8 chain-drive transmission for front wheel drive and disc brakes all round.

It was also fitted with the diesel engine as standard with 350 and 368 cu.in petrol engines as options. The diesel engine was not a success and most people chose petrol engines; by 1982 the diesel engine had become the option alongside a new aluminium 250 cu.in V-8 with 147 bhp for Europe, and 10 bhp less in America where catalytic converters were mandatory.

The diesel engine was also offered with the other GM equivalent cars, Cadillac's own Eldorado, the Oldsmobile Toronado and the Buick Riviera. These three and the Seville shared the same platform, but the Seville was the only one with four doors; the two door cars all used the de ville style with an almost upright rear screen, heavy rear quarter panels and a long trunk deck. The Seville's style was a complete contrast with full side glazing for the rear passengers, a thinner quarter panel and a trunk-back tail where the trunk is narrower than the body after the style of the English coachbuilder Hooper. It was certainly the most elegant of GM's big sedan cars of the period

and came in two forms; the standard car used chrome strips and contrasting roof finish to suggest a convertible – faux-cabriolet – while the limited edition Elegante used two tone finish and coachlines for the more formal limousine appearance.

The Seville arrived during the 1979 oil crisis but demand rose steadily throughout its life and nearly 40,000 were built in its final year.

TECHNICAL DESCRIPTION OF THE CADILLAC SEVILLE	
YEARS OF PRODUCTION	1980-1985
MODELS	4-DOOR SEDAN
ENGINE	FRONT-MOUNTED V-8
BORE X STROKE, CAPACITY	3.4 x 3.3 INCHES, 249 CU.IN
VALVEGEAR	PUSHROD OVERHEAD VALVES
FUEL SYSTEM	FUEL INJECTION
POWER	137 BHP AT 4400 RPM
TRANSMISSION	4-SPEED AUTO FRONT-DRIVE
BODY/CHASSIS	STEEL FRAME CHASSIS, UNITARY BODY
SUSPENSION	FRONT, WISHBONES AND TORSION BARS
	REAR TRAILING ARMS AND COIL SPRINGS
TIRES/WHEELS	205/75 x 15 ON 6 IN. STEEL WHEELS
WHEELBASE, TRACK (F), TRACK(R)	114 x 59.3 x 60.6 INCHES
LENGTH, WIDTH, HEIGHT	204.7 x 71 x 54.3 INCHES
MAX SPEED	109 MPH
WHERE BUILT	DETROIT, USA

NB FROM 1980-82 A 347 CU.IN 105 BHP DIESEL ENGINE WAS FITTED AS STANDARD WITH 347 CU.IN AND 366 CU.IN PETROL ENGINES AS OPTIONS.

1981 - 1990

MODERN CLASSIC DEFINITIONS

Before going further, we need to return to one of our original definitions of a classic car – a post-1945 car with some feature which set it apart from its peers, and not just the mere fact of its survival. Such is the level of protection and durability in the Eighties car that many more will survive to great ages without restoration; where the Fifties car would be worn out after 80,000 miles, many Eighties cars are mechanically and bodily capable of over 200,000 miles with reasonable care and maintenance along the way. So we have to be more selective. Performance with style is what makes a latter-day classic.

One of the ways of enjoying classic car ownership is to be a member of a car club for that particular make or model. The long-standing classic makes are well represented. World-wide clubs for Aston Martin, Bentley, BMW, Ferrari, Jaguar, Lotus, MG, Mercedes, Porsche, Rolls-Royce and many others are open to all ages of the model. There are more specialized clubs too for such as Ford RS Owners or Fiat Dinos. But can you imagine a group of Vauxhall Cavalier or Nissan Bluebird owners enjoying each other's company in ten years time? Not classics, however long they survive.

A DECADE OF CHANGE

By the Eighties, the global car was becoming a reality. Manufacturers were all heading in the same direction as classifications became an international currency – A-class, B-class, C-class. Many were making the same car in different countries under different names or setting up factories in distant lands to take advantage of local conditions, like Honda, Toyota and Nissan in Britain.

The big three American manufacturers each had factories in every continent and most European countries; all had a stake in Japanese companies. The fourth, American Motors, had joined forces with Renault.

Inter-manufacturer co-operation increased in the search for economies of scale as design and development costs became ever greater. Peugeot, Renault and Volvo had co-built the Douvrin V-6 from 1974. Fiat and Saab shared platforms for the transverse front wheel drive Lancia Thema (1984), Saab 9000 (1985), Fiat Croma (1985), and Alfa Romeo 164 (1987).

Some famous names retained their ability to produce classics but lost their independence. Fiat bought Alfa Romeo from its state ownership in late 1986. Ford took over Aston Martin in 1987 and Jaguar in 1989, to the lasting benefit of both companies. Ford had also taken a majority share in AC in 1987 when the new Ace was under development, but gave it back to Cobra builder Brian Angliss in 1992.

Toyota had a stake in Lotus, but General Motors took over in early 1986 and then acquired control of Saab in 1990.

206-207 *Toyota Supra was the six cylinder derivative of the Celica. This new body style came in 1986; 183 cu.in straight-6 developed 204 bhp or 230 bhp with turbo.*

The outcome of all this rationalization and co-operation was that classics still came from the traditional low volume manufacturers, whoever now owned them, or as genuine but expensive coupes or sports cars from the volume producers.

Sedans would only be classics if the model was built for competition – the limited production rally cars like the RS and Cosworth from Ford, or the Lancia Delta Integrale – or from such accepted tuning agents as Mercedes AMG or the BMW M-series. Special editions, merely a different mix of established options under a short-term model name, did not make a classic out of a boring sedan. A few of the chic superminis, like the Peugeot 205GTI or the MG Metro turbo, could survive into classic status.

The trouble with the medium-size sedans was that the Eighties was the era of soap-bar styling and loss of make identity. All began to look the same as they sought to achieve the same object,

hatchback 4/5 seaters with low drag factors; they looked as if they came from the same wind-tunnel and were shaped by perpetually squeezing a bar of soap. In the process the distinctive face of the car – the grille – disappeared into a common radiator intake slot. In the UK these were the repmobiles – company-owned transport for the sales representative – which were as likely to come from Nissan or Toyota as Ford or Vauxhall.

It was the era when all companies expanded their own styling departments and placed offices in important markets around the globe. The traditional Italian styling houses had a difficult time. They could function as styling studios with prototype build facilities like Giugiaro's ItalDesign or IDEA, but any production area had to be capable of producing at least 25,0000 cars a year – supermini cabriolets were a popular product for volume producers to contract out to Pininfarina and Bertone in Italy, Karmann in Germany or Heuliez in France.

Ghia and Vignale were safe as de Tomaso had sold them to Ford back in 1973. It was Zagato who was to suffer, particularly as the company was at the Milan end of Auto Valley and control of such regular customers as Alfa Romeo and Lancia had passed to Fiat in Turin. With facilities for only 1000 cars a year, Zagato survived the Eighties thanks to de Tomaso reshaping Maserati around a number of variations on a Biturbo theme – the Spider and the 228 were built at Zagato – and to Aston Martin who reopened an old association to create the Vantage Zagato and Volante Zagato from 1985-90. Such supercars were very much a product of the late Eighties.

A new breed of exclusive car came through International rallying which had seen increasing participation from factory teams. The FIA rules laid down minimum production numbers, 500, 400 or 200 over 1975-1986. So factories built these quantities of specialist high performance cars. And since the Audi Quattro had shown the way, most of these Eighties cars used four wheel drive. They were not as comfortable and refined as the supercars, but they had a lot of performance and were very much classics of their period.

1981 - 1990

The advanced technology that we see in the cars of today was largely born in the Eighties. Not only did engines receive increasing levels of electronics but so too did transmissions and suspensions. Turbochargers were seen regularly in the Seventies (the 1962 Corvair Monza was probably the first) but the Eighties saw their driveability much improved; electronic ignition and injection combined with smaller, lighter rotating parts to cut the turbo-lag. Turbos were seen particularly in hot hatchbacks and as a means of providing petrol levels of power for diesel engines.

Most manufacturers had at least one model in their ranges equipped with twin-cam four-valve cylinder heads. Four wheel drive, spearheaded by the Audi Quattro, moved on from fixed ratios of torque split between front and rear, to more sophisticated limited slip center differentials with viscous couplings or Torsen worm-and-wheel differentials through to electronic control of center differential clutches. Anti-lock braking (ABS) was still the preserve of more expensive cars, but an increasingly widespread option on the rest. Rear wheel steering had long been understood and achieved by controlled suspension movement, but the Japanese introduced electronic control. Power steering and air-conditioning had

been around for a long time but these were increasingly fitted lower down the market.

The bi-product of all this technology is that it will be much harder to keep your Eighties classic going through the ages, as any restoration required will be beyond the ability of most home mechanics. Original dealers will have to keep servicing older cars and providing replacement parts for much longer than before.

THE BIG SEDANS

Although the rally world contributed some memorable special sedans, there were a few others to catch the eye as future classics. Inevitably the Rolls-Royce and Bentleys will live on; the Silver Shadow and Bentley T were finally replaced by the Silver Spirit and the Bentley Mulsanne in 1980, but what marked the Eighties was the belated reconition that a Bentley should be a sporting Rolls, not just a Rolls with a Bentley radiator. The Mulsanne Turbo came in 1982, followed by the Bentley 8 with firmer suspension in 1984; a merger of the two came in 1985 with the Turbo R. At last, high performance more suited to a history that includes five victories at Le Mans. And the Continental name returned on the convertible that had been called Corniche from

1971. There was still a Lincoln Continental in Ford's premier range. While the Lincolns possessed a certain Fifties style, like an Austin A135, the mechanical elements were also pretty dated – live rear axles and a pushrod V-8. Far more appealing was the Cadillac range with front wheel drive and independent rear suspension; the Seville 4-door was particularly elegant. The Eldorado coupe and convertible had matching Buick Rivieras with more performance.

Jaguar finally unveiled the XJ40 as the new XJ6 in 1986 using a single-cam 176 cu.in 'six' and the new AJ6 4-valve 219 cu.in, which had already been seen in the XJS. The previous XJ12 models had to continue as the V-12 wouldn't fit into the new car until major changes were made in 1992. At that point Jaguar, Mercedes S-class and BMW 7-series all had 12-cylinder versions and competed for the title of best in the world; good cars maybe, classic perhaps, but not cars that you might cherish in your garage in twenty years time.

Good cars emerged from the Club of Four who had shared a common transverse-engined platform. The top Lancia Thema used a Ferrari 308 4-valve engine for the 8.32 which was announced in 1986 to give 150 mph performance. From Saab,

the 9000 Turbo was almost as fast and three of them averaged 132 mph to cover 62,000 miles in 20 days at Talladega, creating a new limited edition model name. Alfa Romeo were the last to introduce their version as the 164 in 1987; with Pininfarina styling, it was one of the best-looking sedans on the market and, with the 183 cu.in V-6 was a worthy rival to such as the BMW M3.

De Tomaso was still in control of Maserati and the 1976 Quattroporte was to continue to 1988 using a 256 cu.in version of one of the earlier V-8 engines. From 1985 this was increased to 298 cu.in and the car became a Royale in 1987. In the latter half of the Seventies there had been a shorter two-door derivative called the Kyalami. Both cars had exceptionally clean lines, but were little known outside Italy. For the Eighties, de Tomaso developed the entirely new Maserati Biturbo range using different chassis lengths for a rear wheel drive platform with derivatives of a new 4-cam 90-degree V-6 which had three or four valves per cylinder and twin turbochargers. All had variations on the same basic three-volume body style; stylistically they were not the most exciting to look at but the mechanical specification was worthy of the best of Maserati tradition.

But perhaps the most memorable sedan of the Eighties was the Vauxhall Lotus Carlton, also sold as the Opel Lotus Omega, a product of General Motors' ownership of Lotus. The standard 183 cu.in 24-valve 204 bhp engine was increased to 221 cu.in with a new crankshaft and given twin turbochargers to develop 377 bhp. With the Corvette's six-speed gearbox, various aerodynamic additions and much improved suspension, the Lotus Omega/Carlton was capable of over 170 mph, the fastest ever 5-seater sedan car. After a 1989 launch, production started in 1990 but finished in 1992 when Lotus was sold on, so only 950 were built.

THE COUPES

The major manufacturers continued to produce coupe versions of their sedans, or at least use their sedan platforms, and these have traditionally acquired classic status. At the lower end of that market, Volkswagen had introduced the Scirroco in 1974 as a Golf coupe in the Ford Capri market.

It had a revised body in 1981. Giugiaro designed both that and the Isuzu Piazza (rear-drive 122 cu.in coupe) with near identical styling. The Scirroco continued until 1991 but the best addition to the Golf range was the slightly bigger Corrado in 1988,

a 2-door hatchback based on the latest Golf GTI; initially offered with the G-Lader supercharged 109 cu.in, as also used in the limited edition 4WD Golf GTI G60 Rallye, the Corrado matured when the VR6 170 cu.in came in 1992. It was VW's sports car, a genuine 2+2, with Porsche 944S2 performance.

As Germany was the only country to allow unrestricted speed on some of its autobahns, sports machinery was an important part of their market; Mercedes took it seriously and used a purpose designed platform, rather than an adapted sedan one, for the new SL300 (183 cu.in 'six') and the SL500 (305 cu.in V-8) in 1989. Like Mercedes, BMW do not change their coupes very often; the 6-series came in 1976 and the 218 bhp BMW 635CSi was added in 1976. It was 1983 before the M-series M635CSi came out with the 286 bhp 24-valve 213 cu.in to make one of BMW's most desirable classics. The replacement 850i arrived in 1989 with a 300 bhp 305 cu.in V-12 as a superb-looking successor; the engine was increased to 341 cu.in in 1992 and a 244 cu.in V-8 made the 840Ci in 1993.

Cadillac tried to take back some of the European coupe market in 1987 by using Italian styling for the Allante convertible. They sent shortened Eldorado

208-209 Corvette ZR-1 of 1989 brought in the new wheels and convex tail panel with its 380 bhp Lotus-developed engine.

chassis to Pininfarina in converted 747 jumbo-jets; the production line was completed when the body-chassis units returned to Detroit for the running gear, which included a 170 bhp 250 cu.in V-8. The power was increased to 200 bhp with a 274 cu.in for 1989, and to 299 bhp with the new 280 cu.in 32-valve V-8 in 1992, but the model was never a major seller. Chrysler tried a similar exercise with Maserati receiving a Le Baron chassis with a turbocharged 134 cu.in 'four'. Although Maserati installed a 16-valve head to get 205 bhp, and a less-stressed 183 cu.in V-6 was offered in 1990, the Chrysler TC by Maserati was not a commercial success.

The one-time kings of the American pony-cars recovered from their disastrous downsizing and power losses of the late Seventies. A new Chevrolet Camaro and sleeker-looking Pontiac Firebird came in 1981 with 88 bhp from a 152 cu.in 'four' or 155 bhp from a 305 cu.in V-8; power was increased steadily throughout the Eighties and by 1990 the range was

142-248 bhp. Ford's Mustang underwent a similar performance transformation, but lacked the style of the GM cars. The Mercury Cougar, which was once a luxury Mustang, became aligned to the Ford Thunderbird; the new styles of 1988 considerably improved both of them. More striking was the new Ford Probe based on a chassis from the Mazda MX-6 using 'fours' or V-6s; launched in 1988, it might have been a Capri replacement but it never had the same appeal in the European market. The last of 1.9 million Capris was built in 1986, one of the final 1000 Capri 280 Special Editions.

While Vauxhalls were very much Opel-based, from 1988 the two ranges had identical cars, although not all Opels had a Vauxhall equivalent. However, Calibra, launched in 1989, was the name given to the coupe derivatives of both the Opel Vectra and Vauxhall Cavalier shown a year earlier. Initially with 122 cu.in engines in 115 bhp 8-valve and 150 bhp 16-valve forms, both were also

offered with four wheel drive; however, when the 204 bhp Turbo 4x4 Calibra arrived in 1991, General Motor's European divisions had a serious 152 mph classic coupe.

BL Cars (British Leyland) had been government owned from 1975, but at the beginning of the Eighties they had forged technical links with Honda, which revitalized aged technology and production methods. Having lost Triumph production, sold Jaguar and kept the MG badge for faster Austins, the company became the Rover group in 1986. The new Rover 800 range (Sterling in America) was a joint Rover-Honda development based on the Honda Legend using a 122 cu.in 4-cylinder for the 820. A 177 bhp 164 cu.in V-6 engine came in 1988 (827), followed by a fastback coupe; it was the 827 Vitesse coupe, with style changes, which was the potential classic. In 1992, the front was changed to include a pronounced Rover-style grille and this is the

210-211 *Aston Martin Vantage Volante came in 1986 with skirts and spoilers but some retained the original body shape.*

most appealing version of the 827 Vitesse. Meanwhile the company had been taken over by British Aerospace in 1988; it was sold on to BMW in 1994 and Honda links were quickly severed.

SPORTS AND SPORTING COUPES

By the end of the Seventies, it seemed as if American emission legislation was going to stifle all sporting machinery, but the engineering challenge was taken up around the world and the Eighties saw a steady performance increase as engines became more and more efficient.

Mid-engined small cars remained a rarity despite the success of Fiat X1/9, but two emerged in the Eighties, the Toyota MR2 and the Pontiac Fiero. The Midship Runabout 2-seater was a product of Toyota's change to a transverse front wheel drive power train for the Corolla, with development through Toyota's early Eighties liaison with Lotus. The MR2 used a monocoque chassis and the Corolla engines, a 16-valve 97 cu.in 130 bhp and an 8-valve 91.5 cu.in 83 bhp unit for the home market. Neat, compact yet spacious, the MR2 did all that was expected of a mid-engined coupe. A supercharged 145 bhp

model was available in some markets from 1986 and a T-bar roof variant arrived in 1987.

The Pontiac Fiero was not quite in the same mold. Within General Motors, Chevrolet produced the sports car – the Corvette – so the Fiero was labelled as a commuter car. With a steel sub-frame covered in plastic panels, it was a good design let down by its basic engine, a 152 cu.in 'four' with 92 bhp at its 1983 launch. By 1985, it had a 170 cu.in V-6 option with 140 bhp, a more appealing proposition. Sadly, the American market was not receptive to a mid-engined commuter car and the Fiero ceased production in 1988.

It was Pontiac's former Chief Engineer and General Manager, John De Lorean who was behind the De Lorean DMC-12. When he left General Motors in 1973, he wanted to build an ideal sports coupe with gull-wing doors. Lotus were eventually entrusted with its development. A fuller story is told later, but what finally emerged at the end of 1980 was a Lotus – steel backbone chassis with fiberglass underbody – with stainless steel panels to Giugiaro's design; it was powered by a rear-mounted Douvrin V-6 in its 173 cu.in Volvo form. The ambitious project failed at the end of 1983 after 8583 examples had been built – a classic might-have-been.

For their own models of the Eighties, Lotus increased their engine size to 134 cu.in for the Elite S2 and Eclat S2 in 1980; these only lasted two

years before the Excel replaced the Eclat, using a number of Toyota components, and stayed in production until 1992. The Turbo Esprit also arrived in 1980; its original angular shape was modernized in 1987 with rounder lines and various versions were available by the end of the decade, still based on the 134 cu.in engine.

For many years, Lotus had wanted a new small sports car to recapture the old Elan market. While this might have shared engines with the Lotus-developed Toyota MR2, the 1986 take-over by General Motors caused a change to a front-wheel-drive Isuzu package, a 97 cu.in with 132 bhp or, for the SE, 167 bhp with a turbocharger; this delayed the Elan's arrival until late 1989. The power train was used by Isuzu for the Impulse coupe which had replaced the Piazza. Despite an enthusiastic reception, Elan world-wide sales never hit their targets in a recessionary period. When General Motors pulled out and sold Lotus to Bugatti president Romano Artioli in 1992, only 3857 had been built; the new owners had to use up the 800 power trains in stock for the Elan S2 which was completed in 1994-1995. Kia then bought the rights and built the Kia Elan in South Korea from 1995 using their own ex-Mazda engines.

The car that really replaced the old Elan was the Mazda MX-5 Miata, which arrived just before the new Lotus Elan. Conceived by Mazda North America, the MX-5 followed the original Elan concept with a 97 cu.in front engine in a rear-drive chassis with all-independent suspension. A 130 bhp 109 cu.in engine came in 1993; it had all the charm and now most of the performance of the original Elan.

Mazda had heavily revised the RX-7 in 1985 with a new Porsche 944-style body, independent rear suspension and a Wankel engine enlarged to 158 cu.in to give 150 bhp, or 200 bhp with a turbocharger, enough to give it 150 mph performance. Adding a convertible in 1987 for the first time was a classic addition to the RX-7 story. An interesting extension to the Wankel range from 1990 was the Eunos Cosmo coupe on a longer wheelbase and with the option of a 3-rotor engine to make237 cu.in.

The Japanese companies were very active in the sporting sector. Mitsubishi had introduced the

Starion 2+2 coupe into the Nissan Z-car market in 1982 with a 144 cu.in Turbo, and a 4WD Rally version followed a year later. The Starion handed over to the 3000GT with 4WD, four-wheel-steering (4WS) and twin-turbocharged 183 cu.in V-6 in 1990; this was sold in the USA as the Dodge Stealth.

Nissan had brought the 240Z concept through to the 300ZX in 1983, but launched an all-new 300ZX 2+2 in 1989 using a 183 cu.in V-6 with twin turbos (280 bhp) or without (230 bhp). Like the Mitsubishi it also had 4WS. It actually became a classic in its own production period which ended in 1996. The smaller 200SX used four-cylinder engines in another attractive little coupe. Meanwhile in 1987, Nissan had started their Skyline GT-R run with 4WD, 4WS and incredible turbocharged performance.

Toyota's 1981 Celica grew into a Supra derivative with a six-cylinder engine of 144 or 170 cu.in in a slightly longer chassis. From this came the even longer Soarer with a 144 cu.in turbo or a 183 cu.in dohc as a more comfortable 2+2 coupe. The Celica changed shape and adopted front wheel drive in 1985; 4WD and a turbocharger followed in late 1986 for the Group A rally team. Supra and Soarer went their own stylistic ways with 144 cu.in or 183 cu.in engines from 1986, presenting attractive alternatives to the equivalent

Nissan and Mitsubishi – good Porsche 944 rivals too. For 1989 the Celica changed shape again and still included the Turbo 4WD. The Soarer was not available on all markets but is a particularly handsome coupe.

And then there was Honda who had ignored sports cars after the S800. Their range had long excelled technically but lacked styling flair – an important part of latter day classic appeal. The Prelude 2+2 coupe arrived in 1982 but we had to wait until the 1987 version for style to match the 145 bhp performance – it also brought in mechanical 4WS. Style and performance continued with the 1991 model which had 185 bhp from its 134 cu.in VTEC engine. What really set Honda apart was the 1990 introduction of the superb mid-engined NSX with all-aluminium chassis and bodywork and a powerful 24-valve 274 bhp V-6 183 cu.in. It was such a good user-friendly car that Ferrari and Porsche 911 owners found it almost unexciting. A Targa-top model came in 1995.

Porsche continued to develop the 911 with increasing engine sizes. The 183 cu.in came in 1980 and the Carrera name was reintroduced in 1983 with a 195 cu.in engine. The Speedster name came back too in 1987. A year later came the Carrera 4 with a 219 cu.in engine and four wheel

drive – a 959 without the turbocharger – and in 1989 the Carrera 2 also gained the 219 cu.in. The Turbo meanwhile continued with a 201 cu.in engine from 1977 which was increased from 300 bhp to 320 bhp in the cleaner Carrera 2 shape. But there was also the more affordable front-engined 944 which had taken over from the 924 in 1981; a 16-valve 944S arrived in 1986 and the 183 cu.in S2 came in 1989 together with a Cabriolet while the 152 cu.in Turbo (1985) moved on from 220 bhp to 250 bhp. The 928 had gone through S2, S3 and S4 versions into the 1990 928 GTS with a 305 cu.in V-8 coming in 1987. The front-engined Porsches may not have the iconic appeal of the 911 series, but they are still worthy future classics.

The 911's French rival, the Alpine Renault A310, became the sleeker and more luxurious GTA in 1985 with the Douvrin V-6 now increased to 173 cu.in (160 bhp) or a 152 cu.in Turbo with 200 bhp. The final Alpine A610 Turbo came in 1991 with a wider body, a more aerodynamic front and 250 bhp from the 183 cu.in Turbo but, by 1996, production had ceased – a sad end to a name that had done so much for French racing and rallying prestige.

However a new French make had arrived in 1986 and has continued in business after a change of ownership in 1991. The Venturi 210 had a

turbocharged version of the 152 cu.in PRV engine but mounted it amidships in a sleek two-seater coupe with composite bodywork on a pressed steel chassis. A neat cabriolet came in 1988 and the 1990 260 used the 173 cu.in V-6 with 260 bhp.

From Germany came the BMW Z1 in 1988, a short-lived sports two-seater powered by the 152 cu.in injection six. With quickly removable fiberglass body panels, its major feature was doors that dropped into the sills. Only just over 8000 were built from 1987-91.

Fiberglass continued to be used for America's only sports car, the Corvette. The latest model arrived in 1983, more compact and more aerodynamic, with a 200 bhp 347 cu.in V-8. This was increased to 230 bhp for 1985 and the following year saw a new convertible. When the ZR1 arrived in 1989 using an entirely special Lotus-designed 347 cu.in 4-cam with 380 bhp, the Corvette finally recovered its 1967 performance; there was a new 6-speed gearbox too. While Alfa Romeo's aged 124 Spider continued to be produced by Pininfarina through to the Nineties, and the 164 was a sporting sedan, the make lacked a mid-size sports coupe following the demise of the Alfetta-based GTV6 in 1987. The Sprint 1.3 with the developed AlfaSud

engine continued a little longer. The new SZ, called Il Mostro from its 1989 launch, was based on the 1985 Alfa 75 sedan. The coupe used a 75 platform with shortened overhangs; its plastic composite bodywork was designed within Alfa Romeo and built by Zagato. When Fiat's then chief, Vittorio Ghidella, was satisfied that the SZ roadholding could match a Porsche 944, the project was given the green light; its V-6 183 cu.in (an option in the 75 from 1987) was tuned to 210 bhp for 152 mph performance.

Zagato set up the production process and built 1000 of the SZ before the Alfa Romeo 75 production was stopped in 1993; Zagato continued with their own roadster version, the RZ until 1994. Meanwhile they had shown the Hyena in 1992 based on the Lancia Delta HF Integrale; in the style of a modernized Giulietta SZ, it was a very good car. Sadly only a handful were built before Zagato finally closed its production doors – a fitting farewell to a company that always produced cars in a classic mold.

In England TVR introduced the sleek new Tasmin as a 2-seater coupe on a new tubular chassis in January 1980, following this up later in the year with the convertible and the 2+2. From 1980-1985 this was available with the 170 cu.in German V-6 and, from 1981-1984, as the Tasmin 200 with the Ford Pinto 144 cu.in. Current owner

Peter Wheeler took over from Martin Lilley in 1982 and dropped the Tasmin name a year later in favor of engine-related numbers – 280i. A further engine variation began in 1983 with the Rover V-8; initially in 213 cu.in form (350i) for the same body range, this was increased for the 237 390SE and then to 256 cu.in for the 420 in 1986.

This came in 300 bhp SEAC sports form (Special Equipment Aramid Composite) or as a 265 bhp sports sedan with genuine space for two adults in the back. Fearing they were getting out of the enthusiast price range TVR brought back an old shape – the Seventies 3000S – widened it and gave it a new chassis with the 280i engine; this S convertible was half the price of the 420SEAC. By the end of the Eighties, the S2 was using the 176 cu.in Ford V-6, the Speed Eight convertible with 237 cu.in had replaced the rest and the Rover engine had been enlarged to 274 cu.in for the 450SE. And there was the racing Tuscan too, but that belongs to the Griffith story of the Nineties.

After a promising start in the specialist GT

212-213 *This 1988 Porsche Carrera Cabriolet has various non-standard items – new wheels, an intake ahead of the rear wheels and a rear wing – but it is still very much a Porsche.*

COMPETITION IMPROVES THE BREED

world in the Sixties, Marcos hit problems. A factory move, the failure to get cars into America and a UK tax change that affected cars sold in kit form, all conspired to close the company down in 1971. However founder, Jem Marsh, continued a business in Marcos spares and gradually reintroduced limited kit-car production of the Ford 1600 and 183 cu.in models from 1981. Then Marcos, too, adopted the Rover V-8 and came up with the Mantula in 1984 in the same basic shape as the original 1800, which was still as striking 20 years later – just flared rear wheel arches for a wider axle – and available in kit form for home assembly. A Spyder convertible followed in 1986 with wishbone independent rear suspension finally available in 1989.

The aim, though, was still to build complete cars for which Type Approval was necessary – the Mantara was finally homologated in 1993 as coupe and Spyder with the 237 cu.in Rover V-8.

In the interim Marcos continued to offer well-made cars in kit form. The Martina used running gear from old Ford Cortina Mk 4 or Mk 5 in a Mantula body/chassis and the Mini-Marcos returned as a Mark V using new molds for Mini components. Not many kit cars deserve classic status, but these were just modernized versions of previous classic production shapes.

Morgan never stopped making classics. They too had continued with Rover power for the Plus 8, with the 237 cu.in in 1990. The 4/4 continued with Ford 97 cu.in engines while the Plus Four returned in 1985 with a Fiat 122 cu.in twin-cam engine; this was replaced by the Rover 16-valve 122 cu.in in 1988.

By now there were many small companies building replicas of some of the more famous shapes of the past. Some, as below, have achieved a classic status of their own, others are just specials. Lynx and Wingfield built Jaguar D-type replicas that were very close to the original designs. GT Developments built the GTD40 looking very like a proper GT40 but with a space-frame and a more modern Ford V-8. AC continued to make the Cobra as a Mark IV – copies from other companies were less desirable.

And Caterham continued to make ever faster variations on the theme of the Lotus 7 to which they had acquired the rights in 1973.

While the rules of the rallying and racing worlds had been responsible for a number of limited edition classic sedans throughout the Seventies, the International rally rules of the Eighties resulted in an amazing collection of specialist machines which were destined to be instant if expensive classics. However, because they were produced in limited numbers and many of them were used in competition, it is not easy to find good standard examples.

Early Seventies rallies were run to FIA Appendix J group 2; 1000 4-seater cars had to be built, but the modifications allowed were considerable, provided enough parts were made to equip 100 cars. Late Seventies rallies were run to Appendix J group 4 which called for cars of at least two seats of which 400 had been produced over 24 months. Modifications allowed were fewer but 400 special editions for rallying was well within the capability of most manufacturers. The Lancia Stratos was one such specialist car; Ford Escort Mk.II RS, Fiat Abarth 131 Rallye, Sunbeam-Lotus, Vauxhall Chevette, Opel Ascona 400 were less specialized but heavily modified. But they were all two-wheel-drive cars as the FIA had banned four wheel drive. For whatever reason, the FIA reinstated four wheel drive for 1979 by which time Audi were already working on the Quattro with intent to go rallying. The rest soon had to follow.

For 1982 new rules came in; Group B only

asked for 200 examples. Special Evolutions of these (another 10 per cent production) were allowed for the competitions, but 200 standard road cars had to be built first – all destined to be future classics. Group A (5000-off) ran alongside but didn't challenge for outright victory. By 1986, the Group B cars had become too fast for rallying, so the rules were changed to limit the power to 300 bhp; the World Rally Championship was limited to Group A (5000 examples) or Group B cars with a 97 cu.in limit.

Audi's first Quattro was launched in March 1980; it was based on the two-door fastback Audi GT with a new floorpan and its turbocharged five-cylinder 128 cu.in engine gave 200 bhp. Audi had previously tried to rally the front-drive Audi 80, but, as the engine was mounted ahead of the front axle line, it was ill-suited to rallying on loose surfaces – it needed four wheel drive. Audi duly built 400 Quattros and had an impressive 1981 season.

For the Group B regulations Audi continued their developments and a new model, the A2, arrived in mid-1983 with many lightweight panels and an engine that could produce as much as 340 bhp.

The end of 1983 saw the Sport Quattro with wide wheelarches, a short wheelbase and new cylinder head with four valves per cylinder; in standard turbocharged form it had 306 bhp which could be increased to over 400 bhp for rallying.

In Group A, Audi ran the 200 Quattro Turbo for

1987 with a somewhat more sophisticated torque split arrangement using Torsen differentials. Any of the Quattros that provided the basis for the rally cars is a likely classic.

Ford were rather left behind in Group B. Having tried to develop the RS1700T within the Escort Mk.III body, following old Escort front-engine rear-drive principles, they decided on the all-new RS200 as a mid-engined four-wheel-drive coupe with a turbocharged 109 cu.it giving 200-350 bhp. The 200 were finally built by January 1986; while the car proved effective, it was only to have one year of International rallying. They went on to develop the 1985 Sierra XR4x4 (176 cu.it V-6 and 4WD) and then the 1987 5000-off Sierra Cosworth using a turbocharged 144 cu.in four-cylinder 16-valve engine with 220 bhp; the RS500 (500-off) Evolution came in 1987 but that could only be used for racing or national rallying. The Sierra Cosworth is a likely classic too. As the competition arm for the Fiat Empire (excluding Ferrari in Grands Prix),

Lancia took rallying very seriously throughout the Seventies and Eighties. The purpose-built Stratos, which won the World Rally Championship from 1974-6, was succeeded by the Fiat-Abarth 131 Rallye, an Escort-type car using the old Fiat 125 twin-cam engine in its 144 cu.in Lancia Beta form. This won the championship in 1977, 1978 and 1980. Their first group B car, the good-looking Rally 037, was loosely based on the mid-engined Lancia Monte Carlo; it used the later 16-valve 131 Rallye engine but with a Volumex supercharger. The necessary 200 were built in time for the 1982 season and the car performed well, but it soon became obvious that four wheel drive was essential to keep up with the Audis and other 4WD machines.

Lancia's response was to take the shape of the normally front-drive 4-door Delta, transfer as many 037 bits as possible to it and add 4WD in its most sophisticated form with three viscous coupling differentials. The engine became a new four-cylinder unit of 107 cu.in but used both a Volumex

supercharger and a turbocharger in series to develop around 400 bhp. This Delta S4 was finally homologated (200 built to a standard specification) for the 1986 season – another Group B car with only a season to run. It won four events, but Peugeot won six and took the cup.

Lancia had introduced the Delta – similar to the Fiat Strada – in 1979. The Delta HF arrived in 1983 with a turbocharged 97 cu.in engine. With an eye to competing in Group A classes before Group B was abandoned, this was developed into the Delta HF 4WD in mid-1986 with a turbocharged 144 cu.in 8-valve engine; following the mid-season announcement 5000 were hurriedly built in time for the first event of 1987. Being best prepared, Lancia duly won the 1987 championship with Sierra Cosworths and BMW M3s as also-rans. For the 1988 season, the second generation HF Integrale came in with flared wheel arches for bigger wheels and brakes and another 5000 were built. A 16-valve version followed in 1989 by which time, 200 bhp was available.

214-215 Lotus 7 successor, the Caterham 7 is a popular track car; this is a 1985 Super 7 Sprint with a 97 cu.in 110 bhp Ford engine.

Championship wins continued from 1988-90. More Evolutions followed and Integrales won in 1991 and 1992, six in succession. Production finally ceased in November 1994 after 44,300 had been sold with various special edition models on the way including rally replicas in Martini colors. Any of the Integrale models is a classic worth keeping.

The Peugeot combine had included Citroen from 1974 and Chrysler-Talbot from 1978. Peugeot themselves had taken part in such events as the East African Safari with some success, but left sprint rallying to the Coventry-based Talbot-Sunbeam-Lotus after the take-over. That rewarded them with the Manufacturers championship in 1981, the last year of Group 4. For Group B the operation was run from France and a purpose-built rally machine was designed to fit under a slightly stretched version of the 205 which was launched in 1983. The 205 Turbo 16 was homologated later that year with the 200 cars laid out alongside the extra 20 Evolution specials. Using the strong light-alloy diesel block with a twin-cam 16-valve head on top, the turbocharged 109 cu.in produced a standard 200 bhp or 335 bhp in Evolution 1 form. The engine was mounted transversely at the rear, offset to the right, with a Citroen SM gearbox coupled to four wheel drive.

Successful enough in 1984, the 205 T16 came out for 1985 in Evolution 2 form with front fins and a rear wing with up to 450 bhp and won the Championship in both 1985 and 1986. With no group A car available, Peugeot took wilder versions of the T16 into long distance rally-raids like the Paris-Dakar. In appearance, the 205 Turbo 16 managed to retain the chic charm of the 205 – an attractive and very effective little classic.

Despite being from the same company as Peugeot, Citroen also went into Group B. The Visa 1000 Pistes was built as a class contender for 1984 using a Peugeot 82 cu.in transverse engine and 4WD with 145 bhp in Evolution form. It never achieved success and Citroen switched to the BX 4TC for 1986 using a Peugeot 505 128 cu.in engine, turbocharged with an oversimplified 4WD system that lacked a center differential. That too failed and the cars joined Peugeot in Paris-Dakar events. A classic pair of failures.

BMC, BMLC, British Leyland, BL Cars had become Austin Rover in 1982. Under its various guises the company had a long tradition of rallying from the big Healeys, through the Minis and into the Triumph TR8, which had its last rally in 1980. For Group B, they eventually chose to use a mid-engined derivative of the MG Metro with four wheel drive. The basic design was carried out in 1982 by the Williams Grand Prix Engineering offshoot of the F1 team. Unlike all its rivals, the car did not use a turbocharged engine as the designers wanted a more user-friendly power delivery; the team elected to develop an entirely new 183 cu.in V-6 engine, having initially used a shortened Rover V-8. In basic 'Clubman' 200-off form this developed 250 bhp with around 400 bhp for the 20-off Evolution model. After considerable development, which included the addition of an ugly front spoiler and rear wing, the MG 6R4 was finally homologated in mid-1985. A succession of minor problems prevented it gaining any great results before the end of Group B, but it became a popular and effective UK rally car from 1987 onwards. Not the most appealing of classics, but still a significant machine. Among the Japanese, the Nissan 240RS (2-door sedan) and Toyota Celica Turbo had made some impact in the early days of group B, but they were only rear-drive machines.

Mazda aimed at Group A and produced a 323 Turbo 4WD using the 97 cu.in engine with a four valve head and a simple 4WD system; the necessary 5000 were completed by mid-1986. The 323 wasn't a great success in 1987 but had some better outings in 1988 with X-trac transmission; for 1989 the mechanical components were transferred to the new shape 323 and the engine increased to 112 cu.in and 180 bhp. In the same mold as the Integrale, it was a neat compact design.

THE RACING REVOLUTION

When Group B was announced for 1982, it was expected that there would soon be a World Championship for racing GT cars as well as for rallying. In the event, there was only a Group C championship for sports-racing cars which lasted well into the next decade. However Ferrari decided to build a 200-off road car from which 20 Evolution racers would be made available for private entrants. The 288GTO is more fully described later but the way in which it was announced was to prove significant.

When the car was first shown at Geneva 1984, it was stated that the model was to be a limited edition of only 200 cars and that deposits would be taken from those wishing to reserve a car. As the 1962 Ferrari 250GTO had proved to be an appreciating classic, many buyers appeared and the planned 200 cars became 273 before the end. The principle was subsequently used for all the supercars that followed, the deposits making a useful contribution to the production process.

Porsche too were hoping for a Group B racing championship when they produced their Gruppe B 959 prototype in 1983. And they had a history of rallying too from the Sixties, so it was envisaged as a dual-purpose car.

The 959 was based on the 911, so the flat-six engine was mounted behind the rear axle with the gearbox ahead; like the Audi Quattro in reverse, it needed four wheel drive to improve stability. The 173 cu.in engine used twin turbochargers to develop 450 bhp and the transmission used computer control to vary the torque split of the

center differential. A prototype won the 1984 Paris-Dakar rally-raid and a production 959 won it again in 1986, but it was to be 1988 before the 200th car was completed and group B rallying had finished. The model was rarely raced but served as a very effective development car for the four-wheel-drive Porsches that were to follow.

Jaguar too conceived the XJ220 as a Group B contender when it was announced in 1988 with a 500 bhp V-12 and Ferguson-designed four-wheel-drive. Deposits were taken, more than the 200 plus 20 Evolutions, so Jaguar had to build the car. By then Group B racing was not going to displace Group C, so JaguarSport redeveloped it without 4WD and replaced the heavy V-12 with a turbocharged 213 cu.in V-6 based on the Metro 6R4 power unit.

THE SUPERCARS

First of the Eighties supercars with no competition pretension was the Aston Martin Vantage Zagato. Aware of Ferrari's success in taking deposits for the 288GTO, Aston Martin took deposits for the proposed 50 cars, based on a Zagato sketch at Geneva 1985 and a scale model at Frankfurt. Working prototypes were shown at Geneva 1986 and deliveries started soon after.

A convertible Volante Zagato followed on.

Production of the faithful V-8, Volante and Vantage continued until 1989 when Aston Martin finally replaced them with the Virage, a more modern car with using the existing 323 cu.in V-8 with new 4-valve cylinder heads. After the success of the 288GTO launch, Ferrari found another excuse for a low volume supercar.

The F40 celebrated 40 years of Ferrari in 1988. As there had been no Group B racing available for the 288GTO, the 20-off Evolution model was still-born. The F40 used that as its basis for over 1300 F40s. Meanwhile normal Ferrari production continued with the 512 becoming 512i (for injection) in 1981 and the Testarossa with four valve heads and new style in 1984. The Bertone-bodied 308GT4 was replaced in 1981 by Pininfarina's Mondial 8 with a longer wheelbase to be a more serious 2+2; a year later came the 308 Qv and Mondial Qv with four valve heads to retain the power while improving emissions. A very attractive cabriolet arrived in 1984.

All the smaller cars changed from 308 to 328 in 1985 and 348 in 1989. As the capacity of the V-8 engine rose from 183 to 195 to 207 cu.in, the names changed to 328 or 3.2 Mondial and 348 or Mondial T. With the 348 the chassis changed from tubular to monocoque and the engines were changed from transverse to longitudinal mounting. Lamborghini's Countach grew from LP400S to LP500S in 1982 with the V-12 becoming a 289 cu.in. LP5000S QV came in 1985 with a 317 cu.in and four-valve heads.

Of their smaller cars, the Urraco 2+2 had been joined by the Silhouette 2-seater targa-top in 1976, both bring replaced in 1981 by the Jalpa 350 which continued in production to 1989.

After a difficult period, the company was taken over in 1987 by Chrysler, who were able to bring in the Diablo in 1990. Meanwhile Bugatti and McLaren had started work on their supercars for the next decade.

216-217 The 4-valve 317 cu.in engine arrived for the Countach 5000S in 1985. Rear wings were an option.

Mazda Rx-7

With the RX-7 Mazda achieved two things. They consolidated their faith in the new Wankel rotary engine and produced a sporting car that did much to raise the Mazda profile. Mazda only started producing 4-wheeled cars in 1960 but they learnt fast. Early car production was of small cars for the Japanese market; the new light and compact Wankel power unit looked like an ideal replacement for their existing vee-twins so Mazda signed a licence agreement with NSU.

German manufacturers of motor cycles and small cars, NSU had developed the rotary power unit from a compact supercharger designed for them by Dr. Felix Wankel in 1956. After slow development, they introduced a single rotor unit in the Sport Prinz Spyder in 1963, before going onto their definitive twin-rotor powered Ro80 introduced in 1967 – a superb car even without its fascinating power unit.

Early Wankel power units had suffered from excessive wear of the rotor tip seals and poor combustion, and it took NSU some time to eradicate these problems; however what no-one ever cured was heavy fuel consumption. When the 1973 fuel crisis came, most manufacturers stopped their Wankel work. NSU had been absorbed by Volkswagen in 1969; even they ceased Wankel production in 1977.

Citroen went into limited production in 1969 with 500 Ami 8 coupes using a single rotor, followed by the GS Birotor in 1973, but they too dropped out in 1975.

Mazda were more persistent. Having taken on the licence, they worked faster than NSU and showed their first prototype in 1964, the two seater 110S Cosmo with twin rotors and a 122 cu.in equivalent capacity. This attractive coupe was sold from 1967-1972.

The R100 followed a year later with the same engine installed in a coupe version of the smallest sedan – a good engine in search of a chassis. It was a pattern that Mazda would repeat with the RX-2 (1970 Capella 616), RX-3 (1971 Grand Familia 808), 140 cu.in RX-4 (1972 Luce 929) and 158 cu.in RX-5 (1975 Cosmo 121). In fact, the Cosmo coupes were nicely styled but not available in all markets.

By the time the RX-7 came out in 1978, Mazda had made the Wankel unit as reliable as any conventional engine, so the world could enjoy its real benefits of smooth high performance in a compact package, particularly in America where the high consumption was offset by low fuel costs; America was the first overseas market for the the RX-7 (Savanna), which was very much aimed at the Datsun 240Z.

For the RX-7 the Wankel was a twin-rotor unit of 140 cu.in developing 100 bhp. In other respects, the RX-7 was really just a conventional 2+2 sports coupe with a 5-speed gearbox and a live rear axle with coil springing. But the lightweight engine gave good weight distribution and handling, and its size allowed a low bonnet line, which gave it distinctive styling and a low drag factor. It was a great success and Mazda made over half a million of this model before the second generation came along in 1985. The power output had been increased to 115 bhp in 1981 and a 165 bhp turbocharged version came along in 1983, enough for nearly 140 mph. The turbocharged engine was also offered in the Cosmo.

With the new RX-7 came an increase to 158 cu.in, turbocharged for 185 bhp or normally aspirated at 150 bhp.

It had independent rear suspension too and became a strong rival to the Porsche 944 whose style it also resembled. A convertible became available in 1987 and the output from the turbocharged version was increased to 200 bhp in 1989. That year saw the new Eunos Cosmo, a good-looking 4-seater coupe, with a 3-rotor 237 cu.in Wankel turbocharged to give 280 bhp; it was the family man's sporting RX-7 and continued to be available until 1998. The third generation RX-7 came along in 1991 with its 158 cu.in Wankel fitted with twin turbochargers to gave a remarkable 255 bhp, rising to 280 bhp for the fourth generation RX-7 in 1999.

Over the years, the RX-7 has also been successful on the race-track and the Wankel engines have also been used in sports-racing cars; when they finally won Le Mans in 1991, they were using a 4-rotor 317 cu.in engine developing around 700 bhp at 9000 rpm – a pair of RX-7 units. Although the Wankel engine has been seen in a number of different models over the years, the popularity of the RX-7 alone has justified Mazda's faith in the rotary engine.

TECHNICAL DESCRIPTION OF THE MAZDA RX-7

YEARS OF PRODUCTION	1978-1985 (1981)
MODELS	COUPE 2-SEATER
ENGINE	FRONT-MOUNTED 2-ROTOR WANKEL
BORE X STROKE, CAPACITY	EQUIVALENT TO 139 CU.IN
VALVEGEAR	PORTS IN CASING
FUEL SYSTEM	ONE 4-BARREL CARBURETOR
POWER	115 BHP AT 6000 RPM
TRANSMISSION	5-SPEED
BODY/CHASSIS	STEEL MONOCOQUE
SUSPENSION	FRONT, WISHBONES AND COIL SPRINGS
	REAR, LIVE AXLE AND COIL SPRINGS
TIRES/WHEELS	185/70 X 13 ON 5 IN. ALLOY WHEELS
WHEELBASE, TRACK (F), TRACK(R)	95 X 56 X 55 INCHES
LENGTH, WIDTH, HEIGHT	169 X 65 X 49 INCHES
MAX SPEED	125 MPH
WHERE BUILT	HIROSHIMA, JAPAN

218-219 *In 1981, the RX-7 had a minor face-lift which included the rear spoiler. Turbo version came in 1983 with 165 bhp.*

Chevrolet Corvette 1983 - 1996

When the latest Corvette was announced in 1983, it was still America's only home-grown sports car. Although it was the fifth distinct body style, it was arguably only the third chassis design. The previous model had lasted since 1968; despite the anti-performance attitudes of the Seventies, it continued to sell well at its own 40,000 a year level and was still selling 25,000 in 1981-1982, so the planned launch for the 1982 model year was deferred for two years.

Work on the new car started in the late Seventies when the decision was finally taken to maintain the front-engine rear drive configuration. They had been looking at mid-engined designs since 1970, using transverse V-8s, or two and four-rotor Wankel engines in what became the Aerovette show car, but any stylistic advantages were outweighed by the practicality of the conventional layout, which could be made to hold the road just as well. A mid-engined V-8 had actually been given the production go-ahead for 1980 but its main supporters moved on and the project was cancelled.

The philosophy of the new Corvette was to make it the best sports car in performance terms; acceleration, top speed, handling, braking had to be as good as possible and they were starting with a clean sheet of paper. Good suspension demands a stiff chassis; previous Corvette coupes had a steel cage, bonded to the fiberglass body and rubber-mounted to a simple perimeter frame. The new one united the steel sections to make a single welded sheet steel monocoque running from front to rear, incorporating a substantial roll-over hoop behind the cockpit and a strong windscreen surround section. The whole structure was built of galvanized steel. Fiberglass sections for the rear roof, the sills, scuttle and parts of the underbody were bonded to the frame to add stiffness.

An aluminized steel subframe carried the engine, transmission and front suspension while the final drive and rear suspension were carried on their own cast aluminium sub-frame. The two sub-frames were joined by a 'torque-tube' which was actually a cast aluminium channel-section encasing the aluminium prop-shaft. With the exhaust system also suspended under this channel, the complete running gear could be assembled separately. Keeping weight down, aluminium was also used for fixed length drive shafts, wheel uprights, the forged front wishbones, the rear suspension trailing arms and the transverse lower link; and fiberglass was used for the transverse leaf

springs front and rear. The maximum Goodyear Eagle tire size played a considerable part in the car's overall scheme; 255/50VR x 16 tires were mounted on 8.5 and 9.5 in. wide alloy wheels.

For the engine, Chevrolet retained the existing 347 cu.in pushrod V-8 which was producing a very unstressed 205 bhp at 4300 rpm using a pair of single point injectors. The four-speed Borg Warner gearbox was mated to a very high overdrive (0.67:1) whose engagement was electronically selected by the engine's ECU (electronic control unit) according to engine speed and throttle position – a useful device to register good fuel economy for the EPA (environmental protection agency) tests. This would eventually be replaced in 1989 by a six-speed gearbox providing similarly long ratios. A GM 4-speed automatic was always an option.

220-221 The ZR-1 (main picture) arrived in 1989 with new wheels with over 50% more horsepower than the best of the rest. Inset, a convertible shows the LCD dashboard.

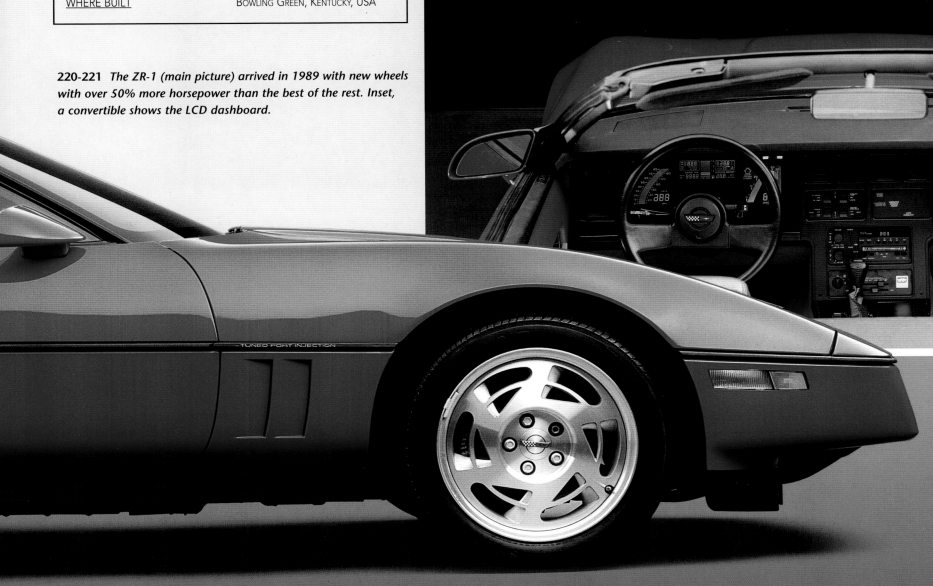

A superb-looking body style was conceived within GM, still made of fiberglass but with a particularly good finish due to the injection of resin into the mold during the curing process. Early studies showed that the radiator could get enough air from underneath the nose which all helped to produce a good drag factor of 0.34; this was much better than the previous car and enabled a 140 mph maximum on 205 bhp. The original plan had been to continue with the T-bar roof of the previous car but a late change was made to make the roof into a single removable panel; the chassis side members were deepened to compensate for the loss of roof stiffness.

A change to multi-port injection in 1985 boosted the power to 230 bhp at 4000 rpm and in 1986 the full convertible arrived. By the time the 6-speed gearbox arrived in 1989, the standard 347 cu.in was producing 250 bhp, but there was a new all-aluminium 347 cu.in V-8 developed by Lotus using four-valve heads with 380 bhp; this Corvette ZR-1 moved into the supercar category with a 175 mph maximum. By the last year of the 1983 Corvette, the two engines were pushing out 304 and 411 bhp respectively. There was a stylish beauty about those 4th generation Corvettes; it is for sure that the ZR-1 is a collectable classic.

TECHNICAL DESCRIPTION OF THE CHEVROLET CORVETTE

YEARS OF PRODUCTION	1986-1996
MODELS	2-SEATER TARGA-COUPE AND CONVERTIBLE
ENGINE	FRONT-MOUNTED V-8
BORE X STROKE, CAPACITY	3.9 x 3.4 INCHES , 349 CU.IN
VALVEGEAR	PUSHROD OHV
FUEL SYSTEM	FUEL INJECTION
POWER	1986 233 BHP AT 4000 RPM
TRANSMISSION	SPEED + O/D, 6-SPEED, 4-SPEED AUTO
BODY/CHASSIS	STEEL FRAME, FIBERGLASS BODY
SUSPENSION	FRONT, WISHBONES AND LEAF SPRING
	REAR, WISHBONE, DRIVE-SHAFT AND
	LEAF SPRING
TIRES/WHEELS	255/50VR x 16 ON
	8.5 OR 9.5 IN ALLOYS
WHEELBASE, TRACK (F), TRACK(R)	96 x 59 x 60 INCHES
LENGTH, WIDTH, HEIGHT	176 x 71 x 46 INCHES
MAX SPEED	144 MPH
WHERE BUILT	BOWLING GREEN, KENTUCKY, USA

222-223 *The convertible arrived in 1986 by which time the power had risen from the 1983 205 bhp to 233 bhp. This is an early example.*

Ferrari Testarossa 1984 and BB512

transverse V-12 arrangement, so chose to use a flat-12 engine to maintain a low center of gravity despite its width. Ferrari had been using 183 cu.in flat-12 engines in the Grand Prix cars from 1970 and the same unit would be used in the 312PB sports-racing car.

To create a road-going flat-12 engine, Ferrari opened out the V-12 Daytona engine into a boxer unit – hence the 365GT4BB (Berlinetta Boxer) – and changed the cam drive from chain to toothed belt. Racing cars have their gearboxes in line with the crankshaft and usually behind the axle line, which would produce a long wheelbase for a road car with the gearbox taking up space required for the transverse silencers. Ferrari mounted the gearbox alongside the engine with the drive to the opposite wheel passing under the penultimate main bearing; for the Countach, Lamborghini turned the engine through 180 degrees and had a conventional gearbox at the

224-225 *The mid-engined Ferrari Testarossa was a striking Pininfarina design with the theme of the side strakes carried round to the rear of the car.*

TECHNICAL DESCRIPTION OF THE FERRARI TESTAROSSA

YEARS OF PRODUCTION	1984-1996
MODELS	COUPE 2-SEATER
ENGINE	MID-MOUNTED FLAT-12
BORE X STROKE, CAPACITY	3.2 X 3 INCHES, 301 CU.IN
VALVEGEAR	TWIN OHC PER BANK, 4-VALVES
FUEL SYSTEM	BOSCH K-JETRONIC FUEL INJECTION
POWER	390 BHP AT 6300 RPM
TRANSMISSION	5-SPEED
BODY/CHASSIS	STEEL TUBE FRAME, STEEL BODY
SUSPENSION	FRONT, WISHBONES AND COIL SPRINGS
	REAR, WISHBONES AND COIL SPRINGS
TIRES/WHEELS	FRONT, 225/50VR X 16 ON 8 IN.
	ALLOYS REAR, 255/50VR X 16 ON 10
	IN.ALLOYS
WHEELBASE, TRACK (F), TRACK(R)	100 X 59.8 X 65.2 INCHES
LENGTH, WIDTH, HEIGHT	177 X 77.8 X 44.6 INCHES
MAX SPEED	182 MPH
WHERE BUILT	MARANELLO, ITALY

front, driving the differential at the rear via a shaft in the sump. Both therefore had to lift their engines above the axle line; the Countach power train mass was further forward than for the BB, but Ferrari had the lower center of gravity. A further benefit of the raised engine was that there was more space to provide an exhaust system for the ports on the underside of the heads; for this engine the spark plugs were on the upper face rather than between the cams. Four Weber triple-choke carburetors sat on top of the engine which produced 344 bhp, enough to match the Daytona's 172 mph top speed.

The BB frame was a conventional Ferrari construction with a tubular frame carrying all-round wishbone independent suspension. The BB's Pininfarina body style was an obvious forerunner to the 308 but lacked the later car's more slender elegance; to break up the depth of the side panels a deep belt line ran the length of the car merging into the tops of the fiberglass front and rear bumpers. On many cars the lower area was painted matte black but they looked far better when the whole car was the same color.

The BB was first shown at the 1971 Turin Show as a concept car to test potential purchaser opinion. Production then started in 1973. After some 380 cars, the first update came in 1976 with the capacity increased to 305 cu.in to overcome the effects of emission controls; the 512BB followed the new system of capacity followed by the number of cylinders and included dry sump lubrication, wider rear tires and a front bumper with an air-dam to counteract high speed lift. Fuel injection was added in 1981 to make the 512i. Then came the Testarossa in 1984 and it was a Pininfarina masterpiece whose major feature was the horizontal strakes leading to the radiator intakes just ahead of the rear wheels. The 305 cu.in engine had been fitted with four-valve heads so the power had increased to 390 bhp; this required bigger radiators for which the side location was better than the previous front mounting. The front intake still fed air to the brake cooling ducts. Rear radiators, plus bigger rear tires, made the car six inches wider than the BB; two inches were added to the wheelbase and five inches to the overall length.

The Testarossa stayed virtually unchanged until 1992 when the 512TR arrived with 428 bhp and anti-lock brakes; a new front showed a family identity that would be carried across to the 355. Only two years later came the 512M, with 440 bhp in slightly less weight, new wheels and a revised front with headlights now visible behind clear plastic, but the overall shape was unchanged from the 512TR. And two years later, 1996 saw the flat-12 Ferrari replaced by the Maranello.

226-227 *This 1980 BB512 has been mildly tailored for competition with a bigger air dam, a lip on the tail, scoops feeding air to sealed air intakes and wider wheels. Most, but not all, had the fiberglass sill panel and the rear wing painted matte black.*

TECHNICAL DESCRIPTION OF THE FERRARI BB512

YEARS OF PRODUCTION	1976-1981
MODELS	COUPE 2-SEATER
ENGINE	MID-MOUNTED FLAT-12
BORE X STROKE, CAPACITY	3.2 x 3 INCHES, 301 CU.IN
VALVEGEAR	TWIN OHC PER BANK, 2-VALVES
FUEL SYSTEM	BOSCH K-JETRONIC FUEL INJECTION
POWER	360 BHP AT 6500 RPM
TRANSMISSION	5-SPEED
BODY/CHASSIS	STEEL TUBE FRAME, STEEL BODY
SUSPENSION	FRONT, WISHBONES AND COIL SPRINGS
	REAR, WISHBONES AND COIL SPRINGS
TIRES/WHEELS	FRONT, 215/70 x 15 ON 7.5 IN ALLOYS
	REAR, 225/70 x 15 ON 9 IN ALLOYS
WHEELBASE, TRACK (F), TRACK(R)	98.4 x 59 x 61.5
LENGTH, WIDTH, HEIGHT	173 x 72 x 44
MAX SPEED	172 MPH
WHERE BUILT	MARANELLO, ITALY

Aston Martin Vantage and Volante Zagato

By 1984 Aston Martin had been producing the DBS shape for 17 years through four changes of ownership, and, for 15 of those years, the car had been powered by the same 323 cu.in aluminium four-cam V-8 engine. The Lagonda had finally gone into production but its appeal was limited. The company needed a new product but couldn't afford the major capital investment needed. The answer was a new suit of clothes for the top Vantage model.

David Brown had taken the company through DB1 to DB6 models, from being a maker of small sports cars through to a world-renowned manufacturer of the finest Grand Tourers. The DB4 and DB5 had been four seaters with a reasonable space in the back for adults.

The DB6 had provided more rear seat space, but David Brown wanted his next model to be a full four-seater and faster than the previous range. The new wider shape was designed by Aston Martin's own William Towns; extra weight and frontal area demanded a new engine, a big V-8 with twin overhead camshafts.

Although work had started on the V-8 engine in 1963, it wasn't ready for production when the DBS was announced in 1967; so this had to use the 6-cylinder DB6 engine until the V-8 was ready in 1969. With 315 bhp, the DBS V-8 was the 160 mph car that David Brown wanted.

Two owners later, the Vantage high performance version arrived in 1977 with 375 bhp and an aerodynamically improved body with a front air-dam, filled-in front grille and a tail spoiler. The convertible Volante followed a year later in response to American demand and remained a very popular model until it was replaced in 1989.

While the Vantage was capable of 170 mph, the new breed of supercar was aiming for even higher speeds. It was the renewal of an old association which brought Aston Martin back into the supercar league. Zagato of Milan had built a limited series of 19 bodies on the DB4GT chassis from 1962-1964. Twenty-five years on, the new owners were looking for an extension to the Vantage range at the time of the 1984 Geneva Motor Show and visited the Zagato stand. Soon afterwards, the general performance criteria for a new Aston Martin Zagato were agreed – a maximum speed of 185 mph and the ability to reach 60 mph in under 5 seconds, with just two seats and a probable production of 50 cars. The engine would be the trusty V-8 developed to produce 435 bhp with bigger carburetors, new camshafts, higher compression and larger exhaust manifolds; as this was to be an after-market conversion, fitted together with a higher axle ratio, not every Vantage Zagato would match the figures.

228-229 *Vantage Zagato was Aston Martin's supercar challenger and achieved 185 mph. Bonnet hump was needed to hide downdraft carburetors.*

The Zagatos could have had a prototype ready for the 1985 Geneva show if Aston Martin had not enforced a 6-month delay in the middle. However a drawing plus the Aston Martin and Zagato reputations were enough to persuade 50 buyers over the next six months to place deposits, a major contribution to the development costs. Three prototypes were shown at Geneva in 1986 and production of the 50 cars began shortly afterwards. Zagato received the working platforms, built new superstructures, fitted the aluminium bodywork, trimmed the interiors, painted the cars and sent them back to Newport Pagnell.

Zagato had originally drawn a flat bonnet around the lower profile of the planned injection system but had to insert a bulge to clear the original downdraft Weber carburetors. Although Zagato introduced a relatively unobtrusive bulge for the production cars, the first press tests were conducted on a factory prototype with a very unsightly hump which the press never forgot. The French

230-231 *Volante Zagato had less power but used fuel injection to allow a flat bonnet and hid its headlights behind shutters.*

magazine Sport Auto was the only one able to find enough road to check the maximum speed – a piece of unopened motorway. They achieved 185 mph – near enough – with 0-60 mph in 4.8 seconds. In fact, 51 Vantage Zagatos were built; it might have been 52 but the car assigned to Aston Martin Chairman, Victor Gauntlett, was used as the prototype for another limited series. The convertible Volante Zagato was shown at Geneva in 1987; this time the fuel injection engine was used, so the Volante looked very much as the Vantage should have looked with an almost flat bonnet and concealed headlights.

Although the Zagato-bodied V-8s never achieved the accolades accorded to the DB4GT Zagato, their contribution to the company finances was far greater; without them, Ford's 1987 takeover might never have happened.

TECHNICAL DESCRIPTION OF THE ASTON MARTIN VOLANTE ZAGATO

YEARS OF PRODUCTION	1988-1990
MODELS	CONVERTIBLE
ENGINE	FRONT-MOUNTED V-8
BORE X STROKE, CAPACITY	3.9 x 3.3 INCHES, 325 CU.IN
VALVEGEAR	TWIN OVERHEAD CAMSHAFT PER BANK
FUEL SYSTEM	FUEL INJECTION
POWER	305 BHP AT 5500 RPM
TRANSMISSION	AUTO OPTION
BODY/CHASSIS	STEEL PLATFORM, ALUMINIUM BODY
SUSPENSION	FRONT, WISHBONES AND COIL SPRINGS
	REAR, DE DION AXLE AND COIL SPRINGS
TIRES/WHEELS	255/50VR x 16 ON 8 IN. STEEL WHEELS
WHEELBASE, TRACK (F), TRACK(R)	103 x 59 x 59 INCHES
LENGTH, WIDTH, HEIGHT	173 x 74 x 51 INCHES
MAX SPEED	150 MPH
WHERE BUILT	NEWPORT PAGNELL, ENGLAND

Ferrari F40

The 288GTO and the F40 were both based on the desire of Ferrari to stem Porsche's domination of GT racing. Ferrari had withdrawn from factory participation in sports car racing at the end of 1973 when FIA sports cars were just two-seater Grand Prix cars. When this was changed in favor of modified GT cars for 1976, some private owners wanted to race their 512BBs; Ferrari produced seven special 512BBs over 1978/9 but none achieved any success. The rules changed again for 1982 with Group B – GT cars – requiring 200 identical units for homologation. While these were not for racing, they had to be produced before the necessary 10 per cent of competition (evolution) models could be used.

As it turned out, Group B racing failed to capture any following. Fortunately Ferrari was well under way with the project and introduced the 288GTO at the 1984 Geneva Show as a Limited Edition of 200. The initials deliberately evoked memories of the 250GTO, where O stood for Omologato. To be sure that 200 such cars could be sold, they started taking deposits at the show, setting a

new trend in the process. Inevitably demand exceeded the intended 200 supply and over 270 were finally built.

It wasn't necessary for homologation purposes but Ferrari chose to use the 308GTB as the basis for the new car. A small light car was obviously better for racing than the big Boxer, and Porsche had shown that turbocharging was the way to go for endurance racing. Ferrari were also using a turbocharged 91.5 cu.in engine in the 126C Grand Prix car from 1981 and had chosen to turbocharge the Italian market 2-valve 208 when the 308 was given four-valve heads in 1982 – this raised the 144 cu.in output from 170 bhp to 220 bhp with 0.6 bar pressure. The 308 engine had further development when it was used to power the Lancia LC2 Group C car from 1983-1986; it withstood over 700 bhp when turbocharged to 1.5 bar.

232-233 *Ferrari F40 was derived from the Evolution version of the 288GTO but with all-new composite bodywork.*

233

TECHNICAL DESCRIPTION OF THE FERRARI F40

YEARS OF PRODUCTION	1987-1992
MODELS	COUPE
ENGINE	MID-MOUNTED V-8
BORE X STROKE, CAPACITY	3.2 X 2.7 INCHES, 179 CU.IN + TURBO
VALVEGEAR	FOUR OVERHEAD CAMSHAFTS
FUEL SYSTEM	WEBER-MARELLI FUEL INJECTION
POWER	478 BHP AT 7000 RPM
TRANSMISSION	5-SPEED
BODY/CHASSIS	TUBULAR FRAME, COMPOSITE BODY
SUSPENSION	FRONT, WISHBONES AND COILS
	REAR, WISHBONES AND COILS
TIRES/WHEELS	FRONT, 245/40ZR X 17 ON 8 IN. ALLOYS
	REAR, 335/35ZR X 17 ON 13 IN. ALLOYS
WHEELBASE, TRACK (F), TRACK(R)	96.5 X 62.7 X 63.8 INCHES
LENGTH, WIDTH, HEIGHT	172 X 77.6 X 44.5 INCHES
MAX SPEED	200 MPH
WHERE BUILT	MARANELLO, ITALY

234-235 *Small venturis are used at the rear to provide some downforce. Bodywork was wider than for the 288GTO as the F40 used the latest Pirelli P Zero tires.*

To run the V-8 engine in the 244 cu.in category of a future Group B, the capacity had to be set at 173 cu.in, allowing for the 1.4 turbo equivalence factor. With twin IHI turbochargers the GTO engine produced 400 bhp at 7000 rpm using 0.8 bar with air-to-air intercooling. Using two small turbochargers reduces turbo-lag – the time taken for the turbines to speed up – and leaves scope for bigger ones for more power. For racing, you need to be able to change gear ratios quickly, which is not possible with a transverse gearbox in unit with the final drive, so the engine was swung through 90 degrees to allow a conventional gearbox behind the axle line; this also eased the installation of the twin turbos. As a result, an extra 4 inches was added to the wheelbase, and the rear of the body was flared out by seven inches to accommodate wider wheels and tires. The chassis was just a stretched version of the 308's tubular frame, but the body was a mixture of materials using fiberglass, Kevlar for the bonnet, and carbon/Kevlar for the roof. The homologated weight was 2550 lbs; although production ones with full interior trim were nearer 2860 lbs they were still 110 lbs lighter than the 308GTB. The GTO looked very like the 308, just longer and wider, until you came to the vertical slots behind the 288GTO's rear wheels, classic reminders of those behind the front wheels of the 250GTO twenty years earlier.

In parallel with the design of the 288GTO, Ferrari also developed the Evolution version which would have been used for racing. When the decision was taken to produce a special car to celebrate the 40th anniversary of Ferrari, the Evo was an obvious basis.

The chassis was a similar tubular space-frame but used fibercarbon bonded to the sills, rather than welded sheet steel, to give a lighter stronger structure; body panelling used Kevlar and fibercarbon while the interior displayed a lot of bare fibercarbon and little sound-deadening. The suspension was modified for Pirelli's latest P Zeros which were considerably wider, adding further to the width of the body, for which Pininfarina created a superbly aggressive style. The power was increased to 478 bhp by adjusting the capacity slightly but with the twin turbos running up to 1.1 bar.

The F40 was duly launched in July 1987, appropriately the last car launched in Enzo Ferrari's presence. The plan was to build around 750 with perhaps a quarter going to the USA which had not been included in GTO sales; the run finally ended in 1992 with 1310 built.

The BMW Z1 marked a turning point in the BMW philosophy, the return of the sports car. Over 1988-1991, 8000 of these neat little two-seaters were built and their success led directly to the launch of the Z3 roadster in late 1995, and the Z3 coupe in 1998.

Although BMW's pre-war reputation was founded on the competition successes of its two-seater sports cars, no open two-seaters had been produced since the 1960 rebirth. Only 252 of the classic 507 had been produced in the Fifties. From then BMW had concentrated on refined sedans and coupes until the launch of the Motorsport division in 1973; the 2002 Turbo wore M-Sport colors but their first product was the mid-engined M1 in 1978.

It wasn't until the 1984 launch of the M635CSi, followed in 1985 by the M3, that the division's activity focussed on producing high performance versions of the sedan cars, taking a leaf from the book of BMW tuning specialists, Alpina. Seeking more creative input from their engineers, BMW set up BMW Technik in 1985 to look at new production processes and vehicle technologies. As a visible product of the new department, they wanted to show a car designed for a new market sector, one that could also be produced if the public response was favorable. The Z1 was the result, Z being the abbreviation for Zentral Entwicklung or Central Development. Based on the 325i, it was a mixture of the old and the new.

The platform used elements from the 3-series, with built-up sill boxes, strong A-pillars for roll-over protection, and an engine compartment revised to allow the engine to be mounted further back in the search for a 50:50 weight distribution. The engine and gearbox came from the 170 bhp 325i but an aluminium torque-tube was used between the aluminium casing used for the gearbox and the final drive

BMW Z1

unit. Strut-type front suspension followed the 3-series but the rear suspension used a geometrical equivalent to a double wishbone set-up; called the Z-axle this would be used by the 1990 3-series cars. This modified chassis was then zinc-coated for maximum corrosion resistance.

Further chassis stiffening was provided by a full-length resin-foam sandwich undertray, shaped to manage underbody air-flow and produce some downforce. Wind-tunnel work also produced a clean overall shape that returned a drag factor of 0.32 with the soft-top erected, and 0.44 without. Air diverters on the top of the screen and a carefully shaped tail minimized wind buffeting for the occupants.

The principle of a stiff monocoque chassis with detachable body panels had been exploited by such as Citroen with the DS19; BMW avoided the usual weight penalty by using lightweight plastic panels. In style, its frontal aspect would appear on the 8-series and the rear

panel was adopted for the 3-series. The sills were high enough to provide side impact protection and restrain the driver, so the doors were very shallow and could safely be left open; this was made possible by designing them to drop down between the sill and the outer body, only after the side windows had retracted first.

There was actually little to be gained from such an exercise as it was more difficult to get in and out over the high sill, but it was different from other cars and it proved to the company that they were capable of making appealing two-seaters; from there to the Z3 was a relatively small step.

236-237   BMW made just 8000 of the clever Z1 from 1988 to 1991. Small front grille was copied by the BMW 850.

TECHNICAL DESCRIPTION OF THE BMW Z1

YEARS OF PRODUCTION	1988-1991
MODELS	ROADSTER 2-SEATER
ENGINE	FRONT-MOUNTED IN-LINE SIC
BORE X STROKE, CAPACITY	3.3 X 2.9 INCHES, 152 CU.IN
VALVEGEAR	SINGLE OVERHEAD CAMSHAFT
FUEL SYSTEM	BOSCH MOTRONIC FUEL INJECTION
POWER	170 BHP AT 5800 RPM
TRANSMISSION	5-SPEED
BODY/CHASSIS	STEEL MONOCOQUE, PLASTIC BODY
SUSPENSION	FRONT, STRUTS AND COIL SPRINGS
	REAR, SEMI-TRAILING ARMS AND COILS
TIRES/WHEELS	225/45ZR X 16 ON 7.5 IN. ALLOYS
WHEELBASE, TRACK (F), TRACK(R)	96.3 X 57 X 58 INCHES
LENGTH, WIDTH, HEIGHT	154 X 66 X 50 INCHES
MAX SPEED	135 MPH
WHERE BUILT	MUNICH, GERMANY

238-239 *Doors dropped down inside the sill which was deep enough to allow driving with the doors down. Inset shows three door positions, up, down and intermediate.*

Nissan 300ZX

The second generation 300ZX was a widely respected car, acknowledged as a classic while it was still in production. It had the right combination of performance, handling, practicality and comfort to appeal to a wide range of people.

Nissan had entered the serious sports coupe market in 1969 with the Datsun 240Z, which quickly established a wide USA following and a reputation in Europe as the new Austin-Healey 3000. Over the next twenty years it developed through 260Z, 280ZX and (Nissan) 300ZX, each of these being available as a 2-seater or 2 + 2.

The first Nissan 300ZX had arrived five years after the 280ZX in 1983. The engine this time was a two-cam 183 cu.in V-6 in normally aspirated 170 bhp and turbocharged 225 bhp forms, the American turbo version having 205 bhp while the Japanese market had a 122 cu.in V-6 turbo with 170 bhp (Fairlady Z200). While the 300ZX was essentially a revised 280ZX, the body panels were all new and the shape considerably cleaner – the European cars would reach 140 mph. Japanese market cars had a foretaste of the next model in 1986 when the V-6 gained four-cam four-valve heads to get 190 bhp. The Japanese 122 cu.in reverted to a straight six with turbo for 180 bhp. Further shape revisions took place in 1987 making the final version seem outwardly remarkably similar to its successor, but underneath it was time to start again.

The new 300ZX was launched at the 1989 Chicago Show, the same show that saw the Honda NSX in prototype form, mid-engined versus the conventional front engine rear drive Nissan. Everything was changed for the new generation 300ZX, which was going to be produced as a 2-seater or 2+2 (5-inches longer), with or without turbochargers. Although the T-bar roof was an option, most cars had it. The European markets only had 300ZX Turbo 2+2, while Americans could only have the Turbo as a 2-seater, but could have either body with the non-turbo engine.

The basic 183 cu.in V-6 engine was almost the same as that used in the previous 300ZX but the cylinder block was lightened and stiffened, although still of cast iron. New 4-cam 4-valve cylinder heads were fitted with variable valve timing used for the inlet camshafts. In normal form, the engine developed 230 bhp, but a turbocharger for each cylinder bank produced 280 bhp for the Europeans, or 300 bhp for the USA with higher octane fuel. There was nothing special about the transmission which used either a 5-speed manual or a 4-speed automatic.

Monocoque design too was conventional, with strong box sections surrounding the cockpit and running to each end of the car. It was all steel with most of the inner sections being zinc-nickel plated. Aluminium was used for the large bonnet and inside the polyurethane bumpers. Where the previous model had carried on the old 240Z strut-type front suspension, it had picked up the semi-trailing arm rear suspension from the 280ZX.

The new car used double-wishbone geometry, but with three links at the front and double wishbone plus a track control arm at the rear. The latter was used for the Super HICAS electro-hydraulic rear steering system fitted to the Turbo model – depending on speed and steering angle it countersteers the rear wheels by up to 1 degree to improve the turn-in before settling back to the straight ahead position. Both front and rear brakes use ventilated discs with twin calipers and have ABS control.

The body shape was evolved in house with help from the wind-tunnel to achieve a drag factor of 0.31, giving the Turbo a maximum around 160 mph. The philosophy was to capture the appearance of a Group C sports-racing car with a forward cockpit and short overhangs outside the wheelbase; the designers succeeded in this as the first impression is that it could be a mid-engined car. The sloping bonnet placed a premium on space for the engine and its ancillaries, but the short length of a V-6 made this possible and also served to keep the weight evenly distributed – 55:45 on the 2-seater and 53:47 on the 2+2. The wheelbase was 5 inches longer than before but the overall length was shorter. For access to the luggage space, the 300ZX retained a hatchback.

During its lifetime there were no significant changes, apart from the introduction of a convertible version in 1992. Having become a classic in its own production lifetime the 300ZX was dropped in 1997 after around a quarter million had been built in various forms.

TECHNICAL DESCRIPTION OF THE NISSAN 300ZX TURBO 2+2	
YEARS OF PRODUCTION	1989-1996
MODELS	COUPE 2+2
ENGINE	FRONT-MOUNTED V-6, TWIN-TURBO
BORE X STROKE, CAPACITY	3.4 X 3.2 INCHES, 180 CU.IN
VALVEGEAR	DOUBLE OVERHEAD CAMSHAFT
FUEL SYSTEM	FUEL INJECTION
POWER	280 BHP AT 64000 RPM
TRANSMISSION	5-SPEED MANUAL
BODY/CHASSIS	STEEL MONOCOQUE
SUSPENSION	FRONT, WISHBONES AND COILS
	REAR, WISHBONE, LINKS AND COILS
TIRES/WHEELS	FRONT, 225/50 X 16 ON 7.5 IN. ALLOYS
	REAR, 245/45 X 16 ON 8.5 IN. ALLOYS
WHEELBASE, TRACK (F), TRACK(R)	101 X 58.9 X 61.2 INCHES
LENGTH, WIDTH, HEIGHT	178 X 70 X 50 INCHES
MAX SPEED	158 MPH
WHERE BUILT	TOKYO, JAPAN

240-241 Nissan's second generation 300ZX became a classic in its own production life-time; the convertible was added to the range in 1992 and used the shorter wheelbase.

Honda NSX

While Honda developed their sedans and coupes cars to perform better and better, the NSX was the welcome return to the sports car market which they had ignored from 1965-1990. The 1999 S2000 showed they mean to stay there.

Honda built up their engineering reputation through their motorcycles which pushed the British and Italian bikes out of the top positions during the Sixties. Their first cars came in 1962, mini-cars for the Japanese market. They went into Formula One in 1965 with a 91.5 cu.in V-12, and built cars for the 183 cu.in formula, gaining a single Grand Prix success with each. But it was the performance of the 61 cu.in Formula Two engines with which Brabham dominated the class in 1966 that really established their reputation in the car racing world. Once they returned to Grand Prix racing as an engine supplier in 1983, their success became legendary.

Honda, perhaps more than anyone else, understood the science

of combustion. The 1971 introduction of CVCC (Compound Vortex Controlled Combustion) used a pre-combustion chamber to produce a stratified charge and very clean exhaust emissions. Because the rest of the American industry were unable to match this, the adopted solution was to continue to produce inefficient engines and then strangle the exhaust with catalytic converters.

The arrival of V-TEC (Variable Valve Timing and Electronic Control) engines in the Mid-eighties was another demonstration of Honda's engineering superiority which would be copied by all; Honda used four valves per cylinder with one inlet valve inoperative until the driver demanded more power, at which point hydraulic controls brought that valve into use and changed the cam timing giving a pronounced power increase.

With such race and technology backgrounds, it was not surprising that Honda felt able to challenge the established supremacy of

Ferrari and Porsche in the ultimate sports car market. The NSX (New Sports eXperimental) was first shown in 1989, with production to start a year later. The technological triumph of this car was the extensive use of aluminium in the suspension and monocoque chassis-body unit, some 5 years before Audi's much acclaimed A8.

Such a car had to be mid-engined, so Honda mounted a 183 cu.in V-6 transversely with the gearbox on the end, giving a compact unit that gave plenty of cockpit space and also allowed luggage space behind. The engine used Honda's V-TEC variable valve timing (belt drive) and added the VVIS (Variable Volume Intake System). In this form it produced 274 bhp at 7300 rpm; although the peak torque was produced at 5500 rpm, the V-TEC system ensured that it was extremely tractable at low speeds. Transmission choices were a manual 5-speed gearbox or a 4-speed automatic.

Traction control and ABS braking were to be expected in such a

design; electrically operated speed-sensitive assistance was provided for the power steering in cars fitted with automatic transmission, but this became a no-cost option for manual transmission cars in 1994. This all helped to ensure that the NSX was easy to drive and the suspension was well designed to provide superb roadholding with no drama if the limits were exceeded. Early reports suggested that it was so good that it was unexciting, but it was certainly safe.

Although Honda used Pininfarina as a consultant on some of their projects, the NSX was created in-house with wind-tunnel assistance.

It has a longer rear deck than most mid-engined cars, but at least this is used to provide useful space for luggage.

242-243 Honda's new sporting flagship used an aluminium body and many of the castings were in aluminium; the NSX was marketed as an Acura in the USA.

The tail carries a rear wing which blends into the body sides. The resulting shape obviously works as the car achieves 160 mph on its 274 bhp. The NSX is virtually hand-built, so Honda set up a special factory, capable of producing up to 25 cars a day.

Although the car was not built for racing, Honda produced the lightweight NSX-R in 1992 weighing 2710 lbs instead of 3020 lbs. Three ran in the 1994 Le Mans and all finished. Further appeal had been added with the introduction of the targa-style T-Roof in 1995; at the same time, came the press-button semi-automatic transmission using drive-by-wire connection between engine and accelerator pedal.

For 1997, there were two versions, depending on the transmission chosen. The automatic transmission retained the 183 cu.in engine with a lower compression ratio to give 256 bhp, but manual transmission cars had a 6-speed gearbox with the engine capacity increased to 195 cu.in to bring the power output to 280 bhp with a slight increase in torque.

The NSX will eventually be replaced but it will be a hard act to follow such a perfect classic.

244-245 *The long tail concealed a useful space for luggage.*
The 183 cu.in V-6 gave 274 bhp but this was increased to 195 cu.in
and 280 bhp in 1997. The T-roof also came in 1997.

TECHNICAL DESCRIPTION OF THE HONDA NSX

YEARS OF PRODUCTION	1990-PRESENT
MODELS	TWO-SEATER COUPE AND TARGA
ENGINE	MID-MOUNTED V-6
BORE X STROKE, CAPACITY	3.5 X 3 INCHES, 181 CU.IN
VALVEGEAR	FOUR OVERHEAD CAMSHAFTS
FUEL SYSTEM	HONDA FUEL INJECTION
POWER	274 BHP AT 7300 RPM
TRANSMISSION	5-SPEED MANUAL
BODY/CHASSIS	ALUMINIUM MONOCOQUE
SUSPENSION	FRONT, WISHBONES AND COILS
	REAR, WISHBONES AND COILS
TIRES/WHEELS	FRONT, 205/50 X 15 ON 6.5 IN. ALLOYS
	REAR, 225/50 X 16 ON 8 IN.ALLOYS
WHEELBASE, TRACK (F), TRACK(R)	99.6 X 59.4 X 60.2 INCHES
LENGTH, WIDTH, HEIGHT	174.4 X 71.3 X 46.1 INCHES
MAX SPEED	160 MPH
WHERE BUILT	TOCHIGI, TOKYO, JAPAN

1991 - 2001 and beyond

MORE CARS FEWER MANUFACTURERS

The Nineties saw further rationalization across the global motor industry as manufacturers merged companies and interests to remain competitive in a market that was producing too many cars.

In 1998 Daimler (Mercedes-Benz) merged with Chrysler and bought a 34 per cent stake in Mitsubishi a year later; Chrysler already had an agreement with the Japanese company and various Mitsubishis had been sold under Chrysler/Dodge names in the USA for some time. Renault took a major stake in Nissan in 1999. Fiat Auto acquired Maserati in 1993 and, in 1999, merged technical interests (excluding Ferrari) with General Motors who already had partnership agreements with Isuzu, Suzuki and Subaru as well as major shareholdings in Saab and Holden; GM also signed an engine exchange agreement with Honda in 1999. General Motors tenure of Lotus came to an end in 1992 when the company was bought by Romano Artioli, the Bugatti president, but Malaysian company Proton took over in 1996.

Volkswagen bought several supercar manufacturers in 1998. Lamborghini was owned by Chrysler from 1987-1993, then by MegaTech (an associate company of South Korea's Kia) until 1998. The remains of Bugatti were also acquired in 1998. From England, Volkswagen took Bentley Motors, while being forced to cede Rolls-Royce Motors to BMW from 2003. Rolls-Bentley's previous owners Vickers also sold Cosworth Racing to Ford and Cosworth Engineering to VW-Audi. Seat and Skoda also came under VW control during the Nineties.

BMW's 1994 purchase of Rover went sour towards the end of 1999 when the new Rover 75 sold poorly on its home market and found difficulty overseas through the weakness of the Euro. BMW kept their new Mini project but sold Land Rover to Ford while Rover was taken over by an English consortium.

While such movement guaranteed the continuation of many famous names, it is difficult to extol the classic heritage of, say, an Aston Martin DB7, when it is a Jaguar under the skin or a Rolls Royce Silver Seraph when it owes all its mechanical elements to a 7-series BMW. But part of the appreciation of classic motoring is an appreciation of style, the ability to turn the heads of bystanders;

to them it matters little that the parts underneath do not necessarily match the badge on the car. To the owner too, it is the badge that matters most; provided that the overall behavior of the car still matches the aspirations, sharing platforms and drive-trains with other makes is no deterrent.

Badge engineering was a dirty word when different grilles were put on the same basic car; at least the bodies now tend to be unique to a single make. Classic makes will continue to produce classic cars.

A major technical feature of the Nineties was the rapid increase in the level of computer involvement in every aspect of the car's running gear, interior comfort, vehicle security and infotainment. Engines became ever more efficient with high specific power outputs and low emissions. By the middle of the first decade (2005) new cars will be using 36-volt batteries with 42-volt systems in a bid to reduce fuel consumption still further by using electrical assistance for such as steering, brakes and climate control. While computers have become extremely reliable, they are impossible to restore. We can only wait and see how the classic car owner of the future will be able to replace an ECU in twenty years time; the cars will last but will the systems?

A CLASSIC HICCUP

The dawn of the Nineties saw the temporary bursting of the classic car bubble.

Through the second half of the Eighties, prices had risen dramatically and almost any old car suddenly acquired a value. The enthusiastic classic car owner found himself involved in the investment market as those with money to burn sought new ways of making even more. Any Ferrari became a blue chip investment.

The rarer Aston Martins and Jaguars doubled or tripled in price over five years and the cost of a full restoration was easily recouped in the selling price.

246-247 Mazda RX-7 was reshaped in 1991; this 1998 version has minor changes to lights and rear wing.

1991 - 2001 and beyond

When orders were taken for the Jaguar XJ220, investors rushed to place their deposits, convinced they could make an easy profit.

Jaguar laid down 350; by the time the first cars were coming out in 1992, the bubble had burst. Stock market indices worldwide had fallen steadily from 1989-1992; investors retreated and tried to sell on their deposits. Jaguar finally produced 280.

McLaren had intended to make 300 of their technical masterpiece, the F1, when they planned the project in 1990; but they were too late and built just over 100 of which some 30 cars were special competition versions. Yamaha had tried to join in at the same time with their Grand Prix supercar but stopped development in 1993 when the supercar market had evaporated. The Bugatti name was revived in 1987 to build another hi-tech supercar; the EB110 went into production in 1993, but four years later the factory closed after just 139 cars had been built.

All this had a knock-on effect in the general classic car market and prices dropped back, almost to where they had started in 1985. For the genuine classic car enthusiast it was good news and sense prevailed again on what constituted a classic car.

SEDANS

Future classics from the Nineties can only follow past trends. What stands out in a crowd now has a chance of being a future classic. Sedan cars will be appreciated if they have a performance heritage. Inevitably some of the Nineties hot hatchbacks will also reach the level of classic appreciation, such as the Renault Clio Williams (1993-1995). With a 150 bhp 122 cu.in engine, this was produced in three mini-series to celebrate the Williams-Renault Grand Prix partnership. With the next generation Clio, Renault went on to produce the even more powerful Clio 172 (bhp) from 1998. Peugeot's three GTI models – 106, 206, 306 – are also likely to have some future appeal.

Volkswagen's trend-setting Golf GTI had become ever quicker, bigger too; the 1974 Mk.I was replaced by the Mk.II in 1983. With the 1991 Mk.III came a new top of the range 170 cu.in 174 bhp VR6 – a desirable 140 mph small sedan.

The Mk.IV arrived in 1997 and 4WD (4MOTION) became available in 1998; in late 1999 the previous top model 140 cu.in VR5 was displaced by the new 170 cu.in V6 (V6 not VR6 denotes the 24-valve version) with variable valve timing and 204 bhp coupled with a 6-speed gearbox and 4MOTION transmission – the most classic Golf yet.

As in the Eighties, International rallying was responsible for some desirable cars, but it was getting very expensive for manufacturers to produce a further ten per cent of evolution models on top of 5000 Group A specials. So, in an attempt to keep production costs down, World Rally Championship (WRC) rules changed again in 1997. The production volume required for group A was cut to 2500 cars, provided it was part of a model family of which 25,000 had been produced.

As every WRC car was expected to have 4WD and turbocharger, entrants could then use a Group A car with approved modifications or produce 20 kits of special parts to convert a conventional two-wheel-drive car into a turbocharged 4WD rally car, although the power limit was still set at 300 bhp for both types.

So Mitsubishi and Subaru continued to run group A cars while others just produced WRC cars for their own use – Ford Focus, Peugeot 206, Seat Cordoba, Toyota Corolla, Hyundai Accent. It is the genuine group A cars and the rally car replicas that are likely to be the future classics.

Mitsubishi's Lancer started as a front wheel drive compact in 1983. By 1991 it had gone through two body revisions and the top version had four-wheel-drive and a 109 cu.in turbo 'four' with 195 bhp. Then they went rallying with the four-door GSR and produced an Evolution version with a 122 cu.in engine and 250 bhp for 1993 – GSR Evo I. Evo II to Evo VI followed from 1994-1999 by which time the four wheel drive systems had been refined,

there was a six-speed gearbox, the 122 cu.in engine was producing 280 bhp and Tommi Makinen had won the world rally championship from 1996-9. Mitsubishi's motorsport arm Ralliart produce various special editions of the Evo models. Evo VII arrived in 2001 Subaru had used four-wheel-drive and flat-four engines from 1979. Nothing classic emerged until 1985 when the neat XT coupe appeared with a flat-four 109 cu.in turbo; for 1987 it had the option of a flat-six 164 cu.in non-turbo version to make an appealing GT package. This was replaced by the attractive SVX coupe in 1991 with the flat-six taken out to 201 cu.in with 240 bhp.

The sedan Impreza came in late 1992 as a shortened Legacy with the flat-four in turbocharged

122 cu.in form with 240 bhp for the rally replica WRX. Like Mitsubishi they have produced an evolution model each year, won the world championship in 1995 and, by 1998, the twin-turbo WRX had 280 bhp – a Japanese limit for road cars. The first Impreza can not be called beautiful but the rally-derived models, WRX and STI (Subaru Tecnica Industries), are future classics on pure driving appeal. In 2000, Subaru UK produced 1000 Impreza P1 rally replicas – improved versions of the WRX – to pass UK road regulations: P stood for Prodrive who have run the Subaru rally teams in the WRC. A new Impreza is came in 2001.

Ford missed out on rally success in the late Eighties as the Sierra-Cosworth was too big for rallying, but they returned in 1992 with the Escort RS Cosworth equipped with the running gear of the Sierra Cosworth 4x4, a 220 bhp turbo 'four' and four wheel drive. As this was intended for group A rallying 5000 examples had to be built; once this was completed the ugly rear wings became an option. The RS2000 also returned to the scene in 1991 with a 150 bhp 122 cu.in Zetec engine and 130 mph performance; a 4WD option came in 1993. When the Escort came out in its final form in 1995, 4WD remained as an option with the RS2000 4x4 for another two years to make one of the nicest of all the RS models – already a classic. The rallying mantle has now passed to the Ford Focus WRC, for which a 4WD Cosworth derivative is expected in 2002.

For most of the Nineties, Toyota were also part of the rally scene, using the Celica coupe as a base, winning the WRC in 1993 and 1994. A new shape had come along in 1989, and the 122 cu.in 208 bhp turbo 4WD was added in 1991. When the model was revised again in 1993, the Turbo 4WD had 242 bhp. However the 1999 7th generation Celica just has front-wheel drive and a new 140 bhp 109 cu.in engine as the company has withdrawn from rallying to put its competition effort into Grand Prix racing, but its new-edge wedge styling looks like a future classic.

248-249 Jaguar XK8 arrived in 1996 with the new all-aluminium 32-valve 244 cu.in V-8 engine.

1991 - 2001 and beyond

Nissan were not involved in world championship rallying, but developed a very effective track car with the Skyline GT-R series. Although there had been a limited series of GT-Rs in the late Sixties, the new hi-tech series started in 1987 as a Group A evolution of the 1985 GTS for competition.

The GTS gave 190 bhp from a turbocharged straight six 24-valve 122 cu.in.

When the 8th generation Skyline came in 1989, there was a special GT-R with the engine increased to 158 cu.in and 280 bhp with 4WD and the Nissan rear wheel steering system HICAS; this was R-32. The 9th Skyline included R-33 from 1995 with the same basic specification but many improvements; in 1997, an R-33 took the unofficial production car lap record round the 13-mile Nurburgring circuit. NISMO (Nissan Motorsport) produced an R400 version with 400 bhp. In the 10th Skyline series, the R-34 arrived in 1999 with further technical changes – a stiffer bodyshell, 6-speed gearbox, electronic torque-split on the 4WD and, for the V-spec, underbody aerodynamics.

These competition cars may not be the most elegant of vehicles, but they are such remarkable pieces of engineering that they deserve permanent reconition.

COUPES AND CABRIOLETS

Two door coupe versions of regular sedans will only be appealing if they really look good, like the Peugeot 406 Coupe which was designed and built at Pininfarina; in its top 190 bhp 176 cu.in V-6 form, it goes as well as it looks. But there are more potential classic coupes which use all-new skins on sedan car platforms – Mercedes CLK, Jaguar XK8, Pontiac Firebird, Ford Mustang and Mercury Cougar, Toyota Soarer (Lexus SC in America) Volvo C70. Many of these also have high performance options and most have cabriolet versions.

Starting from smaller platforms, the Coupes and Spiders from Alfa Romeo and Fiat will also find a classic niche – both with interesting styling. The Fiat Coupe (1993) and the shorter Barchetta (1995) are based on the Tipo which became the Bravo in

1995, while the Alfa Romeo GTV (1994) and Spider (1994) stemmed from the same platform using Pininfarina styling with the GTV having the option of the 183 cu.in V-6. Cabriolets created from such sedans as the Saab 9-3 and BMW M3-series will also be worth keeping.

Aston Martin's big V-8s continued throughout the Nineties but the 1993 arrival of the DB7, then heavily based on the Jaguar XJS, put production numbers up to the highest ever at 1000 a year; they added a convertible in 1996 and installed a V-12 for the new-look Vantage in 1999.

Bristol was still an independent and continued to produce a handful of luxury cars per year. The Blenheim, still powered by 366 cu.in Chrysler V-8, replaced the Brittania in 1993; Blenheim 2 had minor revisions for 1997. And at the end of 1999 Bristol revealed plans to build a new coupe due for production in 2001; the Fighter will use the Chrysler Viper 488 cu.in V-10 in a lightweight aluminium chassis – its proportions are reminiscent of the early Fifties Le Mans racing Bristol 450.

250-251 Lamborghini Diablo roadster was seen as a prototype in 1993 and went into production in 1995.

Maserati's final variations on the original Biturbo theme were the Ghibli (1992) with the familiar V-6 in 122 cu.in 306 bhp or 170 cu.in 284 bhp forms and the Shamal (1989) using a 326 bhp 195 cu.in V-8. A stretched Biturbo, the Quattroporte, continued with the 170 cu.in V-6.The first model since the Ferrari takeover, the 3200GT 2+2, joined the luxury coupe market in 1998 using the 195 cu.in V-8 with 280 bhp – styled by Giugiaro who had been responsible for the original Ghibli when he was at Bertone.

Mercedes' 1989 SL range continued throughout the Nineties, adding the V-12 SL600 in 1992, and replacing the in-line sixes with 90 degree V-6s in 1998. A new range of SLs is expected for 2001 to be followed by the hi-tech McLaren-Mercedes SLR from 2003.

THE SUPERCARS

Certainly all Porsches and Ferraris will continue to be revered in the purpose built GT category. In the Mid-nineties, Porsche dropped their front-engined range, the 968 (the 1991 replacement for the 944) and the 928, to produce ever more sophisticated variations of the 911 – the 993 from 1993 and the 996 from 1997. Competition produced its own models; the limited mid-engined GT1 came in 1997, the GT2 in 1998 and the GT3 in 1999.

Ferrari developed the Testarossa into the 512TR in 1992 and 512M in 1994, but reverted to front engines for the 550 Maranello in 1996 as their performance flagship. This followed on from the successful launch of the front-engined 456GT 2+2 in 1992. The 'little' Ferrari became the 355 in 1994 and the 360 Modena in 1999, although the 355 Spider continued for another year until the 360 cabriolet arrived. After the success of the F40, Ferrari produced the F50 in 1995 – less than ten years later; like its predecessor, the F50 was a road-going racer with all the appropriate technology, but was not designed for racing. An F60 will soon follow.

Honda continued to be the major rival to the Ferrari 355/360 with the NSX; an even lighter limited edition of the aluminium body/chassis unit was used for the NSX-R in 1992, a T-roof came in 1995, and the V-6 engine was increased to 195 cu.in in 1997. With Honda's more active return to formula one in 2000, albeit still only as an engine supplier, we can expect more sporting models – like the type R Integra – and a new NSX is expected in 2001.

Lamborghini had been reduced to a single model when the Diablo replaced the Countach in 1990; various versions followed including the 4WD VT in 1991 and a roadster in 1995. Audi's influence became apparent in 2000 with the Diablo 6.0 VT brought back to its original smooth shape which was further refined; almost every detail, inside and out , was improved. The Lamborghini is the classic king of the road, which the VW-Audi group will challenge themselves when they eventually bring the Bugatti name to the market. Bugatti had been a classic name from its foundation at Molsheim in 1910. While a few type 101 cars were built after the war, the make was effectively dead from the time of Ettore Bugatti's death in 1947 until it was revived in 1987; Romano Artioli, with moral support from the son of Bugatti's second marriage, set up a brand new

1991 - 2001 and beyond

hi-tech factory near Modena in Italy. The EB110 (110 years from Bugatti's birth in 1881) was launched in 1991 as an engineering masterpiece; the body was in aluminium but fibercarbon was used for the chassis, which carried a mid-mounted 213 cu.in V-12 with four turbochargers, coupled to a six-speed gearbox and a four-wheel drive system. It would comfortably exceedut the failure of the supercar market killed the project and the company by 1997.

Inevitably the McLaren F1 has to be considered a classic, a rare and expensive one. With its central driver seat, all fibercarbon body and chassis, and mid-mounted BMW V-12 engine it was very much a road-going Grand Prix car, but with some very sophisticated refinement. A racing version was also built. Production had started in 1993 but stopped in 1997 after just 100 of the planned 300 had been built.

Venturi too were still active in the luxury mid-engined category; they produced the twin-turbo 408 bhp 400GT for a one-make racing series in 1992 and the 3183 cu.in Douvrin V-6 came in 1994 for the Atlantique. Lotus finally became a serious rival when

they added the twin turbo 354 bhp 213 cu.in V-8 to the long-running Esprit in 1996; the 243 bhp 122 cu.in turbo 'four' was still offered in the more sporting GT3. Lotus will finally replace the Esprit in 2002 with what is currently (2000) called the M250 using Elise chassis technology.

Another English rival will be the Spectre R45. This started as the GTD R42 in 1993; GTD had made some 350 GTD40s as steel-framed fiberglass-bodied replicas of the famous GT40 from 1985-1992, and they were very good cars in their own right, usable on road or track. Seeking a move into the world of homologated production road cars, they evolved the mid-engined R42 using an aluminium and steel monocoque with the 280 cu.in quad-cam Ford V-8 with their own gearbox. As with the GT40 the number reflected the height in inches. GTD never reached the production stage and the company was reformed as Spectre Cars. The restyled Spectre R45 was shown in 1997 and production is expected to start in 2000. As a roadgoing evolution of the classic GT40 it deserves to succeed.

Another classic name of the Fifties returned when Osca was revived in 1998 by the heirs of Touring, Zagato and Maserati with Japanese backing. The Osca 2500 uses a steel frame chassis with a mid-mounted Subaru 190 bhp 152 cu.in flat-four under neat-looking two-seater aluminium bodywork. Production was scheduled for late 2000. Of a similar specification is the Vemac RD180 which uses a 180 bhp 109 cu.in Honda V-TEC; with engineering by Tokyo R&D, it will be developed and built in England by the company that produced the Yamaha-powered tandem-seater Rocket of the early Nineties, designed by McLaren's Gordon Murray. Subsequently the only supercars have been those built to take part in World Championship Sports car racing which demanded a production of 25 for the GT1 category. Mercedes and Porsche were the only major manufacturers to get involved. Porsche produced the 911 GT1 in 1997 but made it mid-engined and Mercedes made the CLK-GTR using fibercarbon chassis and bodywork with a mid-mounted 421 cu.in V-12 developing over 600 bhp – the 25 were built in 1998-1999.

252-253 *Porsche Boxster started production in 1996 with the 204 bhp 152 cu.in flat six*

SPORTS 2-SEATERS, OPEN AND CLOSED

Two small companies that were also involved in sports-car racing of the Nineties were Lister and Panoz. Panoz had built old-style roadsters from 1996 but made a new front-engined design for racing. Engineering company Lister had produced successful sports-racing cars in the Fifties; although the engineering side has continued throughout, the Lister make was revived in the Eighties using highly modified Jaguar XJS V-12 with enlarged engines, improved handling and revised bodywork. The 1994 Lister Storm took the Jaguar V-12 several stages further with a supercharged 427 cu.in derivative in an all-new chassis and body with luxury interior at a high price. Racing versions followed.

In Germany Isdera, which started to make cars in 1981, continued to make a handful of mid-engined Imperators and Commendatores using Mercedes V-8s and V-12s. Mercedes V-12 power was also used for the Italian Pagani Zonta announced in 1999 while a new French company, Mega, had joined the scene in 1998 also using Mercedes V-12 power for the mid-engined Montecarlo.

Despite increasing restrictions on using performance, sports cars have regained popularity and there are many more on the roads now. Although many sporting drivers prefer the practicality of a closed roof, the near-universal speed limits have brought the open car back into favor. Necessarily owned by driving enthusiasts, they are all likely to become classics in time.

Most sports cars continued to use the classic front engine rear drive principle, although greater attention was paid to keeping the weight distribution evenly balanced for better handling. Mazda redesigned the MX-5 Miata in 1998 and continued to show their faith in the Wankel engine with a new RX-7 coupe in 1999. After many years, Honda finally returned to this market with the S2000 in 1999 using a variable cam 122 cu.in engine and 6-speed gearbox in a classic two-seater; with 240 bhp available it is impressively quick.

Mercedes surprised the market by joining the small sports-car sector with the SLK roadster in 1996; initially with only four cylinders (136 bhp or 192 bhp

with a supercharger) it became a serious performer when the 195 cu.in V-6 was installed for 2000.

Audi continued to make high performance S versions of their A sedans but finally turned their TT concept sports coupe into the production 2-seater TT in 1998, following this with the roadster a year later. Using the 5-cylinder turbocharged 109 cu.in (180 or 225 bhp), it broke new ground in offering Audi's highly-developed 4WD in a small sporting car. It is not the most beautiful future classic being based on the lines of the retro VW Beetle, but it is a classic piece of engineering.

Morgan only produce classics. Even the new Aero 8 announced in 2000 looks like a traditional Morgan, but underneath all is new. New extruded aluminium chassis, wishbone suspension and a BMW 268 cu.in V-8 are covered by the first Morgan body to visit a wind-tunnel.

BMW, themselves, had joined the sports car fraternity with the Z3 roadster in 1995 using a shortened 3-series chassis; within a year the basic 109 cu.in 'four' was joined by the 170 cu.in 'six'

1991 - 2001 and beyond

from which came a 195 cu.in M version with 320 bhp in 1997. A coupe model was added in 1998, together with a more extreme-looking M coupe.

While the Z3 was just a classic style, BMW's Fifties 507 gave the 1999 Z8 some more evident design cues and the Nineties M5 305 cu.in V-8 with 394 bhp gave it remarkable performance – a real classic of the future.

Ford continued to be a major engine supplier to specialist manufacturers, the 280 cu.in aluminium quad-cam V-8 being particularly well suited. The classic Jensen name reappeared in 1998 with the prototype SV8, a traditional looking comfortable two-seater; production is still awaited. Earlier Jensens were Chrysler powered but the new sports car used the Ford V-8 producing 330 bhp.

The same engine was also used for the de Tomaso (now Qvale) Mangusta, a similar style of car now being produced through an association with California based BMCD which once had a major shareholding in the original Jensen firm; the de Tomaso Guara, previously using BMW V-8 power, also used the Ford quad-cam V-8 from 1998. And yet another similar car to use that power plant was the AC Ace from 1997; the old Cobra shape came back into production in 1997 and from 1999 was available with fibercarbon bodywork. And finally, Marcos made further revisions to the original shape for the Mantis and Manta Ray using the Ford quad-cam with the 237 cu.in Rover V-8 remaining as an option.

Still from the UK, TVR restyled their range around the Griffith in 1990 using Rover V-8 power in 237 cu.in and 262 cu.in forms with the softer Chimaera arriving in 1992. TVR finally increased the Rover unit to 305 cu.in before bringing in their own 256 cu.in V-8 for the Cerbera 2+2 in 1995. Their own 244 cu.in straight six was used for the 1996 Tuscan Speed Six which was further restyled in 1999. Through the Nineties TVR became a performance icon well able to accelerate faster than many more established supercars.

From Japan, Mitsubishi's 4WD 3000 GT with up to 280 bhp remained in production through the Nineties and was joined by a spyder in 1995. Toyota's Supra changed shape in 1993, gaining an aggressive rear wing, with in-line six-cylinder engine options of 152 and 183 cu.in with twin turbos and 280 or 324 bhp giving remarkable performance.

And after many years of solo representation the Chevrolet Corvette finally found an American rival in the Dodge Viper. Starting life as a 1989 show car, the Viper was conceived by Chrysler chief Bob Lutz with Cobra creator Carroll Shelby in the original AC mold – tubular steel chassis but fiberglass bodywork and a big engine, an 488 cu.in V-10 Chrysler commercial unit. By the time the Viper went into production in 1992, the V-10 had been reworked in aluminium by Lamborghini to give 400 bhp at 4600 rpm. A coupe version came in 1996 with V-10 power up to 455 bhp. Successful also in International GT racing, the Viper has become an a classic in its own time. Chrysler's other classic offerings of the Nineties were the sports two-seater Plymouth Prowler based on Thirties American hotrods with separate front wings and the four-door coupe PT Cruiser; both are more retro than classic now, but will become future classics.

The Corvette itself moved on to its fifth generation in 1997 with restyled bodywork, still using a small-block Chevrolet engine but now increased to 347 cu.in with 350 bhp. The use of a rear transaxle was the major mechanical change. With a cabriolet in 1998 and a targa-style roof in 1999, the latest Corvette will continue well into the new millenium – as classic as ever. And from 2003 the world is hoping to see a new Jaguar sports car, the F-type, nearly 30 years after the final E-type. The XJS and XK8 were aimed at E-type owners who wanted more comfort, but they did not replace the E-type.

The F-type concept car, shown by Jaguar at the 2000 Detroit show, was based on the running gear from the S-type sedan which had been introduced

in 1998. If the production car looks as good as the concept, the F-type will be an instant classic.

While the Morgan had long ruled as the traditional minimalist sports car – all performance and few comforts – a new breed has taken over. The Caterham 7 continues to provide exciting dynamic behavior but is really more at home on the race track. Westfield and Donkevoort (Holland) followed the same theme but without the original Lotus blessing. The Rocket was even less of a road car, looking more like a Late-fifties Cooper GP car; designed by McLaren's Gordon Murray, it had tandem seating for two and a 143 bhp 61 cu.in Yamaha 4-cylinder unit ahead of the rear axle. Renault joined the fray with the Sport Spider in 1996 using a mid-mounted 122 cu.in 'four' with 150 or 175 bhp and a race championship was organized for them. And 1999 saw the Lotus 340R; Elise with cycle front wings and skimpy bodywork.

254-255 BMW Z-8 Roadster has an aluminium space frame and 400 bhp; limited production started in 2000.

At the end of 2000 a new name entered the ring – Strathcarron – on a lightweight two-seater powered by a Triumph 73 cu.in motorcycle 'four' producing up to 140 bhp. Low volume cars built for enthusiasts usually become classics in time.

Mid-engined sports cars were still a rarity. MG returned to the market in 1995 with the MGF using the Rover K-series engine and transmission mounted behind the driver. Lotus used the same power unit when they presented the Elise in 1995; this pioneered new extruded aluminium technology in the chassis, which has also been adopted by Vauxhall and Opel for the VX220. Toyota too still had faith in mid-mounted engines for sports cars and redesigned the MR-2 for 2000. Having dropped the 968, Porsche created a new entry-level sports car in the Boxster (1996) with the 152 cu.in flat-six engine mounted amidships, another classic Porsche destined for a long life. Still the home of the low-volume sports car, England produced the Noble M10 V6 in 1998. Designer Lee Noble had been familiar to racing enthusiasts for his Ultima, Prosport and Ascari track cars. The M10 was his road car; using a mid-mounted Ford Duratec 152 cu.in aluminium V-6 in a steel chassis with fiberglass composite bodywork, it is built to a remarkably high standard: Based on past experience, all the cars from the Nineties that we have mentioned are likely to become future classics.

However, many of them are still in production and will depreciate in value like any new car. Classic reconition can take up to 15 years, so catch them before the prices go up.

Lamborghini Diablo 5.7

By the time the Countach ceased production, it had been around for 16 years. It may not have been the most beautiful of supercars but it was unquestionably the most dramatic. Two changes of ownership had slowed the funds available for its replacement, but Chrysler's takeover in 1987 contributed considerably to the birth of the Diablo, finally launched in January 1990.

The Countach had been drawn by Bertone's Marcello Gandini. It was Gandini who styled the Diablo, long, low and with none of the sharp edges of the Countach. Where the Countach grew scoops and air-ducts during its development, the Diablo used the wind-tunnel to get the air flowing where it was wanted.

During the Diablo's gestation period, four-wheel-drive had become fashionable for supercars, starting with the Porsche 959; the prototype Jaguar XJ220 and the Bugatti EB110 followed. The Countach layout was particularly suitable for this; the gearbox was ahead of the engine with the shaft to the final drive running via drop-gears through the sump; the shaft could easily be extended forward to drive the front wheels through a center differential. The Diablo had

an extra six inches in the Countach-style chassis to allow the four-wheel-drive option – the Diablo VT (Viscous Traction).

Inevitably the new car had to produce more power. The Countach's V-12 was increased from 315 to 347 cu.in, and 455 bhp to 492 bhp. With the smoother body shape, this took the Diablo to 205 mph at the Nardo test track in southern Italy. The VT, launched a year later, recorded 202 mph; some power is lost through the four-wheel-drive system.

By mid-1992 the recession was biting and Lamborghini were suffering from a lack of orders. By the end of the year Chrysler were ready to sell. But it was a year before the company was taken over by Megatech, a Bermuda-based company under Indonesian control. Meanwhile Lamborghini were trying to boost sales with limited editions; the factory could build 650 cars a year but had only produced 300 in 1992.

256-257 Gandini and the wind tunnel ensured that the Diablo did not requite wings and ugly scoops. The shape is almost a single volume.

The SE30, shown in September 1993, was a Special Edition of 150 cars only to celebrate 30 years of production in 1994. It used two-wheel-drive with a traction control system to manage power increased to 525 bhp; strategic use of magnesium castings and fibercarbon reduced the weight from 3470 lbs to 3220 lbs. Externally, the spoiler under the nose had been reshaped to provide an air intake, and a slatted fibercarbon engine cover filled the hollow behind the rear window. A rear wing had an adjuster flap in the center; Lamborghini claimed 207 mph.

Then in 1995 came the Jota, a Diablo for private entrants in GT racing with 590 bhp available from the 347 cu.in. engine. Engine air scoops over the cabin were the most obvious sign that this wasn't just an SE30. At the end of 1995, the Bologna Motor Show saw the first production Roadster; the open Diablo, with four-wheel-drive, had first been shown as a prototype at the 1993 Geneva Show.

In 1998, Lamborghini standardized the output at 530 bhp for all models, the VT, the Roadster and the SV (originally the Jota); by 1998 the SV was available in GT2 form with 640 bhp. Audi acquired the company during that year. For the following year, the Diablo VT was mildly restyled with air intakes cut into the front spoiler, exposed headlights while the track was widened front and rear. At the Frankfurt Show in September 1999, they launched the evolution of the SV into the limited edition 366 cu.in. GT (80 cars) and GT-R (30 cars).

The 366 cu.in. unit became standard with 550 bhp for the Diablo 6.0 (ex-VT) for 2000, while the Roadster retained the 530 bhp 347 cu.in. Production of the Roadster and GT are scheduled to finish in 2001, leaving the single model Diablo to evolve into the next generation.

**TECHNICAL DESCRIPTION
OF THE LAMBORGHINI DIABLO 5.7**

YEARS OF PRODUCTION	1991-2000
MODELS	COUPE AND ROADSTER
ENGINE	MID-ENGINED V-12
BORE X STROKE, CAPACITY	3.4 X 3.1 INCHES, 348 CU.IN
VALVEGEAR	FOUR OVERHEAD CAMSHAFTS
FUEL SYSTEM	FUEL INJECTION
POWER	492-530 BHP AT 7100 RPM
TRANSMISSION	5-SPEED (SV MODEL WITH 4WD)
BODY/CHASSIS	STEEL FRAME, ALUMINIUM AND COMPOSITE BODY
SUSPENSION	FRONT, WISHBONES AND COIL SPRINGS REAR, WISHBONES AND COIL SPRINGS
TIRES/WHEELS	FRONT 235/35 X 18 ON 8.5 IN. ALLOYS REAR 335/30 X 18 ON 13 IN. ALLOYS
WHEELBASE, TRACK (F), TRACK(R)	104.3 X 60.6 X 64.6 INCHES
LENGTH, WIDTH, HEIGHT	175.6 X 80.3 X 43.3 INCHES
MAX SPEED	205 MPH
WHERE BUILT	MODENA, ITALY

258-259 *Additional side window allows better visibility than many mid-engined cars. Diablo continues the Countach's beetle-wing door system.*

Bugatti EB110

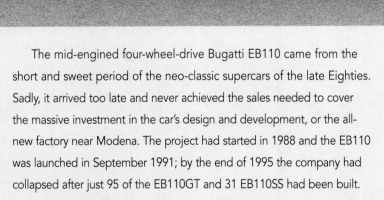

The mid-engined four-wheel-drive Bugatti EB110 came from the short and sweet period of the neo-classic supercars of the late Eighties. Sadly, it arrived too late and never achieved the sales needed to cover the massive investment in the car's design and development, or the all-new factory near Modena. The project had started in 1988 and the EB110 was launched in September 1991; by the end of 1995 the company had collapsed after just 95 of the EB110GT and 31 EB110SS had been built.

Everything on the EB110 was designed to the highest available standards. The fibercarbon chassis was designed by Aerospatiale; Messier Bugatti, aircraft undercarriage specialists, developed the racing style adaptive suspension; Bosch collaborated on the anti-lock brakes; Weber provided the fuel injection and Michelin built special tires for the car. Engine and transmission were the products of Bugatti's own engineers, led by former Lamborghini designer Paolo Stanzani.

To provide the power to achieve at least 200 mph, Bugatti chose to use a relatively small 213 cu.in V-12 engine with turbocharging to 1 bar pressure which produced 560 bhp for the 110GT and, with 1.2 bar, 610 bhp for the 110SS. To minimize turbo-lag and provide good low down performance they chose to use four small IHI turbochargers, one for each trio of cylinders. Helping to maintain a low center of gravity, the engine had a very short stroke of just 2.2 inches; the 3.1 inches bore

allowed the use of five valves per cylinder, three inlet and two exhaust.

Having worked at Lamborghini from the beginning, Stanzani had considerable experience of making compact mid-engined packages. The V-12 engine was mounted longitudinally but offset to the left – the driver's side – to allow a two-shaft 6-speed gearbox on the right, such that the main-shaft provided drive to the front wheels through a torque tube in the center of the car. The main-shaft also carried the epicyclic center differential and the Torsen differential for the rear wheels. The two block-crankcase castings, split across the centers of crankshaft and gearbox shafts, were works of art on their own.

Clothing all these mechanical marvels was largely the work of Lamborghini sculptor Marcello Gandini with adjustments by Giampaolo Benedini, who had designed the new factory. Not beautiful, it was certainly dramatic and contained such original Bugatti styling cues as the little horseshoe intake set within the grille and the style of the aluminium wheels. The fibercarbon chassis was further reinforced by a steel roof section, but the aluminium body panels were bolted into position. Scissor-action doors were chosen to keep the open-door width down and ease payment of motorway tolls.

At Bugatti's last Geneva Show in 1995, the company displayed three examples of the EB110, each proclaiming a world record.

260-261 *In the later shade of Bugatti blue, the EB110 was launched 110 years after the birth of Ettore Bugatti.*

The EB110SS had achieved 218 mph during its official ministry testing at the Nardo test-track in southern Italy; another claimed to be the fastest car using methane gas as a fuel – 214.2 mph. And the third claimed the fastest speed ever recorded on ice – 184.1 mph. The Bugatti EB110 was a very fast car of exceptional stability.

The Bugatti name had a long history. Italian-born Ettore Bugatti set up his factory in Molsheim in 1909; over the next thirty years he produced a selection of delectable motor cars for competition and road use. After WW2, with Ettore's health failing, the company failed to regain its former glories and it was finally taken over by Messier. While attempts to revive the name included the Grand Prix type 251 in 1956 and a sports car in 1960, the name passed into history for nearly 30 years.

Its revival was due to a consortium of businessmen led by Romano Artioli, with Bugatti's son Michel (by his second marriage) as the family connection. In 1988, a new factory was set up at Campogalliano near Modena, the home of Ferrari and Lamborghini. The EB110 was announced in 1991, 110 years after the birth of Ettore. Following its extravagant series of launches in September 1991 in Paris and Molsheim, it moved into slow production. Two years later, the 4-seater sedan EB112 was shown, but it never reached the production stage.

Artioli took over Lotus in mid-1993 to promote the image of an engineering group capable of working for others, but it did nothing to change the overall post-recession situation. The final end came with the auction of the factory and its contents in April 1997. A large fortune had been spent with litle return.

Subsequently the VW group gathered the remains and intend to use the name, together with those of Bentley and Lamborghini, on a new generation of supercars.

TECHNICAL DESCRIPTION OF THE BUGATTI EB110GT

YEARS OF PRODUCTION	1992-1995
MODELS	COUPE 2-SEATER
ENGINE	MID-MOUNTED V-12
BORE X STROKE, CAPACITY	3.1 X 2.2 INCHES, 213 CU.IN
VALVEGEAR	FOUR CAMSHAFT, FIVE VALVES
FUEL SYSTEM	QUAD-TURBO FUEL INJECTION
POWER	560 BHP AT 8000 RPM
TRANSMISSION	6-SPEED WITH FOUR WHEEL DRIVE
BODY/CHASSIS	FIBERCARBON CHASSIS, ALUMINIUM BODYWORK
SUSPENSION	FRONT, WISHBONES AND COIL SPRINGS
	REAR, WISHBONES AND COIL SPRINGS
TIRES/WHEELS	FRONT 245/40 X 18 ON 9 IN. ALLOYS
	REAR 325/30 X 18 ON 12 IN.ALLOYS
WHEELBASE, TRACK (F), TRACK(R)	10.4 X 61 X 63.7 INCHES
LENGTH, WIDTH, HEIGHT	173.2 X 76.4 X 44.3 INCHES
MAX SPEED	212 MPH
WHERE BUILT	MODENA, ITALY

262-263 Small horseshoe in the grille was an original hall-mark; 4WD had last been used by Bugatti in 1930 with two racing type 53s.

Jaguar XJ220

When the mid-engined Jaguar XJ220 was first shown at the 1988 Birmingham Show, it instantly attracted a flock of people trying to place orders. It was the height of the classic and supercar boom. As first shown it had a 500 bhp 4-cam 378 cu.in V-12 mated to a 5-speed four-wheel-drive transmission. When deliveries finally started in 1991, it looked much the same but it had rear wheel drive only and a turbocharged 213 cu.in V-6 engine with 542 bhp.

Although this was an engine that Jaguar had used in sports-car racing, many people felt it was not a real Jaguar engine and tried to reclaim their deposits. It was the depth of the trough after the boom. They needed their money back and were prepared to give up their S70,000 deposits as long as they did not have to pay the rest of the money. In the end fewer than 300 of the projected 350 cars were built.

The design of the XJ220 started some four years before its first showing. It was planned for International GT racing (Group B) for which only 200 had to be built. Porsche had announced their 959 but had not built any, and Ferrari had started producing the 288 GTO. Jaguar had already allowed the American Group 44 team to fly the flag in the American IMSA version of Group C and Tom Walkinshaw Racing (TWR) was going to take Jaguar back on the world's tracks in Group C during 1985.

264-265 XJ220 was very long and wide but beautifully styled.

The XJ220 would be a useful addition to the Jaguar armoury should Group B replace Group C, and it would be a flagship road car.

The first prototype was built away from Jaguar after working hours by a few dedicated employees, with a lot of help from suppliers around Coventry, particularly FF Developments who designed the transmission and provided the secret assembly area. With this part-time work, it was not surprising that it took three years to produce. It was finished a week before the 1988 show and that was the first time that the Jaguar chairman, John Egan, had seen it, but he was happy to allow it to be shown.

After the successful reception, Jaguar wanted to give the green light to the production of at least 200, but they had nowhere to build it. So the project was given to JaguarSport, which Jaguar had set up with TWR to make niche-market versions of Jaguar road cars and to go racing.

While Group B had been adopted by the rally world, it never became a force in racing, so TWR simplified the design; they removed

the 4WD and changed the engine to the turbocharged 213 cu.in V-6, which was to be used in Group C racing for 1989/90. It had been the power unit for the MG Metro 6RV rally car. The XJ220 was shortened but it still looked much the same, had even more power and was 606 lbs lighter than the original.

Meanwhile Ford had taken over Jaguar but approved the project and confirmed that the heavily revised car would cost $420,000

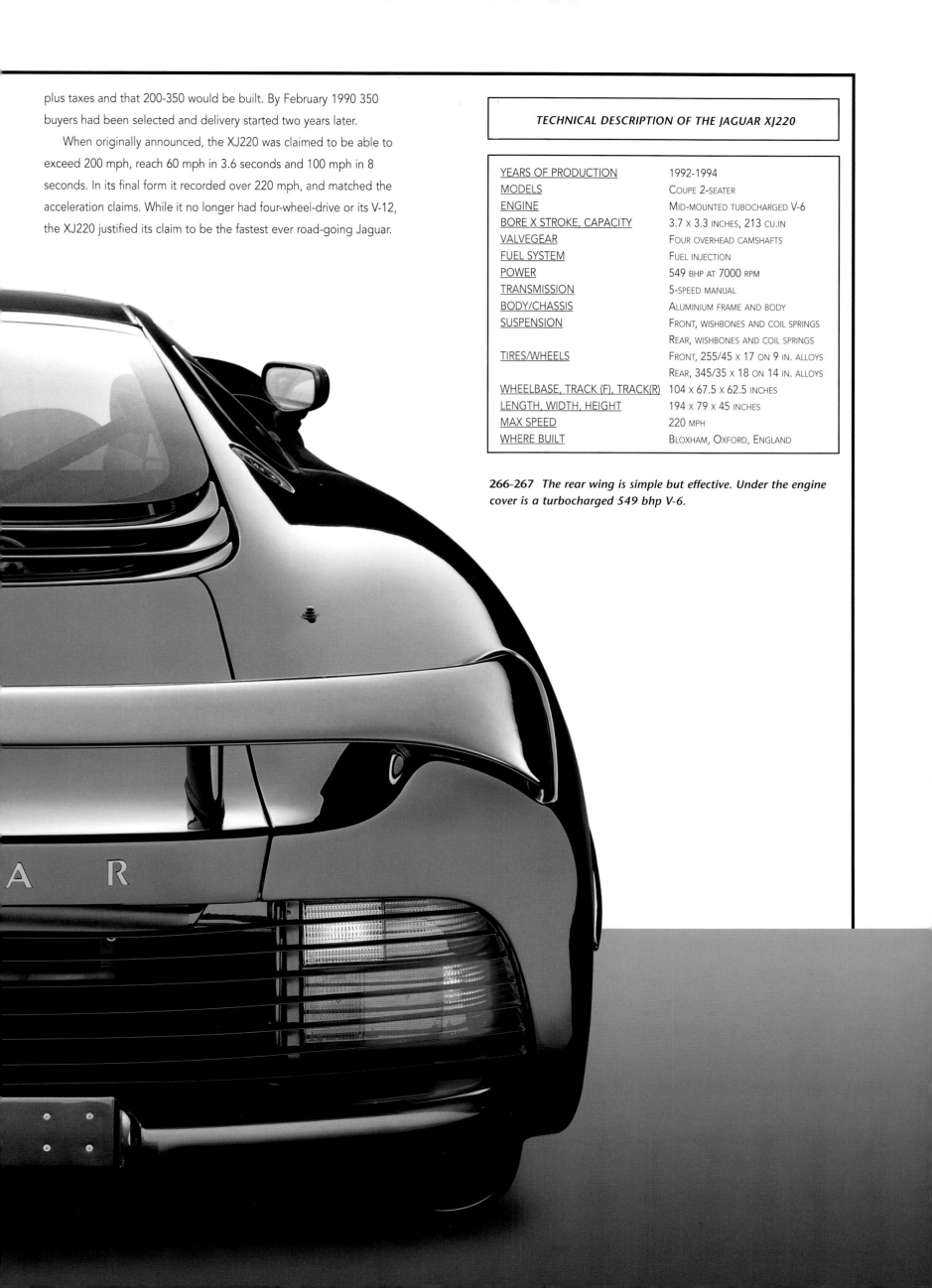

plus taxes and that 200-350 would be built. By February 1990 350 buyers had been selected and delivery started two years later.

When originally announced, the XJ220 was claimed to be able to exceed 200 mph, reach 60 mph in 3.6 seconds and 100 mph in 8 seconds. In its final form it recorded over 220 mph, and matched the acceleration claims. While it no longer had four-wheel-drive or its V-12, the XJ220 justified its claim to be the fastest ever road-going Jaguar.

TECHNICAL DESCRIPTION OF THE JAGUAR XJ220

YEARS OF PRODUCTION	1992-1994
MODELS	COUPE 2-SEATER
ENGINE	MID-MOUNTED TUBOCHARGED V-6
BORE X STROKE, CAPACITY	3.7 x 3.3 INCHES, 213 CU.IN
VALVEGEAR	FOUR OVERHEAD CAMSHAFTS
FUEL SYSTEM	FUEL INJECTION
POWER	549 BHP AT 7000 RPM
TRANSMISSION	5-SPEED MANUAL
BODY/CHASSIS	ALUMINIUM FRAME AND BODY
SUSPENSION	FRONT, WISHBONES AND COIL SPRINGS
	REAR, WISHBONES AND COIL SPRINGS
TIRES/WHEELS	FRONT, 255/45 x 17 ON 9 IN. ALLOYS
	REAR, 345/35 x 18 ON 14 IN. ALLOYS
WHEELBASE, TRACK (F), TRACK(R)	104 x 67.5 x 62.5 INCHES
LENGTH, WIDTH, HEIGHT	194 x 79 x 45 INCHES
MAX SPEED	220 MPH
WHERE BUILT	BLOXHAM, OXFORD, ENGLAND

266-267 The rear wing is simple but effective. Under the engine cover is a turbocharged 549 bhp V-6.

European sports cars have always sold well in the USA but Americans like their home-grown sports cars big. Once the Corvette gained V-8 muscle-power, it could outperform any other American product – until the Cobra came along in the Mid-sixties. The Corvette almost kept pace with the Cobra until the latter retired in the face of safety legislation, leaving the Corvette to regain its place as King of the American Road – until the Viper came along. Once more a snake. And behind it was the man who created the Cobra, Carroll Shelby, encouraged by Chrysler's President at the time, Bob Lutz. The roadster first appeared in public as the Dodge Viper concept car at the 1989 Detroit Show. It was 5 inches lower and 7 inches wider than the Cobra. Like the Cobra it had a separate chassis, side exhausts and a big lazy engine, an 488 cu.in V-10 from a Chrysler truck; the chassis is made of sheet steel with strong box section in the sills and around the transmission tunnel. By the time the production Viper arrived in 1992, the engine had been transformed by Lamborghini – owned by Chrysler at the time – with aluminium castings replacing the cast iron cylinder block and heads; it still only had two valves per cylinder but

Chrysler Viper

was able to produce over 400 bhp. Although the car is heavy at over 3300 lbs, it has good performance, reaching 100 mph in just over ten seconds, a match for a tuned Cobra 427. And there are six gears with the highest ratio allowing 70 mph cruising at just 1400 rpm – it reaches its maximum speed in fifth gear. On the road, cornering power is very high due to its massive tires and low center of gravity, but the

268-269 *Viper RT-10 is the Roadster, here. The 488 cu.in V-10 was a truck engine transformed by Lamborghini.*

roadster's ride is very harsh and uncomfortable. It is a fair weather sports car as it only had removable side-screens and a simple soft-top. But despite that, it is a great sporting machine for the serious enthusiast. The GTS, which was added in 1996, was modelled on the Cobra Daytona coupe, the car that gave Ford the FIA Manufacturer's GT Championship in 1965, even down to its blue paintwork with twin white stripes – American racing colors.

It is a two-seater fixed head coupe with a separate hatchback luggage area and it has roll-up side windows. Improvements in the chassis, together with the stiffer body, have allowed the ride to be improved and there is even more power available, if you live in America.

The American market gets 455 bhp, but the Europeans aren't allowed side exhaust outlets and also have to be quieter. The result is just 384 bhp; this is still enough to make the European GTS faster than the roadster, thanks to a more slippery shape, but the 0-100 mph time has slipped from 10.7 to 11.7 seconds.

Where the roadster was impractical for anything but fine days or the race track, the GTS is an all-weather car which can even be used for commuting.

TECHNICAL DESCRIPTION OF THE CHRYSLER VIPER RT-10 (1992)

YEARS OF PRODUCTION	1992-2002
MODELS	2-SEATER ROADSTER AND COUPE
ENGINE	FRONT-MOUNTED V-10
BORE X STROKE, CAPACITY	3.9 X 3.8 INCHES, 487 CU.IN
VALVEGEAR	PUSHROD OHV
FUEL SYSTEM	ELECTRONIC FUEL INJECTION
POWER	406 BHP AT 4600 RPM
TRANSMISSION	6-SPEED MANUAL
BODY/CHASSIS	SHEET STEEL CHASSIS, ACRYLIC BODY PANELS
SUSPENSION	WISHBONES AND COIL SPRINGS, FRONT AND REAR
TIRES/WHEELS	FRONT 275/40 X 17 AND ON 10 IN ALLOY WHEELS REAR 335/35 X 17 ON 13 IN ALLOY WHEELS
WHEELBASE, TRACK (F), TRACK(R)	96.2 X 59.5 X 60.6 INCHES
LENGTH, WIDTH, HEIGHT	176.7 X 77.7 X 47 INCHES
MAX SPEED	167 MPH
WHERE BUILT	DETROIT, USA

270-271 *US side exhausts had to be replaced by power-robbing longer quieter pipes for Europe.*

Being attractive little GT cars produced in small numbers, TVRs have always had a following among dedicated classic enthusiasts, but it was only in the Nineties that they reached the level of instant reconition by the man in the street, even though the company had been producing cars for 40 years. The modern TVRs are instantly eye-catching even before the raucous sound of a powerful engine turns the heads. They are very fast but usable every-day cars that are seen in increasing numbers in Europe and around the world, except in America.

Ironically, it was American importer, Jack Griffith, who first installed a big V-8 in a TVR – a 1962 Mk.IIA with Ford power. From this came the Griffith 200, a Mark III TVR using a strengthened chassis with the 286 cu.in Ford V-8. The Griffith 400 followed in early 1964. Although few Griffiths were sold outside America, the replacement Tuscan V-8, the first of the new Lilley management, was a success and gave over 150 mph in 1967. Tuscan V-6s, Vixens, M-series and Taimars took the company through the Seventies without recapturing that performance level.

The design for the Eighties was the wedge-shaped Tasmin, initially with Ford V-6 power which also temporarily returned the cars to the US market. Current owner Peter Wheeler had taken charge from 1981. The Tasmin name was dropped when the Rover unit arrived in 1983 for the 350i convertible. By the Mid-eighties the Rover engine had grown further to extend the range, providing the 145 mph 390SE (1984) and the 150 mph 420SEAC (Special Edition with Aramid Composite bodywork) in 1986; by 1989 these were 400SE and 450SE and a new Speed Eight came in, a longer more aerodynamic cabriolet, with 3.9 and 262 cu.in Rover engines.

Motor Show 1986 had seen the launch of the TVR S as a low cost alternative. While the chassis used the familiar steel tubes, it was powered again by the Ford V-6, and clad in a body more reminiscent of the Seventies cars. The Tuscan name returned when the Rover unit was inserted into the S3 as a basis for the one-make TVR-sponsored Tuscan Challenge for 1989; the body was changed, the chassis uprated and the engines reworked to develop 350 bhp from 268 cu.in. The equivalent road-car became the TVR S3C V8 (or SV8) in 1991 using a 240 bhp 244 cu.in Rover V-8. By now TVR had developed their own engine shop, TVR Power, to work on the Rover engines and develop their own new AJP V-8.

When the new Griffith finally arrived in mid-1992, it had a 262 cu.in Rover unit with 280 bhp installed in a chassis that had learnt the lessons of Tuscan racing; its curvaceous body had an extremely effective quick-action soft-top. The Chimaera followed a year later, a little longer for more luggage space and a little softer for more comfort, with similar lines carrying different detailing. As this was given the option of 244 and 262 cu.in units, the Griffith moved up to a 305 cu.in Rover developing a massive 340 bhp; the acceleration of the Griffith 500 is brutally quick with 0-100 mph in just over 10 seconds.

T TVR Griffith 500

Griffith and Chimaera have continued through 2000, Chimaera with a choice of the 244, 280 and 305 cu.in Rover-based engines, Griffith with the 305 cu.in.

The first sign of TVR's own engine came with the long-wheelbase Cerbera 2+2 first shown in 1994; production started two years later. Engineer Al Melling designed a compact 256 cu.in 75-degree V-8 using single overhead cams and only two valves per cylinder to develop 350 bhp at 6500 rpm, proving that complication was not an essential part of efficiency.

A 274 cu.in version came in 1996 for which the Cerbera chassis was uprated with bigger brake discs and tires.

Melling followed up his V-8 with a new straight six 244 cu.in engine with twin-cam four valve heads developing 355 bhp; this was an optional engine for the Cerbera, but it was also installed in yet another new model, the Tuscan Speed Six, which went into production in 1999.

In concept it is a shortened Cerbera with a clever two-piece detachable hard-top giving coupe, Targa-top and roadster in one design. The new style has the rounded sides of the Griffith but very striking detail in its front and rear panels; the interior is pretty striking too with nothing conventional in switchgear or instrumentation.

It is the best looking TVR so far and the performance is amazing, with 0-100 mph in 9.3 seconds and a maximum speed towards 180 mph. TVR will continue to produce classics for many years.

TECHNICAL DESCRIPTION OF THE TVR GRIFFITH 5.0	
YEARS OF PRODUCTION	1992-PRESENT
MODELS	TWO-SEATER ROADSTER
ENGINE	FRONT-MOUNTED V-8
BORE X STROKE, CAPACITY	3.7 x 3.5 INCHES, 304 CU.IN
VALVEGEAR	PUSHROD OVERHEAD VALVES
FUEL SYSTEM	LUCAS FUEL INJECTION
POWER	326 BHP AT 5250 RPM
TRANSMISSION	5-SPEED MANUAL
BODY/CHASSIS	STEEL TUBE FRAME, FIBERGLASS BODY
SUSPENSION	FRONT, WISHBONES AND COILS
	REAR, WISHBONES AND COILS
TIRES/WHEELS	FRONT, 205/55x 15 ON 7 IN. ALLOYS
	REAR, 245/45 x 16 ON 7.5 IN.ALLOYS
WHEELBASE, TRACK (F), TRACK(R)	90 x 57.5 x 57.5 INCHES
LENGTH, WIDTH, HEIGHT	153 x 76 x 47.6 INCHES
MAX SPEED	160 MPH
WHERE BUILT	BLACKPOOL, ENGLAND

272-273 The Griffith grew from the Tuscan racing car and was made with Rover engines of 244, 262 and 305 cu.in.

Aston Martin DB7

Aston Martins are like Ferraris; every one is a classic. In fact, Aston Martins are rarer. Over the past decade Ferrari has produced around 3000 cars a year; Aston Martin have only recently reached 1000 cars a year, of which perhaps 100 have been based on the old V-8, built by hand at Newport Pagnell. The balance has been the DB7, made possible by Ford's acquisition of Aston Martin in 1987 and of Jaguar in 1989. Without Ford and Jaguar, Aston Martin would have died. Ten years on Ford use the company as the prototype for new technologies. In the old days this would have spelled a reversion to development by customer, but Aston Martin compete for sales with Porsche and Mercedes, so new model development is just as thorough as these, but is considerably assisted by the availability of all the Ford facilities.

The old V-8 range had been somewhat revitalized with the Virage in 1988, for which the 323 cu.in V-8 had four valves per cylinder and electronic fuel injection, but the construction was no lighter; Volante (1990) and Vantage (1992) followed before the Virage name was quietly dropped in 1994, but the old cars continued, still in low numbers. Throughout the Eighties, Aston Martin's owners – Victor Gauntlett and Peter Livanos – were well aware that a new smaller car was needed to increase production levels, and knew that this would require considerable contributions from other manufacturers. While Jaguar had supplied Aston Martin with parts over the years, they were

not prepared to help if Aston Martin were going to produce a rival in their own market. The Ford take-over changed all that.

Initially, Ford had left Aston Martin management alone to get the Virage into production but they finally assumed full control in 1991, by which time they had also taken control at Jaguar, who happened to have the ideal basis for a new Aston Martin. Jaguar had taken a long time to put the 1986 XJ6 – XJ40 – into production and had been working on XJ41, the replacement for the XJS. After several XJ41 prototypes had been built, Jaguar decided that it was not a viable proposition in terms of the probable numbers and attempted to salvage the situation by marrying the new car with the old XJS platform. With Ford in charge, one of these became the prototype for the new small Aston, starting in 1991; it became the DB7 when Sir David Brown was invited to be patron of the company.

With the project came the six-cylinder four-valve AJ-6 engine which would form a logical extension to the DB2-6 range of cars with six-cylinder engines. It had to be an engine unique to Aston Martin, so a 195 cu.in version was chosen and supercharged to give the 335 bhp necessary to take on the 500SL and Porsche 928. The body was reworked and given a distinctive Aston appearance that reflected the earlier DB cars – its designer Ian Callum is now the design chief at Jaguar. The DB7 was duly launched in 1993 and received high acclaim.

Meanwhile Jaguar had developed the next XJ-6 (X300) which was launched in October 1994 as an evolution of the previous model, but with revised rear suspension.

It had taken a long time but the XJS replacement, the XK8 (X100), finally came in March 1996. It still used much of the XJS floorpan which meant that it fitted neatly under the DB7. Although this had previously used its own rear suspension, it now shares more components with the XK8. The convertible DB7 Volante had followed on in January 1996.

The lines of the DB7 and XK8 were very similar, they had the same interior space, but the XK8 had a new four-valve V-8 engine; as it developed 284 bhp against the 335 bhp of the DB7 and was only available with automatic transmission, the two models were not in conflict. But when the supercharged XKR appeared in 1998 with 363 bhp and 5-speed manual transmission, the DB7 needed to restore its superiority.

The answer appeared in 1999; the DB7 Vantage had a new 366 cu.in V-12 engine with 420 bhp and a 6-speed gearbox, as used in the latest Chevrolet Corvette. Developed from Ford's modular engine series by Cosworth, the new V-12 is a remarkably compact piece of machinery weighing very little more than the six-cylinder unit. Brakes, tires and suspension were also uprated to make the Vantage a truly modern supercar with 180 mph performance. It will be worth keeping.

TECHNICAL DESCRIPTION OF THE ASTON MARTIN DB7

YEARS OF PRODUCTION	1993-PRESENT
MODELS	COUPE AND CONVERTIBLE 2+2
ENGINE	FRONT-MOUNTED STRAIGHT-6, SUPERCHARGED
BORE X STROKE, CAPACITY	3.5 x 3.2 INCHES, 197 CU.IN
VALVEGEAR	TWIN CAMSHAFT, FOUR VALVES
FUEL SYSTEM	FUEL INJECTION
POWER	335 BHP AT 6000 RPM
TRANSMISSION	5-SPEED
BODY/CHASSIS	STEEL MONOCOQUE
SUSPENSION	FRONT, WISHBONES AND COIL SPRINGS REAR, WISHBONES AND COIL SPRINGS
TIRES/WHEELS	245/40ZR x 16 ON 8 IN. ALLOYS
WHEELBASE, TRACK (F), TRACK(R)	102 x 60 x 60 INCHES
LENGTH, WIDTH, HEIGHT	182 x 71.5 x 50 INCHES
MAX SPEED	160 MPH
WHERE BUILT	BLOXHAM, ENGLAND

274-275 Aston Martin DB7 used a prototype XJS replacement as its starting point, but developed a very different style and character.

Ferrari 355

With the 1999 arrival of the 360 Modena, Ferrari's small car grew up. The Testarossa line had ceased in 1996, so the new car had to outperform the old by such a margin that it would appeal to those who wanted their mid-engined Ferraris to have twelve cylinders. In fact, the 360 is just as big as the Testarossa – a big car.

The range had started with the V-6 Dino 246GT in 1969. The replacement 308 – 183 cu.in V-8 – stayed in production for ten years in various forms, which included changes to fuel injection and four-valve cylinder heads. Increasing the capacity to 195 cu.in in 1985 brought a significant power increase from 240 to 270 bhp for the 328, which only had a few body detail changes to distinguish it from its predecessor. However it had moved with the times and had such details as air conditioning and ABS brakes.

The 308 and 328 were among Pininfarina's finest shapes, taken to their ultimate in the 288GTO.

The first major change came with the 348 in 1989. The engine was further enlarged to 207 cu.in to produce 300 bhp, but mounted fore-and-aft. Behind it, the transmission unit contained a transverse gearbox under the limited slip differential with the clutch at the rear. With a dry sump system, this allowed the mass of the engine to be set lower to give better roadholding. As a result the wheelbase was lengthened by 4 inches. There were important changes to the chassis as well. The 348 was the first Ferrari to have a pressed steel welded chassis rather than the tubular frame designs that had served the company for so long.

The 308 had been styled to look like a scaled down 365GT4/BB but the lines were far better balanced in the smaller car.

276-277 *Ferrari 355 Spider was launched in 1995 a year after the coupe Old P264/265.*

The 348 followed the Testarossa and also used side radiators with strakes lining the intakes, but it lacked the fluid curves of its big brother and was not as appealing. Both coupe and spider (targa-roof) versions were launched in 1989 as 348 tb and 348 ts with the 't' referring to the transverse gearbox. The 2+2 Mondial was uprated at the same time with the 348 layout, but retained the tubular chassis and its existing bodywork; the Mondial T cabriolet came in 1991. When the open and better-looking 348 Spider arrived in early 1993, the other models became 348GTB and GTS; a few months later the engine output was increased to 320 bhp across the range.

The 348 Spider stayed in production until May 1995, by which time the new F355 Berlinetta and GTS had been on sale for a year. The number this time referred to 213 cu.in 5-valve.

277

Ferrari lifted the performance of the new car considerably. The five-valve head design, three inlet and two exhaust, was part of an improved efficiency which included titanium connecting rods to allow higher engine speeds. As a result, the 355 developed 380 bhp at 8250 rpm, compared with 320 bhp at 7200 rpm; with the latest Bosch engine management system it still retained surprising tractability, but it needed six speeds squeezed into the transverse gearbox to make the best use of the higher rev range. Although the car looked quite different, the body was unchanged above the waistline; new front and rear lower sections were deeper to include underbody venturis and the side radiator intake shape was changed with the strakes removed. Bigger tires and electronic damper control were among the changes to the chassis.

All these gave the 355 a quite different character, almost a racing car for the road. This impression was further heightened by the option in 1997 of F1-style two-pedal control with clutch and gear selection operated electro-hydraulically via levers each side of the steering column. As with the 348, the Spider had followed in 1995 and continued in production alongside the 360 which came in 1999. The new 360 set out to be even faster with its 219 cu.in V-8 engine using variable-length inlet tracts, variable exhaust cam timing to produce 400 bhp at 8500 rpm.

The chassis uses extruded aluminium sections for stiffness and light weight while the outer skin has more extreme underbody venturis for greater downforce; the radiators have been moved to the front where the intakes help to create the front end of a GP car. This time there was no GTS equivalent. The 360 Modena is a spectacularly fast car capable of 180 mph and reaching 100 mph in under 9 seconds.

Sooner or later, they will all be classics, but you can still have a very good and practical Ferrari for less money with a Mondial; they were dropped when the F355 came out.

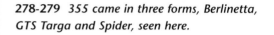

TECHNICAL DESCRIPTION OF THE FERRARI F355

YEARS OF PRODUCTION	1994-1999
MODELS	COUPE AND SPIDER 2-SEATER
ENGINE	MID-MOUNTED V-8
BORE X STROKE, CAPACITY	3.3 X 3 INCHES, 213 CU.IN
VALVEGEAR	FOUR CAMSHAFT, FIVE VALVES
FUEL SYSTEM	BOSCH MONO-MOTRONIC M5.2 INJECTION
POWER	381 BHP AT 8250 RPM
TRANSMISSION	6-SPEED
BODY/CHASSIS	STEEL MONOCOQUE
SUSPENSION	FRONT, WISHBONES AND COIL SPRINGS
	REAR, WISHBONES AND COIL SPRINGS
TIRES/WHEELS	FRONT 225/40 X 18 ON 7.5 IN. ALLOYS
	REAR 265/50 X 18 ON 10 IN.ALLOYS
WHEELBASE, TRACK (F), TRACK(R)	926.5 X 59.6 X 63.6 INCHES
LENGTH, WIDTH, HEIGHT	167.3 X 74.8 X 46.1 INCHES
MAX SPEED	183 MPH
WHERE BUILT	MARANELLO, ITALY

278-279 *355 came in three forms, Berlinetta, GTS Targa and Spider, seen here.*

The Venturi is a French sporting car that deserved to succeed, and may still do so. When such respected names as Bugatti, Delage, Delahaye, and Talbot died as a result of post-war luxury taxes, France lost its performance heritage. Since then small bands of enthusiasts have tried to keep the sporting flag flying. Alpine lasted from 1956-1994, having been absorbed into Renault during the Seventies; Ligier road cars came and went in the Seventies; Matra lasted a little longer before being absorbed into Peugeot-Citroen in 1979. And the latest to try and resuscitate a tradition that stretched back to the beginning of motor racing was Venturi. By 1996 it had changed hands for the second time but the new owners had run out of money by 1999; it has now been taken on by a group in Monaco who have yet to revive production or development. Around 1000 cars have been built over the 15 years.

Venturi was founded in 1984 by two racing enthusiasts, Claude Poiraud and Gerard Godfroy; the first prototype was shown later that year but it was not until the 1986 Paris Show that the first of the high quality mid-engined sports cars was launched. As they were doing for Alpine, Renault provided turbo-charged V-6 engines and transmissions for which Venturi increased the power output with higher boost pressures. Unlike Alpine, though, Venturi mounted the engine ahead of

the rear wheels in the classic racing position, like the equivalent Ferrari 308. The chassis was well designed with a full length pressed steel frame and racing-style wishbone geometry front and rear. This was clothed in composite bodywork of an effective yet simple low-drag shape. It was luxuriously trimmed inside with all the care that goes into hand-made bespoke cars with leather upholstery and polished wood veneers. Although it didn't have the design skills of Ferrari behind it, the Venturi was arguably better built and certainly had appropriate performance.

The first model, which became the 210, used the 152 cu.in PRV V-6 with a single Garrett T3 turbocharger at 0.85 bar pressure to give 210 bhp with a maximum speed around 150 mph. The 260 used the 173 cu.in V-6 with 1 bar of boost pressure to give 260 bhp and a maximum over 160 mph; the Atlantique was a lightweight 260 without such heavyweight luxuries as air conditioning, electric seat adjustment and radio/cassette system, thereby saving 320 lbs. By 1988, both 210 and 260 were available in coupe and "Transcoupe" form – removable roof panels and a rear window assembly that swings forward, down and back to hide partly under the rear deck.

Over 1992 and 1993, Venturi organized the Gentleman Drivers Trophy, a one-make series to promote the name of Venturi. For this they prepared and maintained a number of identical 400 GTs; these

Venturi 210

used twin turbos with the 183 cu.in V-6 producing 408 bhp attached to a racing style gearbox. The chassis was 4 inches longer and the rear body section adopted a full width rear wing; the whole body was widened to accept bigger wheels and provide scoops for brakes and the rear radiators. They had two seasons of successful racing for the two seasons before producing a road-going equivalent 400GT. Some of the 400's features were carried across to the 1995 Atlantique 300, which used Peugeot's new all aluminium 183 cu.in single-cam V-6 with a single turbo to generate 270 bhp; this had the longer wheelbase but narrower rear tires than the 400, so the it was only 5.5 inches wider than the 210/260.

By 1998, the cars had been restyled at the front and the Atlantique came in two forms both using Peugeot's latest 4-cam, 4-valve V-6. The standard one had 210 bhp without the turbocharger, and was mated to a ZF 4-speed automatic transmission. The 300 had twin turbochargers for 302 bhp and still used a 5-speed manual gearbox. The 400GT continued with the two-valve heads and twin turbos. While the same basic car has been around for over ten years, the engines have been progressively updated and the specification is still modern. Inevitably there are very few dealers but many of the components come from other cars, or can be obtained from original suppliers. As a classic, the Venturi is a good Ferrari substitute and very much more rare.

280-281 *The French Ferrari. With the revised shape of 1997 came a longer and wider car to give more space and comfort.*

McLaren F1

While the McLaren F1 was and is unattainable by all but a few, it stands as the ultimate classic supercar. Designed and built regardless of cost, it was superbly engineered to be perfect in every detail. Despite the fact that it was not designed to be a track car, a privately-entered McLaren F1 won Le Mans in 1995. That fully justified its claim to be a true Grand Prix car for the road. While the Ferrari F50 can lay the same claim, it was not a road car in the McLaren sense of comfort and practicality alongside tremendous performance. While McLaren intended to build 350 F1s over seven years, the market had gone by the time the first cars were delivered in 1994; just 100 were built and the unamortised engineering costs had to be written down to advertising the company's ability for future projects. The F1 was a first class advertisement.

Most classics started their lives as cars with a price that reflected the costs involved in their production, whether it was a sports-racing Ferrari or a Jaguar E-type, and their prices then depreciated. The market decreed that they had become classics when the prices rose. Prices for the rarer and more desirable classic cars rose very rapidly during the Eighties, such that a number of specialist manufacturers built their own instant classics, whatever the cost. Ferrari started it with the 288GTO when they launched the concept in 1984; Aston Martin

Vantage Zagato (1985), Porsche 959 (1987), Ferrari F40 (1988), Jaguar XJ220 (1989), McLaren and the TWR Jaguar XJR-15 (1990) followed on while the old name of Bugatti had been relaunched in 1987 to produce supercars from 1991 but only lasted until 1997.

Although the McLaren F1 became the fastest ever road car with a recorded speed of 240 mph, high speed wasn't the main purpose behind the concept of the McLaren. Designer Gordon Murray wanted to make the best possible car to his own ideals; as he had designed so many successful Grand Prix cars in the past, the ultimate road car was bound to be interesting. It had to be agile, easy to drive, practical, comfortable and be able to out-corner and out-accelerate anything else on the road.

Extensive use of Grand Prix-style fibercarbon in the construction of the chassis and body kept it small and light. A 372 cu.in V-12, purpose-built by BMW, gave it plenty of torque throughout the rev range and 627 bhp for a car

282-283 *Fastest production car ever, the McLaren F1 achieved 240 mph. Chassis and body are made of fibercarbon composites.*

weight of around a ton ensured electrifying performance. It was a 3-seater with a central driver seat set ahead of two passengers; luggage could be stored in special compartments behind its upward-hinging doors and it was quiet enough to hear the stereo.

A comfortable ride without loss of high speed stability was achieved with firm springing, special absorption-mounted sub-frames, and high speed aerodynamic control – a wing-shaped under-body gave negative lift. A small rear wing lifted under high speed braking to maintain braking balance, and a suction fan controlled the under-body air for optimum aerodynamic downforce.

Only after everything was packaged around the chassis in the best possible position was the body shrink-wrapped around the hard points with no wasted space. Style engineer Peter Stevens controlled the wind-tunnel tests and had a little freedom to create a shape that is supremely functional. To an engineer, that is also beautiful.

Unfortunately all this technology is necessarily expensive. Fibercarbon is a very costly material before you start to mold it in high temperature ovens over long periods, and there were nearly 100 separate fibercarbon components, ranging from large chassis components to little door trims. All the metal components like suspension links are made to Grand Prix standards. And the F1 took some 700 man-hours spread over 4 months per car. It wasn't difficult to see where a large part of the £530,000 asking price went.

The result was a very fine car which fulfilled all its designer's aspirations. What else can reach 60 mph in just 3.2 seconds and go on to clock 100 mph three seconds later? It is more a work of art than mere transport.

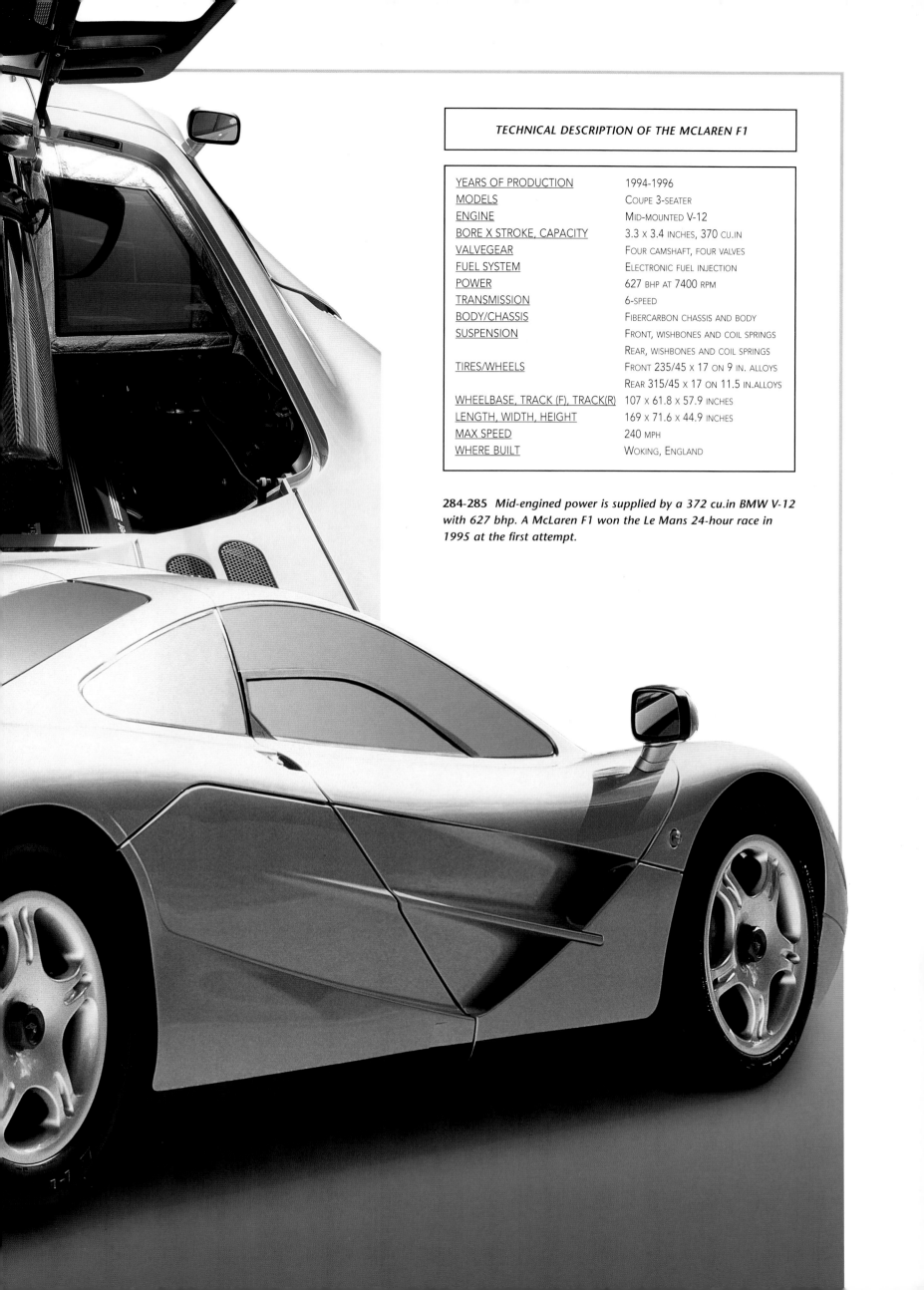

TECHNICAL DESCRIPTION OF THE MCLAREN F1

YEARS OF PRODUCTION	1994-1996
MODELS	COUPE 3-SEATER
ENGINE	MID-MOUNTED V-12
BORE X STROKE, CAPACITY	3.3 x 3.4 INCHES, 370 CU.IN
VALVEGEAR	FOUR CAMSHAFT, FOUR VALVES
FUEL SYSTEM	ELECTRONIC FUEL INJECTION
POWER	627 BHP AT 7400 RPM
TRANSMISSION	6-SPEED
BODY/CHASSIS	FIBERCARBON CHASSIS AND BODY
SUSPENSION	FRONT, WISHBONES AND COIL SPRINGS
	REAR, WISHBONES AND COIL SPRINGS
TIRES/WHEELS	FRONT 235/45 x 17 ON 9 IN. ALLOYS
	REAR 315/45 x 17 ON 11.5 IN.ALLOYS
WHEELBASE, TRACK (F), TRACK(R)	107 x 61.8 x 57.9 INCHES
LENGTH, WIDTH, HEIGHT	169 x 71.6 x 44.9 INCHES
MAX SPEED	240 MPH
WHERE BUILT	WOKING, ENGLAND

284-285 *Mid-engined power is supplied by a 372 cu.in BMW V-12 with 627 bhp. A McLaren F1 won the Le Mans 24-hour race in 1995 at the first attempt.*

Throughout the Seventies and Eighties, the major European manufacturers virtually ignored the open two-seater sports car.

They left that niche market to the specialists and made convertible versions of their high volume cars. But by the Mid-nineties the demand for sports cars had returned and BMW had already put a toe in the water by making 8000 of the Z1. The Z1 was a low volume product of BMW's own specialist department, but its success led to the introduction of the 2-seater Z3; it was a pleasantly practical two-seater with normal doors, comfortable and with an electrically powered soft-top.

Using a conventional BMW-style platform with the same wheelbase as the Z1, it was built in their South Carolina factory. Initially it was offered with two four-cylinder engines, the 2-valve 116 bhp 109 cu.in and a new 4-valve 140 bhp 115 cu.in, but the car could take more power and the Z3 2.8 followed in March 1996 with the six-cylinder 192 bhp engine. That raised the top speed from 123 mph with 140 bhp to 136 mph. In early 1997 came the M roadster, a Z3 with the 321 bhp 195 cu.in six cylinder which BMW's M-Sport division produced

for the M3. This was accompanied by some frontal restyling and outlet vents behind the front wheels. Suspension was reworked too with wider wheels under flared arches.

This all transformed the Z3 into a fast sporting machine, capable of reaching 100 mph in just 12 seconds and going on to a maximum speed limited to 155 mph.

Later in 1997, BMW showed the Z07 design study; although it appeared to be based on the Z3, it had an aluminium space frame and aluminium bodywork, and was powered by the 400 bhp 298 cu.in V-8 that would later be used in the M5.

It appeared in production form as the 193 bhp Z3 and 321 bhp M coupes in late 1998; the coupe was only available with the six-cylinder engines. In 1998, the roadsters had a minor restyle at the rear with the now typical flat panel, and the 2.8 engine adopted the variable valve timing which improved the performance.

Over the next two years engine options increased; the 4-cylinder 115 cu.in engine remained, but there were no fewer than four 24-valve six-

BMW Z3

cylinder versions available – 134 cu.in 170 bhp, 152 cu.in 187 bhp, 183 cu.in 231 bhp with the 195 cu.in M giving 325 bhp; only the latter two were offered in the coupe.

While the Z07 concept car provided a shape for the coupe, it went on to provide a chassis for the new Z8 in 2000. This retained the aluminium space-frame and the 400 bhp V-8 engine. In style, it is like a Z3 with such classic cues from the Fifties BMW 507 as the twin wide radiator intakes.

The wheelbase is slightly longer than that of a Z3 and the car is some 585 lbs heavier, but it is more sophisticated, and faster than even the M Roadster with 0-100 mph in 11 seconds before going on to the same 155 mph limited top speed. The Z8 is hand-built and only a few will be made, just like the Z1.

286-287 *The BMW M Roadster is a Z3 with a revised front spoiler, wider wheels and the M5 engine.*

TECHNICAL DESCRIPTION OF THE BMW Z3 M ROADSTER

YEARS OF PRODUCTION	1997-DATE
MODELS	ROADSTER AND COUPE
ENGINE	FRONT-MOUNTED IN-LINE SIX
BORE X STROKE, CAPACITY	3.4 x 3.5 INCHES, 195 CU.IN
VALVEGEAR	TWIN OVERHEAD CAMSHAFTS
FUEL SYSTEM	SIEMENS MOTRONIC FUEL INJECTION
POWER	321 BHP AT 7400 RPM
TRANSMISSION	5-SPEED
BODY/CHASSIS	STEEL MONOCOQUE
SUSPENSION	FRONT, MACPHERSON STRUTS AND COIL SPRING
	REAR, SEMI-TRAILING ARMS AND COIL SPRINGS
FRONT TIRES/WHEELS	225/45 x 17 ON 7.5 IN. ALLOYS
REAR TIRES/WHEELS	245/40 x 17 ON 9 IN. ALLOYS
WHEELBASE, TRACK (F), TRACK(R)	96.3 x 55.9 x 58.7 INCHES
LENGTH, WIDTH, HEIGHT	158.5 x 68.5 x 50 INCHES
MAX SPEED	155 MPH (LIMITED)
WHERE BUILT	NORTH CAROLINA, AMERICA

Ferrari F50

With the F50, Ferrari set out to build the ultimate two-seater, a Grand Prix supercar for the road, including passing worldwide emission and noise tests . Where the F40 had been a development of the 'evolution' version of the 288 GTO Group B car, and was then used to celebrate 40 years of Ferrari production, the F50, launched at Geneva in 1995, celebrated nothing more than Ferrari technology. Production of the 1311 F40s had been completed over 1988-1992 and the engineers needed a fresh challenge.

The heart of any Ferrari is the engine. Much was made of the fact that this was a copy of the 1990 Grand Prix engine, but you can't turn a short stroke 213 cu.in F1 engine with gear-driven cams and four main bearings into a long-stroke 286 cu.in engine with chain-driven cams and seven main bearings. Sure, the cylinder block was made of the same nodular cast-iron, the cylinders were inclined at the same 65-degree angle, the bore was very close to that for the F1 engine, and the cylinder heads had five valves, but this was just F1 technology applied to a new engine. It wasn't even a prototype for the 456GT engine, as that used an aluminium block, four-valve-heads and belt-driven cams. However, it is a very powerful engine, developing 520 bhp at 8500 rpm from 286 cu.in, a higher specific output than the Ferrari 355. Thanks to the Bosch Motronic engine management system, it remains very tractable at low engine speeds, although the peak torque comes at 6500 rpm. Some of this tractability is due to the variable geometry inlet tracts, and a computer choice of two tuned exhaust system lengths before the gases reach the silencers and catalysts. Five valves per cylinder, three inlet and two exhaust, allow 10,000 rpm to be reached, despite chain-driven camshafts and spring-operated valve closure.

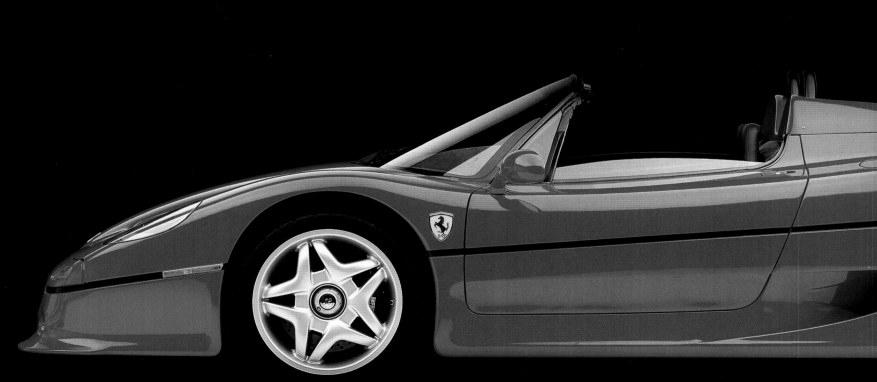

As with a Grand Prix car, this unique engine was bolted directly to the fibercarbon monocoque which contains an F1-style rubberised fuel tank; the 6-speed synchronised gearbox is attached to the bell-housing which incorporates a dry-sump oil tank. The rear suspension followed F1 principles with long wishbones and push-rods operating inboard electronically adjustable dampers with coil springs around them; the same system was used at the front, attached directly to aluminium inserts bonded into the monocoque. Inevitably, with no rubber in the mounting system, a lot of engine noise is transmitted to the interior, but Ferrari made a virtue out of this by arguing that it was part of the car's appeal. Similarly the only elements to absorb road shocks were the low profile tires, Goodyear Fioranos specially designed for this car, but the electronic damping works well and the ride is better than that of the F40. Maintaining the purity of feedback, there is no servo-assistance for the steering or the brakes.

288-289 *The black belt-line and the rear wing were design cues taken from the F40, but the tightly curved windscreen echoes Group C racing practice.*

Inside the car, composite seats are trimmed in leather but most of the fibercarbon surfaces are left bare although the rear bulkhead is covered in sound-deadening panels. The LCD instruments are computer controlled to display analogue rev counter and speedometer with bar graphs for the other instruments. There is even a gear selection indicator which the computer works out according to revs and road speed. Inevitably, Pininfarina designed the body, a mixture of curves evocative of both the F40 and racing Group C designs. It also adopted Grand Prix car technology in its aerodynamic solutions; the raised section under the nose, later adopted for the 360, allows the air to flow along a flat underbody until it reaches the venturis each side of the

gearbox. The downforce created at each end is balanced by a rear wing sweeping across the car from curved sides, just like the F40. It is this increased downforce and the electronically controlled suspension that justifies the creation of the F50. It was designed to be faster than the F40 in its ability to go round a race circuit. It came in two forms, open Barchetta or closed Berlinetta. The front section of the engine cover is interchangeable between a roof and a faring, which also includes twin roll bars to be bolted to the monocoque. Both the 288GTO and the F40 exceeded their planned production numbers. This time it was a strictly Limited Edition; 349 were built, many of which went to the USA – a worldwide classic.

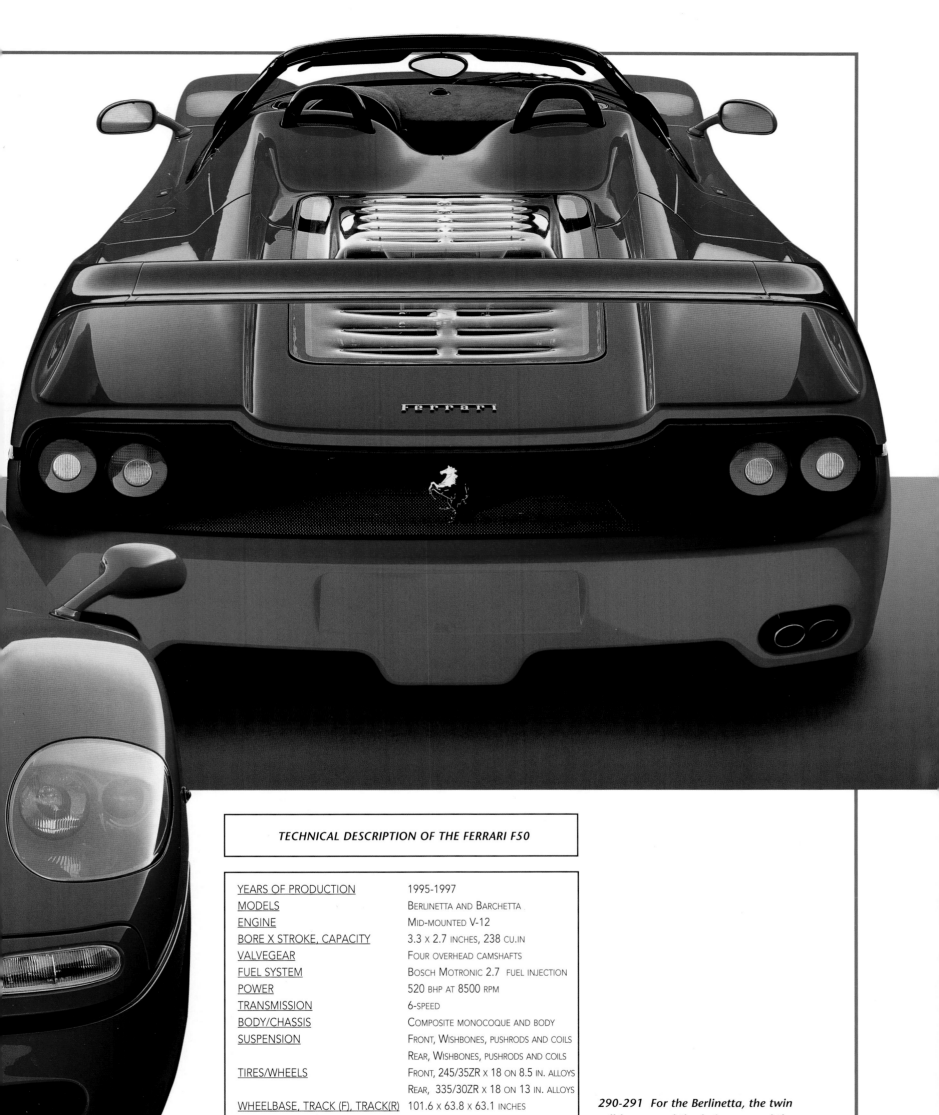

YEARS OF PRODUCTION	1995-1997
MODELS	BERLINETTA AND BARCHETTA
ENGINE	MID-MOUNTED V-12
BORE X STROKE, CAPACITY	3.3 X 2.7 INCHES, 238 CU.IN
VALVEGEAR	FOUR OVERHEAD CAMSHAFTS
FUEL SYSTEM	BOSCH MOTRONIC 2.7 FUEL INJECTION
POWER	520 BHP AT 8500 RPM
TRANSMISSION	6-SPEED
BODY/CHASSIS	COMPOSITE MONOCOQUE AND BODY
SUSPENSION	FRONT, WISHBONES, PUSHRODS AND COILS
	REAR, WISHBONES, PUSHRODS AND COILS
TIRES/WHEELS	FRONT, 245/35ZR X 18 ON 8.5 IN. ALLOYS
	REAR, 335/30ZR X 18 ON 13 IN. ALLOYS
WHEELBASE, TRACK (F), TRACK(R)	101.6 X 63.8 X 63.1 INCHES
LENGTH, WIDTH, HEIGHT	176.4 X 78.2 X 44.1 INCHES
MAX SPEED	202 MPH
WHERE BUILT	MARANELLO, ITALY

290-291 For the Berlinetta, the twin roll-hoops and the faring around them are replaced by a fixed roof. The raised section under the front intake allows air to flow smoothly to the rear venturis.

Chevrolet Corvette 5th Generation

The latest Corvette, launched at Detroit in 1997, is once again a much more refined car than its predecessor. There is more space inside and the ride is more comfortable. Its faster too. With automatic transmission it will reach 100 mph in 13 seconds, or 11.5 seconds with the manual gearbox. The coupe will go on to over 170 mph, and the convertible, in production from 1998, is only 5 mph slower.

It always takes a long time to develop a new Corvette. Given that its production rate is around 40,000 a year it doesn't justify a large design and development team. They say it took seven years to bring C5 to production, the fifth generation Corvette – 1953, 1963, 1968 and 1983 being the start points for previous generations. Like its predecessor, it is all new apart from some drive-train elements.

But this time even the major components are different. The 347 cu.in V-8 may look like a continuation of previous engines, as it is near enough the same capacity as the previous LT1 (349 cu.in) or the Lotus-designed LT5 for the ZR1(350 cu.in), but the new LS1 (345 cu.in) is a cross between the two; the Lotus-style aluminium block has the same 3.8 inches bore as the LT5 but retains a central camshaft, pushrods and two valves per cylinder in the aluminium head. With sequential fuel injection and a new composite intake manifold, power was increased to 350 bhp, midway between the LT1 at 304 bhp and the LT5 at 411; given that the new car is 3% lighter and has a 15% lower drag factor, that gives a useful performance increase over the previous standard car.

The gearbox too is different. The 6-speed manual version now comes from Borg Warner; while the 4-speed automatic is still GM-Hydramatic, both types are now mounted in unit with the rear transaxle. This improves the weight distribution and reduces the transmission hump in the cockpit. They've made the car wider and the wheelbase longer, further increasing interior space; as intended, this has made the handling more user friendly.

The suspension has received considerable attention. To start with, the new chassis frame is much stiffer than the previous one, so the suspension can work more effectively. At the front there are still twin wishbones but the rear suspension now uses the same system, rather than making the drive-shaft act as a transverse link – the principle used since 1963. The latest Goodyear Eagle Tires have a run-flat capability which saves carrying a spare wheel.

Like most high performance cars, the Corvette has anti-lock brakes and the associated traction and stability controls.

There is a choice of suspension options too from comfortable to adaptive to sport modes. Its rack and pinion steering is servo-assisted and the steering wheel position is adjustable.

Since the launch, a hard-top coupe was added to the range in 1999, together with head-up display for some of the information; although the facia now has dials with needles, a projection onto the bottom of the screen shows engine speed and oil pressure as bar graphs and a digital road speed.

A little more power was added in 2001 with improved fuel consumption, and it is now possible to get a Corvette C06, a hard-top coupe with 390 bhp, 110 lbs less and wider wheels. Meanwhile the Corvette has also been out on the International GT race-tracks, taking on the Vipers and Porsches; the C5-R won the 2001 Daytona 24-hour race outright. Impressive as previous Corvettes have been in their day, this one is equally sure to become a future classic, worth the seven-year wait.

TECHNICAL DESCRIPTION OF THE CHEVROLET CORVETTE

YEARS OF PRODUCTION	1997-PRESENT
MODELS	COUPE AND CONVERTIBLE 2-SEATER
ENGINE	FRONT-MOUNTED V-8
BORE X STROKE, CAPACITY	3.8 X 3.6 INCHES, 345 CU.IN
VALVEGEAR	CENTRAL CAMSHAFT
FUEL SYSTEM	BOSCH SEQUENTIAL INJECTION
POWER	350 BHP AT 5600 RPM
TRANSMISSION	4-SPEED AUTO OR 6-SPEED MANUAL
BODY/CHASSIS	STEEL FRAME, FIBERGLASS BODY
SUSPENSION	FRONT, WISHBONES AND LEAF SPRING
	REAR, WISHBONES AND LEAF SPRING
TIRES/WHEELS	FRONT, 245/45 X 17 ON 8.5 IN. ALLOYS
	REAR, 275/40 X 17 ON 9.5 IN. ALLOYS
WHEELBASE, TRACK (F), TRACK(R)	104.5 X 62 X 62.2 INCHES
LENGTH, WIDTH, HEIGHT	179.7 X 73.6 X 47.6 INCHES
MAX SPEED	171 MPH
WHERE BUILT	KENTUCKY, USA

292-293 *The latest generation Corvette was launched in 1997, followed a year later by the Cabriolet.*

Porsche Boxster

From the time that the mid-engined Boxster was shown as a concept car at Detroit in 1993, the front-engined 968's days were numbered. This was the new entry-level Porsche, a real sports car packed with all the latest Porsche technology including a new version of Porsche's hallmark engine, the flat-6 'boxer'. Boxer roadster produced Boxster. Although the concept car was styled after the fashion of the mid-engined 550 Spyder of 1953, with no luggage space and little room for crash absorption, the mechanical elements stayed with the design through the next three years of development.

The Boxster will inevitably become a classic one day; like all Porsches, the relatively low production rate ensures some rarity.

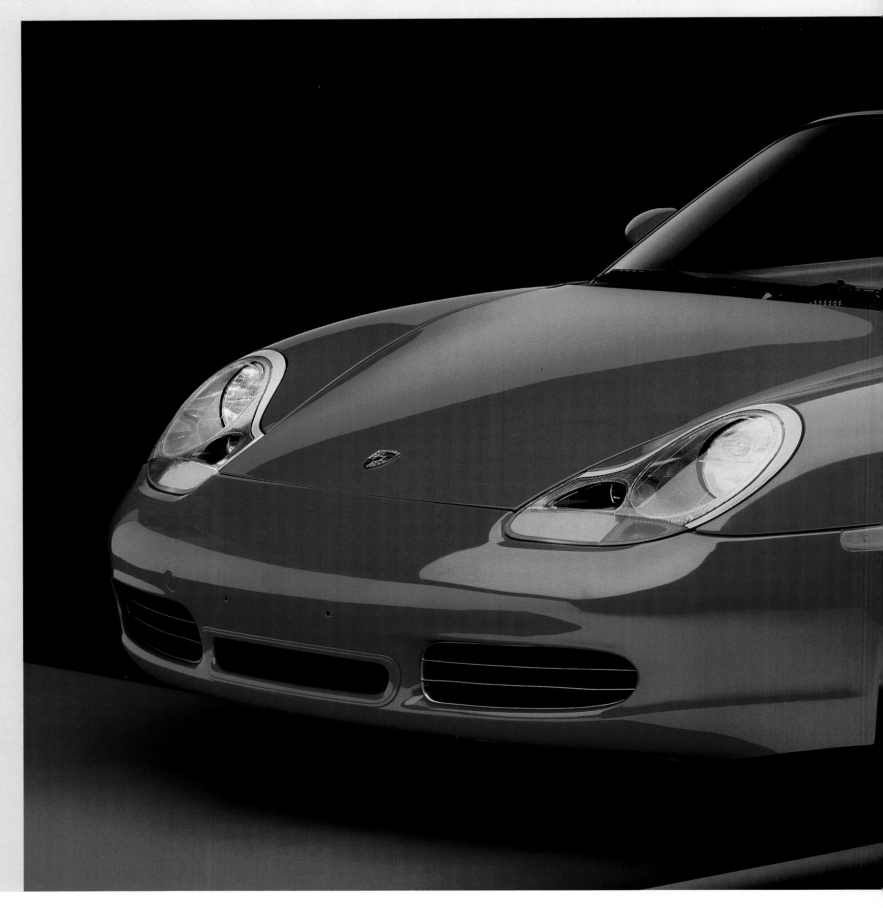

Just before the Boxster went into production in Finland, the millionth Porsche was produced covering a period of exactly 50 years; a quarter have been open cars. In round figures, there have been 77,000 of the 356, 118,000 of the 914/916, 325,000 of the 924/944/968, 61,000 of the 928 with the 911 still running after 419,000 had been produced by July 15, 1996. That average rate of 20,000 per year has now been almost doubled to around 40,000, with the Boxster contributing approximately half.

The heart of any car is the engine, particularly with a Porsche.

The Boxster has a new flat-6 with full water-cooling, integral dry sump lubrication and four-valve heads.

The two-piece alloy crankcase clamps a central cast-iron bearing bridge, containing the seven main bearings and a layshaft which takes the drive to the camshafts; chain wheels are mounted at each end of the layshaft to drive the exhaust camshafts. These drive the inlet camshafts through separate chains via Porsche's Variocam system which alters the inlet timing. Aluminium cylinder blocks use Silumin cylinder coating, and the heads too are aluminium castings.

294-295 With the 1999 Boxster S came the 195 cu.in engine and wider wheels and tires.

TECHNICAL DESCRIPTION OF THE PORSCHE BOXSTER S

YEARS OF PRODUCTION	1999-PRESENT
MODELS	ROADSTER 2-SEATER
ENGINE	MID-MOUNTED FLAT-6
BORE X STROKE, CAPACITY	3.6 X 3 INCHES, 193 CU.IN
VALVEGEAR	FOUR CAMSHAFT, FOUR VALVES
FUEL SYSTEM	BOSCH MOTRONIC FUEL INJECTION
POWER	252 BHP AT 6250 RPM
TRANSMISSION	6-SPEED
BODY/CHASSIS	STEEL MONOCOQUE
SUSPENSION	FRONT, STRUTS AND COIL SPRINGS
	REAR, STRUTS AND COIL SPRINGS
TIRES/WHEELS	FRONT 205/50 X 17 ON 7 IN. ALLOYS
	REAR 255/40 X 17 ON 8.5 IN.ALLOYS
WHEELBASE, TRACK (F), TRACK(R)	95.1 X 57.7 X 60.2 INCHES
LENGTH, WIDTH, HEIGHT	170 X 70 X 50.8 INCHES
MAX SPEED	164 MPH
WHERE BUILT	STUTTGART, GERMANY

Ignition and the sequential injection are controlled by the latest Bosch Motronic system.

As launched the engine was a 152 cu.in developing 204 bhp at 6000 rpm with maximum torque of 181 lb.ft at 4500 rpm but it maintained over 80 per cent of that between 1750 and 6500 rpm. The Boxster S came in early 1999 with the engine increased to 195 cu.in, 252 bhp and 225 lb.ft at 4500 rpm; and later the same year, the standard engine was increased to 164 cu.in in 1999, increasing the power to 220 bhp and torque to 192 lb.ft at 4750 rpm. The standard transmission is a 5-speed manual gearbox but Porsche's 5-speed Tiptronic box allows manual override by push-buttons on the steering wheel. The 195 cu.in S has a six-speed gearbox.

Galvanized steel is used for the unitary chassis; this carries MacPherson strut suspension front and rear, chosen for its compactness, while the brakes use 4-piston calipers.

Features of the body include a rear aerofoil that rises at over 50 mph and a remarkable electrically-operated folding roof that can be raised or lowered in just 12 seconds. There are also two luggage compartments, one under the bonnet and another over the gearbox. The style retains the traditional broad sloping front which produces a very low 0.31 drag factor with the hood raised; a hard-top is one of the many options available.

There are many other features both standard and optional which add together to make the Boxster such an exceptional car.

It is above all a driver's car providing maximum enjoyment in safety; top speeds of the three versions range from 145 mph to 160 mph and the acceleration is very quick thanks to an overall weight of only 2750 lbs. Early reports praised the handling and roadholding and said that the chassis could easily handle more power.

The 252 bhp Boxster S is just the first of probably many higher power derivatives – the more power the more classic.

296-297 *Styling is simple and effective and is unlikely to show signs of age in the future.*

AERODYNAMIC TERMINOLOGY

- **Air dam (bib)** - A transverse lip or bib, mounted under the nose of the car, which diverts air around the car and reduces the flow under the body.
- **Downforce** - The overall downward force exerted by aerodynamic attachments on the upper surface of the car.
- **Drag** - The overall aerodynamic force encountered by the body as it goes through the air. The drag coefficient gives the measure of efficiency of the shape compared with a vertical flat plate of coefficient 1.
- **Eddy** - The turbulent air created in the wake of the car as it moves through the air. Eddies increase drag.
- **Kamm tail** - A sharp vertical cut-off at the rear of the car. This retains the streamlining effect of a long shapely tail but provides quick separation from the drag-inducing eddies created by a conventional notchback.
- **Lift** - Air flowing over surfaces creates a pressure. If the pressure below a body is greater than above, the result is lift. The opposite is usually referred to as negative lift. The pressure difference multiplied by the surface area gives the overall upwards or downwards force.
- **Spoiler** - Usually fitted at the rear of the car, this acts like a Kamm tail and interrupts the air flow; by its shape it also acts to provide downforce. Front spoilers are shaped to provide front downforce, rather than just act as air diverters.
- **Rear wing** - A wing across the rear of the car, shaped to give some downforce and straighten the air-flow to reduce the turbulence behind the car.
- **Skirt** - Technically this refers to plastic sheet hanging down under the sills to ensure that underbody air is directed to the rear of the car. On road cars, the skirt refers to any moulding mounted below the sills and is usually only for cosmetic purposes.
- **Venturi** - Underbody ducts at the rear of the car which are shaped to create negative pressure and therefore downforce.

BODY TERMINOLOGY

- **Barchetta** - A little boat is the Italian term for the full-width bodies used on sports cars after the period of cycle-wings.
- **Berlina** - After the horse-drawn Berlin coach, Berline (Fr) or Berlina (It) is a closed car capable of carrying at least four people. Saloon (Eng) and Sedan (US) are the equivalent terms.
- **Berlinetta** - A little saloon, therefore a two-seater fixed head coupé. The equivalent Salonette was only ever used by MG.
- **Brougham** - Coachwork term referring to a size half way between a limousine and a saloon, but with an open section over the front seats and a relatively small rear compartment for two.
- **Cabriolet** - The non-English equivalent to the drop-head coupé, usually only on a 2-door car. It implies that the folding hood is permanently fixed to the car giving better weather protection than the removable hood of a roadster. When down it will be concealed beneath a cover.

- **Convertible** - TThe American term for a drop-head coupé but now used for the two-door 4-seater hatchbacks. Convertible sedans are the 4-door equivalents (US).
- **Coupé** - Pronounced "coupay", this is a French term for a shortened saloon, now much used by English-speaking manufacturers; American speech ignores the acute accent on the 'e' and refers to it as a 'coop'. Since the Sixties it has become the 2-door sporting version of a 4-seater saloon car. Before that the coupé was usually a 2-seater, or 2+2; drop-head coupés (dhc) had soft tops that folded down (as cabriolets) and fixed-head coupés (fhc) were the solid roof equivalent of a dhc. Drop-head coupés, cabriolets and convertibles all have roll-up side windows - Roadsters did not in the Fifties.
- **De Ville** - A town carriage with the front seats covered by a removable panel, giving rise to Coupé de Ville or Limousine de Ville.
- **Facia** - The complete padded panel with instruments, and controls for heating, radio etc. The old dashboard just carried instruments and switches.
- **Fairing** - A panel added to lessen aerodynamic drag as in the covering of rear wheel arches or in the head-fairing behind the seats of some open two-seaters.
- **Fastback** - A body with a rear section that slopes from roof to tail in a straight or convex line - as the pre-war Airline designs.
- **GT** - Gran Turismo or Grand Touring was a fixed-head coupé with, probably, a fastback, giving sports car performance in comfort for two people and luggage. The initials have been abused over the years to imply high performance without style.
- **Hatchback** - A body with an opening rear panel.
- **Homologated** - FIA-recognized
- **Limousine** - Originally a six-light large saloon - three windows per side - now any large car capable of carrying six or more people.
- **Notchback** - A body with separate rear luggage compartment
- **Roadster** - American name for open two-seater with sporting lines and, originally, a soft-top carried in the car for occasional use. English equivalent used to be Sports Car. Now used when the lowered soft-top is completely concealed beneath a flat panel.
- **Saloon** - English equivalent to Sedan (US) and Berlina (It), derived from the room in a house.
- **Sedan** - American name for Saloon.
- **Sedanca** - The same as a Coupé de Ville. Sedanca de Ville is effectively a Limousine de Ville with a rear compartment taking four people.
- **Sill** - The boxed panel below the bottom of the door opening. Called the rocker panel in America.
- **Spider** - Italian equivalent of Roadster or Sports Car.
- **Strake** - a curved strip on the side of the bodywork. This comes from the full-length wooden planks used on in boat-building.
- **Targa roof** - Fixed head coupé with removable roof section. Triumph TR4

referred to it as a Surrey Top which originally applied only to the fabric covering, which Triumph also provided.

- **Tonneau** - Originally an open body with access to the rear compartment through a small door, either in the side or rear. Now only used in 'tonneau cover' referring to the soft material covering some or all of the seats of an open car.
- **Tourer** - An open 2-door car with four seats and a cabriolet top. Twenties Tourers often had smaller doors for the rear compartment.

POWER-TRAIN TERMINOLOGY

- **4-cam** - Term used to show that a vee-engine has twin overhead camshafts for each bank of cylinders. Also quad-cam.
- **4-choke** - Each intake hole in a carburetter is called a choke because the air-flow is choked to create the low pressure to suck the fuel out of the jets. With big V-8s, a single carburetter with four chokes is a very efficient means of supplying the mixture. Most have progressive later opening of the larger pair of chokes.
- **4WD** - Four-wheel-drive. FWD means Front-wheel-drive.
- **4WS** - Four wheel steering, the computer-controlled system. that actively steers the rear wheels by small amounts to improve handling.
- **ABS** - Anti-Block System, the original term for Anti-lock Brakes.
- **BHP** - Brake Horsepower, or the rate at which an engine can work. One brake horsepower is 550 pounds-feet per second. Pounds-feet is a measure of torque; the time per cycle is shorter so the power is greater as engine speed rises. It is called Brake Horsepower because it is measured against a braking torque on a dynamometer.
- **ESP** - Electronic Stability Programme. Porsche's term for the overall computer control that can apply individual brakes or decrease the power to maintain traction on slippery roads, or to recover a potentially dangerous cornering situation. Other manufacturers use different initials for the same functions.
- **Oversteer** - Handling term to denote that the tire slip angle is greater at the rear than at the front. The car tightens its line in a corner and less steering lock is required.
- **Slip angle** - When a tire is subjected to a cornering force it runs at an angle to the direction it is pointing. This is known as the slip angle.
- **Supercharger** - Engine-driven air-pump or compressor which supplies air under pressure to the engine's intake system.
- **Traction Control** - Original form of ESP where braking or power can be adjusted to maintain traction, but not to correct cornering problems.
- **Turbo(charger)** - Compressor, driven by a turbine which is powered by the engine's exhaust gases.
- **Understeer** - Handling term to denote that the tire slip angle is greater at the front than at the rear. The car runs wide in a corner and more steering lock is required.

BIBLIOGRAPHY

Alfa Romeo Tradition, Griffith Borgeson, Haynes Publishing, Somerset, UK, 1990.

Alfa Romeo, Le Vetture dal 1910, Luigi Fusi, Editrice Adiemme, Milan, Italy, 1965.

America, Great Marques of, Jonathan Wood, Octopus Books, London, UK, 1986.

American Automobile, Art of, Nick Georgano, Cadogan Publishing, London, UK, 1985.

Austin Healey, Original, Anders Clausager, Bay View Books, Devon, UK, 1990.

BMW, A History, Halwart Schrader, Osprey Publishing, London, UK, 1979.

Boss Wheels, Robert C.Bowden, TAB Books, Pennsylvania, USA, 1979.

Bristol Cars and Engines, L.J.K.Setright, Motor Racing Publications, Surrey, UK, 1974.

Bristol Cars Gold Portfolio, Various Road Tests, Brooklands Books, Surrey, UK, 1988.

British Post-war Classic Cars, Jonathan Wood, Osprey Publishing, London, UK, 1980.

Camaro (Chevrolet), The Great, Michael Lamm, Lamm-Morada Publishing, California, USA, 1978.

Cars of the Fifties & Sixties, Michael Sedgwick, Grange Books, London, UK, 1983.

Cars of the Seventies & Eighties, Nick Georgano, Grange Books, London, UK, 1990.

Classic Cars around the world, Michael Bowler, Parragon, Bristol, UK, 1995.

Corvette (Chevrolet), Karl Ludvigsen, Automobile Quarterly, New Jersey, USA, 1977.

Corvette, Cream of the Crop, Henry Rasmussen, Top Ten Publishing, California, USA, 1991.

Corvette, The Newest, Michael Lamm, Lamm-Morada Publishing, California, USA, 1984.

Corvettes (Chevrolet) 1953-88, Richard Langworth, Motor Racing Publications, Surrey, UK, 1988.

De Tomaso Pantera Gold Portfolio, Various Road Tests, Brooklands Books, Surrey, UK, 1992.

Decade of Dazzle, Fifties America, Henry Rasmussen, Motorbooks International, Wisconsin, USA, 1987.

Encyclopaedia of Motorcars, N. Georgano et al, Ebury Press, London, UK, 1973.

Fastest Cars around the world, Michael Bowler, Parragon, Bristol, UK, 1995.

Ferrari, the Complete, Godfrey Eaton, Cadogan Books, London, UK, 1986.

Ferrari, The Machines and the Man, Pete Lyons, Foulis, Somerset, UK, 1989.

Fiat Sports Cars, Graham Robson, Osprey Publishing, London, UK, 1984.

Fifty years of classic Cars, Jonathan Wood, Colour Library Books, Surrey, UK, 1994.

Ghia, Ford's Carrozzeria, David Burgess-Wise, Osprey Publishing, London UK, 1985.

Giugiaro and Ital Design, Akira Fujimoto, Car Styling Publishing, Tokyo, Japan, 1981.

Jaguar Saloon Cars, Paul Skilleter, Haynes Publishing, Somerset, UK, 1988.

Jaguar Sports Cars, Paul Skilleter, Haynes Publishing, Somerset, UK, 1983.

Japanese Car, Complete History, Marco Ruiz, Foulis, Somerset, UK, 1988.

Jensen and Healey Stories, Browning & Blunsden, Motor Racing Publications, Surrey, UK 1974.

Lamborghini, Stefano Pasini, Automobilia, Milan, Italy, 1984.

Lamborghini, the Complete Book, Pete Lyons, Foulis, Somerset, UK, 1988.

Lotus Book, The, William Taylor, Coterie Press, London UK, 1998.

Maserati 1965-75, Various Road Tests, Brooklands Books, Surrey, UK, 1985.

Maserati from 1926, Richard Crump, Foulis, Somerset, UK, 1983.

Mercedes-Benz Motor..Engines, Anon, Daimler-Benz Ag, Stuttgart, Germany, 1973.

MG - Britain's Favourite Sports Car, Malcolm Green, Haynes Publishing, Somerset, UK, 1998.

MG by McComb, Wilson McComb, Osprey Publishing, London, UK, 1990.

Mille Miglia, la storia della, Giovanni Lurani, I G de Agostini, Novara, Italy, 1979.

Nissan 300ZX, Ray Hutton, Motor Racing Publications, Surrey, UK, 1990.

On Four Wheels, Anon - part work, Orbis Publishing, London, UK, 1975.

Pininfarina, Cinquantanni, Anon, Industrie Pininfarina SpA, Turin, Italy , 980.

Porsche 911 Turbo, Various Road Tests, Brooklands Books, Surrey, UK, 1988.

Porsche Catalogues, Malcolm Toogood, Apple Press, London, UK, 1991.

Porsche Specials, Boschen & Barth, Patrick Stephens, Northants, UK, 1986.

Renault, Romance of, Edouard Seidler, Edita SA, Lausanne, Switzerland, 1973.

Rootes Group, Cars of the, Graham Robson, Motor Racing Publications, Surrey, UK, 1990.

RS, The Faster Fords, Jeremy Walton, Motor Racing Publications, Surrey, UK, 1987.

Saab, The Innovator, Mark Chatterton, David & Charles, London, UK, 1980.

Touring Superleggera, Anderloni & Anselmi, Autocritica srl, Rome, Italy, 1983.

Triumph TRs, The Complete Story, Graham Robson, Crowood Press, Wiltshire, UK, 1991.

TVR Collectors Guide, Graham Robson, Motor Racing Publications, Surrey, UK, 1987.

TVR Portfolios 1959-94, Various Road Tests, Brooklands Books, Surrey, UK, 1996.

World Car Catalogue 1975-2001, Anon, Hallwag AG, Berne, Switzerland, Annual.

Zagato, Settant'anni, Michele Marchiano, Giorgio Nada Editore, Milan, Italy, 1989.

MAGAZINES

Autocar, Iliffe - IPC Business Press - Haymarket, UK. *Autosport*, Autosport - Haymarket, UK.
Classic Car, IPC Business Press - EMAP, UK.
Motor, Temple Press - IPC Business Press, UK.
Autocritica srl, Rome, Italy.
Motor Sport, Teesdale Press - Haymarket, UK.
Crowood Press, Wiltshire, UK.
Road and Track, CBS Publications, California, USA.

INDEX

c= caption
bold= chapter's title

─────────── A ───────────

AAC (Auto Avio Costruzioni), 36
AACA (Antique Automobile Club of
    America), 8, 11
Abarth, 55, 120, 123
Abarth, Carlo, 55
Abarth-Simca 1300GT, 123
Abarth-Simca 2000 Coupe, 123
Abbots of Farnham, 50
Abingdon, 94, 97
AC 289, 122, 131
AC 428, 119, 184
AC, 20, 128, 129, 131, 152, 206, 254
AC Ace, 58, 122, 128, 129c, 206
AC Ace-Bristol, 129
AC Cobra, 58, 122, 127, **128-131**, 206
AC Cobra Daytona Coupe, 130
AC Frua, 184
Adams, Denis, 122
Aerovette, 220
Aldington, H.J., 46
Alfa Romeo, 18, 20, 26, 28, 54, 57,
    80, 82, 115, 120, 144, 145, 174,
    177, 182, 206, 207, 209, 213
Alfa Romeo 164, 206
Alfa Romeo 2000 GTV, 145
Alfa Romeo 6C-2500, 19c, **26-29**
Alfa Romeo 75, 213
Alfa Romeo Alfasud Sprint, 177
Alfa Romeo Alfetta GT, 145
Alfa Romeo Duetto Spider, 120, 144,
    145, **174-175**
Alfa Romeo Giulia, 82, 120, 144
Alfa Romeo Giulia TZ, 144, 145
Alfa Romeo Giulietta, 54, 81, 82,
    120, 145
Alfa Romeo Giulietta Spider, 59, **80-
83**
Alfa Romeo Giulietta Sprint, 52, 58,
    80-83, 144
Alfa Romeo Giulietta SS, SZ, 82, 145
Alfa Romeo Giulietta Veloce, 81
Alfa Romeo GTV Spider, 250
Alfa Romeo GTV6, 213
Alfa Romeo Junior Z 1300, 145
Alfa Romeo Sprint GT, **144-145**
Alfa Romeo SZ Il Mostro, 213
Alfa Romeo Tipo 159, 80
Allard, 21, 99
Alpine, 21, 59, 115, 156, 157, 280
Alpine-Renault 1600S, **156-157**
Alpine-Renault A108-110, 156, 157
Alpine-Renault A310 Turbo, 212
Alvis, 18, 53
American Motors, 206
Amon, Chris, 166
Andruet, 156
Arkus-Duntov, Zora, 74, 137
Artioli, Romano, 211, 246, 251, 262
Aston Martin, 10, 21, 44, 45, 52, 56,
    66, 102, 136, 152, 179, 182, 200,

201, 206, 207, 217, 228, 229c,
    229, 230, 231, 247, 274
Aston Martin Atom, 44
Aston Martin DB1, 6c
Aston Martin DB2, 21c, **44-45**, 57
Aston Martin DB2/4, **44-45**, 102
Aston Martin DB3S, 44, 45
Aston Martin DB4, 45, 52, 58, **102-
107**, 119, 124
Aston Martin DB4 GT, **102-107**, 119,
    120, 134
Aston Martin DB4 GT Zagato, 118c
Aston Martin DB5, 103, 105, 107, 119
Aston Martin DB6, 107, 119
Aston Martin DB6 Volante, 107
Aston Martin DB7, 246, **274-275**
Aston Martin DB7 Volante, 275
Aston Martin DBR1, 44
Aston Martin DBR2, 103
Aston Martin DBS, 119
Aston Martin Lagonda, **200-201**
Aston Martin V8, 201
Aston Martin Vantage, 44c, 44, 45,
    107
Aston Martin Vantage Volante, 210c
Aston Martin Vantage Zagato, 207,
    217, **228-231**, 282
Aston Martin Virage, 201
Aston Martin Volante Zagato, 207,
    217, **228-231**
Audi, 115, 214, 215, 253
Audi 200 Quattro Turbo, 214
Audi 80, 214
Audi A8, 243
Audi Quattro, 207, 208, 214, 215,
    217
Austin, 68, 70, 94, 115, 210
Austin 7, 18
Austin A30, 19
Austin A40, 58, 94, 114, 198
Austin A50, 114
Austin A90 Atlantic, 68
Austin-Healey, 21, 25, 58, 59, 69, 94
Austin-Healey 100, 24, 58, **68-71**, 72
Austin-Healey 100M, 69c, 69
Austin-Healey 100S, 70
Austin-Healey 3000, 70, 114, 240
Austin-Healey 300S, 70
Austin-Healey Sprite, 59
Austin Maxi, 184
Austin Rover, 216
Austin-Morris, 24, 58, 60
Autenreith, 47
Auto Union, 60
Autoar, 34
Auto-Avio Costruzioni, 20
Autobianchi A112, 177

─────────── B ───────────

Bantam, 18
BAT (Berlina Aerodinamica Tecnica), 82
Baur, 182
Benedini, Giampaolo, 260
Bentley, 17, 53, 88, 89, 206, 208,
    246, 262

Bentley R-type, 88
Bentley Continental, 52, 53
Bentley Continental R-type, 88
Bentley Continental S-type, **88-89**
Bentley Mulsanne, 208
Bentley T, 117, 208
Bentley, W. O., 21, 44
Berkeley, 55
Bernabei, 34
Bertone, 21c, 52, 80, 81c, 82, 104c,
    107, 115, 118, 120, 121, 144,
    145c, 145, 146, 147, 152, 153c,
    153, 166, 177, 181, 182, 184, 207,
    217
Biondetti, 37
Bitter CD, 182
Bitter, Erich, 182
Bizzarrini 5300GT (Strada), 153
Bizzarrini, Giotto, 146, 152, 153
BL Cars (British Leyland), 210, 216
Blydenstein, Bill, 178
BMC (British Motor Corporation), 19,
    53, 59, 94, 115, 140
BMW, 18, 20, 28, 46, 47, 48, 55, 57,
    115, 118, 181, 185, 196, 202, 203,
    206, 208, 209, 211, 236, 246, 252,
    253, 254, 282, 285c, 286
BMW 2000C, 118
BMW 2000CS, 118
BMW 2800CS coupe, 118
BMW 3200CS, 118
BMW 326, 47
BMW 327, 47
BMW 327 coupe, 18
BMW 327/80, 46
BMW 328, 20, 47
BMW 507, 287
BMW 850, 237c
BMW M1, **202-203**, 236
BMW M3, 209, 215, 250
BMW Z1, 213, 236, **236-239**, 286,
    287
BMW Z3, 253, 254, **286-287**
BMW Z8, 254c, 287
Boano, 111, 112
Bond, 55
Bond, James, 105
Bonnet, Rene, 123, 185
Borgward Hansa, 18
Brabham, 242
Bristol, 16, 20, 47, 48, 50, 128, 129,
    152, 179, 250
Bristol 400, **46-51**
Bristol 401, 48c, 48
Bristol 402, **46-51**
Bristol 403, 48, 50
Bristol 404, **46-51**
Bristol 405, 50
Bristol 406, 50
Bristol 407, 50
Bristol 450, 250, 48
Bristol Blenheim, 250
Bristol Brittania, 179, 250
British Leyland, 140, 142, 183
Broadley, Eric, 192
Brown, David, 44, 45, 103, 228

Bugatti, 10, 211, 217, 246, 251, 260,
    262, 263c, 280, 282
Bugatti EB 110, 252, 248, 256,
    260-263
Bugatti EB112, 262
Bugatti, Ettore, 251, 252, 261c,
    262
Bugatti, Michel, 262
Buick, 98, 117
Buick 3.5, 122
Buick Riviera, 117, 201, 205, 208

─────────── C ───────────

Cadillac, 17, 21, 98, 99, 100, 101,
    177c, 208, 209
Cadillac Allante, 209
Cadillac Coupe de Ville, 99, 100
Cadillac Eldorado, 13c, 55, **98-101**,
    117, 204, 205, 208, 209
Cadillac Eldorado Brougham, 101
Cadillac Eldorado de Ville, 100c
Cadillac Fleetwood, 100, 117, 176,
    177c
Cadillac Fleetwood Brougham, 101
Cadillac Sedanca de Ville, 99, 100
Cadillac Seville, **204-205**, 208
Callum, Ian, 274
Carrozzeria Sargiotto, 146
Castagna, 26
Caterham, 7, 58, 214, 215c
CCCA (The Classic Car Club
    of America), 8, 9
Chapman, Colin, 58, 148, 149
Chevrolet, 93, 98, 116, 122, 136,
    137, 152, 153, 181, 182, 196,
    221
Chevrolet Biscayne, 101
Chevrolet Camaro, 11, 116, 117,
    172c, 172, 173
Chevrolet Corvair, 55, 116, 172
Chevrolet Corvair Monza, 208
Chevrolet Corvette, 11, 20, 55, 59,
    72-75, 90, 122, 136, **136-139**,
    211, **220-223**, 254, 275, **292-293**
Chevrolet Corvette ZR1, 209c, 221c,
    222
Chinetti, Luigi, 37, 44
Chrysler, 50, 55, 57, 116, 117, 119,
    172, 173, 177, 179, 180, 183,
    185, 188, 210, 217, 246, 254,
    256, 267
Chrysler 300, 55
Chrysler, Le Baron, 210
Chrysler Viper, 250, **268-271**
Chrysler-Talbot, 216
Cisitalia, 36, 52, 56, 59
Cisitalia Gran Sport, **32-35**, 65, 89
Cisitalia Tipo Nuvolari, 35c
Citroen, 18, 115, 121, 155, 182, 184,
    185, 187, 216, 280
Citroen 2CV, 7, 11, 19, 55, 115
Citroen Ami 8, 218
Citroen DS19, 54, 115, 118
Citroen DS21, 115
Citroen SM, 121, 185, 216

Citroen Visa, 216
Coker, Jerry, 69
Colombo, 36, 56, 111, 154, 26
Cooper, 20
Cooper-MG, 128
Cosworth, 118, 185, 275, 246
Coventry Climax, 30, 58, 115, 148, 198
Cunningham, Briggs, 126

———————— D ————————

Daimler, 54, 59, 246
Daimler Barker Special Sport Coupe, 59
Dallara, Giampaolo, 146, 158, 192
Daninos, Jean, 52
Darraq, 57
Datsun, 18, 185
Datsun 240Z, 240
Datsun Fairlady S211, 114
Davis, Cliff, 128
DB, 18
De Lorean DMC 12, 211
De Lorean, John, 211
De Tomaso, 115, 120, 180, 184, 187, 192, 193c, 207, 209
De Tomaso, Deauville, 120
De Tomaso Guara, 254
De Tomaso Mangusta, 120, 254
De Tomaso Pantera, 120, 187, **192-193**
De Tomaso, Alejandro, 192
De Virgilio, 64
Delage, 21, 52, 57, 280
Delahaye, 21, 57, 280
Dixi, 18
DKW, 18, 19
Dodge Challenger, 172
Dodge Charger, 117
Dodge Viper, 254, 287
Donkevoort, 254
Drogo, Piero, 153
Dusio, Piero, 20, 33, 34

———————— E ————————

Egan, John, 266
Enever, Syd, 94

———————— F ————————

Facel Vega, 52, 57, 58, 152
Farina, 37
Feeley, Frank, 44
Ferrari, 7, 20, 33, 34, 37, 38, 56, 57, 85, 108, 111, 112, 115, 120, 121, 130, 132, 134, 135, 136, 146, 154, 150, 160, 161c, 161, 162, 164, 165c, 165, 166, 168, 170, 171, 180, 184, 192, 193, 206, 212, 215, 217, 226, 226, 232, 235, 243, 246, 247, 251, 262, 274, 276, 278, 279, 281c, 281, 282, 288, 289
Ferrari 125, 34
Ferrari 166, **36-39**, 44, 128
Ferrari 250, 121, 146
Ferrari 250GT, 58, 102, **108-113**, 124, 126, 132, 133c, 134, 135

Ferrari 250GT Berlinetta, 112
Ferrari 250GT Berlinetta Tour de France, 56
Ferrari 250GT Cabriolet, 112
Ferrari 250GT California Spyder, 109c, 112
Ferrari 250GT Europa, 56
Ferrari 250GT Lusso, 117c, **132-135**
Ferrari 250GT SWB, 56, 108, 109c, 110c, 112, 119, 132, 134, 135
Ferrari 250GT SWB (short wheelbase), 56
Ferrari 250GT SWB Berlinetta, 110c
Ferrari 250GTE, 112
Ferrari 250GTO, 119, 127, **130-135**, 152, 161, 162, 217
Ferrari 250GTS (Spider), 161, 162
Ferrari 250LM, 134, 158
Ferrari 275GTB (Berlinetta), 161
Ferrari 275GTB4, 161, 162
Ferrari 275LM, 119
Ferrari 288GTO, 217, 264, 224, 232c, 232, 234c, 235, 282, 288, 290
Ferrari 308, **194-195**, 208, 232, 235, 280
Ferrari 328, 184, 217, 295
Ferrari 330, 121
Ferrari 330P4, 162
Ferrari 348, 217, 276, 277
Ferrari 355, **276-279**
Ferrari 360, 251, 279
Ferrari 365GT4, 179
Ferrari 365GT4/BB, 276, 255
Ferrari 365GTB4 Daytona, 121 **160-163**, 180, 184
Ferrari 400, 181
Ferrari 512 TR, 251
Ferrari BB512 **224-227**, 232
(Ferrari) Dino 246GT, **164-167**, 170, 184, 187, 194
Ferrari F40, 217, 224, **232-235**, 251, 282, 288, 289c, 289, 290, 291c
Ferrari F50, 224, 251, 282, **288-291**
Ferrari Mondial 8, 195, 217
Ferrari Mondial T Cabriolet, 277
Ferrari Testarossa, 217, **224-227**, 251, 276, 277
Ferrari, Alfredino, 164
Ferrari, Enzo, 36, 146, 235
FIAT, 18, 20, 33, 35, 36, 54, 55, 56, 59, 115, 120, 165, 168, 170, 177, 178, 184, 194, 206, 207, 213, 214, 215, 246, 250
FIAT 1100, 20
FIAT 1100S, 59
FIAT 1100TV, 59
FIAT 124, 168
FIAT 124 Spider, 177
FIAT 124 Sport, 120, 170, 171
FIAT 125, 215
FIAT 127, 177
FIAT 128, 177
FIAT 130, 180
FIAT 131 Abarth Rally, 177, 184, 214, 215
FIAT 500, 7, 18, 21, 55, 128
FIAT 508C MM, 33
FIAT 600, 18
FIAT 2300, 119
FIAT Barchetta, 250

FIAT Bravo, 250
FIAT Coupe, 250
FIAT Croma, 206
FIAT Dino 2.4, 164, 165, 166, **168-171**, 206
FIAT Dino 206GT, 121
FIAT Nuova Cinquecento, 18, 55
FIAT Strada, 215
FIAT Tipo, 250
FIAT X1/9, 123, 184, 211
FIAT-Abarth, 55
Fiedler Fritz, 46
Fissore, 180
FIVA (Federation Internationale des Voitures Anciennes), 10, 11, 13
Ford, 17, 21, 30, 31, 57, 58, 59, 76, 90, 93, 115, 117, 199, 122, 128, 129, 131, 150, 180, 181, 184, 185, 192, 193, 206, 207, 208, 215c, 215, 249, 252, 254, 266, 272, 274, 275
Ford 105E, 150
Ford 1600, 214
Ford Anglia 105E, 117, 123, 184
Ford Big Bird, 91, 92c
Ford Capri, 117, 118, 121, 209, 210
Ford Capri RS2600, 118
Ford Capri RS3100, 118
Ford Corsair, 117
Ford Cortina, 117, 119, 192
Ford Cortina GT, 7, 117, 122, 123
Ford Cortina-Lotus, 117
Ford Cosworth, 207
Ford Escort, 117, 177
Ford Escort Mk.II RS, 214
Ford Escort RS Coswirth, 249
Ford Escort Twin Cam, 156
Ford Fairlane, 117
Ford Falcon, 116, 117, 172
Ford Fiesta, 177
Ford Focus WRC, 249
Ford Galaxy, 116, 117
Ford GT40, 116, 119, 130, 135, 158, 192
Ford Mexico, 117
Ford Model T, 19
Ford Mustang, 9, 11, 93, 116, 117, 118, 172, 173, 181, 192, 204, 210, 250
Ford Mustang Boss 351, 117
Ford Pinto, 213
Ford Probe, 210
Ford Sierra Cosworth, 215, 249
Ford Taunus, 118
Ford Thunderbird, 55, 59, **90-93**, 117, 204, 210
Ford XR3 Escort, 177
Ford Zephyr, 129
Ford, Edsel, 17
Ford, Henry, 19
Frazer Nash, 20, 40, 46, 47

———————— G ————————

Gandini, Marcello, 158, 189c, 193, 260
Ganz, Josef, 18
Gauntlett, Victor, 231, 274
Ghia, 37, 120, 121, 154, 168, 180, 181, 187, 192, 207

Ghidella, Vittorio, 213
Giacosa, Dante, 18, 19, 20, 33, 34
Gilbern, 183, 184
Ginther, Richie, 24
Giugiaro, 104c, 152, 153, 155, 187, 192, 202, 203, 207, 209, 211, 251
GM (General Motors), 17, 72, 90, 98, 115, 117, 121, 122, 172, 178, 204, 206, 209, 210, 222, 246
Godfroy, Gerard, 280
Goertz, 57
Gordini, 177
Gordon GT, 152
Gordon Keeble, 152, 153
Gordon, John, 152
Graber, 53
Gregoire, J.A., 18
Griffith, 122, 198, 254
Griffith, Jack, 272
GSM Delta, 123

———————— H ————————

Hanomag, 18
Hawthorn, Mike, 164
Healey, Donald, 21, 70, 183
Henry J, 72
Hershey, Frank, 90
Heuliez, 207
Hill, Phil, 24
Hillman, 115
Hillman Husky, 59
Hillman Imp, 115
Hoffman, Max, 86
Holden, 246
Honda, 114, 115, 206, 210, 211, 242, 243c, 243, 246
Honda Acura, 243c
Honda Legend, 210
Honda NSX, 240, **242-245**, 251
Honda Prelude, 212
Honda S2000, 253
Honda S500, 115
Honda S800, 115, 212
Horseless Carriage Club, 8
HRG, 44
Humber, 115
Hyundai Accent, 249

———————— I ————————

IDEA, 207
Isdera, 253
Isetta, 55, 115
Iso, 55
Iso Fidia, 153, 181
Iso Grifo A3C (Corsa), 153
Iso Grifo A3L (Lusso), **152-153**
Iso Grifo GL365, 153
Iso Grifo GL400, 152, 153
Iso Grifo Rivolta, 119
Iso Lele, 153
Iso Rivolta, 146, 152
Issigonis, Alec, 19
Isuzu, 211, 246
Isuzu Piazza, 209
ItalDesign, 155, 177, 184, 185, 187, 207
Italy, 20, 56, 59, 115, 177, 184, 207, 252, 262

——————— J ———————

Jaguar, 18, 21, 58, 59, 72, 76, 84, 94, 115, 119, 120c, 124, 126c, 126, 142, 152, 180, 206, 208, 210, 247, 248, 253, 254, 266, 274, 275
Jaguar 2.4, 54
Jaguar D-type, 59, 124, 126, 214
Jaguar E2A, 126
Jaguar E-type, 11c, 86, 87, 115, 119, 120c, **124-127**, 134, 282
Jaguar XJ220, 217, 256, **264-267**, 282
Jaguar XJ6, 118
Jaguar XJS, 138, 275c
Jaguar XJS V12, 253
Jaguar XK 120, **40-43**, 56, 58, 124
Jaguar XK 120C, 58
Jaguar XK 140, 40, 42, 43, 55c
Jaguar XK 150, **40-43**, 58
Jaguar XK8, 249c, 250
JaguarSport, 217
Jano, Vittorio, 64
Jeep, 24
Jensen, 58, 119, 152, 254
Jensen-Healey, 183
Jowett Javeline, 18, 44

——————— K ———————

Kaiser-Frazer, 72
Karmann, 122, 207
Keeble, Jim, 152
Kia, 211, 246
Kimber, Cecil, 22

——————— L ———————

Lagonda, 21, 44, 58, 179, 200, 228
Lamborghini, 115, 120, 146, 147, 158, 161, 184, 188, 190, 193, 203, 251, 256, 258, 260, 262
Lamborghini 350GT, **146-147**
Lamborghini 400GT, 146, 147
Lamborghini Countach, 159, 184, **188-191**, 217c, 217, 225, 226, 251, 256, 258c
Lamborghini Diablo 5.7, **256-259**
Lamborghini Espada, 121, 147, 182
Lamborghini Islero, 120
Lamborghini Miura, 120, **158-159**, 160, 184, 187, 188
Lamborghini Urraco P250, 194
Lamborghini, Ferruccio, 146, 158, 159, 188
Lampredi, 56, 11, 168, 170
Lancia, 18, 20, 64, 65, 66, 115, 120, 207, 215
Lancia Aprilia, 18
Lancia Ardea, 18
Lancia Aurelia, 18, 52, 66, 89, 120
Lancia Aurelia 2500GT, 65c, 66
Lancia Aurelia B10, 64
Lancia Aurelia B20, 35, **64-67**
Lancia Aurelia B24 Spyder, 65, 66c
Lancia Beta Monte Carlo, 184, 215
Lancia Delta HF Integrale, 207, 213, 215
Lancia Delta S4, 215
Lancia Flaminia, 120
Lancia Flavia, 120

Lancia Fulvia HF, 156
Lancia Fulvia Sport, 145
Lancia Lambda, 64
Lancia LC2, 232
Lancia Stratos, 166, 177, 184, 185c, 214, 214, 215
Lancia Thema, 206, 208
Land Rover, 246
Lawrence, Chris, 179
Lea-Francis, 18
Leland, Henry, 98
Leyland, 115
Ligier, 184
Ligier, Guy, 185
Lilley, Martin, 213
Lincoln, 17, 91, 93
Lincoln Continental, 55, 101, 117, 176, 208
Lincoln Mercury, 17, 192, 193c
Lincoln Zephyr, 17, 18
Lindner, Peter, 126c
Lister, 20, 253
Lister Storm, 253
Livanos, Peter, 274
Loewy, Raymond, 55, 122
Lola GT, 192
Lord, Leonard, 68
Lotus, 20, 58, 150, 183, 198, 206, 209c, 211, 246, 252, 262, 292
Lotus 36, 151
Lotus 50 Elan +2, 151c, 151
Lotus 7, 214, 215c
Lotus Cortina, 7c, 156
Lotus Eclat S2, 211
Lotus Elan, 117, 122, **148-151**, 211
Lotus Elan S2, 150, 151
Lotus Elise, 252, 254, 255
Lotus Elite, 58, 122, 123, 148
Lotus Elite S2, 211
Lotus Esprit, 211, 252
Lotus Europa, 122
Lotus Excel, 211
Lurani, Count "Johnny", 12
Lutz, Bob, 254, 267

——————— M ———————

Marazzi, 120
Marazzi, Mario, 147
Marcos, 114c, 122, 123, 213, 214, 254
Marcos Manta Ray, 254
Marcos Mantis, 254
Marek, Tadek, 103
Marsh, Jem, 214
Maserati, 18, 56, 57, 115, 120, 121, 146, 155, 182, 184, 187, 209, 210, 246, 252
Maserati 3500 GT, 56
Maserati A6 CGS, 34
Maserati Biturbo, 207, 209, 251
Maserati Bora, 155, 184, **186-187**
Maserati Frua, 121
Maserati Ghibli, 121, **154-155**, 182, 187, 192
Maserati Ghibli SS, 155c
Maserati Indy, 182
Maserati Merak, 155
Maserati Mexico, 182
Maserati Mistral, 121, 187
Maserati Sebring, 121

Matra, 123, 280
Matra Djet, 123
Matra MS530, 123
Matra-Simca Bagheera, 185
Mazda, 115, 185, 211, 253
Mazda 110S Cosmo, 218
Mazda 323, 216
Mazda Capella, 218
Mazda Cosmo, 185
Mazda Eunos Cosmo, 219
Mazda Luce, 218
Mazda MX5 Miata, 211, 253
Mazda R100, 218
Mazda RX7, 247c, **218-219**
McLaren, 13c, 196, 202, 217, 248, 252, 254, **282-285**
McLaren-Mercedes SLR, 251
Mega, 253
Mega Tech, 246, 256
Mercedes-Benz, 18, 57, 60, 84, 115, 117, 121, 181, 206, 208, 209, 246, 252, 253, 274
Mercedes-Benz 300SEL, 117
Mercedes-Benz 300S, 85
Mercedes-Benz 300SL (Gullwing), 57, 59c, **84-87**, 102, 121
Mercedes-Benz CLK, 250
Mercedes-Benz CLK-GTR, 252
Mercedes-Benz SLK, 253
Mercedes-Benz 190SL, 9c, 121
Mercedes-Benz 230SL, 119, 121
Mercedes-Benz 250SL, 121
Mercedes-Benz 280SL, 121
Mercury, 17
Mercury Cougar, 117, 172, 210, 250
Messerschmitt, 55
Messier, 262
MG, 22, 23, 25, 53, 58, 94, 95, 115, 122, 182, 206, 210
MG Magnette, 94, 95
MG Metro, 216, 266
MG Metro Turbo, 207
MG Midget, 10, 22, 59, 122
MG TA, 22, 128
MG TB, 21, 22c, 23
MG TC, 40, 21, **22-25**, 58
MG TD, 24, 25, 94
MG TF, 6c, **22-25**
MGA, 21, 25, 56, 58, 59, 94, 95, 96, 122, 140, 142c, 198
MGA 1600, **94-97**
MGA EX175, 94
MGB, 97, 122, **140-143**, 198
MGC, 122, 140, 142
Michelotti, 77, 122, 123c
Milestone Car Society, 8, 9
Mini, 55, 56, 177, 246
Mini Cooper, 55, 56
Mini Cooper S, 11, 55, 117, 156
Mini-Marcos, 123
Mitchell, Bill, 137
Mitsubishi, 211, 212, 246, 249, 254
Monroe, Marilyn, 91c
Monteverdi, Peter, 180
Moretti, 21
Morgan, 17, 21, 30, 31, 76, 114, 122, 179, 214, 253, 254
Morgan 4/4, **30-31**
Morgan Aero 8, 253
Morgan Plus-4, 58, 76
Morgan Plus 8, 122

Morris, 18, 23, 53, 94, 115
Morris Cowley, 22
Morris Garages, 22
Morris Minor, 7, 19
Moss, Stirling, 126
Mulliner Park Ward, 117
Mulliner, H.J., 53, 88, 89
Munday Harry, 150
Murray, Gordon, 252, 282

——————— N ———————

Nader, Ralph, 55
Nash, 58
NISMO (Nissan Motorsport), 250
Nissan, 114, 206, 207, 211, 212, 216, 240, 250
Nissan 1600SSS, 114
Nissan 240Z, 114
Nissan 300ZX, **240-241**
Nissan Fairlady Z200, 240
Nissan Bluebird, 206
Nissan Skyline, 250
Nissan Skyline GT-R, 212
Noble M10, 255
Noble, Lee, 255
NSU, 115, 118
NSU Sport Prinz, 118
Nuvolari, Tazio, 34, 35c

——————— O ———————

Oakland, 98
Ogle Design, 119
Oldsmobile, 98, 117, 204
Oldsmobile F85, 117
Oldsmobile Toronado, 116, 117, 121, 204, 205
Olley, Maurice, 72
Opel, 115, 121, 182, 210, 255
Opel Ascona, 178
Opel Ascona 400, 214
Opel Calibra, 210
Opel Commodore, 121
Opel GT, 121
Opel Kadett, 121
Opel Lotus Omega, 209
Opel Manta, 178
Opel Rekord, 121
Opel Vectra, 210
Orsi, 56, 154
Orsi, Omer, 154
OSCA, 56, ·154, 252
OSCA 1500S, 59
OSCA 2500, 252

——————— P ———————

Pagani Zonta, 253
Panhard, 57, 123, 153
Panhard, Dyna, 18
Panoz, 253
Pegaso, 57
Peugeot, 18, 115, 177, 182, 206, 216, 248, 280, 281
Peugeot 205 GTI, 207
Peugeot 205 Turbo, 216
Peugeot 206, 249
Peugeot 406, 250
Peugeot 504 Coupe, 115

Phillips, George, 94
Pinin Farina, 34, 35, 38, 64, 65, 80, 82, 89, 111
Pininfarina, 13c, 20, 28, 33, 33c, 34, 52, 56, 59, 65, 82, 83c, 101, 117, 120, 121, 132, 145, 160, 161c, 164, 165, 168, 170, 174, 174c, 180, 194, 195, 207, 209, 213, 217, 226, 235, 243, 250, 276, 290
Plymouth, 17, 18
Plymouth Barracuda, 117
Plymouth Belvedere, 117
Plymouth Cuda, 172
Plymouth Prowler, 254
Plymouth Superbird, 117
Poiraud, Claude, 280
Pontiac, 117, 172
Pontiac Fiero, 211
Pontiac Firebird, 117, **172-173**, 210, 250
Pontiac Judge, 173, 181
Pontiac Tempest GTO, 117
Porsche, 18, 20, 21, 34, 44, 57, 60, 61, 62, 121, 156, 185, 196, 197, 206, 213c, 217, 232, 243, 251, 252, 255, 264
Porsche 356, 56, **60-63**
Porsche 911, 121, 156, 165, 181, 185, 194
Porsche 911 GT1, 252
Porsche 911 Turbo, **196-197**
Porsche 911SC Targa, 180c
Porsche 917, 196
Porsche 924, 185
Porsche 928, 181, 274
Porsche 944, 211, 212, 213, 219
Porsche 959, 256, 282
Porsche Boxter, 252c, 255, **294-297**
Porsche Carrera, 185, 212
Porsche Carrera Cabriolet, 213c
Porsche Carrera RS, 196
Porsche Speedster Carrera, 57c, 62, 63c
Porsche Turbo 930, 196, 197c
Porsche, Dr., 19
Porsche, Professor Ferdinand, 60
Proton, 246

——————— Q ———————

Qvale, Kjell, 254

——————— R ———————

Radford, Harold, 119
Redele, John, 156
Reliant, 55, 119
Reliant Scimitar GT, 55, 119
Renault, 19, 55, 115, 123, 156, 157, 185, 206, 248, 280
Renault 16, 115, 122, 156
Renault 30, 185
Renault 4CV, 19
Renault R5, 177
Renault 750, 156
Renault Caravelle, 115
Renault Clio Williams, 248
Renault Dauphine, 19, 115, 123, 156
Renault Dauphine Gordini, 55

Renault Floride, 115
Renault R4, 115
Renault R5 Alpine, 157, 177
Renault R8, 19, 115
Renault R8 Gordini, 115, 156
Ricart, Wilfredo, 57
Riley, 16c, 18, 53, 115
Rivolta, Count Renzo, 152
Rivolta, Piero, 152, 153
Rochdale Olympic, 123
Rodger, Bernie, 152
Rolls-Royce, 17, 88, 206, 208, 246
Rolls-Royce Camargue, 117
Rolls-Royce Corniche, 208
Rolls-Royce Shadow II, 117
Rolls-Royce Silver Cloud, 89
Rolls-Royce Silver Cloud II, 53
Rolls-Royce Silver Cloud III, 53
Rolls-Royce Silver Dawn, 88
Rolls-Royce Silver Seraph, 246
Rolls-Royce Silver Shadow, 53, 117, 208
Rolls-Royce Silver Spirit, 208
Rootes group, 18, 115
Rosengart, 18
Rover, 17, 53, 122, 180, 183, 210, 213, 214, 255, 272, 273c, 273
Rover 2000, 118
Rover TVR 420SEAC, 272
Rover 75, 246
Rover SD1, 180
Rover V-8, 254
Rover 827 Vitesse, 210
Rudd, Ken, 128, 129

——————— S ———————

Saab, 16, 20, 54, 118, 182, 206, 208, 246
Saab 900, 206
Saab 900 Turbo, 209
Saab 9000, 178
Saab 92, 19
Saab 9-3, 250
Saab Monte Carlo, 118
Saab Sonett II, 123
Saab Sonett III, 123
Saoutchik, 57
Savonuzzi, Giovanni, 20, 33, 34
Sayer, Malcom, 126c
Schlesser, Jo, 185
Scuderia Ferrari, 36
Seat, 246
Seat Cordoba, 249
Shelby Cobra, 128
Shelby Mustang GT350, 117
Shelby Mustang GT500, 117, 172
Shelby, Carrol, 129, 254, 267
Siata, 56
Simca, 57
Simca 1000, 123
Simca 1100, 177
Singer, 115
Singer Chamois coupe, 115
Skoda, 246
Società Autostar, 152
Spada, Ercole, 145
Spectre Cars, 252
Spectre R45, 252
Sport Auto, 231
St.Louis, Missouri, 72

Stabilimenti Farina, 28, 35, 38c
Standard, 76, 115
Standard Flying Ten, 30
Standard Vanguard, 21, 58, 122
Stanzani, Paolo, 146, 128, 260
Stevens, Peter, 284
STI (Subaru Tecnica Industries), 249
Studebaker, 55, 122
Studebaker Champion, 17
Studebaker Golden Hawk, 117
Subaru, 246, 249
Subaru 190, 252
Subaru Impreza, 249
Subaru Legacy, 249
Sunbeam, 115, 177
Sunbeam Alpine, 59
Sunbeam Lotus, 183, 214
Sunbeam Rapier, 59
Sunbeam Stiletto, 115
Sunbeam Tiger, 122
Sunbeam-Talbot, 18
Sunbeam-Talbot 90, 59
Suzuki, 246

——————— T ———————

Talbot, 17, 21, 52, 57, 177, 280
Talbot Murena, 185
Talbot-Sunbeam-Lotus, 216
Tastevin, Jean, 179
Tickford, 45, 105
Tjaarda, Tom, 180, 192
Tojeiro, John, 128
Tornado Talisman, 123
Touring, 20, 26, 36, 52, 57, 102, 146
Towns, William, 179, 200, 201c, 228
Toyota, 115, 206, 207, 211, 255
Toyota 2000GT, 115
Toyota Celica, 115, 206c, 212, 216, 249
Toyota Corolla, 211, 249
Toyota MR2, 211
Toyota Soarer (Lexus SC), 250
Toyota Supra, 206c, 212
Triumph, 17, 21, 58, 76, 77c, 78, 94, 115, 118, 122, 152, 178, 182, 184, 255
Triumph 2000, 78
Triumph 2500, 122, 123
Triumph Dolomite, 182
Triumph Italia, 78
Triumph Spitfire, 122
Triumph Stag, 119, 142
Triumph TR1, 76
Triumph TR2, 25, 31, 58, **76-79**
Triumph TR3, 77, 122
Triumph TR3A, **76-79**, 122
Triumph TR4, 56, 76, 78, 122, 123c
Triumph TR4A, 122
Triumph TR5, 78, 122
Triumph TR6, 78, 122, 198
Triumph TR7, 140, 182
Triumph TR8, 216
TVR, 58, 122, 184, 198, 213, 254, 272
TVR 3000, **198-199**
TVR Cerbera, 254, 273
TVR Chimaera, 254, 273
TVR Convertible, 199c

TVR Grantura, 58
TVR Griffith 500, **272-273**
TVR Taimar, 272
TVR Tuscan, 122, 213, 272, 273c, 273
TVR Vixen, 272
TWR (Tom Walkinshaw Racing), 264
TWR Jaguar XJR-15, 282

——————— U ———————

Ultima, 255

——————— V ———————

van Vooren, 89
Vanguard, 18, 31, 76
Vauxhall, 115, 121, 207, 210, 255
Vauxhall Cavalier, 206, 210
Vauxhall Chevette, 214
Vauxhall Chevette HS2300, 177
Vauxhall Firenza, 178
Vauxhall Lotus Carlton, 209
Vauxhall Victor, 7
VCC (Veteran Car Club), 10
Venturi, 212, 280, 281
Venturi 210, **280-281**
Veritas, 18
Vignale, 35, 56, 57, 121, 122, 155, 181, 192, 193, 207
Volkswagen, 18, 19, 60, 115, 118, 121, 198, 209, 246, 248, 262
Volkswagen Beetle, 7, 18, 19, 21, 54, 55, 60, 61, 62, 116, 253
Volkswagen Corrado, 209
Volkswagen Golf, 177
Volkswagen Golf GTI, 177, 248
Volkswagen K70, 118
Volkswagen Scirocco, 177, 209
Volvo, 18, 54, 114c, 119, 206, 211
Volvo B120 (Amazon), 54
Volvo B122S (Amazon Sport), 54
Volvo C70, 250
Volvo P1800, 119
VSCC (Vintage Sports-Car Club), 10, 11, 13
VW Audi, 181, 185, 246, 251

——————— W ———————

Wallace, 158
Wankel, 115, 118, 185, 211, 219, 220, 253
Wankel, Dr. Felix, 218
Warwick GT, 152
Wheeler, Peter, 213, 272
Williams, 216
Williams-Renault, 248
Wolseley, 23, 53, 94, 115

——————— Y ———————

Yamaha, 115, 252, 254

——————— Z ———————

Zagato, 56, 82, 107c, 107, 120, 134, 144, 145, 207, 213, 229, 230, 252
Zagato, Elio, 56

PHOTOGRAPHIC CREDITS

Page 1: NEIL BRUCE AUTOMOBILE PHOTOLIBRARY;
Pages 2-3: FOTOSTUDIO ZUMBRUNN;
Pages 4-5: RON KIMBALL STOCK PHOTOGRAPHY;
Pages 6-7: FOTOSTUDIO ZUMBRUNN;
Pages 8-9 top: FOTOSTUDIO ZUMBRUNN;
Pages 8-9 bottom: NEIL BRUCE AUTOMOBILE PHOTOLIBRARY;
Pages 10-11: FOTOSTUDIO ZUMBRUNN;
Pages12-13: RON KIMBALL STOCK PHOTOGRAPHY;
Pages 14-15: MAGGI & MAGGI;
Pages 16-17: FOTOSTUDIO ZUMBRUNN;
Page 19: ARCHIVIO STORICO ALFA ROMEO;
Pages 20-21: FOTOSTUDIO ZUMBRUNN;
Page 22 top: NEIL BRUCE AUTOMOBILE PHOTOLIBRARY;
Page 22 bottom: NEIL BRUCE AUTOMOBILE PHOTOLIBRARY;
Pages 22-23: FOTOSTUDIO ZUMBRUNN;
Page 23 bottom: NEIL BRUCE AUTOMOBILE PHOTOLIBRARY;
Pages 24-25: FOTOSTUDIO ZUMBRUNN;
Pages 26-27: FOTOSTUDIO ZUMBRUNN;
Pages 28-29: FOTOSTUDIO ZUMBRUNN;
Pages 30 and 31: MAGGI & MAGGI;
Pages 32 and 33: FOTOSTUDIO ZUMBRUNN;
Pages 34 and 35: FOTOSTUDIO ZUMBRUNN;
Page 36 bottom: NEIL BRUCE AUTOMOBILE PHOTOLIBRARY;
Pages 36-37: RON KIMBALL STOCK PHOTOGRAPHY;
Page 37 bottom: NEIL BRUCE AUTOMOBILE PHOTOLIBRARY;
Page 38 top and bottom: GIORGIO NADA EDITORE;
Pages 38-39 and 39 bottom: MIDSUMMER BOOKS LTD;
Pages 40 and 41: NEIL BRUCE AUTOMOBILE PHOTOLIBRARY;
Pages 42 and 43: MIDSUMMER BOOKS LTD;
Pages 44-45: FOTOSTUDIO ZUMBRUNN;
Page 45 top: NEIL BRUCE AUTOMOBILE PHOTOLIBRARY;
Pages 46 and 47: GIORGIO NADA EDITORE;
Pages 48-49: MIDSUMMER BOOKS LTD;
Pages 50 and 51: MIDSUMMER BOOKS LTD;
Pages 52-53: FOTOSTUDIO ZUMBRUNN;
Pages 54-55: FOTOSTUDIO ZUMBRUNN;
Pages 56-57: RON KIMBALL STOCK PHOTOGRAPHY;
Pages 58-59: MAGGI & MAGGI;
Pages 60 and 61: MIDSUMMER BOOKS LTD;
Pages 62 and 63: RENE' STAUD STUDIOS;
Pages 64 and 65: MIDSUMMER BOOKS LTD;
Pages 66 and 67: MAGGI & MAGGI;
Pages 68 and 69: MIDSUMMER BOOKS LTD;
Pages 70 and 71: MIDSUMMER BOOKS LTD;
Pages 72 and 73: MAGGI & MAGGI;
Pages 74 and 75: MAGGI & MAGGI;
Pages 76-77 top: MIDSUMMER BOOKS LTD;
Pages 76-77 bottom: ARCHIVIO WHITE STAR;
Pages 78-79 top: MIDSUMMER BOOKS LTD;
Pages 78 bottom and 79 bottom: MAGGI & MAGGI;
Pages 80 and 81: MAGGI & MAGGI;
Pages 82 and 83: MAGGI & MAGGI;
Pages 84 and 85: RENE' STAUD STUDIOS;
Pages 86-87: RENE' STAUD STUDIOS;
Pages 88-89: FOTOSTUDIO ZUMBRUNN;
Page 88 bottom: NEIL BRUCE AUTOMOBILE PHOTOLIBRARY;
Pages 90 and 91: FOTOSTUDIO ZUMBRUNN;
Pages 92-93 top: RON KIMBALL STOCK PHOTOGRAPHY;
Pages 92-93 bottom: FOTOSTUDIO ZUMBRUNN;

Pages 94 and 95: MIDSUMMER BOOKS LTD;
Page 96 top and bottom: MIDSUMMER BOOKS LTD;
Pages 97: MAGGI & MAGGI;
Pages 98-99: RON KIMBALL STOCK PHOTOGRAPHY;
Pages 100 and 101: FOTOSTUDIO ZUMBRUNN;
Pages102 and 103: ATELIER SCHLEGELMILCH;
Pages 104 and 105: FOTOSTUDIO ZUMBRUNN;
Pages 106 and 107: FOTOSTUDIO ZUMBRUNN;
Pages 108-109 top and bottom: MAGGI & MAGGI;
Page 109 bottom: NEIL BRUCE AUTOMOBILE PHOTOLIBRARY;
Pages 110 and 111: MAGGI & MAGGI;
Pages 112 and 113: FOTOSTUDIO ZUMBRUNN;
Pages 114-115: FOTOSTUDIO ZUMBRUNN;
Page 116: FOTOSTUDIO ZUMBRUNN;
Pages 118-119: FOTOSTUDIO ZUMBRUNN;
Pages 120-121: FOTOSTUDIO ZUMBRUNN;
Pages 122-123: MIDSUMMER BOOKS LTD;
Pages 124 and 125: MAGGI & MAGGI;
Pages 126-127: MIDSUMMER BOOKS LTD;
Pages 128-129: MIDSUMMER BOOKS LTD;
Pages 130-131: MIDSUMMER BOOKS LTD;
Pages 132 and 133: FOTOSTUDIO ZUMBRUNN;
Pages 134-135: PETER VANN;
Pages 136-137: MIDSUMMER BOOKS LTD;
Pages 138-139: MIDSUMMER BOOKS LTD;
Pages 140 and 141: NEIL BRUCE AUTOMOBILE PHOTOLIBRARY;
Pages 142 and 143: NEIL BRUCE AUTOMOBILE PHOTOLIBRARY;
Pages 144-145: RENE' STAUD STUDIOS;
Pages 146-147: NEIL BRUCE AUTOMOBILE PHOTOLIBRARY;
Pages 148 and 149: ATELIER SCHLEGELMILCH;
Pages 150 and 151: MIDSUMMER BOOKS LTD;
Pages 152-153: PETER VANN;
Pages 154-155: NEIL BRUCE AUTOMOBILE PHOTOLIBRARY;
Pages 156-157: MAGGI & MAGGI;
Pages 158-159: RON KIMBALL STOCK PHOTOGRAPHY;
Pages 160-161: RON KIMBALL STOCK PHOTOGRAPHY;
Pages 162-163: RON KIMBALL STOCK PHOTOGRAPHY;
Pages 164 and 165: MAGGI & MAGGI;
Pages 166 and 167: MAGGI & MAGGI;
Pages 168 and 169: MIDSUMMER BOOKS LTD;
Pages 170-171: MIDSUMMER BOOKS LTD;
Pages 172 and 173: MIDSUMMER BOOKS LTD;
Pages 174 and 175: MAGGI & MAGGI;
Pages 176-177: FOTOSTUDIO ZUMBRUNN;
Pages 178-179: MIDSUMMER BOOKS LTD;
Pages 180-181: RON KIMBALL STOCK PHOTOGRAPHY;
Pages 182-183: NEIL BRUCE AUTOMOBILE PHOTOLIBRARY;
Pages 184-185: NEIL BRUCE AUTOMOBILE PHOTOLIBRARY;
Pages 186 and 187: MAGGI & MAGGI;
Pages 188 and 189: GIORGIO NADA EDITORE;
Pages 190 and 191: MAGGI & MAGGI;
Pages 192 and 193: RON KIMBALL STOCK PHOTOGRAPHY;
Pages 194-195: RENE' STAUD STUDIOS;
Pages 196-197: RON KIMBALL STOCK PHOTOGRAPHY;
Pages 198 and 199: MIDSUMMER BOOKS LTD;
Pages 200-201: MIDSUMMER BOOKS LTD;

Pages 202-203: NEIL BRUCE AUTOMOBILE PHOTOLIBRARY;
Pages 204-205: RON KIMBALL STOCK PHOTOGRAPHY;
Pages 206-207: NEIL BRUCE AUTOMOBILE PHOTOLIBRARY;
Pages 208-209: FOTOSTUDIO ZUMBRUNN;
Pages 210-211: FOTOSTUDIO ZUMBRUNN;
Pages 212-213: RON KIMBALL STOCK PHOTOGRAPHY;
Pages 214-215: NEIL BRUCE AUTOMOBILE PHOTOLIBRARY;
Pages 216-217: FOTOSTUDIO ZUMBRUNN;
Pages 218-219: MIDSUMMER BOOKS LTD;
Pages 220 and 221: FOTOSTUDIO ZUMBRUNN;
Pages 222 and 223: FOTOSTUDIO ZUMBRUNN;
Pages 224-225 top: RENE' STAUD STUDIOS;
Page 224 bottom: FOTOSTUDIO ZUMBRUNN;
Pages 226-227: FOTOSTUDIO ZUMBRUNN;
Pages 228 and 229: NEIL BRUCE AUTOMOBILE PHOTOLIBRARY;
Pages 230 and 231: MIDSUMMER BOOKS LTD;
Pages 232 and 233: FOTOSTUDIO ZUMBRUNN;
Page 234 top: FOTOSTUDIO ZUMBRUNN;
Pages 234-235: RENE' STAUD STUDIOS;
Pages 236-237: FOTOSTUDIO ZUMBRUNN;
Pages 238 and 239: FOTOSTUDIO ZUMBRUNN;
Pages 240-241: RON KIMBALL STOCK PHOTOGRAPHY;
Pages 242-243: JIM FETS;
Pages 244-245: RON KIMBALL STOCK PHOTOGRAPHY;
Pages 246-247: MAGGI & MAGGI;
Pages 248-249: ARCHIVIO WHITE STAR;
Pages 250-251: RON KIMBALL STOCK PHOTOGRAPHY;
Pages 252-253: RON KIMBALL STOCK PHOTOGRAPHY;
Pages 254-255: ATELIER SCHLEGELMILCH;
Pages 256 and 257: MAGGI & MAGGI;
Pages 258 and 259: FOTOSTUDIO ZUMBRUNN;
Pages 260 and 261: FOTOSTUDIO ZUMBRUNN;
Pages 262 and 263: FOTOSTUDIO ZUMBRUNN;
Pages 264 and 265: RENE' STAUD STUDIOS;
Pages 266-267: FOTOSTUDIO ZUMBRUNN;
Pages 268-269: FOTOSTUDIO ZUMBRUNN;
Page 269 top: NEIL BRUCE AUTOMOBILE PHOTOLIBRARY;
Pages 270 and 271: FOTOSTUDIO ZUMBRUNN;
Pages 272-273: NEIL BRUCE AUTOMOBILE PHOTOLIBRARY;
Pages 274-275: NEIL BRUCE AUTOMOBILE PHOTOLIBRARY;
Pages 276-277: MIDSUMMER BOOKS LTD;
Pages 278 and 279: MIDSUMMER BOOKS LTD;
Pages 280-281: MIDSUMMER BOOKS LTD;
Pages 282 and 283: NEIL BRUCE AUTOMOBILE PHOTOLIBRARY;
Pages 284 and 285: NEIL BRUCE AUTOMOBILE PHOTOLIBRARY;
Pages 286-287: RON KIMBALL STOCK PHOTOGRAPHY;
Pages 288 and 289: RON KIMBALL STOCK PHOTOGRAPHY;
Pages 290 and 291: FOTOSTUDIO ZUMBRUNN;
Pages 292-293: JIM FETS;
Pages 294-295: RON KIMBALL STOCK PHOTOGRAPHY;
Pages 296-297: RON KIMBALL STOCK PHOTOGRAPHY.

AKNOWLEDGEMENTS

The foundation of all research is the contemporary report. I would like to thank all the motoring journalists, including many former colleagues, for their dedicated work in getting their stories whether it be from the manufacturers for new cars and road tests or by recording motor sport events. Following the absorption of my original employer, *Motor*, into *Autocar*, the latter has been my modern bible. I would also like to thank all the fellow motoring historians who have combed through these magazines and whose works now grace my reference library; I hope they are all included in the Bibliography.
Some thanks are also due to those club secretaries who have unwittingly helped me by setting up useful web-sites.
But my main thanks have to be reserved for my father, who brought me up to appreciate the finer points of vintage and classic motoring, and my family who have allowed me to maintain that interest.

Michael Bowler

The Publisher would like to thank:

Archivio Storico Alfa Romeo;
Vittorio Berzero;
Archivio Ferrari;
Porsche Archives, Germany;
Maserati S.P.A.;
Stefano Mazza;
Mercedes-Benz Classic Archives Team;
TR Register Italy